THE GLEA

THE RISALE-I NUR COLLECTION

THE GLEAMS

Reflections on Qur'anic Wisdom and Spirituality

BEDİÜZZAMAN SAİD NURSİ

Translated by Hüseyin Akarsu

TUGHRA
BOOKS
New Jersey

16 15 14 13   2 3 4 5

Published by Tughra Books
345 Clifton Ave., Clifton,
NJ, 07011, USA

www.tughrabooks.com

Library of Congress Cataloging-in-Publication Data

Nursi, Said, 1873-1960.
[Risale-i nur. English. Selections]
The gleams : reflections on Qur'anic wisdom and spirituality / Bediuzzaman Said Nursi ; translated by Huseyin Akarsu.
p. cm.
Includes index.
ISBN 978-1-59784-132-0 (cloth)
1. Koran--Criticism, interpretation, etc. 2. Islam--Prayers and devotions. I. Akarsu, Huseyin. II. Title.
BP252.S86213 2008b
297.8'3--dc22

2008050107

Printed by
Numune Matbaacılık ve Cilt San. Tic. Ltd. Şti.
Yüzyıl Mah. Matbaacılar Sitesi 2. Cad. No:192 Istanbul-Turkey
www.numune.com.tr

Table of Contents

THE TWENTY-NINTH GLEAM

THE THIRTIETH GLEAM

Said Nursi and the Risale-i Nur

Said Nursi's (1877–1960) achievements, personality, character, and continuing influence make him an important twentieth-century Muslim figure. A most effective and profound representative of Islam's intellectual, moral, and spiritual strengths, he spent his life overflowing with love and ardor for Islam, pursuing a wise and measured activism based on sound reasoning, and following the Qur'an and the Prophetic example. Much has already been said and written about the lofty ideal he pursued and his deep familiarity with the world and his times, as well as his simplicity, austerity, tenderness, loyalty, chastity, modesty, and contentedness.

Said Nursi lived during a global crisis. Materialism was triumphant, communism was widespread, and Muslims were being urged to reject Islam. Shocked by the West's scientific and military victories and influenced by modern thought, Muslims were facing a challenge of losing connection with their roots and sometimes their belief. Said Nursi, however, pointed people to the source of belief and inculcated in them a strong hope for an overall revival. His writings showed Islam's truth and opposed the growing deviation. Relying on God and his firm conviction in Islam's truth, and driven by his powerful hope about the future of the Muslim world, he defended Islam and sought to raise a new generation that would represent Islam correctly.

Voicing the sighs and laments of the whole Muslim world, as well as its belief, hopes, and aspirations, he said:

> I can bear my own sorrows, but the sorrows arising from the calamities visiting Islam and Muslims have crushed me. I feel each blow delivered to the Muslim world as delivered first to my own heart. That is why I have been so shaken.... During my life of over eighty years, I have tasted no worldly pleasure. My life has passed on battlefields, in prisons or other places of suffering. They have treated me like a criminal, banishing me from one town to another, keeping me under constant surveillance. There has been no persecution I have not tasted, no oppression I have not suffered. I neither care for Paradise nor fear Hell. If I see my nation's belief secured, I will not even care about burning in Hell, for while my body is burning my heart will be as if in a rose garden. (Tarihçe-i Hayat [Biography], Nesil, Istanbul: 1996, vol 2, p. 2206)

At a time when science and philosophy were used to produce young atheists and nihilism was widespread; when such things were done in the name of civilization, modernization, and contemporary thinking; and when resisters were persecuted, Said Nursi worked for a people's revival, infusing them with modern and traditional education as well as spiritual training.

Many contemporaries explicitly or tacitly acknowledged him as the most important thinker and writer of twentieth-century Turkey, or even of the Muslim world. Despite this and his leadership of a new Islamic religious and intellectual revival, he remained a humble servant of God. His life exemplified his understanding of humility: "Desire for fame is the same as show and ostentation, a 'poisonous honey' extinguishing the heart's spiritual liveliness.

Said Nursi diagnosed the Muslim world's long-standing "diseases" and offered the most effective cures. Basing his activity on the Qur'an and Sunna (the Prophet's way or traditions), as well as the Islamic tradition and natural phenomena (considered signs of Divine Existence and Unity), he concentrated, respectively, on proving the pillars of Islam; the necessity of belief, worship, morality, and good conduct; and certain socio-economic issues facing contemporary Muslims.

Bediüzzaman Said Nursi's life story

In the Ottoman period

Said Nursi was born in Nurs, Bitlis, in 1877, eastern Anatolia, and educated by the district's best scholars, completing the normal madrasa (traditional religious school) education when he was fourteen. He soon surpassed his teachers and earned the title Bediüzzaman (Wonder of the Age). Believing that modern science and logic was the way of the future, he advocated teaching religious sciences in secular schools and modern sciences in religious schools.

Following the uprising on April 13, 1909, he was one of the many scholars indiscriminately arrested and court-martialed for inciting the unrest. However, as he managed to restore some calm, he was acquitted. Returning to eastern Anatolia, he taught that Islam allowed freedom in government and rejected dictatorship. He later collected these speeches in *Munazarat* (The Discussions).

In 1911, while preaching in Damascus' Umayyad mosque, he stated that Muslims were being defeated due to the growth of despair, the loss of truthfulness in social and political life, love of belligerence, ignoring bonds among believers, pervasive despotism, and egocentricity. He then offered his cure: hope, truthfulness, trustworthiness, mutual love, consultation, solidarity, and freedom in accordance with Islam. Building on these, he asserted that the true civilization contained in Islam would dominate the world.

Returning to Istanbul to seek the new Sultan's support for a university in Van, eastern Anatolia, he finally secured sufficient funds—19,000 gold liras. Unfortunately, World War I broke out before the university could be completed.

During World War I, Said Nursi commanded a volunteers' regiment on the Caucasian front and in eastern Anatolia. His heroism was admired by the commanders. He also dictated (to his students) his famous introduction to the Qur'anic commentary, *Isharat al-I'jaz* (Signs of Miraculousness), during the war.

Eventually captured, he spent over two years in a prisoners' camp in Kostroma, northwestern Russia. Amid the Russian revolution, Said Nursi escaped and returned to Istanbul. After receiving a medal and rejecting all government appointments, he joined the *Dar al-Hikmat al-Islamiya* (the religious academy) on the army's recommendation. When imperial Europe invaded the collapsed Ottoman State to grab what it could, Said Nursi protested against the British presence in Istanbul and the invasion of Turkey.

In 1922, after receiving eighteen official invitations, Said Nursi went to Ankara and was given an audience at the Grand National Assembly. On

January 19, 1923, he delivered an influential address to the Assembly emphasizing the importance of observing religious obligations. Eight months later he moved to Van and devoted himself to prayer and teaching.

In the Republic of Turkey

After the collapse of the multi-ethnic, multi-religious Ottoman State and the Turkish War of Independence, the new Republic of Turkey was founded (1923). Following the founding of the republic a large number of cultural, social and political reforms were enacted in the period up to the end of the 1930s. Eventually, the principles of republicanism, nationalism, populism, statism, secularism, and revolution (meaning continuing change in the state and society) were "officially" accepted as the essential principles to guide the new Turkey.

When a revolt broke out in southeastern Turkey in 1925, Said Nursi rejected the rebels' call to support them, saying that Muslims should not fight each other and that many innocent people would die for the benefit of a few criminals. However, because of his influence on people, the government exiled him to Burdur, south-western Anatolia, where he was kept under surveillance. Then he was sent to Barla, an out-of-the-way village surrounded by mountains within the borders of Isparta, situated to the north-west of Burdur. However, he found true consolation in the Omnipresence of God and in complete submission to Him. The basic works of the *Risale-i Nur* Collection (Epistles of Light), *The Words* and *The Letters*, were written in Barla. Handmade copies soon circulated throughout Turkey.

In 1935 he was arrested and remained in prison for eleven months with 125 of his students throughout the period of their trial at Eskişehir Criminal Court. Although he always opposed revolt and breaches of public peace and order, and stressed that one person's rights could not be violated even for society's sake, he was accused of working to destroy public order. When asked his opinion of the Republic, he replied: "My biography, which you have in your hands, proves that I was a religious republican before any of you were born." After eleven months' detention, he was acquitted.

Following his release, from 1936–1943, he endured seven years of exile in Kastamonu (a small town in the Black Sea region near the north coast of Turkey). During these years, he wrote a major part of the *Risale-i Nur*. In

1943 he was tried with 126 of his students at the Denizli Criminal Court trials for having had a treatise on God's existence printed secretly in Istanbul. Said Nursi was accused of forming a Sufi order and organizing a political society. Once again he was remanded in custody until 1944, during which time he taught the other prisoners and produced some parts of the *Risale-i Nur*. He was eventually acquitted but he was once more subjected to internal exile, this time in Emirdağ in Afyon, central Turkey.

In 1948 a new case was opened against him and 53 students in Afyon Criminal Court, and he was jailed for 20 months in Afyon Prison. However, in 1956, he and his students were declared innocent by the Supreme Court.

After his release, he stayed for brief periods in Emirdağ, Isparta, Afyon, Istanbul, and elsewhere. In 1950, the multiparty system was introduced and restrictions on the Religion were relaxed. Said Nursi was arrested only once after this in 1952, when he was tried for his publication of *Guide for Youth*. He was acquitted by unanimous decision.

On Bediüzzaman's death in Urfa on March 23, 1960, the coroner fixed his estate as a simple garment, and 20 lira. He left this world with complete honor, dignity and victory. His works, the real legacy of this hero of Islam and humanity, the 6,000-page *Risale-i Nur* Collection, remain highly influential and a lighthouse guiding us on our way back to God.

The Risale-i Nur

The problems of Muslims from Said Nursi's viewpoint

In the *Risale-i Nur* Said Nursi identifies the cause of the Muslim world's decline as the weakening of belief's foundations. Together with the unceasing attacks of scientific materialism and atheism, this weakening was seen by Said Nursi as a great cloud of denial and doubt hovering over the Muslim world. To neutralize it, having decided that when the freedom of conscience or belief and thought was accepted in the world under the principle of secularism, Islam no longer demanded physical "*jihad*," he undertook a "*jihad* of the word with the diamond principles of the Qur'an" designed to strengthen belief by reconstructing Islam from its foundations of pure belief.

During his time and our own, ignorance of God and the Prophet, upon him be peace and blessings, heedlessness of religious commands, indifference to the Islamic dynamics of prosperity in both worlds, and ignorance of modern scientific knowledge were leading causes of Muslim backwardness. He stated that Muslims could escape this backwardness only through modern scientific and religious knowledge as well as systematic thought, and could protect themselves against deviation only by acquiring true knowledge.

Ignorance was a source of Muslim poverty, internal conflict, and other problems. Ignorance of Islam's truth, when added to ignorance of science and technology, resulted in vast uncultivated plains and the Muslims' poverty.

Said Nursi explained the Ottoman collapse in the following terms in his *Sunuhat* ("Inspirations") and the Treatise of *Lemeat* ("The Treatise of Gleams") at the end of *Sözler* ("The Words"):

> Destiny allowed this calamity because we did not adhere to Islam's commandments. The Almighty Creator wanted us to perform the daily prescribed Prayers, which would occupy us for only one hour out of every twenty-four-hour day. But we neglected to do so. In return, by subjecting us to four years of training, troubles, and continuous mobilization, He forced us to a kind of Prayer. He wanted us to force our carnal souls to fast one month a year, but we pitied them. In return, He made us fast for four years. He wanted us to allocate one-fortieth of the wealth He bestowed on us to the needy and poor, but we were stingy. In return, He took from us the accumulated zakah of many years. He wanted us to go on Hajj once during our lives but we did not do so. In return, He caused us to run from front to front for four years.

At the same time, those Muslim intellectuals to whom the masses looked for guidance and salvation were attracted by the violent storm of denial based on scientific materialism and materialist philosophy. Emerging in the previous century from a human-centered worldview rooted in scientism, rationalism, and positivism, as well as from the contradictions between modern science and an anti-science Church, this storm gradually robbed Europe of most of its belief in Christianity.

This process, unparalleled in history, shook the "building" of an Islam that was already old and decayed in many hearts and minds (individual and communal). Said Nursi believed that this "building" could be protected by presenting Islam's essentials to all the faculties of modern people. Also, Muslims' actions had to display the perfection of Islamic moral qualities and the truths of belief.

Belief, knowledge of God, and worship

Before the republic, Said Nursi had already changed from "Old Said" to "New Said"; that is to say, he withdrew from public life, and began to devote himself to defending and explaining Islam's main principles of thought, belief, worship, and morality. His words reached numerous people through the copies of the *Risale-i Nur* handwritten by him and his students.

Bediüzzaman's sound, scholarly knowledge of Islam, coupled with his life experience of enduring hardship and persecution alongside ordinary but pious people and teaching them, enabled him to explain Islam and belief to modern people in apparently simple terms and in a way that could account for their experiences and worldview. Analyzing both belief and unbelief, he used clearly reasoned arguments to explain and prove the Qur'anic conception of God and His Unity, Prophethood and bodily Resurrection, and human duty of worship.

Using easily understood "parables," comparisons, and explanations, Said Nursi produced categorical proofs showing that modern scientific discoveries actually support and reinforce the truths of the Religion. He used the Qur'anic methodology of addressing each person's intellect, and all inner and outer facilities, to encourage people to study the universe and its functioning in order to understand creation's true nature and purposes. This, in turn, leads to learning the One Creator's Attributes and our own duties as God's servants.

Said Nursi explained the universe's true nature as being a comprehensive sign of its Creator, and showed via clear arguments that all fundamentals of belief can be proven rationally when the universe is read in this way. As belief is then grounded in modern science, it remains firm and immune to materialism, naturalism, and atheism.

In this framework of belief all scientific and technological advances merely uncover the workings of the cosmos. If the cosmos is thus viewed as a vast and infinitely complex and meaningful unified book describing its Single Author, all discoveries and advances reinforce, deepen, and expand belief. So, the believers' most fundamental needs—to worship God by recognizing Him with His Most Beautiful Names and Attributes, and to obey Him—are met. He focused on the essentials of belief and worship and the Qur'an's main purposes: explaining and proving Divine Existence and

Unity, Prophethood, Resurrection, and the need for worship and justice. He explains in various places of his *The Words*, *The Letters*, and *Lahikalar* (Addenda):

> Creation's highest aim and most sublime result is belief in God. The most exalted rank of humanity is knowledge of God. The most radiant happiness and sweetest bounty for jinn and humanity is love of God contained within knowledge of Him; the spirit's purest joy and the heart's purest delight is spiritual ecstasy contained within love of God. All true happiness, pure joy, sweet bounties, and unclouded pleasure are contained within the knowledge and love of God.
>
> Belief is not restricted to a brief affirmation based on imitation; rather, it has degrees and stages of development. It is like a seed growing into a fully grown, fruit-bearing tree; like the sun's image in a mirror or in a drop of water to its images on the sea's surface and to the sun itself. Belief contains so many truths pertaining to God's Names and the realities contained in the universe that the most perfect science, knowledge, and virtue is belief and knowledge of God originating in a belief based on argument and investigation. While belief based on imitation can be refuted through doubt and questions raised by modern thought, belief based on argument and investigation has as many degrees and grades of manifestation as the number of Divine Names. Those who attain certainty of belief coming from direct observation of the truths on which belief is based study the universe as a kind of Qur'an.
>
> The Qur'an, the universe, and humanity are three kinds of manifestations of one truth. The Qur'an, issuing from the Divine Attribute of Speech, may be regarded as the written or composed universe. The universe, originating in the Divine Attributes of Power and Will, may be considered as the created Qur'an. Since the universe is the Qur'an's counterpart and, in one respect, the collection of Divine laws of creation, sciences that study the universe must be compatible with Islam. Therefore now (when science prevails) and in the future (the age of knowledge), true belief should be based on argument and investigation; on continual reflection on God's "signs" in the universe; and on natural, social, historical, and psychological phenomena. Belief is not something based on blind imitation; rather, it should appeal to both the intellect or reason and the heart, for it combines reason's acceptance and affirmation with the heart's experience and submission.
>
> There is another degree of belief: certainty coming from direct experience of its truths. This depends on regular worship and reflection. Those with such belief can challenge any objection. So, our first

> and foremost duty is to acquire such belief and, in complete sincerity and purely for God's sake, spread it to others. A hadith relates that it is better for you if one embraces belief through you than for you to possess the world.

In short, Said Nursi argues that belief consists of acquiring Islam in its entirety.

The role of knowledge

Said Nursi emphasized that true knowledge yields happiness in this world and in the one to come, and that humanity came to this world to be perfected through knowledge and prayer. Thus "knowledge without the heart's insight is ignorance," for our minds need to absorb revealed religious truth, to which our heart is a mirror. "Revealed truth is reasonable, but reason on its own cannot attain it."

The heart's insight comes from the Qur'an; the mind's insight comes from the other sciences. He writes:

> The reality of the universe and all beings is based on the Divine Names. The reality of every being is based on one or many Names. All sciences and arts are based on and rely upon a Name. The true science of philosophy is based on the Name the All-Wise (al-Hakim), true medicine on the Name the All-Healing (ash-Shafi), geometry on the Name the All-Determining (al-Muqaddir), and so on. Just as each science is based on and ultimately ends in a Name, the realities of all arts, sciences, and human perfections are based on the Divine Names.

Said Nursi concludes that knowledge gained by studying the universe in God's name is true knowledge. Science interprets the universe, which is a symbolic creation of God pointing to a Truth beyond itself.

The Gleams

A look at the contents of *The Gleams* shows that in accordance with the Qur'anic way described above, it proves and explains the main truths of belief. At the same time, it answers atheists' criticisms of these truths and of Qur'anic verses. Examples of this are parts of the Twelfth, Fourteenth, and Sixteenth Gleams, which were written in reply to questions put to

Bediüzzaman by his students. Others of the Gleams, particularly the Twenty-Third, the celebrated Treatise on Nature, and in the Sixth Point of the Thirtieth, the discussion on Divine Self-Subsistence, refute in readily understandable manner naturalist and materialist philosophy.

In the face of attempts to substitute Islam with such philosophy and the innovations that accompanied these attempts, Bediüzzaman's stress on adherence to the Practices (*Sunna*) of the Prophet Muhammad, upon him be peace and blessings, may be seen notably in the Eleventh Gleam, and his solving of one of the chief points of conflict between the Sunnis and Shi'a in the Fourth—the question of "the Imamate."

The First and Second Gleams are a powerful reinforcement for faith in that they address and answer clearly one of the key questions of monotheism, that is, the true wisdom and purpose in the creation of suffering and apparent evil. Bediüzzaman moves from a simple recounting of the tales of Jonah and Job onto the inner meaning and significance of these stories and the correct attitudes and conduct to adopt when encountering suffering and tribulation in this life. The third Gleam describes how God has equipped humans with the capacity for love and the longing for eternity and how human experience of the mysteries of time is a sign of the reality of the Everlasting One and the Afterlife.

The Gleams is distinguished from the first two volumes (*The Words* and *The Letters*) of the *Risale-i Nur* in so far as it considers social effects of belief to a greater extent. For example, the Twentieth Gleam, On Sincerity, demonstrates that sincerity is the means of healing the divisions in society and achieving union. The Nineteenth encourages the important Islamic principle of frugality, of which Bediüzzaman himself was the finest example. The Twenty-Fifth addresses the sick, and the Twenty-Sixth, the elderly. These two Gleams are full of sincere and warm condolences for the sick and elderly.

In addition to this, it may be noted that in the Sixth Section of the Twenty-Ninth Letter, Bediüzzaman points out that of the six main sections of society, irreligion can offer only a superficial and temporary happiness to the youth. For the sick, the elderly, the weak and the poor, the children and the pious it can offer nothing. Thus, on being moved to the more populous centre of Isparta, he wrote the above-mentioned parts of *The Gleams*, demonstrating how true belief and Islam answer the needs of all sections of society, affording true happiness both in this world and the next.

The Twenty-Eighth Gleam, short pieces on various topics, throw important light on Qur'anic verses, the Twenty-Ninth illustrates the essence of the way of the *Risale-i Nur*—reflective thought, and the Thirtieth, another treatise of the greatest importance, expounds the Six Divine Greatest Names, or six Divine Names with all-encompassing manifestations.

Despite being written under particular constraints and in particular conditions, the *Risale-i Nur* and the present work expound a universal Qur'anic way and deal with universal problems in a manner that addresses the needs of contemporary humankind. This may be seen as the reason for its continued spread and acceptance within Turkey and throughout the world.

The
First Gleam

The First Gleam

Taking refuge in God with the supplication of the Prophet Jonah

In the Name of God, the All-Merciful, the All-Compassionate.

Eventually he called out in the veils of darkness (formed of the belly of the fish, the sea, and dark, rainy night): "There is no deity but You, All-Glorified are You (in that You are absolutely above having any defect). Surely I have been one of the wrongdoers (who have wronged themselves)." (21:87)

He called out to his Lord, saying, "Truly, affliction has visited me (so that I can no longer worship You as I must); and You are the Most Merciful of the merciful." (21:83)

*Still, if they turn away from you (*O Messenger*), say: "God is sufficient for me; there is no deity but He. In Him have I put my trust, and He is the Lord of the Supreme Throne (as the absolute Ruler and Sustainer of the universe and all creation, Who maintains and protects it)."* (9:129)

God is sufficient for us; how excellent a Guardian is He! (3:173)

There is no power and strength save with God, the All-High, the All-Mighty.

O the Everlasting, You are the Everlasting, O the Everlasting, You are the Everlasting!

For those who believe, it is guidance and healing. (41:44)

What follows are six *Gleams*, each of which describes one of the many lights emanating from the blessed verses and phrases above. Reciting these verses and phrases each thirty-three times, particularly between the Evening Prayer and the Nightfall Prayer is of great merit.

The supplication of the Prophet Jonah, upon him and our Prophet be peace and blessings, is a most powerful supplication, and a most effective means to receive an answer to our prayers from God. What follows is a summary of the well-known experience of the Prophet Jonah, upon him be peace.

He was cast into the sea, and a large fish swallowed him. The sea was stormy, and the night turbulent and dark; there was no sign of hope from any direction. While in that situation, he prayed:

> *There is no deity but You, All-Glorified are You (in that You are absolutely above having any defect). Surely I have been one of the wrongdoers (who have wronged themselves).*

This supplication was a swift means of salvation for him. The power of his prayer lies in what follows:

In that situation there was no apparent means or causes to which Jonah could have had recourse for salvation; he was in need of one who could command the whale and the sea, and the night and the sky if he were to be saved. The night, the sea, and the whale were united against him. Only one who could subject all three of these to their command could bring Jonah forth on the shore of salvation. Even if all of creation had become Jonah's servants and helpers, this would have been of no avail.

This means that apparent means and causes have no part of their own in the production of results. Since Jonah saw with the eye of certainty that there was no refuge other than the Causer of Causes, and as he, through his utmost conviction of God's absolute Oneness and His dominion over the universe, fully perceived that in addition to His overall manifestations that reign supreme over all of creation, God also has manifestations particular to each thing and being as the All-Compassionate, his supplication served to be a means for the night, the sea, and the whale to be subjected to him. Through the light of his conviction of the Oneness of God, Who has absolute control over everything, the belly of the whale became a submarine for him, and the awesome sea roaring with mountain-like waves became a peaceful plain, a pleasant place for an excursion. His supplication, based on and proclaiming God's Oneness, also served for the sky to be cleared of all clouds and for the moon to shine over his head like a lantern. Those things that had been pressing him from all sides, threatening him, now showed to him a friendly face. So he reached the shore of salvation, where under a gourd plant he fully perceived the great extent to which his Lord had favored him.

Now we are in a situation one hundred times more awful than that in which the Prophet Jonah, upon him be peace, first found himself. Our night is the future. When we look upon our future with heedlessness towards our religious responsibilities, it is a hundred times darker and more fearful than his night. Our sea is this moving, unstable earth. Each wave of this sea bears on it thousands of dead bodies, and so is a thousand times more frightening than his sea. Our fish consists of the lusts and caprices of our evil-commanding soul, which strive to destroy our eternal life. Such a fish is a thousand times more harmful than his. For his fish could have destroyed a hundred-year lifespan, whereas ours seeks to destroy a life that will last hundreds of millions of years.

This being our true state, we should do as the Prophet Jonah, upon him be peace, did; turning away from all means and causes, we should take refuge directly in our Lord, Who is the Causer of Causes. We should say:

> *There is no deity but You, All-Glorified are You (in that You are absolutely above having any defect). Surely I have been one of the wrongdoers (who have wronged themselves).*

We should understand and know with a certainty which comes from observation that only He, our Lord, Who keeps the future under His command, the world under His absolute control, and our evil-commanding souls under His direction, can remove from us the harm of the future, this world, and the lusts and caprices of our evil-commanding souls, all of which are united against us because of our neglect and misguidance.

What agent is there other than the Creator of the heavens and earth who can know whatever occurs in our heart, down to its most subtle and secret thoughts, and illuminate the future for us by establishing the Hereafter, saving us from the countless suffocating waves of the world? Nothing, no one other than the Necessarily Existent One can in any way help us or save us; we can only be saved with His will and permission.

As this was the case, the result of Jonah's prayers was that the whale became a mount or a vessel for him and the sea became a peaceful plain; the night was serenely lit for him by the moon. We too should then make the same supplication:

> *There is no deity but You, All-Glorified are You (in that You are absolutely above having any defect). Surely I have been one of the wrongdoers (who have wronged themselves).*

With the sentence *There is no deity but You*, we should ask for God's mercy upon our future; with the phrase *All-Glorified are You* we should ask for mercy upon our world; with the phrase *Surely I have been one of the wrongdoers (who have wronged themselves)*, we should ask for mercy upon our souls. Thus, our future may be illuminated with the light of belief in an atmosphere that is lit by the Qur'an, and the awe and dread of our night may be transformed into serenity and joy. Also, while we travel this earth amidst the waves of years and centuries, a sea on which countless beings have embarked, and one out of which countless ones have been thrown into nothingness through the alternation of life and death, we should board the vessel of the truth of Islam, constructed in the dockyards of the wise Qur'an, so that we may fulfill our duty of life on the shore of safety and salvation. The tempest and turbulence of the sea will become a series of pleasing, ever-renewed spectacles, like the changing scenes on a screen, and instead of instilling fearful loneliness and dread they will enlighten our minds and urge us to take a reflective look on everything around us and to learn from the lessons. By virtue of the guidance of the Qur'an and the education that the Criterion of Truth and Falsehood gives, our soul will no longer ride us, but will instead become our mount. As we ride it, it will serve us to attain eternal life.

In short, humans have a comprehensive nature; as we suffer from and shiver with the infection of malaria, so also do we suffer from the quakes and tremors of the earth, and will also suffer from the mighty convulsions that all of creation will undergo on the Day of Resurrection. As we fear a microscopic organism, we also fear a shooting star that appears among the heavenly bodies. As we love our home, we also love the entire world. As we love our little garden, we also love the infinite and eternal Paradise, and we love this ardently. Therefore, such a being's object of worship, the Lord, our refuge, our savior, and our goal can only be the One in Whose grasp of Power is the whole universe, and under Whose command are both the atoms and planets, at one and the same time. Human beings therefore need to constantly pray, saying like Jonah, upon him be peace:

> *There is no deity but You, All-Glorified are You (in that You are absolutely above having any defect). Surely I have been one of the wrongdoers (who have wronged themselves).*

All-Glorified are You. We have no knowledge save what You have taught us. Surely You are the All-Knowing, the All-Wise.

The Second Gleam

The Second Gleam

Illnesses and seeking recovery through the prayer of the Prophet Job

In the Name of God, the All-Merciful, the All-Compassionate.

And (mention) Job: He called out to his Lord, saying: "Truly, affliction has visited me (so that I can no longer worship You as I must); and You are the Most Merciful of the merciful." (21:83)

The prayer of the Prophet Job, upon him be peace, the hero of patience, has proved effective as a means of recovery to many who have recited it during their tribulations. Drawing on the verse, we should say in our prayer: "*Truly, affliction has visited me; and You are the Most Merciful of the merciful.*"

What follows is a summary of the well-known experience of the Prophet Job, upon him be peace.

Job was afflicted with numerous wounds and sores over a long period of time, yet he endured his sickness with utmost patience, thinking that a great recompense would be given in return. But later, when he felt he could no longer worship God with his heart and tongue, which are the seat of knowledge and remembrance of God, he feared that his duty of worship would suffer, and so he said in a prayer, not for the sake of his own comfort, but for the sake of his worship of God, "*Affliction has visited me, and You are the Most Merciful of the merciful!*" God Almighty accepted this sincere, disinterested, and devout supplication in the most miraculous fashion. He granted Job perfect good health and made manifest in him an abundance of compassion.

Thus, this Gleam contains five points:

First point

Corresponding to the physical wounds and illnesses of the Prophet Job, upon him be peace, we have inner, spiritual diseases. If our inner being was to be turned to the outside, and our outer being turned inward, we would appear with more wounds and diseases than the Prophet Job. For each sin that we commit and each doubt that enters our mind causes wounds in our heart and our spirit.

The wounds of the Prophet Job, upon him be peace, were of such a nature that they threatened his brief, worldly life, but our inner wounds threaten our infinitely longer, everlasting life. We need the supplication of Job thousands of times more than he did. His wounds and diseases affected his heart and tongue, while the wounds that arise from sins, the temptations and the doubts that arise from these wounds, inflict damage upon the inner dimension of the heart, which is the seat of belief, thus,—we seek refuge in God from such a thing—harming our belief. They also prevent the spiritual joy which comes from religious recitations with the tongue, which interprets the belief in the heart, thus causing it to turn away from recitation in aversion.

Sin penetrates to the heart, darkens and hardens it until it extinguishes the light of belief. Each sin has a path that leads to unbelief. Unless that sin is swiftly obliterated by seeking God's forgiveness, it grows from a worm into a snake that gnaws at the heart.

For example, when a person secretly commits a shameful sin and feels great shame, fearing that others may become aware of this misdeed, they find the existence of angels and spiritual beings too much to endure. They then wish that there were some evidence to deny their existence. Similarly, if one who commits a major sin that deserves the punishment of Hell does not try to shield themselves from the sin by imploring God's forgiveness, they will then wholeheartedly wish for Hell's non-existence, and they dare to deny the existence of Hell if they find any encouragement.

Again, people usually feel hurt and distressed when receiving even the slightest of reproaches from their superiors. So one who shows laziness in fulfilling their duty of servanthood, such as failing to perform the daily obligatory Prayers despite the repeated orders of the Sovereign of Eternity, will feel greatly distressed and wish there were no such duty of servanthood. In turn, there will arise from this wish a desire to deny God, which implies enmity towards Him. If some doubt concerning God's existence occurs in their heart, they will be inclined to cling to it as conclusive proof. Thus, a wide door to destruction will be opened in front of them. That wretched one does not know that even if the duty of servanthood may cause slight discomfort or bother, by denying God's existence, they make themselves the target of spiritual troubles that are millions of times more distressing. While agonizing over the bite of a gnat, they welcome the bite of a snake. Many more examples can be coined, but these three are enough to understand the meaning of *But what they themselves have earned has rusted upon their hearts* (83: 14).

Second point

As was explained in the Twenty-Sixth Word in *The Words* concerning the meaning of Divine Destiny, people have no right to complain about disasters and illnesses for the following three reasons:

FIRST REASON: God Almighty has made the garment of the body with which He has clothed people a manifestation of His Art. He has made people a model by which to cut, trim, and change the garment of the body, thus displaying the manifestations of His various Names. Just as the Name of the All-Healing manifests Itself by favoring the ill with recovery, so too the Name of the All-Providing is recognized through the satisfaction of hunger. He is the Master of all dominion, and is free to operate however He wills in His dominion.

SECOND REASON: Life is refined, perfected, and strengthened through disasters and illnesses, and fulfils its own purpose. Life led monotonously on the couch of ease and comfort cannot be regarded as existence and does not serve it. Rather, it is almost identical with non-existence.

THIRD REASON: This world is the realm of testing, the abode of service. It is not the place of pleasure or being rewarded for things that were performed in God's cause. So diseases and misfortunes—as long as they do not harm the Religion and are patiently endured—conform fully to service and worship, and even strengthen it. Since such diseases and misfortunes make each hour's worship equivalent to that of a day, one should offer thanks instead of complaining.

Worship consists of two kinds, positive and negative. What is meant by positive is the worship we perform regularly. As for negative worship, this is when one who is afflicted with misfortune or disease perceives their own weakness and helplessness, turning to and seeking refuge in their Compassionate Lord, concentrating upon Him, and entreating Him, and thus offers a pure form of worship. Hypocrisy cannot penetrate this kind of worship. If one endures patiently, concentrating on the rewards to be given in return for misfortune, and offers thanks, then each hour that passes will count as a whole day spent in worship.

I once was very anxious because of a severe illness that struck one of my brothers of the Hereafter, Muhajir Hafiz Ahmed. But it occurred to my heart that I should congratulate him because each minute he spent was counted as a whole day's worship. He himself was enduring his illness in patience and thankfulness.

Third point

As we have pointed out in one or two of the Words (included in *The Words*), whenever a person thinks of their past life, an utterance of either agony, joy, or relief comes to their tongue. That is, one either regrets or thanks God, saying, "All praise and thanks are for God."

What causes people to regret is the agony that arises from the termination of former pleasures. The termination of pleasure is a pain in itself. Sometimes a temporary pleasure causes incessant pain, and concentration on it will be like lancing a wound, causing regret to gush forth.

Yet, the continual pleasure felt in the spirit that arises from the cessation of past temporary pains leads one to utter, "All praise and thanks are for God." In addition to this innate tendency of humanity, if one considers the reward to be given in the Hereafter in return for misfortune and thinks that a brief life will count as a long life spent in reward and that it will bring good, then instead of showing just patience, one will be thankful. So one should say, "All praise and thanks are for God for every state, save unbelief and misguidance."

People say, "Hard times seem interminable." Indeed they do, but not because such times are distressing, as people usually imagine, but rather because they yield important results, the same as a long life does.

Fourth point

As was explained in the First Station of the Twenty-First Word, if a person does not waste the power of patience God Almighty has given to them on baseless fears and worries, this patience will suffice for every misfortune. But if one wastes the power of patience on the misfortunes that are past or on imagined ones of the future, instead of concentrating on the present misfortune—a state that is caused by being under the influence of groundless apprehensions and anxieties—as one is unaware of the nature of things and events and perceives this transient life as if it were eternal, then one's patience will not be able to cope with the misfortunes of the present. As a result, people begin to complain. People complain in a manner as if—God forbid!—they were complaining about God Almighty to others. In a most unjustified and even insane manner, they complain and display impatience.

If the day that is past held misfortune, the distress is now gone, and only tranquility remains; the pain has vanished and the pleasure in its cessation remains; the trouble is gone, and the reward remains. Hence one should not complain, but give thanks in joy. One should not resent misfortune but love it. Any part of the transient life that has passed in misfortune comes to be counted as an eternal, blessed life owing to the misfortune. So worrying about the repetition of pains suffered in the past and wasting part of one's patience on such worries is lunacy.

As for the future, since they have not yet arrived, thinking of diseases or misfortune that will probably come and showing impatience by complaining and feeling stressed or wearied is also foolishness. This is as ridiculous as complaining now about future hunger or thirst, as thinking about them now, and eating and drinking all day to avoid such possible afflictions. This self-oppression is so ridiculous that one who is afflicted with it no longer deserves pity and compassion.

In short, just as thankfulness increases Divine bounty, so too complaints increase misfortune, leaving no justified reason for compassion.

During the initial year of World War I, a virtuous person in Erzurum was afflicted with a bad disease. I went to visit him, and he said to me, complaining bitterly, "For a hundred nights I have not been able to place my head on the pillow and sleep." I felt great sorrow and pity for him. Suddenly a thought came to me and I said:

> Brother, your past hundred troublesome days are now just like one hundred happy days. So do not think of them and complain; rather consider them in their true nature and be thankful. As for future days, since they have not yet come, seek refuge in the Mercy of your All-Merciful, All-Compassionate Lord. Do not weep without being beaten, do not be afraid of something that is non-existent, and do not give something non-existent the color of existence. Concentrate on the present hour; your power of patience will suffice for this hour.
>
> Do not act like a foolish commander who, although the left wing of the enemy force has joined his right wing and reinforced him, disperses his forces in the center to the left and the right even before the right wing of the enemy is ready to fight. Thus he weakens his own center, and the enemy destroys it with minimal effort.

I added:

> Brother, do not be like that foolish commander! Mobilize all your forces against the present hour. Think of Divine mercy and the other worldly rewards; consider how you can transform your brief, transient life into a long, everlasting one. So, instead of complaining bitterly, give joyful thanks.

Much relieved, he said, "All praise and thanks be to God, my disease is now a tenth of what it was before."

Fifth point

This point consists of three matters.

FIRST MATTER: Genuine and harmful misfortune is that which affects the Religion and one's religious life. One should always seek refuge in tears at the Divine Court from misfortune in matters of Religion, and cry out for help. However, any misfortune that does not affect the Religion or one's religious life is not misfortune from the perspective of truth. Some such misfortunes are merciful warnings from the All-Merciful One. Consider the shepherd who throws a stone at his sheep when they trespass on another's field; the sheep, feeling that the stone is intended as a warning to save them from a harmful action, turn back gladly. Similarly, there are many apparent misfortunes that are in reality Divine warnings and admonitions; some others serve for atonement for and forgiveness of sins, while yet others arise from heedlessness of religious duties, and remind us of our human helplessness and weakness, thus giving us some sort of peace and serenity.

Diseases regarded as misfortune are, as has already been mentioned, not misfortune, but rather a favor from God and a means of purification. There is a Prophetic Tradition which says, "Just as a tree drops its ripe fruit when shaken, so too do sins fall away through the shivering of a fever."[1]

The Prophet Job, upon him be peace, did not pray for the comfort of his soul, but rather sought a cure for the purpose of worship when his disease began to prevent his remembrances of God with his tongue and his reflection upon the truths of belief and similar topics in his heart. We too should make our primary intent, when making that supplication, the healing of our inward and spiritual wounds that arise from sinning.

If physical diseases hinder our worship, we may seek refuge at the Divine Court from them. However, we should seek refuge in a humble and supplicating fashion, not in a protesting and complaining manner. Since we are pleased with God as our Lord, then we must resign ourselves to all that He gives us as a manifestation of His Lordship.

To sigh and complain in a manner that suggests we object to Divine Destiny and Decree is a form of criticizing Divine Destiny, an accusation leveled against God's compassion. One who criticizes Divine Destiny is hitting their head against an anvil and breaking it. One who finds fault with God's mercy will inevitably be deprived of it. Using a broken hand to take revenge will only induce further damage to the hand. Similarly, a person who when afflicted with misfortune responds to it with protest and complaint, only compounds their misfortune.

SECOND MATTER: Physical misfortunes grow when they are seen to be large, and shrink when they are seen to be small. For example, we think we see something at night. If we concentrate on it as if it were a real thing, it

1 Al-Bukhari, *al-Jami' as-Sahih*, "Marda" 2; Ibn Maja, *Sunan*, "Tibb" 18.

grows bigger, but if we do not, it disappears. As another example, if we attempt to ward off an attacking swarm of bees, they will become more aggressive, but if we go on without paying them any attention, they will disperse. In the same way, physical misfortunes, when perceived as great and given attention, grow, and worry causes them to penetrate the body and take root in the heart. This will additionally give rise to inward affliction, which in turn causes the outward, physical misfortune to perpetuate itself.

However, if the worry is removed through resignation to the Divine Decree and reliance on God, the physical misfortune will gradually decrease, dry up and disappear, just like a tree whose roots have been severed. I once said the following to describe this reality:

> O helpless one, give up lamenting over misfortune and trust in God,
> For know that this lamenting is an error that causes trouble after trouble;
> If you have found the One Who makes you suffer, then know that misfortune is a gift that brings peace and happiness.
> But if you do not find Him, know that the whole world is
> A place of suffering and misfortune doomed to destruction.
> So, when you have such a great responsibility (as to be able to make this transient world the field of the Hereafter),
> Why do you lament over an insignificant misfortune?
> Come, put your trust in God and smile at the face of misfortune
> So that it may also smile, for as it smiles, it lessens and changes.

If, when fighting, one smiles at the enemy, enmity, however bitter it may be, will lessen and change into reconciliation, and will even disappear. Just so, if one confronts misfortune with reliance on God, the result will be the same.

THIRD MATTER: Each age has characteristics particular to itself. In this age of heedlessness of Divine orders misfortune has changed its nature. It is not misfortune, but rather a Divine favor for certain persons at certain times.

I especially regard those afflicted with illness at this time as fortunate—provided their illness does not affect their faith or religious life—and therefore I cannot oppose illness or certain other kinds of misfortune. Nor can I feel pity for them. Whenever a sick young man comes to visit me, I see him, in comparison to his peers, as being more concerned with and devoted to his religious duties and the Hereafter. This gives me the idea that illness is not a misfortune for such people, but rather a Divine favor. For, although illness causes some trouble for such a person in their brief, transient worldly life, in reality it is beneficial for their eternal life. It counts as a form of worship. If this person recovers, they will not be able to maintain the spiritual state they had during their illness and might fall into dissipation because of the intoxicating lures of youth and dissoluteness of the present time.

Conclusion

In order to display His infinite Power and limitless Mercy, God Almighty has created humankind with unlimited innate impotence or helplessness as well as poverty or want. He has also created it to be like a machine that has the capacity to receive unlimited varieties of pain as well as innumerable varieties of pleasure to exhibit the countless examples of His Names. Within that human machine are hundreds of instruments, each of which has its own particular pains and pleasures, duties and rewards. It can be said that all the Divine Names manifested in the universe, which is like an example of the human on a macro scale, also have manifestations in the human, which is the micro-cosmos.

Whatever is beneficial to human beings, such as good health, appetites, and pleasures, leads the human to offer thanks, prompts the machine to carry out its functions in many respects, and thus the human becomes a factory that produces thanks. Likewise, afflictions such as illness, pain, and other things that provoke suffering and trouble set in motion other mechanisms in that machine, working the mines of helplessness, weakness, and poverty that are inherent in human nature. They put human beings in a state where they are ready to seek help and refuge, but not only with a single tongue but with the tongue of all its members. Thus the human becomes like a moving pen that consists of thousands of different pens due to those afflictions. Humans inscribe their life history on the page of their life or on a tablet that belongs to the World of Immaterial Representations or Ideal Forms; they make it a board where the manifestations of the Divine Names can be read and the human becomes like an ode composed by the All-Glorified Being, thus fulfilling the duty required by his or her creation.

The Third Gleam

The Third Gleam

Everything is perishable except God and the good deeds pleasing Him

In the Name of God, the All-Merciful, the All-Compassionate.

Everything is perishable (and so perishing) except His "Face." His alone is judgment and authority, and to Him you are being brought back. (28: 88)

The repeated phrase O *Everlasting One, You are the Everlasting!* O *Everlasting One, You are the Everlasting!*, which echoes the meaning of the above-mentioned verse, expresses two important truths. It is for this reason that some elders of the Sufi Order of Naqshbandiya have made repeating it a certain number of times a special invocation, adopting it as a concise Naqshi supplication. As this phrase echoes the meaning of the mighty verse whose meaning is mentioned above, we will examine some points included in its significant truth.

First point

When recited for the first time, the phrase O *Everlasting One, You are the Everlasting!* cuts the heart from everything other than God, like a form of major heart surgery. The way this happens is as follows:

Because of the comprehensiveness of their nature, human beings are connected with almost all of creation. In addition, a boundless capacity to love is included in the comprehensive nature of human beings. For this reason, humans feel love for the whole of creation. They love the huge world as if it were their house; they love eternal Paradise as if it were their garden. However, whatever of creation the human loves does not remain; it all departs. So human beings continuously suffer the pain of separation, and their boundless love becomes the means of boundless agony.

It is our fault that we suffer such agony, for the boundless capacity to love has been given to us so that we direct it towards the One Who possesses an infinite, everlasting beauty. Human beings are in error when they misuse this capacity to love mortal beings, and in turn suffer the punishment in the form of pangs of separation.

And so, when recited for the first time, the phrase O *Everlasting One, You are the Everlasting!* signifies that the person is cleansing themselves from this error and, freeing themselves from attachment to mortal creation by abandoning it before it abandons them, has restricted their love to the Everlasting, the Beloved. What they are saying is, "The only Truly Everlasting One is You! Everything other than You is mortal. Anything mortal certainly cannot be the object of an enduring love; it cannot be loved eternally by a heart created for eternity. Since those innumerable beloveds are mortal and bound to depart, leaving me, I declare, O *Everlasting One, You are the Everlasting!* and leave them before they leave me. Only You are everlasting, and I know and believe that beings can only subsist by Your making them subsist. Thus, they should be loved because of Your love. They are otherwise not worthy of the heart's attachment."

When in this state, the human heart abandons innumerable objects of love. Seeing the stamp of mortality on the beauty and loveliness of these objects, it severs the attachment. If it does not do this, it will make itself suffer a wound for each beloved.

The second O *Everlasting One, You are the Everlasting!* serves as both an ointment and a cure for those wounds. That is: "O Everlasting One! Since You are everlasting, this is sufficient, You have taken the place of everything, and anything that exists exists only because of Your Existence."

Truly, any beauty, grace, or perfection in creation, which are causes of love, are indications of the Truly Everlasting One's Beauty, Grace, and Perfections, and are their pale shadows reflected through numerous veils. It can even be said that they are the shadows of the shadows of the manifestations of His All-Beautiful Names.

Second point

Human beings innately have a passionate love for immortality. This love is such that, because of the faculty of imagination, humans first fancy a sort of immortality in everything they love, and this is why they love it. Whenever they think of or see the death of what they love, they cry out from the depths of their being. All the lamentations arising from separation are in fact interpretations of the weeping that results from the love of immortality. If human beings were not able to perceive immortality, they could not love anything. It could even be said that one of the reasons for the existence of the everlasting realm and eternal Paradise is that humans cherish a passionate desire for immortality because of the intense love of immortality in their nature, and all humanity innately prays for immortality. It is because the Everlasting One of Majesty has accepted this intense, never-fading, innate desire of humans and their effective, powerful prayer that He has created an everlasting realm for humanity bound to die in this transient world.

Is it possible to think that the Munificent, Compassionate Creator would accept the insignificant desire of our stomachs and the supplication they make through the tongue of disposition for a temporary permanence or life, and create innumerable kinds of delicious foods—is it possible that such a Munificent, Compassionate Creator would not accept the passionate desire of all humanity arising from an overwhelming innate need, and the constant prayer for immortality it offers verbally and innately based on a universal, deep-rooted reality? God forbid, a hundred thousand times! It is impossible that He would not accept it. Its rejection could never be in conformity with His Wisdom, His Justice, His Mercy, and His Power.

Since humans deeply love immortality, all their perfections and pleasures are dependent on immortality. And since immortality is particular to the Everlasting One of Majesty and the Everlasting One's Names are also everlasting, and since the mirrors of the Everlasting One take on the color of the Everlasting One, reflecting His manifestations, and are favored with some sort of immortality, surely the matter most necessary for human beings, their most important duty, is to form a relationship with that

Everlasting One and to hold fast to His Names. For everything expended on the way of the Everlasting One is favored with some sort of immortality.

So, the second O *Everlasting One*, *You are the Everlasting!* expresses this truth. In addition to providing a cure for the countless spiritual wounds of humanity, it satisfies the intense desire for immortality that is inherent in its nature.

Third point

In this world, time has extremely diverse effects on the death and decay of things. Although things and beings exist one within another like concentric circles, they differ greatly in decay and death.

Just as the hands of a clock counting the seconds, minutes, and hours resemble one another in appearance, but differ in respect of speed, so too do the spheres of the body, soul, heart, and spirit in the human differ from each other. For example, while the body has a life, existence, and endurance restricted to each day, or even the hour, and although it has no consciousness of the past or the future, the heart has a wide sphere of existence and life that extends through many days, both the past, the present, and the future. As for the spirit, its sphere of life and existence extends from years before the present day to the years following it.

Considering this reality, when time is spent in worship of the All-Merciful, All-Glorified God, embedded with knowledge and love of Him, pursuing His approval and good pleasure, which is the source of the life of the heart and spirit, our transient life in this world encapsulates the seeds of and results in an everlasting life. It takes on the effect of an eternal life.

Truly, one second spent for the good pleasure of the Truly Everlasting One in knowledge of and love for Him is equivalent to a year. If it is not lived for His sake, a year lasts no longer than a second. It can even be said that a single second spent for His good pleasure gains immortality. A hundred years spent in this world by people heedless of Divine truths and orders are in fact only a second.

There is the famous saying, "A moment's separation is as long as a year, and a year's union passes as swiftly as a second." I say, in complete opposition to this, a moment's union for the sake of God within the bounds of the Everlasting One of Majesty's good pleasure is a window opening onto a perpetual union. Not one year, but perhaps a thousand years, spent in misguidance and heedlessness of Divine truths and orders are like a second. There is another saying which corroborates this: "When in the company of enemies the vast earth is like a cup, while the eye of a needle in the company of friends is like a broad field."

The true meaning of the first saying above is this: since union with mortal beings is transient, however long it is, it is brief. A year in such union passes like a second, and is an illusion. It occurs to one like a daydream causing regret, or like a dream bringing sorrow. The human heart, which desires immortality, can take in one year's union the tiniest pleasure of a moment. As for separation, its one moment becomes as if not one year but many years. For the arena of separation is broad. A heart yearning for eternity suffers years of destruction because of separation, even if this separation is only for a second, for it evokes innumerable separations. All of the past and future are filled with separations from physical and earthly loves.

In connection with this matter we say:

> O people! Do you want to make your brief and useless life long, immortal, beneficial, and fruitful? To want this is a natural requirement of being human; so then spend your life on the way of the Truly Everlasting One. For anything turned to the Everlasting One receives the manifestation of immortality.

Since everyone passionately desires a long life and yearns for immortality, and since there is a means of transforming this transitory life into an everlasting life, surely anyone who still preserves their humanity will seek out that means and try to transform that possibility into a reality, acting accordingly. The means in question are as follows: do whatever you should do for God's sake, meet with others for God's sake, and work for God's sake. Act within the sphere of "for God, for God's sake, and on account of God." Then all the minutes of your life will become like years.

The fact that the Qur'an regards the Night of Power and Destiny as being equal to, or even better than, a thousand months, that is, about eighty years, indicates this truth.[2] Also, the Ascension[3] which our Prophet, upon him be peace and blessings, made in a few minutes but which, by the expansion of time, had the effect of many years—a fact unquestionably accepted by the people of sainthood and truth—proves this truth and factually demonstrates it. The few minutes of the Ascension were as long, broad, and comprehensive as thousands of years. For the Prophet, upon him be peace and blessings, entered the world of permanence by way of the Ascension, and a few minutes of that world comprise thousands of years of this world.

As already mentioned, the expansion of time is a well-known fact that has been experienced by many saints. It is related that some saints did a day's work in a single minute, some performed the duties of a year in an hour, and some others recited the whole Qur'an within a single minute. Such people of truth and honesty would never knowingly stoop to lying. There can be no doubt that they have observed the fact of the expansion of time, which has so far been widely and unanimously reported.

An example of the expansion of time that can be confirmed by all is experienced in dreams. A day in the waking world, or many days, would be necessary to experience the occurrences, words, pleasures, and pains that are sometimes experienced in the dream of a minute.

In short, certainly, humans are mortal, but they have been created for immortality and as the mirrors to an Everlasting One, and they have been charged with duties which produce perpetual fruit, and have been given a form that is a medium for the everlasting Names of the Everlasting One. This being the case, the true duty of such a being is to hold fast with all their ability and faculties to the Names of that Everlasting, Eternal One within

---

2 The Qur'an reads:

We have surely sent it (the Qur'an) down in the Night of Destiny and Power. What enables you to perceive what the Night of Destiny and Power is? The Night of Destiny and Power is better than a thousand months! The angels and the Spirit descend in it by the permission of their Lord with His decrees for every affair—(Being) a sheer mercy and security (from all misfortunes, for the servants who spend it in devotions in appreciation of its worth), (being) until the rising of the dawn. (97:1–5).

God Almighty keeps the Night of Destiny and Power hidden so that people should value every night and worship Him during it. God's Messenger, upon him be peace and blessings, recommends that we look for it among the last ten nights of the holy month of Ramadan. (Tr.)

3 The Ascension (*al-Mi'raj*): The miraculous journeying of the Prophet Muhammad, upon him be peace and blessings, through the realms of existence beyond the limit of forms, during which he witnessed the supreme signs of God.

the bounds of the things that please Him, and to go on towards Him on the way to eternity. As their tongue utters, "O Everlasting One, You are the Everlasting!", so their heart, spirit, mind, and all their other faculties should pronounce:

> *He is the Everlasting! He is the Eternal, uncontained in time! He is the All-Enduring! He is the All-Perpetual! He is the One Sought! He is the Beloved! He is the One Desired! He is the One Worshipped!*

All-Glorified are You. We have no knowledge save what You have taught us. Surely You are the All-Knowing, the All-Wise.

Our Lord, take us not to task if we forget or make mistakes!

The Fourth Gleam

The Fourth Gleam

The highway of the Sunna

The title "The Highway of the Sunna" is appropriate for this treatise.

Although the matter of the Imamate and Caliphate is of secondary importance, it has been given excessive importance and discussed among the matters of belief in theology and the essentials of the Religion. So, since it has a relevance to our basic duty towards the Qur'an and belief, it is worth discussing in part here.

In the Name of God, the All-Merciful, the All-Compassionate.

There has come to you a Messenger from among yourselves; extremely grievous to him is your suffering, full of concern for you is he, and for the believers full of pity and compassion. Still, if they turn away from you (O Messenger), say: "God is sufficient for me; there is no deity but He. In Him have I put my trust, and He is the Lord of the Supreme Throne." (9:128–129)

Say: "I ask of you no wage for it (conveying God's Religion to you), but (I ask of you) love for my near relatives." (42:23)

We will point out in two Stations two of the many mighty truths that are contained in these powerful verses.

First station

This Station consists of four Points.

First point

This highlights God's noblest Messenger's, upon him be peace and blessings, perfect mercy and compassion towards his Community.

As reported through reliable channels of narration in authenticated sources, while everyone else, including even the other Prophets, will feel that they have enough trouble of their own on the Day of Resurrection, God's noblest Messenger, upon him be peace and blessings, will be completely concerned with his people and will call out, "My Community! My Community!" Also, as reliably narrated and affirmed by the saints who have penetration into time and certain secret truths and events, when he was newly born, his mother heard him supplicating for his Community, saying, "My Community! My Community!" In addition, as his whole life history and the laudable, high standards of conduct which he personally exhibited and promulgated demonstrate his perfect compassion and affection, by asking his whole Community to pray for him (so that he could get more strength and be more successful in conveying his Message and dealing with the affairs of his Community), he showed that he was concerned with the happiness of all of them and thus displayed his boundless compassion. So, you can understand what great ingratitude and injustice it would be not to follow the way of such an affectionate and merciful leader.

Second point

Among his universal and all-embracing duties of Prophethood, the noblest Messenger, upon him be peace and blessings, displayed great compassion for certain particular, minor elements. Considered superficially, his great compassion for such elements could appear to be irreconcilable with the supreme importance of the mission of Prophethood. But in reality, since such minor elements were exemplary links in a chain that would become the means of the fulfillment of a universal duty of Prophethood, exceptional importance was attached to such links for the sake of the chain.

For example, the extraordinary compassion the noblest Messenger, upon him be peace and blessings, showed towards Hasan and Husayn[4] in their childhood and the great importance he attached to them did not arise only from his love because of a family relationship; his affection for them was rather because they would act as the origin, example, and index of an exceptionally important community that would carry on the religious duties which had been established through the Prophethood.

Indeed, while the noblest Prophet, upon him be peace and blessings, took Hasan, may God be pleased with him, into his arms out of his exceptional compassion and kissed him on the head, he did so not only out of his love and affection for him personally but also for the sake of the certain *Mahdi*-like[5] heirs to the mission of Prophethood and bearers of the sacred Shari'a of Muhammad such as *Ghawth al-A'zam* Shah Jilani,[6] who would appear among his blessed, light-diffusing descendants. He saw with the eye of Prophethood the sacred service they would render in the future, and approved and applauded them, and as a sign of his approval and encouragement kissed Hasan on the head.

Also, he kissed Husayn, may God be pleased with him, on the neck and thus showed his extraordinary compassion for him and the extraordinary importance he attached to him. This was not only for the sake of Husayn himself but also for the sake of many *Mahdi*-like light-diffusing persons such as Zayn al-'Abidin and Ja'far as-Sadiq who would appear among his radiant progeny as illustrious Imams, and on account of the religion of Islam and the mission of Messengership.

The Prophet Muhammad, upon him be peace and blessings, had a heart that could get certain knowledge from the Unseen, and illumined eyes with which he would observe the Place of the Supreme Gathering on the side of eternity from the Age of Happiness in this world, see Paradise and

---

4 Hasan and Husayn, may God be pleased with them, are the grandsons of God's Messenger, upon him be peace and blessings, through his beloved daughter Fatima and his cousin 'Ali, may God be pleased with them. (Tr.)

5 *Mahdi* is the title of the person promised to come towards the end of time in order to revive the Islamic creed and life and establish justice in the world. (Tr.)

6 'Abdul-Qadir al-Jilani (d. 1166): One of the most celebrated Sufi masters. A student of jurisprudence and Hadith, he became known as the *Qutb* (spiritual pole) of his age and the *Ghawth al-'A'zam* (the greatest succor). He wrote *Kitab al-Ghunyah, Futuh al-Ghayb* and *al-Fath ar-Rabbani*.

watch angels in the heavens from the earth, monitor events that remained concealed in the dark veils of the past from the time of Adam, and penetrate the future.[7] He was also favored with some sort of vision of the All-Majestic One.[8] That illustrious Prophet certainly saw the spiritual poles (spiritual leaders), and the Imams who would be heirs to the duties of Prophethood, and *Mahdi*-like persons, who would descend from Hasan and Husayn, and kissed them on the head on their behalf. So, Shah Jilani has a share of the kiss that Hasan received.

Third point

According to one interpretation, the meaning of the verse, *I ask of you no wage for it (conveying God's Religion to you), but (I ask of you) love for my near relatives* (42:23) is that the noblest Messenger, upon him be peace and blessings, asked for no wage to carry out the duty of Messengership, but he asked for love to be shown to the members of his Family.

It might be interpreted that this means the Messenger was pursuing advantage for his Family, yet, according to Divine declaration, *Surely the noblest, most honorable of you in God's sight is the one best in piety, righteousness, and reverence for God* (49:13), the mission of Messengership considered not family relationships, but nearness to God.

THE ANSWER: With his future-penetrating power of sight, the noblest Messenger, upon him be peace and blessings, saw that his Family would become like a light-diffusing tree in the world of Islam. The overwhelming majority of those who would guide and instruct peoples at every level and stratum in the attainment of human perfections would appear among his descendants. He discerned that his Community's prayer for his Family in the final section of the Prayers, "O God, bestow Your blessings upon our master Muhammad and on the Family of our master Muhammad, as You bestowed Your blessings on Abraham and on the family of Abraham. Indeed, You are the All-Praiseworthy, the All-Sublime," would be accepted. In other words, just as the overwhelming majority of the light-diffusing guides among the people of Abraham were

---

7 al-Bukhari, *al-Jami' as-Sahih*, "Riqaq" 44, "Mawaqit as-Salah" 11, Manaqib, 1; Muslim, *al-Jami' as-Sahih*, "Munafiqun" 28, "Fadail" 136; at-Tirmidhi, *Sunan*, "Zuhd" 9, "Tafsir Sura" 42. (Tr.)

8 *at-Tirmidhi*, "Tafsir Sura" 53; at-Tabarani, *al-Mu'jam al-Kabir*, 11:332; al-Hakim, *al-Mustadrak*, 2:629. (Tr.)

Prophets who emerged from his offspring, he saw amongst his family the greatest of the guides and scholars who would perform the most important Islamic duties and lead along the spiritual paths, teaching Islam and its practice—people who would perform in Islam the function which the Prophets of Israel carried out in the history of the Children of Israel. It is because of this that having been ordered to declare, *I ask of you no wage for it (conveying God's Religion to you), but (I ask of you) love for my near relatives*, he asked his Community to love his Family. In one of several other declarations which corroborate this, he decreed, "I leave you two precious things. If you hold fast to them, you will find salvation. They are God's Book and my Family."[9] For the source and guardians of the Sunna of the Prophet were his Family and they were first of all responsible for adhering to it in every respect.

This truth, declared by the noblest Messenger, upon him be peace and blessings, has been transmitted through later generations under the heading of following the Book and the Sunna—the Prophet's Way. This means that by bringing his Family to the attention of his Community he stressed the importance of his Sunna in respect of his mission of Messengership. So, one who abandons following the Sunna can neither be regarded as belonging to the Prophet's Family nor become a true friend to them.

Also, the reason he desired to gather his Community around his Family was that, with God's leave, he knew his Family would grow over the course of time, and that Islam was going to become weak. Therefore, an extremely strong group of people in solidarity was necessary so that it could be the means of and center for the spiritual and moral progress of the world of Islam. With Divine leave, he thought of this, and desired to gather his Community around his Family.

Even though the members of the Prophet's Family were not always leading others in belief and conviction, they were greatly ahead of them in respect of submission and support for Islam. For they were predisposed to Islam because, first of all, they were of the same family as God's Messenger. The support or partisanship coming from family ties cannot easily be abandoned no matter how weak it is and even though that support or partisanship may cause injustice. So, especially when considered that the truth to which the Prophet's Family adhered and in adherence to which (the truth)

---

9 *Muslim*, "Fadail" 37; *at-Tirmidhi*, "Manaqib" 77; Ahmad ibn Hanbal, *al-Musnad*, 3:14. (Tr.)

their glory lay is the most powerful, fundamental and glorious truth in the world, and for the sake of which many of its members sacrificed their lives, could it ever be possible for them to give up support for it? It was because of their predisposed, unshakeable adherence to Islam that the Family of the Prophet accepted the smallest sign in favor of the Religion of Islam as though it was a powerful proof. For their willful adherence to Islam was supported through family ties. Others become convinced of its truth and gave support only after seeing some powerful proof.

Fourth point

In connection with the Third Point, we will briefly examine a matter which has become a point of dispute between the Shi'a and the Ahl al-Sunna wa'l-Jama'a and which has been exaggerated to such an extent that it is found in the books concerned with principles of faith and among the essentials of belief.

The Ahl al-Sunna wa'l-Jama'a say that 'Ali, may God be pleased with him, was the fourth in merit among the Rightly-Guided Caliphs. Abu Bakr as-Siddiq, may God be pleased with him, became the first caliph because he was more qualified and therefore better suited to be caliph. The Shi'a claim that the caliphate was Ali's right, and that an injustice was done to him. He was superior to all the others. A summary of their arguments is as follows: There are many Prophetic Traditions about 'Ali's merits; 'Ali was the ancestor of the overwhelming majority of the saints and the source of the spiritual paths—he is known as the "King of Sainthood"; the Prophet, upon him be peace and blessings, showed great interest in him and in the members of the Prophet's Family who were to be descended from 'Ali; as the husband of the Prophet's daughter Fatima, he was the father of the Prophet's descendants. All these, according to the Shi'a view demonstrate that 'Ali was superior to the others and that the caliphate was his right; they hold that it was usurped from him.

The Answer to the Claims of the Shi'a: 'Ali, may God be pleased with him, repeatedly acknowledged that the first three caliphs were entitled to caliphate. He obeyed and followed them during their caliphate for a term of more than twenty years, and held the position of Shaykh al-Islam[10] in their caliphate. These realities contradict the claims of the Shi'a. In addi-

[10] The position of Shaykh al-Islam signifies the highest religious authority. (Tr.)

tion, the victories of Islam and the struggles against its enemies in the time of the first three caliphs and the internal conflicts in Ali's time also contradict the Shi'as claims concerning the Islamic caliphate. All these support the Sunni claims.

QUESTION: The Shi'a consist of two groups: one are the Shi'a of sainthood, while the other are the Shi'a of caliphate. Even if we admit that the second group are wrong in their stance, one which originates from their political, purposeful partisanship, the first group do not have any deliberate political attitude. However, they support the others. That is, some of the saints of the Sufi orders consider 'Ali to be superior and more entitled to the caliphate, and have confirmed the Shi'a of caliphate in their claims.

THE ANSWER: We should consider 'Ali, may God be pleased with him, from two perspectives. One concerns his personal perfections and rank, and the other concerns his representing the collective personality of the Prophet's Family. This collective personality manifests, in one way, the essential nature of the noblest Messenger, upon him be peace and blessings.

In regard to the first perspective, all verifying scholars, including first and foremost 'Ali himself, give precedence to Abu Bakr and 'Umar, and see their ranks as higher in the service of Islam and nearness to God. As for the second perspective, as the representative of the collective personality of the Prophet's Family, which represents an aspect of the Muhammadan Truth,[11] 'Ali has no equals. Thus, when we examine the highly laudatory Prophetic Traditions about 'Ali, we can see that they concern this second point. An accurately narrated Tradition which confirms this fact reads, "The descendants of every other Prophet are from himself. My descendants are those of 'Ali."[12]

The reason why the laudatory Traditions about 'Ali are more than those about the other three caliphs and why they have become so widespread is that in the face of the wrongful attack on and denigration of 'Ali

11 Muhammadan Truth is the universal ontological, moral, and spiritual truth or meaning that the Prophet Muhammad, upon him be peace and blessings, represents. (Tr.)

12 at-Tabarani, *al-Mu'jam al-Kabir*, 3:43; ad-Daylami, *al-Musnad*, 1:172.

by the Umayyads[13] and Kharijites,[14] the Ahl al-Sunna wa'l-Jama'a, who stand for the truth, publicized far and wide the Traditions about him. Since the other Rightly-Guided Caliphs were not made targets of such criticism or denigration, no need was felt to spread the Traditions about them.

In addition, God's noblest Messenger, upon him be peace and blessings, saw with the eye of Prophethood that 'Ali, may God be pleased with him, would experience grievous events and internal dissidence in the future, and in order to save him from despair and his Community from forming an ill opinion of him, he consoled him and guided his Community with significant Traditions like "Whosever's master I am, 'Ali, too, is their master."[15]

The excessive love for 'Ali, may God be pleased with him, by the Shi'a of sainthood and their deeming him superior to the first three Caliphs, which occurred under the influence of following a Sufi path, do not make them as accountable as the Shi'a of caliphate. For by reason of their way, those who follow the path of sainthood consider their spiritual guides with love. Love by nature tends to be excessive, and desires to see, in fact sees, the beloved as greater than the rank that beloved actually possesses. Ecstatics may be excused for excesses of love, provided that their deeming 'Ali superior, an emotion that arises from their love, does not lead to the denigration of or enmity towards the other Rightly-Guided Caliphs and does not go beyond the essential teachings of Islam.

As for the Shi'a of caliphate, since their view is under the influence of political prejudice, they are unable to be saved from resentment or aggression, and they lose their right to be excused in this matter. Since Persian national pride was wounded at the hand of 'Umar, they act in a way that

---

13 The Umayyads were a powerful clan belonging to the Quraysh (native people of Makka) during the early history of Islam. Many members of it opposed Islam and the Messenger, but later they generally accepted Islam. Mu'awiya ibn Abi Sufyan, the son of their leader Abu Sufyan, opposed 'Ali during his caliphate and became the caliph after him. Thus, the reign of the Umayyad Dynasty, which would last almost ninety years, began with Mu'awiya's caliphate. (Tr.)

14 The Kharijites were those who supported 'Ali at the beginning of his caliphate but later opposed him and fought with him because he accepted that it might be referred to the decision of the arbiters from his and Mu'awiya's sides who was more entitled to the caliphate. They formed a powerful seditionist group and rebelled against the government many times. (Tr.)

15 *at-Tirmidhi*, "Manaqib" 19; Ibn Maja, *Sunan*, "Muqaddima" 11; Ahmad ibn Hanbal, *al-Musnad*, 1:84, 118; . (Tr.)

seems to confirm the saying, "Not for love of 'Ali but out of hatred for 'Umar"; they display their feelings of revenge in the form of love of 'Ali. In addition to this, 'Amr ibn al-'As' rebellion against 'Ali and 'Umar ibn Sa'd's tragic war against Husayn,[16] may God be pleased with him, caused the Shi'a to feel an intense revulsion and enmity towards the name 'Umar.

The Shi'a of sainthood have no right to criticize the Ahl al-Sunna wa'l-Jama'a, for the Ahl al-Sunna wa'l-Jama'a do not denigrate 'Ali; instead, they love him sincerely. But they avoid going to extremes in their love, as this is described as dangerous in the Traditions.[17] The Prophet's praise of the followers of 'Ali in the Traditions[18] refers to the Ahl al-Sunna wa'l-Jama'a. Those of 'Ali's followers who love him in the way he should be loved are the Ahl al-Sunna wa'l-Jama'a, who are the people of truth. Just as the excessive love of Jesus, upon whom be peace, is dangerous for the Christians who deify him, so it has been clearly stated in authentic Traditions that excessive love for 'Ali is dangerous.

Question: If the Shi'a of sainthood make the objection that once 'Ali's exceptional excellences have been accepted, then it is not possible to place Abu Bakr as-Siddiq above him, the answer is as follows:

The Answer: When the personal excellences of Abu Bakr as-Siddiq al-Akbar and 'Umar al-Faruq al-A'zam, may God be pleased with them, and their accomplishments during their caliphates in carrying out the Islamic duties inherited from the Prophet are weighed on the scales against the extraordinary personal excellences of 'Ali, may God be pleased with him, and his struggles for the caliphate, which he was forced to undergo because of tragic events that were the result of certain distrust, the Ahl al-Sunna perceive that Abu Bakr's, or Umar's, or 'Uthman Dhu'n-Nurayn's weighed heavier, and so they perceive them as having a higher ranking.

Furthermore, as demonstrated in the Twelfth and Twenty-Fourth Words, Prophethood is such an elevated rank that when compared to sainthood, a minuscule manifestation of Prophethood is superior to a great man-

16 Husayn, 'Ali's younger son and the Prophet's younger grandson did not accept the caliphate of Yazid after Mu'awiya and opposed him. He was tragically martyred together with the majority of his family members at Karbala in Iraq in 681. 'Umar ibn Sa'd was the commander of Yazid's army who killed them. (Tr.)

17 an-Nasa'i, *Sunan*, 5:137; Ahmad ibn Hanbal, *al-Musnad*, 1:160. (Tr.)

18 at-Tabarani, *al-Mu'jam al-Awsat*, 6:354–355. (Tr.)

ifestation of sainthood. From this perspective, the Ahl al-Sunna have arrived at the conclusion that the success of Abu Bakr and 'Umar during their caliphates indicates that God gave them a greater share in the succession to the duties of Prophethood and the establishment of the laws brought by God's Messenger, upon him be peace and blessings. Since the personal excellences of 'Ali, may God be pleased with him, did not transcend that greater share that came from succession to the duties of Prophethood, he acted as a Shaykh al-Islam (the greatest scholar and chief *mufti* of Islam) for Abu Bakr and 'Umar—the *Shaykhayn al-Mukarramayn* (the Two Noble Chiefs or Chief Leaders)—in the time of their caliphates, and he esteemed them. How should the Ahl al-Sunna, the people of truth, not love and revere those *shaykhs*, whom 'Ali loved and revered sincerely? Let us make this truth clear through an example:

One of the three sons of a very rich man is given twenty coins of silver and four coins of gold from his father's inheritance, while another one is given five of silver and five of gold, and the third, three of silver and five of gold. Clearly, the last two receive less in quantity, but more in quality. (That is, the extra one coin of gold given to the last two is more in value than the extra fifteen coins of silver the first one receives.) As in this example, the little extra amount of the share of the *Shaykhayn* in the gold of nearness to God which arises from succession to the duties of Prophethood and the establishment of the laws brought by God's Messenger weighs heavier than the far greater amount of 'Ali's share in the silver of nearness to God that comes from his perfections of sainthood and personal excellences. We should consider this point in comparison. But if they are compared with one another from the viewpoint of courage, knowledge, and sainthood, the results change.

Also, 'Ali is beyond comparison in respect of representing the collective personality of the Prophet's Family, and of the Muhammadan Truth, which was manifested in that collective personality in the form of absolute succession to the Messenger, upon him be peace and blessings. For this point concerns the incomparable greatness and universal mission of the Prophet himself, upon him be peace and blessings.

As for the Shi'a of caliphate, they can have no substantial claim in the face of the Ahl al-Sunna wa'l-Jama'a. For although the Shi'a of caliphate claim to have exceptional love for 'Ali, in fact they disparage him, and their doctrines come to mean that 'Ali behaved unethically. For they say that although Abu Bakr and 'Umar, may God be pleased with them, acted unjustly and wronged him, 'Ali pretended that he approved of them. In the terminology of the Shi'a, he dissimulated. That is, he was afraid of them and acted hypocritically. How can love perceive a person who was a hero of Islam, who won the title "Lion of God," and was the commander and guide of the truthful and trustworthy as a hypocritical coward who pretended to love and approve of those whom he did not love out of fear for more than twenty years and who agreed to follow wrongdoers? 'Ali, may God be pleased with him, would disclaim that sort of love.

The creed of the Ahl al-Sunna, the people of truth, in no way disparages 'Ali, nor accuses him of acting unethically. Without attributing any cowardice to such an exceptional person, they say, "If 'Ali had not seen the first three Rightly-Guided Caliphs as rightful, he would not have recognized them even for a moment, nor obeyed them. Since he saw them as rightful and preferable, he submitted the heroism and energy he devoted to Islam to the way of truth."

In short, going into extremes in any matter is not good. The truth lies in the middle way, and this is what the Ahl al-Sunna have chosen. But, unfortunately, even though to a small degree, certain Kharijite and Wahhabi ideas have infiltrated the Sunni thought and creed under the guise of the Ahl al-Sunna, and some adherents of politics and heretics criticize 'Ali, may God be pleased with him. They say—God forbid—since 'Ali did not understand politics, he was not able to display the capacity or competence required for caliphate and therefore did not govern well. Because of their unjustified accusations, the Shi'a or the 'Alawis feel resentment towards the Ahl al-Sunna. Yet the creed or basic beliefs of the Ahl al-Sunna do not give rise to such ideas; indeed, they defend the opposite stance. The Ahl al-Sunna cannot be condemned because of the ideas that belong to the Kharijites or some heretics. Rather, the Ahl al-Sunna are more consistent than the 'Alawis in following 'Ali. In their sermons and prayer they mention 'Ali with the words of praise he deserves. Particularly the saints and the purified scholars, the overwhelming majority of whom have belonged to the Ahl al-Sunna, have recognized 'Ali as a guide and the king of sainthood. The 'Alawis or the Shi'a should not set themselves against the Ahl al-Sunna; they should ignore the Kharijites and heretics who have deservedly earned the enmity of both the 'Alawis and the Ahl al-Sunna.

Some from among the Shi'a have even abandoned the Sunna Prayers only for the sake of opposing the Ahl al-Sunna. What has been said here is more than enough, as this matter has been sufficiently discussed by the scholars.

And so, Ahl al-Sunna, the people of truth, and 'Alawis, who have adopted the love of the Prophet's Family as a way to follow! Put an end to this meaningless, unjust, and harmful dispute and quarrel between you without any delay. Otherwise, the heretical movements which are now so strong and influential will make you a weapon to be used against one another, and both of you will be crushed, one after the other. Since you are believers in God's Oneness and as there are therefore numerous sacred bonds between you which order brotherhood and unity, it is essential that you should leave aside insignificant matters that generate division.

Second station

This is about another truth contained by the verse, *There has come to you a Messenger from among yourselves; extremely grievous to him is your suffering, full of concern for you is he, and for the believers full of pity and compassion. Still, if they turn away from you (O Messenger), say: "God is sufficient for me; there is no deity but He. In Him have I put my trust, and He is the Lord of the Supreme Throne."* (9:128–129).[19]

The Fifth and Sixth Gleams

These two Gleams are about the phrases *God suffices for us, how excellent a Guardian He is* and *There is no strength or power save with God*, respectively. They were written in Arabic and included in the Twenty-Ninth Gleam, as they concern remembrance of God and reflection rather than intellectual knowledge.

19 It was written and included in *The Gleams* as The Eleventh Gleam.

The Seventh Gleam

The Seventh Gleam

The predictions at the end of Surat al-Fath

In the Name of God, the All-Merciful, the All-Compassionate.

God has assuredly confirmed the vision for His Messenger as true (and will certainly fulfill it) in reality: you will certainly enter the Sacred Mosque, if God wills, in full security, with your heads shaven or your hair cut short, and you will have nothing to fear. But He always knows what you do not know, and (therefore, without allowing you to enter the Mosque this year,) granted you a near victory before this. He it is Who has sent His Messenger with the Divine guidance and the Religion of truth that He may make it prevail over all religions. God suffices for a witness (for the truth of His promise and the mission of His Messenger). Muhammad is the Messenger of God; and those who are in his company are firm and unyielding against the unbelievers, and compassionate among themselves. You see them (constant in the Prayer) bowing down and prostrating, seeking favor with God and His approval and good pleasure. Their marks are on their faces, traced by prostration. This is their description in the Torah; and their description in the Gospel: like a seed that has sprouted its shoot, then it has strengthened it, and then risen firmly on its stem, delighting the sowers (with joy and wonder); (thereby) it fills the unbelievers with rage at them (the believers). God has promised all those among them who believe and do good, righteous deeds forgiveness (to bring unforeseen blessings) and a tremendous reward. (48:27–29)

These last three verses of *Surat al-Fath*[20] are miraculous in many respects. Out of the ten comprehensive aspects of the Qur'an's miraculousness or inimitability, its aspect of giving news of the future is displayed in seven or eight ways. (In other words, it contains seven or eight predictions.)

The first prediction

God has assuredly confirmed the vision for His Messenger as true (and will certainly fulfill it) in reality, to the end of the verse, gives us the certain news of the conquest of Makka before it happened. It occurred two years later, just as the verse predicted.

The second prediction

In the beginning, the Treaty of Hudaybiya was considered to be against the interests of Islam and it was thought that the Quraysh were victorious. Whereas, *He granted you a near victory before this* stated that in reality this Treaty would be a great victory and the key to further conquests.

With the Treaty of Hudaybiya, Muslims no longer had to resist the attacks of the Makkans with the sword; instead, the brilliant truths of the Qur'an found a peaceful atmosphere to spread, and it conquered minds and hearts. In this truce, the two sides came to know one another. The virtues of Islam and the light of the Qur'an rent apart the veils of obstinacy and tribal fanaticism and proved to be very effective. For example, people like Khalid ibn Walid, a genius of war, and 'Amr ibn al-'As, a genius of politics and diplomacy, who could not accept defeat, were defeated by the Qur'an, which manifested itself in the truce. Having willingly submitted in perfect obedience to Islam in Madina, Khalid began to serve Islam and its conquests.

AN IMPORTANT QUESTION: What was the wisdom in the setbacks of the Companions of the Pride of creation and the Beloved of the Lord of the worlds, upon him be peace and blessings, at the end of Uhud and beginning of Hunayn[21] in the face of the polytheists?

---

20 *Surat al-Fath* (Chapter 48) was revealed just after the Treaty of Hudaybiya, which was signed between God's Messenger and the Makkans in 627, five years after the Messenger's emigration to Madina. (Tr.)

21 The Muslims suffered a setback in the second stage of the Battle of Uhud, which took place in 625, three years after the emigration of God's Messenger to Madina, at the out-

THE ANSWER: Among the polytheists were many people like Khalid, who in the future would be equal to the leading Companions of that time. Therefore, so as not to disgrace them entirely in consideration of their glorious future, Divine wisdom gave them an immediate reward for their future good works and did not completely destroy their honor. That is to say, the Companions of the past were defeated by the Companions of the future, so that those future Companions would enter Islam, not through fear of the lightning of the sword, but through zeal for the flash of truth, and so that their inherent valor should not be utterly humiliated.

The third prediction

By saying, *You will have nothing to fear*, the verse states, "You will certainly circumambulate the Ka'ba in full security." However, at that time, not only the environs of Makka and the tribe of the Quraysh but also the majority of the desert peoples of the Arabian Peninsula were hostile. So, by predicting, "You will certainly circumambulate the Ka'ba in full security," the verse states that the Muslims would subdue the entire Arabian Peninsula, all the Quraysh would accept Islam, and total security would be established throughout Arabia. All occurred just as had been foretold.

The fourth prediction

He it is Who has sent His Messenger with the Divine guidance and the Religion of truth that He may make it prevail over all religion foretells with utter certainty that the Religion which the noblest Messenger, peace and blessings be upon him, brought would triumph over all religions. However, at that time, Christianity, Judaism, Zoroastrianism, (and Buddhism) had hundreds of millions of followers and were the official religions of world-dominant states like Rome, Persia, and China, which had hundreds of millions of subjects. The verse states that the Religion which Muhammad the Arabian, upon him be peace and blessings, a man who was yet unable to conquer even his own small

---

skirts of Mount Uhud, three miles north from the Prophet's Mosque in the center of Madina. They suffered a similar setback at the beginning of the Battle of Hunayn, which happened just after the conquest of Makka in the valley of Hunayn between the Muslims and the allied forces of certain neighboring tribes. (Trans.)

tribe, brought would prevail over all religions and be victorious over all states. And it does so in the clearest and most definite manner. The future proved this prediction to be true, with the light of Islam diffusing from the Pacific Ocean in the east to the Atlantic Ocean in the west.

The fifth prediction

Muhammad is the Messenger of God; and those who are in his company are firm and unyielding against the unbelievers, and compassionate among themselves. You see them (constant in the Prayer) bowing down and prostrating. These statements inform us of the prominent virtues and elevated characteristics of the Companions which made them the most virtuous human generation after the Prophets. While in their apparent meaning they express the excellent qualities particular to each class of Companions, they implicitly allude to the order of succession of the four Rightly-Guided Caliphs who would succeed the Prophet, upon him be peace and blessings, and mention each with his particular, distinguishing excellences. These are as follows:

Those who are in his company points to Abu Bakr as-Siddiq, who was distinguished and famous for being the closest friend of the Prophet, and the first to die and join him after his death. *Unyielding against the unbelievers* implicitly refers to 'Umar, who in the future would overawe many countries with his conquests, and make the unjust tremble with his justice. With *and compassionate among themselves*, the Qur'an alludes to 'Uthman, who, in the future when the ground for a most serious dissension was being prepared, would prefer to be martyred wrongfully while reciting the Qur'an out of his perfect kindness and compassion in order that the blood of Muslims should not be spilt. Finally, *You see them (constant in the Prayer) bowing down and prostrating, seeking favor with God and His approval and good pleasure* alludes to the conditions in which 'Ali would find himself in the future. We learn that 'Ali was perfectly entitled to the caliphate and undertook it heroically, and that he was not responsible for the wars in which he had to be involved during his caliphate in pursuit of God's good pleasure. It also points to the fact that 'Ali, well-known for his bowing and prostrations in the Prayer, always preferred perfect asceticism and worship of God.

The sixth prediction

The part, *Their marks are on their faces, traced by prostration. This is their description in the Torah* gives two pieces of information concerning the Unseen:

The first: We are informed of the qualities of the Companions mentioned in the Torah, which was unknown to the illustrious Prophet, upon him be peace and blessings, as he was unable to read. As mentioned in the Nineteenth Letter, *And he came with ten thousands of saints* (*Deuteronomy*, 33: 2), the Torah refers to the Companions of the Prophet. That is, his Companions would be pious worshippers, righteous, and saints. Although the Torah has been considerably corrupted through being translated into numerous languages, it confirms with many of its verses the part of *Surat al-Fath*, *Their marks are on their faces, traced by prostration. This is their description in the Torah.*

The second piece of information concerning the Unseen is this: The phrase, *This is their description in the Torah*, foretells that the Companions and the generation that followed them would attain such a degree in worship that their spiritual illumination would shine in their faces, and marks would be apparent on their foreheads, like some sort of stamp of sainthood caused by their repeated prostrations. The future bore out this prediction with all its clarity and certainty. Numerous illustrious persons, such as Zayn al-'Abidin[22] and Tawus al-Yamani,[23] who amidst perplexing events of dissension and political upheaval performed prayers of a thousand *rakahs* day and night and performed the early morning Prayer with the ablution of the night or late-evening Prayer (i.e., they spent the entire night praying), demonstrated the meaning of and proved the prediction in *This is their description in the Torah.*

The seventh prediction

The section, *and their description in the Gospel: like a seed that has sprouted its shoot, then it has strengthened it, and then risen firmly on its stem, delighting the sow-*

22 'Ali ibn Husayn Zayn al-'Abidin (d. 712). The grandson of 'Ali ibn Abi Talib, the fourth caliph, through 'Ali's younger son Husayn, may God be pleased with them. He was famous for his devotions, good nature, generosity, and helping the poor and needy. He was nicknamed Zayn al-'Abidin (The Ornament of God's worshippers). (Tr.)

23 Tawus ibn Kaysan al-Yamani, one of the leading figures among the generation succeeding the Companions. (Tr.)

ers (with joy and wonder); (thereby) it fills the unbelievers with rage at them (the believers), also contains two pieces of information concerning the Unseen:

The first is the Gospel's prediction of the Companions, which was unknown to the unlettered Prophet, upon him be peace and blessings.

In addition to the verses in the Old Testament concerning God's Messenger and his Companions such as those mentioned above and others like *You will break them with a rod of iron* (*Psalms*, 2:9), The Gospels have several such verses as *I will no longer talk much with you, for the ruler of this world is coming* (*John*, 14:30).[24] These verses foretold that a Prophet would come who would be charged with waging *jihad*; that he would be the ruler of the world.

It is thus understood from such verses that at the outset the Companions would appear to be few and weak. Nevertheless, like seeds, they would grow, thicken, and gain strength. When they came to the point where they would cause the unbelievers to be choked by their own rage, they would conquer many peoples and prove their Prophet, upon him be peace and blessings, to be the ruler of the world. So, the descriptions of the Gospels exactly uphold the meaning of the verses of *Surat al-Fath* that we have examined here.

---

[24] The Gospels contain several other verses concerning God's Messenger, upon him be peace and blessings, and His holy Companions, may God be pleased with them. For example, *Nevertheless I tell you the truth. It is to your advantage that I go away; for if I do not go away, the Helper (Paraklit) will not come to you; but if I depart, I will send him to you. And when he has come, he will convict the world of sin, and of righteousness, and of judgment* (*John*, 16: 7–8); *Jesus said to them, "Have you never read in the Scriptures: The stone which the builders rejected has become the cornerstone. This was the Lord's doing, and it is marvelous in our eyes? Therefore, I say to you, the Kingdom of God will be taken from you, and given to a nation bringing the fruits of it. And whoever falls on this stone will be broken; but on whomsoever it falls, it will grind him to powder."* (*Matthew*, 21: 42–4); *When the Helper (Paraklit) comes, ... the Spirit of truth who proceeds from the Father, he will testify of me* (*John*, 15: 26); *I still have many things to say to you, but you cannot bear them now. And when he, the Spirit of truth, has come, he will guide you into all truth, for he will not speak on his own authority; but whatever he hears he will speak, and he will tell you things to come. He will glorify me, for he will take of what is mine and declare it to you* (*John*, 16: 12–14); and *Now this is the testimony of John, when the Jews sent priests and Levites from Jerusalem to ask him, "Who are you?" He confessed, and did not deny; but confessed, "I am not the Christ." And they asked him, "What then? Are you Elijah?" He said, "I am not." "Are you that Prophet?" And he answered, "No." Then said they to him, "Who are you, that we may give an answer to those who sent us? What do you say about yourself?" He said: "I am the voice of one crying in the wilderness: 'Make straight the way of the Lord,' as the prophet Isaiah said."* (*John*, 1: 19–23). (Tr.)

Second aspect: This part of the verse alludes to the fact that even though the Companions were relatively weak and small in number when they accepted the Treaty of Hudaybiya, within a short time they were to grow and gain such strength and magnificence that at a time when humankind, planted in the field of the earth by the Hand of the Divine Power, was like a tree whose shoots are short, weak, defective, and barren of fruit due to their heedlessness of the Divine Religion and knowledge, they would multiply rapidly, grow strong, and yield plenty of fruit. The great powers of the time would be filled with rage at them, struggling in envy and jealousy. The future bore out this prediction in a most brilliant fashion.

This prediction has one more hint: it is expected that the Companions should be promised only a tremendous reward where they are praised with significant qualities. However, the verse ends with the promises of *forgiveness* and a tremendous reward. This suggests that in the future there will appear serious faults among the Companions because of internal conflicts. For forgiveness indicates the existence of faults. At such a time the thing most demanded by the Companions, the greatest favor, would be forgiveness and the greatest reward would be the absence of punishment due to the forgiveness. As the word *forgiveness* suggests this, it also has a connection with the sentence at the beginning of the *Sura*, *That God may forgive you (O Messenger) your lapses of the past and those to follow*. The forgiveness mentioned in this sentence for the Messenger is figurative, for the Messenger is infallible. Even if it is taken literally, it denotes forgiveness suited to the rank of Prophethood. In addition, as it contains the good tidings of forgiveness for the Companions in the person of the Prophet, upon him be peace and blessings, it adds a further subtlety to the verse through the *forgiveness* promised to the Companions at the end of the *Sura*.

The Qur'an has ten basic miraculous aspects. Of the many examples of giving clear tidings of the Unseen which are contained in the above-mentioned three verses at the end of *Surat al-Fath*, only seven examples have been given here. As the last of the three verses refers to the Companions, it also refers to their states and conditions with its phrases. In the same way that this portrays their attributes in its literal meaning, the repetition of its letters in certain numbers alludes to the classes of the famous Companions, like the peoples of Badr, of Uhud, of Hunayn, of the Hall,[25] and the Approved Allegiance[26]. It also contains many other mysteries.

All-Glorified are You. We have no knowledge save what You have taught us. Surely You are the All-Knowing, the All-Wise.

* * *

A Postscript

In connection with certain future events alluded to in the last verses of *Surat al-Fath*, similar predictions are found in the following verses:

> *And indeed We guided them to a straight path (in belief, thought, feeling and action). Whoever obeys God and the Messenger (as they must be obeyed), then those are (and in the Hereafter will be, in Paradise) in the company of those whom God has favored (with perfect guidance)—the Prophets, and the truthful ones (loyal to God's cause and truthful in whatever they do and say), and the witnesses (those who see the hidden Divine truths and testify thereto with their lives), and the righteous ones (in all their deeds and sayings and dedicated to setting everything right). How excellent they are for companions!* (4:68–69)

We will mention two of the numerous fine points to be found in these verses.

---

25 The People of the Hall were the poor Companions who lived in the hall adjacent to the Prophet's Mosque in Madina. They were specially educated by the Prophet to become scholars and transmitters of his hadiths. Abu Hurayra, may God be pleased with him, was the most renowned among them. (Tr.)

26 The People of the Approved Allegiance were the Companions who gave allegiance to God's Messenger, upon him be peace and blessings, under a tree at Hudaybiya before the Treaty of Hudaybiya was signed. When rumors circulated that 'Uthman ibn 'Affan, who had been sent to Makka to negotiate the Muslims' intention to make Minor Pilgrimage, had been killed, God's Messenger, upon him be peace and blessings, called the believers in his company to swear allegiance to him to defend themselves even if they might be killed. They had come with the intention to visit the Ka'ba and to make a Minor Pilgrimage. However, when they met with the unexpected reaction and felt their cause to be under great threat, they united around the Messenger, upon him be peace and blessings, as if a single body. They had no other intention than to serve God's cause in order to gain His approval and good pleasure. God was well pleased with the purity of intention and faithfulness in their hearts. So, this allegiance was later called the Approved Allegiance. (Tr.)

First point

As the Qur'an of miraculous exposition expresses truths through its explicit, clear meanings and concepts, so too does it contain many allusive meanings in its styles and composition. Each of its verses contains numerous levels of meanings. Since the Qur'an originates in the all-encompassing Knowledge of God, it is possible that all of these meanings are intended. The interpretation of the Qur'an cannot be restricted to one or two meanings like human speech, which is the product of limited minds and individual will.

It is for this reason that the scholarly interpreters of the Qur'an have explained innumerable truths contained in its verses. There are still many more truths which the interpreters have left unexplained. In addition to its explicit meanings, the Qur'an contains much significant knowledge, particularly in the letters used and in its allusions.

Second point

The verse, by stating,

> *the Prophets, and the truthful ones (loyal to God's cause and truthful in whatever they do and say), and the witnesses (those who see the hidden Divine truths and testify thereto with their lives), and the righteous ones (in all their deeds and sayings and dedicated to setting everything right). How excellent they are for companions!*

interprets the verse of *Surat al-Fatiha, the Path of those whom You have favored*, and explains who are those among humankind that have been specially favored with God's guidance and whom we are ordered to follow. They are the Prophets, at the head of whom is Muhammad, God's Messenger, upon him be peace and blessings, the truthful ones loyal to God's cause, the witnesses who see the hidden Divine truths and testify thereto with their lives, and those who are righteous in all their deeds and sayings and who are dedicated to setting everything right. These people are the leaders of those on the Straight Path, people who are favored with true Divine blessing. The verse also indicates these types of people as being especially among the first generation of Islam, and suggests that they will be followed by an excellent generation to be called the *Tabiun*—those who succeed the Companions and follow them in an excellent way. The verse also refers to the leaders or chiefs of these five groups with their best-known attributes and the most prominent aspects of their future life, thus displaying an aspect of the miraculous nature of the Qur'an, namely giving news of the future.

As *the Prophets* in the verse explicitly indicates God's Messenger, upon him be peace and blessings, so does *the truthful ones* indicate, first of all, Abu Bakr *as-Siddiq* (the Truthful One), may God be pleased with him. It informs us by allusion that he will succeed the Prophet, upon him be peace and blessings, occupy second position after him, and he will specifically be mentioned with the title of *as-Siddiq* by the Muslim Community as the most prominent of all truthful ones after the Prophet.

With *the witnesses (those who see the hidden Divine truths and testify thereto with their lives)*, the verse alludes to 'Umar, 'Uthman, and 'Ali, may God be pleased with them, together. It hints that they will be favored with the caliphate and that they will bear witness to the truth of Islam by being martyred, thus adding martyrdom to their other virtues.

With the phrase *the righteous ones*, the verse refers to the Peoples of the *Suffa* (the Companions living in a hall adjacent to the Prophet's Mosque in Madina), Badr, and the Approved Allegiance (the Allegiance given to the Prophet at Hudaybiya); and by saying *How excellent they are for companions*, it explicitly encourages us to follow them, alluding to how excellently the generation that succeeded them acted. It also alludes to Hasan, may God be pleased with him, who as the fifth caliph affirmed the Prophetic Traditions which predicted, "After me, the caliphate will last thirty years,"[27] and "This is my grandson Hasan, a noble master of people! God will reconcile two great groups (of Muslims) by means of him."[28] Thus, the verse draws attention to the great value of Hasan's caliphate despite its brief duration.[29]

In short, in the same way that the last verse of *Surat al-Fath* contains references to the four Rightly-Guided Caliphs, so too does this verse, by confirming the former, allude to their future positions and conditions, thus giving some news of the future. The gleams of this miraculous nature, name-

---

27 *at-Tirmidhi*, "Fitan" 48; *Abu Dawud*, "Sunna" 9. (Tr.)

28 *al-Bukhari*, "Sulh" 9; *at-Tirmidhi*, "Manaqib" 30.

29 As the verse alludes to the Prophet, Abu Bakr, 'Umar, 'Uthman, and 'Ali with the words it uses, it also refers to Hasan, 'Ali's older son, with the word "*hasuna*," the verb from which the word "*hasan*" (meaning beautiful, excellent) it contains. (Tr.)

ly giving certain news of the future or a dimension of the Unseen, which is one of the aspects of the miraculous nature of the Qur'an, are so numerous in the Qur'an that they cannot be restricted to a few like those mentioned above. The reason those who only consider the literal meaning of the Qur'an's verses restrict them to forty or fifty is that they approach the Qur'an superficially. Sometimes a single verse can contain allusions to four or five future events.

Our Lord, take us not to task if we forget or make mistakes!

All-Glorified are You. We have no knowledge save what You have taught us. Surely You are the All-Knowing, the All-Wise.

The Eighth Gleam

This has been published as part of *Sikke-i Tasdik-i Gaybî* ("The Confirmation of the Tidings of the Unseen").

The Ninth Gleam

This Gleam is about some subtle matters of the view of the Unity of Being. They are found scattered in some other Treatises.

The Tenth Gleam

This is concerned with some misfortunes that occur as a merciful Divine warning to some who show negligence in striving in God's cause. They have not been included in the translation.

The
Eleventh Gleam

The Eleventh Gleam

The stairway of the Sunna and antidote for the sickness of innovations in the Religion

In the Name of God, the All-Merciful, the All-Compassionate.

> *There has come to you a Messenger from among yourselves; extremely grievous to him is your suffering, full of concern for you is he, and for the believers full of pity and compassion.* (9:128)

This verse opens a highway and establishes a stairway to the Sunna, the way of the Prophet, upon him be peace and blessings.

> *Still, if they turn away from you (O Messenger), say: "God is sufficient for me; there is no deity but He. In Him have I put my trust, and He is the Lord of the Supreme Throne."* (9:129)

> *Say (to them, O Messenger): "If you indeed love God, then follow me, so that God will love you and forgive you your sins."* (3:31)

Of the hundreds of significant points these two mighty verses contain, eleven will be explained concisely.

First point

The noblest Prophet, upon him be peace and blessings, declared, "Whoever follows my Sunna when my Community is corrupted, there is for him (or her) the reward of a hundred martyrs."[30]

---

30 at-Tabarani, *al-Mu'jam al-Awsat*, 5:315; al-Bayhaki, *Sunan*, "Zuhd" 118. (Tr.)

Certainly, following the Sunna of the Prophet, upon him be peace and blessings, is of exceptional value. It is even more valuable particularly at times when innovations in the Religion are prevalent. Especially when the Muslim Community is corrupted, following even an ordinary practice of the Prophet signifies a strong belief in and deep reverence for Islam. Observation of the Islamic rules established by the Prophet and following his Sunna (his way of life) recalls the noblest Prophet, upon him be peace and blessings. This recollection leads one to feel the constant company of God. When one follows the Prophet even in dealings of the least significance and in the practices of daily life such as eating, drinking, or sleeping, such ordinary transactions and natural acts become meritorious acts of worship and actions of the Shari'a. For, a person who follows the Prophet even in such everyday actions has thought about following the noblest Prophet, upon whom be peace and blessings, and considers these to be among the good manners of conduct commended by the Shari'a. Then this thought causes them to recall the Prophet as the one who brought the Shari'a. Through this recollection, their hearts turn to Almighty God, the Legislator of the Shari'a. This gives some sort of spiritual satisfaction and sense of worship.

Thus, one who appropriately follows the Sunna as a way of life transforms even their habitual acts into worship, and can make their whole life fruitful and yielding of reward.

Second point

Imam Rabbani, Ahmad Faruqi,[31] may God sanctify him, says, "While passing through the ranks in my spiritual journeys, I saw the most brilliant, magnificent, appealing, sound, and reliable among the groups of the saints to be those who follow the Sunna of the Prophet, upon him be peace and blessings, as the principle of their path. Even the ordinary saints of this group appeared to be more magnificent than the distinguished saints of other groups."

---

31 Imam Rabbani, Ahmad Faruq al-Sarhandi (d. 1624): Accepted by many as "The Reviver of the Second Millennium," especially in Islamic spirituality. Born in Sarhand (India) and well-versed in Islamic sciences, he removed many corrupt elements from Sufism. He also taught Shah Alamgir or Awrangzeb (d. 1707), who had a committee of scholars prepare the most comprehensive compendium of Hanafi Law. (Tr.)

Imam Rabbani, the Renewer of the Second Millennium, may God sanctify him, speaks the truth. One who takes the Sunna as the basis of their path is on the way to the station of being a beloved of God under the guardianship of God's Beloved, upon him be peace and blessings.

Third point

I once experienced an inner transformation, during which due to being devoid of a guide and to the pride of my evil-commanding soul, my intellect and heart were floundering amidst truths in an awful spiritual storm. They were being tossed about, rising and falling, sometimes from the Pleiades to the ground, sometimes from the ground to the Pleiades.

During this transformation, I observed that, like compasses used in ships to find the direction and to determine the course to follow, the principles of the elevated Sunna of the Prophet, including even those that are concerned with good manners, were like electric switches along the innumerable hazardous, dark ways. And whenever, during that spiritual journey, I found myself under great pressure, weighed down with extremely heavy burdens, I followed the principles of the Sunna concerning that situation and felt relaxed as if I had been freed from all those burdens. By submitting to them, I was saved from doubts, that is, the hesitations or anxieties about whether any certain course of action was right or beneficial. Whenever I abandoned following them, I noticed that there was intense pressure. There were numerous ways for which it was not possible to detect where they led. The burden was heavy, and I was utterly powerless. My sight was short, and the way to follow, dark. Whenever I held fast to the Sunna, everything was illuminated and the safe way to follow appeared. I felt the burden had been lightened and the pressure lifted. Through these observations of mine, I confirmed the conclusion Imam Rabbani drew in his spiritual journey.

Fourth point

Once, because of a mood produced by contemplating death, the affirmation of "Death is a reality," and the transience and passing of the world, I envisioned myself in a strange world. I had a vision in which I was a corpse standing at the head of three huge corpses.

One: I was like a tombstone at the head of the immaterial corpse of all the living creatures that had had a connection with my life and entered the grave of the past.

Two: I was a point which would be swiftly erased, an ant which would quickly die, on the face of this century, which was the tombstone at the head of the grave of the past in the cemetery of the earth, where the huge corpses of all kinds of living creatures that had had a connection with the life of humankind were buried.

Three: Since the universe is certain to die on the Day of Resurrection, I envisioned that it had actually died. I found myself both in terror at the death agonies of that huge entity and in astonishment at its death, and saw my own death, which is certain to occur in the future, as having happened. Upon my death, as declared in *If they turn away from you....*, all beings, all my beloveds, turned their backs on me, abandoning me and leaving me alone. My spirit was being driven towards the future on the side of post-eternity, which resembled a boundless ocean. It would be cast into it willingly or unwillingly.

While in that most strange and sorrowful mood, the verse, *If they turn away from you, say: "God is sufficient for me; there is no deity but He. In Him have I put my trust, and He is the Lord of the Supreme Throne,"* brought belief and the Qur'an to my aid. The verse became like a sound and reliable boat, and my spirit went inside the verse with complete confidence and joy. I came to understand that besides its apparent meaning, the verse had an allusive meaning, which had consoled me and given me satisfaction and serenity.

With its apparent meaning, the verse says to the noblest Prophet, upon him be peace and blessings:

> If the people of misguidance turn away, diverge from your Shari'a and Sunna, and do not heed the Qur'an, do not worry. Say, "God Almighty is sufficient for me. In Him I put my trust. He will raise up others in your place who will follow me. His Throne of rule encompasses everything. Neither the rebellious can escape its bounds, nor are those who ask for help left unaided."

With its allusive meaning, the verse says:

> O human and O leader and guide of people! If all beings abandon you and go to extinction along the way of mortality, if living beings depart from you and race down the way of death, if human beings abandon you and enter the cemetery, and if the people of heedlessness and misguidance do not heed you but fall into darkness, do not worry; say, "God Almighty is sufficient for me. Since He exists, everything exists. Since this is so, those who have left have not gone to non-existence. They are traveling to another of His realms. To replace them, that Owner of the Supreme Throne will send others from among His innumerable soldiers. Those who have entered the cemetery have not been utterly annihilated. They are on the way to another realm. He will send others who are duty-bound in their place. And in place of those who fall into misguidance, He can send His obedient servants who will follow the straight path. He substitutes for everything. All things cannot be equal to a single manifestation of His favor and regard."

And so, thanks to the allusive meaning of the verse, the three awful corpses which had filled me with dread took on other forms. Life and death, and separations and departures, became a movement displaying wisdom, an instructive activity, a journey for the fulfillment of duties, a demobilization, and a charging with duties, under the rule, supervision, and guardianship of an All-Majestic One, Who is also the All-Wise, the All-Compassionate, the All-Just, and the All-Powerful, based on His Wisdom and Mercy. The universe does its duty in a whirl of activities, coming and going.

Fifth point

The mighty verse,

> *Say (to them, O Messenger): "If you indeed love God, then follow me, so that God will love you..."* (3:31)

clearly proclaims how important and necessary it is to follow the Sunna. Among the logical syllogisms, this verse contains the most powerful and clearest of what are called conditional or exclusive syllogisms. It is as follows:

As an example of the conditional syllogism, it is said, "If the sun rises, it will be daytime." The positive conclusion of this syllogism is, "The sun has risen, so it is daytime." The negative conclusion is, "It is not daytime, so the sun has not risen." Both of these conclusions are clear in their logic.

In just the same way, the above-mentioned verse says, "If you love God, you will follow God's Beloved. If you do not follow him, this conclusively means that you do not love God." Love of God entails following the elevated Sunna of God's Beloved. One who believes in God will certainly obey Him. The most acceptable, the most straightforward, and the most direct and shortest way of obedience to Him is undoubtedly the way which God's Beloved demonstrated and followed.

It is self-evident that the All-Generous One of Grace, Who fills up the universe with so many bounties, will demand thanks from conscious beings in return for the bounties. And the All-Wise One of Majesty, Who has adorned the universe with so many miracles of art, will certainly and clearly make the most distinguished of conscious beings His addressee and interpreter and the leader of His servants who will convey to them all that He wants them to do or not to do. Also, the All-Gracious One of Perfection, Who has favored the universe with the uncountable manifestations of His Grace and Perfections, will undoubtedly and clearly assign the most perfect duty of servanthood to the one who is the most comprehensive and has the most perfect measure and means of reflecting His Grace, Perfection, Names, and Art, which He loves and wants to display. He will make this being's personality and conduct an excellent example for others and encourage them to follow him so that his personality and good conduct may also appear in them.

In short, love of God requires and results in following the elevated Sunna. How happy is the person whose share of following the Sunna is great! Woe to the one who does not appreciate the Sunna but indulges in religious innovations!

Sixth point

The noblest Messenger, upon him be blessings and peace, declared, "All innovations in the Religion are misguidance, and all misguidance will be in Hellfire."[32] That is to say, according to the verse, *This day I have perfected for you your Religion* (5: 3), after the rules of the Shari'a and the principles of the Sunna have been completed, making new inventions or producing

---

32 *an-Nasa'i*, "Iydayn" 22; at-Tabarani, *al-Mu'jam al-Kabir*, 9:97. (Tr.)

innovations in the Religion, which mean that one thinks these rules and principles are defective and can be improved upon, is misguidance and deserves Hellfire.

There are degrees in the Sunna. Some of its principles or decrees are imperative; they cannot be ignored or abandoned. They are described in detail in the illustrious Shari'a. They are among the established, unquestionable rules of the Religion and can in no way be altered.

The other degree of the Sunna consists in supererogatory acts of worship and practices. These also fall into two categories. One category is composed of the Prophet's supererogatory practices of worship, which are very meritorious and highly commendable for Muslims to perform. They are also described in the books of the Shari'a. Changing them is innovation.

Another category comprises the Prophet's practices that are regarded as good manners or good, commendable conduct. They are mentioned in the Prophet's biographies. Not following them is not regarded as innovation, but it entails opposition to the Prophetic practices and good conduct and causes deprivation of the light that derives from these acts and from the principles of good conduct or manners. There is still another category of the Prophet's good manners or conduct, which consists in everyday actions, behavior, and dealings of the Prophet, upon him be peace and blessings, which are known through reliable, unanimously reported Traditions. For example, there are numerous Prophetic practices showing good manners in speaking, eating, drinking, sleeping, and concerning social relationships. One who follows these good manners in their daily life transforms their everyday practices into a form of worship, and derives significant spiritual radiations and benefits from them. Observing the least of them recalls the noblest Messenger, upon him be peace and blessings, and imparts a light to the heart.

The most important among the rules and principles of the Sunna are those which are the public symbols or marks of Islam. These are acts of worship that the whole community of Muslims are required to perform, and are therefore included in the general social rights and duties. If some among the community do them, the whole community benefits from it, and, by contrast, if none perform such actions, then the whole community becomes responsible. There can be no hypocrisy or ostentation in the performance of such indications of Islam, and they are openly proclaimed and performed.

Even if they are included in the supererogatory acts of worship, they are socially more important than personal obligatory acts.

Seventh point

Every rule and practice of the elevated Sunna indicates good conduct. There is nothing included in the Sunna that does not bear a light or teach good manners and conduct. The noblest Messenger, upon him be peace and blessings, declared, "My Lord has taught and educated me, and how well He has taught and educated me!"[33] One who studies the Prophet's biography and knows his conduct will certainly understand that God Almighty collected all varieties of good conduct in His Beloved. One who abandons his Sunna abandons good manners, and becomes the object of the saying, "An ill-mannered person is deprived of Divine favor." This means self-ruin.

QUESTION: How can one preserve good manners before the Knower of whatever is unseen, Who sees and knows everything? Situations which cause shame and embarrassment cannot be kept hidden from Him. One sort of good manners is covering the parts of the body which we must cover and veiling the detestable states. It is impossible to conceal anything from the Knower of all that is unseen.

THE ANSWER: First of all, the All-Majestic Maker, Who especially wills that His Art be shown as beautiful, veils detestable things and draws attention to His bounties by decorating them; He also wills that His creatures and servants be shown as beautiful to other conscious beings. Their appearance in ugly situations is a form of opposition to His Names, such as the All-Gracious, the All-Decorating, the All-Subtle, and the All-Wise, and is contrary to good manners. So, good manners according to the elevated Sunna of the Prophet, upon him be peace and blessings, is to take on a purely good manner within the bounds of the All-Majestic Maker's Names.

Secondly, as far as doctors are concerned, they may look at the most private member of someone who is not canonically forbidden to marry them; when necessary these can be shown to the doctor. This is not regarded as being opposed to good manners; rather, the nature of medicine requires this. But this same doctor cannot look at the forbidden members of

33 al-Munawi, *Fayd al-Qadir*, 1:225; al-Qurtubi, *al-Jami' li-Ahkam al-Qur'an*, 18:228. (Tr.)

that person outside their professional calling, nor do good manners allow them to be shown.

The All-Majestic Maker has numerous Names, and each Name has particular manifestations. For example, the existence of the Name the All-Forgiving means that there are sins to be forgiven, and the existence of the Name the All-Veiling indicates the existence of defects to be hidden. Likewise, the Name the All-Gracious and Beautiful does not desire that ugliness be seen, while Names that indicate beauty, grace, and perfection such as the All-Subtle, the All-Munificent, the All-Wise, and the All-Compassionate require that all beings should be beautiful and act in the best possible manner. The Names of grace, beauty, and perfection will the exhibition of beauties in front of angels, spirit beings, jinn, and humankind through the beautiful states and good manners of beings. Thus, the principles of good conduct or manners contained in the elevated Sunna are the indications and samples of these lofty manners.

Eighth point

Preceding, *Still, if they turn away from you (O Messenger), say, "God is sufficient for me...,"* the verse,

> *There has come to you a Messenger from among yourselves; extremely grievous to him is your suffering, full of concern for you is he, and for the believers full of pity and compassion.* (9:128)

shows the perfect affection and kindness of God's noblest Messenger towards his Community, and with *Still, if they turn away from you....*, it states as follows:

> O humankind, and O Muslims! The affectionate Messenger guides you with boundless affection, expends all his power and energy for your benefit, and cures your spiritual wounds with the rules He brings and the principles of his elevated Sunna. Therefore, you must know how unfair and unreasonable it is to turn away from his Sunna and the rules he conveys in a way that means the denial of his self-evident affection and condemnation of his most visible kindness.
>
> And O affectionate Messenger, O kind Prophet! If they do not recognize this immense affection and kindness of yours and if out of foolishness they do not support or listen to you, do not worry. The All-Majestic One, under Whose command are the hosts of the heavens and the earth, and the sovereignty of Whose Lordship rules from

> His all-encompassing Supreme Throne, is sufficient for you. He will muster around you His truly obedient troops, and make them heed you and accept your decrees.

Truly, there is no matter included in the Shari'a of Muhammad and his Sunna which does not have numerous instances of wisdom. Despite all my defects and helplessness, I make this claim and am ready to prove it. In fact, the seventy to eighty Treatises of the Light (*Risale-i Nur*) that have been written so far are seventy to eighty truthful witnesses bearing testimony to how full of wisdom and true are the matters of the Sunna and Shari'a of Muhammad, upon him be peace and blessings. Not seventy, but even seven thousand treatises would not, if I were capable of writing them, be able to describe these instances of wisdom.

I have numerous experiences and observations that the rules of the Shari'a and principles of the elevated Sunna are each the most beneficial cures for the diseases of the spirit, mind, and heart, and particularly for diseases of society. I have personally observed and explained, to the extent that I am capable, in the Treatises of the Light that other social and philosophical principles and theories cannot take their place. If there are some who doubt the truth of my claim, let them refer to the relevant parts of the *Risale-i Nur*.

It may be understood from this how profitable it is to follow, as far as possible, the Sunna of such a person, and how favorable and advantageous for our eternal life, how beneficial for our worldly life, this is.

Ninth point

Strictly following the entire Sunna in all its degrees and aspects can only be achieved by those most advanced in the Religion and in nearness to God. However, it is possible for all to follow it by intention and by supporting and admitting it as their way of life. We are religiously obliged to follow its imperatives or obligatory rules and principles. Even if there is no sin in not carrying out the supererogatory acts of worship established by the Sunna, such neglect causes considerable loss of reward. To change them is a grave error. As for the Prophet's everyday practices, if we follow them, these practices become acts of worship. If we do not follow them, no punishment is incurred, but we benefit less from the light of the good conduct of God's Beloved, upon him be peace and blessings.

New inventions in the ordinances concerning worship mean innovation, and since innovation is opposed to the verse, *This day I have perfected for you your Religion* (5:3), they must be rejected. However, the regular recitations and invocations adopted by the sound Sufi ways, even if they are in various forms and manners, are not considered to be innovations, provided they are originally based on the Qur'an and the Sunna and do not oppose the principles and fundamentals of the Sunna. Nevertheless, some scholars have included even these as innovations, but call them "acceptable innovations." Imam Rabbani, the Reviver of the Second Millenium, may God be pleased with him, says:

> While passing through the ranks in my spiritual journeys, I saw that the words reported from God's noblest Messenger, upon him be peace and blessings, have a particular light; they are shining with the rays of the elevated Sunna. When I saw other bright and powerful regular recitations that were not reported from him and when I observed the spiritual states that belong to those who do not take following the Sunna as the absolute basis of their way, I saw that there was no such light from them. Even the brightest of this sort was not equal to the least of the former. I understood from this that the rays of the elevated Sunna are an elixir. Also, the Sunna is sufficient for those who seek light; there is no need to seek light outside it.

This conclusion of a hero of the truth and the Shari'a such as Imam Rabbani shows that the elevated Sunna is the foundation of happiness in both worlds and the source of all excellence and perfection.

O God! Favor us by enabling us to follow the elevated Sunna.

Our Lord! We believe in what You have sent down and we follow the Messenger, so record us among the witnesses (of Your Oneness and Lordship, and of the truth You have revealed). (3:53)

Tenth point

The verse,

Say (to them, O Messenger): "If you indeed love God, then follow me, so that God will love you, is a miracle of conciseness, for there are many sentences in this verse that is comprised of only three phrases. They are as follows:

The verse declares as follows:

> If you have faith in God, may His Majesty be exalted, you will certainly love Him. If you love God, then you will act in the manner He loves. Doing so means resembling the person whom God loves in his acts. Resembling that person is possible by following him. If you follow him, God will love you. You must love God so that He will love you.

All of these sentences form only a brief, concise interpretation of the verse. What is being said here is that the most important and exalted goal for humans is being favored with the love of God Almighty. The verse decrees and shows that the way of achieving this most exalted goal is following God's Beloved, following his elevated Sunna. The following three points will clearly demonstrate this truth.

FIRST POINT: Humankind has been created with a limitless, innate love for the Creator of the universe. For humankind innately loves beauty and grace, and adores excellence, perfection, and favor. This love increases in proportion with the degrees of beauty, grace, excellence, and favor, stretching up to its final point.

Furthermore, the tiny heart of the human can contain a love as great as the universe. The fact that the faculty of memory, which occupies a place in the mind the size of a lentil, can hold as many writings as there are in a library demonstrates that the human heart can contain the whole universe and bear love that great.

So, since human nature has a capacity to feel limitless love for favor, grace, beauty, and perfection; and since, as decisively demonstrated by His works exhibited in the universe, and as self-evidently established by the embroideries of His Art that is apparent in beings, and as clearly and demonstrably proved by the countless varieties of His bounties observed in animate creatures, the Creator of the universe has infinite holy grace, beauty, perfection, and favor, then it is certain that these demand limitless love from humankind, which is the most comprehensive, the most needy, the most thoughtful, and the most yearning of conscious beings.

Indeed, just as every human being has a capacity to love the All-Majestic Creator infinitely, so, too, due to His grace, beauty, perfection, and favor, the All-Majestic Creator has a greater right than everybody else to be infinitely loved. It can even be said that all the varieties of love and intense attachment a believing person has for their life, subsistence, and existence, and for their world and self, and for all creatures, are in fact manifestations of this capacity. More than that, the various intense emotions of humans are reflections of that capacity which have taken on different forms.

As humans take pleasure in their own happiness, so too do they receive happiness from the happiness of others with whom they are connected. Also, as they love one who saves them from a disaster, so too do they love those who save their loved ones. If, considering this state of mind, out of the infinite varieties of Divine favor, a person should think about what follows:

> As my Creator has saved me from non-existence, which is eternal darkness, and given me a particular, beautiful world, so too will He save me from going into non-existence, which is eternal extinction, when the appointed time comes for me to die, and accord me an eternal, most splendid world in the everlasting realm. Again, as He has also granted me external and inner senses and faculties with which to benefit from all the varieties of delight and beauty of that world and to wander throughout it and take pleasure in it, so too does He bestow countless bounties on all my relatives, loved ones, and fellow-persons whom I love much and to whom I feel great attachment. These bounties are also accorded to me, as I feel happy and pleased with their happiness.

A person should think thus and say:

> Since, as stated in the adage, "The human is the slave of kindness done to them," everyone adores kindness, and if I had a heart as vast as the universe, it should be filled—indeed I wish to fill it—with love for all those countless bounties. Even if I am unable to feel that love, I feel it through my capacity and intention, and through belief in their Bestower and through appreciation of them, and through yearning for Him.

One should consider the love for the bounties I have briefly mentioned and conclude how great a love we should feel for the Divine Grace, Beauty, and Perfection. As for those who do not believe in God, because of their unbelief they are infinitely hostile to Him, and even bear a pitiless and insulting enmity towards the whole universe.

SECOND POINT: Love of God necessitates following the Sunna of Muhammad, upon him be peace and blessings. For loving God means doing whatever pleases Him. The things that please Him are manifested and reflected in their perfect form in the person of Muhammad, upon him be peace and blessings. We can resemble the Prophet Muhammad in his acts in two ways:

The first: As required by His love, obeying God's commands and acting within the sphere of the things that please Him necessitate following the Prophet, for the perfect leader in obedience to God is Muhammad, upon him be peace and blessings.

The second: Since the person of Muhammad is the most important means for God's favors upon humanity, he certainly deserves limitless love for God's sake. A person wants, by nature, to resemble the one whom they love if it is possible for them to do so. Thus, those who love God's Beloved must certainly try to resemble him by following his elevated Sunna.

THIRD POINT: Just as God Almighty has infinite compassion, so too does He have infinite love. As He makes Himself infinitely loved through the fine qualities and varieties of beauty He gives to all the creatures in the universe, so too does He love His creatures, including particularly the conscious ones who respond with love to His causing Himself to be loved. It can clearly and definitely be understood how important and exalted an aim it is to draw upon oneself the view of love of the One a single manifestation of Whose Mercy forms all of the subtleties, beauties, pleasures, and bounties of Paradise. Since He definitely decrees in His Word—the Qur'an—that one can be favored with His love only by following the Sunna of Muhammad, upon him be peace and blessings, then it is evident that following it should be the ultimate aim of humanity and its most important duty.

Eleventh point

This Point consists of three matters.

FIRST MATTER: The Sunna of the noblest Messenger, upon him be peace and blessings, has three sources: his words, his acts, and his states or his conduct. With respect to the degrees of religious responsibilities, they fall into three categories: imperative, supererogatory, and good manners or his customary practices.

We are religiously obliged to follow those that are imperative; abandoning them incurs punishment and retribution.

As believers, we are also responsible for carrying out the supererogatory acts as meritorious decrees. However, there is no punishment or retribution for not doing them. If we perform such acts, we gain great rewards, but making any alteration in them is a great error, and misguided.

As for the Prophet's customary practices or laudable manners, following or imitating him in his everyday life or manners is highly commendable from the perspective of wisdom and considering human personal and social life. For in each of his customary practices lie many benefits for life, and by following them, our everyday practices become like acts of worship.

Since, as both friends and foes agree, the Prophet Muhammad, upon him be peace and blessings, had all good morals or virtues to the highest degree; and since, as is unanimously agreed, he is the most distinguished and excellent member of humanity; and since, as his numerous miracles show, his personal excellences and the world of Islam that he founded bear witness, and the truths of the wise Qur'an, which he conveyed and explained, confirm, he is the most excellent, perfect person and the most perfect guide; and since, as a result of following him, hundreds of millions of people have ascended through the degrees of perfection and attained the happiness of both worlds; then surely his elevated Sunna, his way of life, is the most excellent example to follow, the safest guide to employ, and soundest set of laws to adopt. Happy is he whose share in following the Sunna is great. If one does not follow the Sunna because of laziness, this incurs a tremendous loss; considering the Sunna to be unimportant is a tremendous crime, and criticizing it in a way to suggest that one does not accept it is serious misguidance.

SECOND MATTER: God Almighty proclaims in the wise Qur'an: *You are surely of a sublime character and do act by a sublime pattern of conduct* (68: 4). According to authentic, reliable narrations, when a distinguished Companion like 'A'isha, may God be pleased with her, described the Prophet, upon him be peace and blessings, she would say, "His character is the Qur'an."[34] That is, the concrete example of all virtues or excellent moral qualities that the Qur'an mentions is the Prophet Muhammad, upon him be peace and bless-

---

34 *Muslim*, "Musafirun" 139; *Ibn Maja*, "Ahkam" 14; Ahmad ibn Hanbal, *al-Musnad*, 6:91, 163. (Tr.)

ings. He is the one who conforms to them best of all; it is he whose nature is a perfect embodiment of them.

Thus, while every one of the deeds, states, words, and acts of such a person is worthy to be a model for humankind, even the insane can understand how unfortunate are those heedless people who believe in him and belong to his Community, yet attach no importance to his Sunna or who want to change it.

THIRD MATTER: The noblest Messenger, upon him be peace and blessings, had a perfect nature that was perfectly balanced, and he strictly obeyed the Divine order, *Pursue, then, what is exactly right (in every matter of the Religion) as you are commanded (by God)* (11: 112), and his biography clearly demonstrates that he was always balanced and straightforward in all his actions and states. He continuously avoided going to all sorts of extremes.

For example, completely free of both stupidity and demagogy or sophistry, the two extreme points of intellect that entail its corruption, his intellect or power of reason always worked in accordance with wisdom; this is the point of balance, upon which uprightness is based. Likewise, his power or faculty of anger, completely removed from both cowardice and rage, the extreme points of this power which signify its corruption, always acted with blessed courage, which is the middle point. Similarly, his power of passion, absolutely purified of both frigidity and dissipation, which are the extreme points of this power, and therefore indicate its corruption, always and strictly followed chastity as the middle way or the point of balance. And so on.... In short, in all aspects of his Sunna, his natural states and everyday practices, including his speech, eating, and drinking, and in all the ordinances of the Shari'a, he always chose the balanced way and avoided all kinds of extremes and wastefulness, which entail wrongdoing and cause "darkness." Thousands of books have been written about the details of this matter. Following the adage, "A hint is enough for one who is wise and intelligent," we see this drop from the ocean as being sufficient and cut the story short here.

> O God, bestow blessings on the one who has all moral excellences, and was honored with the Divine declaration, "You are surely of a sublime character and act by a sublime pattern of conduct." It is he who said: "Whoever follows my Sunna when my Community has been corrupted, there is for him (or her) the reward of a hundred martyrs."

They say: "All praise and gratitude are for God, Who has guided us to this (prosperity as a result of the guidance with which He favored us in the world). If God had not guided us, we would certainly not have found the right way. The Messengers of our Lord did indeed come with the truth." (7:43)

All-Glorified are You. We have no knowledge save what You have taught us. Surely You are the All-Knowing, the All-Wise.

The
Twelfth Gleam

The Twelfth Gleam

• *The sustenance God undertakes to provide*
• *The seven levels of the heavens and the earth*

This Gleam expounds two fine points concerning the Qur'an, written in connection with two questions asked by Rafet Bey.

In His Name, All-Glorified is He.

There is nothing but it glorifies Him with His praise.

Peace be upon you, and on your brothers, and God's mercy and blessings!

My dear, faithful brother, Rafet Bey,

Your questions coming at this difficult time put me in a difficult position. Your two new questions are of little importance, but since they relate to two points concerning the Qur'an, and the question about the earth is connected with criticism of the geography and astronomy of the Qur'anic statement that God has created *seven heavens* and *of the earth the like of them* (65:12), they seemed to be significant to me. For this reason, without considering that the questions are of little importance, two issues concerning two verses of the Qur'an will be scientifically explained.

First issue

This consists of two Points.

FIRST POINT: According to the verses,

How many a living creature there is that does not carry its own provisions (in store), but God provides for them, and indeed for you. He is the All-Hearing, the All-Knowing. (29: 60)

Surely God—it is He Who is the All-Providing, Lord of all might, and the All-Forceful. (51: 58)

sustenance is directly in the hands of the All-Powerful One of Majesty and comes from the treasury of His Mercy. Since the provision for every living creature has been undertaken by Him as the Lord of the whole creation, no one should die of hunger. But we can see that many die of hunger or lack provisions. The reality of this matter is as follows:

The Lord's guarantee is a reality, and no one dies because of a lack of provisions. For the All-Wise of Majesty stores up as reserves in the form of fat some of the provisions He sends to the bodies of living creatures. He even stores up some of the sustenance He sends to each cell in the cell, and keeps it there as a reserve stock to be spent when no sustenance comes from outside. Those whom we perceive as dying of hunger die before this store has been completely consumed. This means that they do not die of a lack of provisions; they rather die from a habit acquired through wrong choices and practices or because of an illness resulting from that wrong choice and practice and giving up that habit.

The natural sustenance stored up in the bodies of living creatures in the form of fat generally suffices for forty days. It may even exceed twice forty days as a result of certain illnesses or spiritually ecstatic states. Years ago (in 1921) it appeared in a newspaper that a man in prison in London managed to live healthily for seventy days without eating anything.

Since, then, the natural sustenance lasts for forty to seventy or eighty days, and since the Divine Name, the All-Providing manifests Itself throughout the earth in an all-inclusive, extensive way; and since food flows forth from breasts and wood in an extraordinary, unexpected fashion, then, if wicked humanity does not interfere out of wrong choice or misuse, the Name, the All-Providing should come to the aid of the starving living creature before the natural sustenance is consumed, and not allow death out of hunger. So, those reported to die of hunger definitely do not die from a lack of provision if they die in less than forty days. Rather, as stated in the adage, "The abandoning of habits is one of the causes of destruction," their death is either because of a habit acquired through wrong choice or of an illness resulting from abandoning that habit. Therefore, it may be said that there is no death from hunger.

Indeed, it is observed that provision is not in direct proportion to power and will. For example, when utterly deprived of will and power in the womb before coming to the world, babies are given their provisions in such a way that they do not even need to move their mouths. Then when they come into the world, they still do not have power or will, but since they have some sort of capacity or potential senses, they need only to move to fasten their mouths to the breast, and are provided through the fountains of the breasts with the perfect, the most nutritious, and easily digestible sustenance in the kindest and strangest fashion. As they grow in power and will, that fine, readily available sustenance starts to be gradually withdrawn from the infants. The fountains of the breasts dry up, and the child's sustenance comes from somewhere else. But since they still do not have enough will or power to obtain their sustenance, the All-Providing of Munificence sends their parents' care and compassion to their assistance. Whenever they have enough power and will, then their sustenance is not sent them in a readily available way.

Sustenance remains in its place and says, "Come and search for me, take me!" Sustenance is not always directly proportional to will or power. In addition to the example of infants above, the fact that the animals weakest in will and power live better and are better provided for proves this.

SECOND POINT: There are different sorts of possibility, such as "possibility in reason," "possibility by way of practice," and "ordinary possibility." If an event is not possible in reason, that is, if sound reason does not see it as being possible, it is rejected. If it is not of the sort that can be obtained through practice or efforts, it can only be a miracle (created by God through a Prophet). It cannot easily be a wonder that can be worked by saints. If something is not possible either through practice or in principle but has been reported to have taken place, it can only be accepted if there is a decisive proof for its occurrence based on direct observation.

It is for this reason that the extraordinary states of Sayyid Ahmad Badawi,[35] who managed to live without eating for forty days, are of the sort of possibility obtained through practice. It may have been both an exceptional wonder worked by him and a habitual practice of his. It is unani-

35 Sayyid Ahmad Badawi (d. 1276) was one of the most famous saints in the history of Islam. (Tr.)

mously reported that Sayyid Ahmad Badawi, may God sanctify him, had wondrous and ecstatic states of spiritual absorption. He occasionally, but not always, ate once in forty days as a way of working a wonder. He may well have done so because his states of spiritual absorption caused him not to feel the need to eat, in which case, it became a habitual practice. It has reliably been reported that many other saints have worked this sort of wonder. So, as we explained above, since the reserves of sustenance stored up in the body last for more than forty days, and managing without eating for such a length of time is possible by way of practice, and it has been reliably narrated about exceptional people, then it cannot be denied.

Second issue

Two important matters will be explained in connection with the second question, because with the narrow-ranging laws of geography and astronomy and their incomplete principles and tiny measures, scientists have been unable to ascend to the heavens of the Qur'an and discover the seven levels of meanings in the stars of its verses, and thus they have criticized the verses (related to the issues discussed and which we are explaining,) and foolishly even attempted to deny them.

The First Important Matter

This is about the earth having seven levels, like the heavens. Modern scientists, or the sciences concerned with the earth and heavens, deny this. They make this a pretext to oppose some of the truths in the Qur'an. We will briefly mention some points related to this matter.

FIRST POINT: First of all, the apparent, basic meaning of a verse is one thing, and other meanings or connotations inferred from it and the things that confirm it are another. If one of the numerous connotations or meanings inferred cannot yet be confirmed or appears to lack necessary evidence, the basic meaning cannot be denied. Of the numerous parts of the basic meaning regarding the seven levels of the heavens and the earth with its points of resemblance to them, as will be explained below, there are seven apparent realities to point to and confirm it.

Secondly, the verse does not explicitly state that the earth has seven layers. In its apparent meaning, the verse, *God is He Who has created seven heavens and of the earth the like of them* (65:12), states that God has created the earth like the seven heavens, and made it a dwelling place for His creatures. It does not explicitly state that God has created seven levels of the earth. The likeness in the verse between the heavens and the earth is in regard to both being created and made habitations for creatures.

SECOND POINT: Compared with the heavens, the earth is in fact very small. But in the same way that the heart is equal to the body in one respect, the earth, as the place of exhibition and the focus of countless Divine works of art, can be equal to the heavens as the heart of the universe and, with the meaning it has, its center. From this perspective, (1) the earth has seven climes, as has been understood from early times; (2) it is universally accepted that there are seven continents, namely Europe, Africa, Oceania, the two Asias (at the present, one Asia and Antarctica), and the two Americas; (3) there are the seven great seas or oceans and the parts of the earth they surround in both or either of its hemispheres; (4) the earth has seven contiguous layers from its center through to its outer crust;[36] (5) the famous seven universal elements called "the seven levels," comprise simple, particular elements that are the means of living for animate creatures; (6) there are seven levels or realms comprising the three animal, vegetable, and mineral kingdoms, and the four basic elements of water, air, fire, and soil; (7) there are seven realms of various living and conscious beings, such as jinn, devils, and humans, as discovered by numerous saints of spiritual discovery and observation; and (8) there are seven other spheres or globes resembling ours, and on which living beings particular to each live—and all these facts have been inferred from the above-mentioned verse, which says *God is He Who has created seven heavens and of the earth the like of them.*

Thus, we have been able to establish in seven ways that the earth has seven levels or layers of seven kinds. The last, eighth meaning is important from another perspective but not included in our discussion.

---

36 The earth has several distinct layers, each of which has its own properties: the inner core, the outer core, the lower mantle, the outer mantle, the asthenosphere, the lithosphere, and the crust. The earth can also be seen in its surroundings. The atmosphere which surrounds it is divided into the troposphere, the ozone layer, the stratosphere, the mesosphere, and the thermosphere. The solid earth can be divided into the biosphere, the hydrosphere, and the internal structure of the earth, which includes the crust, mantle and core. (Tr.)

THIRD POINT: Since the Absolutely Wise One wastes nothing and creates nothing in vain, and since other creatures serve conscious beings, and attain perfection, gain liveliness, and are saved from futility through them, and since the Absolutely Wise and All-Powerful One of Glory has caused the element of air, the world of water, and the layer of earth to be inhabited with innumerable living creatures, and since just as air and water do not prevent the movement of animals, so also dense matter like earth or rock do not impede the conduction of electricity, X-rays, or the like, for sure the All-Wise of Perfection, the Immortal Maker, will certainly not have left uninhabited the seven adjoining layers, with all their parts and places, from the inner core of the earth to the outer crust, where we exist. He has certainly caused these areas to be inhabited by living, conscious creatures particular to each. Among those conscious beings are angels and other spirit beings. For them, the densest and hardest layer is like the sea is for the fish and the air for birds. Even the terrible heat in the core must be for these conscious beings like the sun's heat for us. Since these conscious spirit beings are created from light, fire is like light for them.

FOURTH POINT: In the Eighteenth Letter, a comparison is mentioned to clarify the irrational descriptions made by some saints of spiritual discovery of some strange marvels concerning the earth's layers. Its gist is as follows:

The earth is a seed in the corporeal realm, while in the Intermediate Realm or the World of Immaterial Representations or Ideal Forms it is like a huge tree that has stretched its branches as far as the corners of the heavens. Some saints of spiritual discovery have seen demons dwell in a realm of the earth that stretches billions of square miles, but this is not in the corporeal earth itself, but rather on the branches or levels of the earth that are reflected in the World of Ideal Forms. Since an apparently insignificant level of the earth has such a vast reflection in another world, it may surely be said that the earth has seven levels or layers corresponding to the seven levels of the heavens. Thus, by showing the tiny earth as corresponding to the heavens, the relevant Qur'anic verses draw attention to the above-mentioned and other similar points in a miraculously concise way.

The Second Important Matter

> *The seven heavens and the earth, and whoever is therein, glorify Him.* (17: 44)

Then He directed (His Knowledge, Will, Power, and Favor) to the heaven, and formed it into seven heavens. (2: 29)

Many verses like the ones above describe the heavens as seven heavens. A brief explanation of this matter, which was explained in detail in *Isharat al-'Ijaz* ("The Signs of the Qur'an's Miraculousness"), is as follows:

Muslim philosophers and scientists (of the Middle Ages) included in the heavens what the Shari'a calls the Divine Supreme Throne and the Divine Supreme Seat, and so mentioned the nine heavens in a strange way. The impressive descriptions of those geniuses of philosophy and science continued to influence people for many centuries. This influence was such that many interpreters of the Qur'an felt compelled to reconcile the apparent meanings of the relevant verses with their way of thought. This caused the Qur'an's miraculousness to be veiled to an extent. In contrast to this classical approach, which it is neither possible to ignore nor to rectify, the modern scientific approach went to the extreme opposite and nearly denied the (plural) existence of the heavens. Both being extreme, these approaches have been unable to portray the reality in its entirety.

As for the sacred wisdom of the wise Qur'an, as always, it chooses the middle, straight way and declares that God Almighty has created seven levels in the heavens. The movable stars move in the heavens like fish (moving in the water), and glorify God. A Prophetic Tradition says, "The sky is a wave held back."[37] That is, it is an ocean in which the waves are stationary.

We will explain this Qur'anic truth decisively, in a brief way, by presenting seven facts and seven aspects of meaning.

The first fact: Science and wisdom do and should admit that this boundless space is not an infinite vacuum, but rather that it is filled with a sort of matter called ether.

The second fact: It is a scientific, logical, and indeed observable reality that there is a kind of matter that fills space and which serves as a link for such laws as gravitation and repulsion among the celestial bodies and which is the conductor of light, heat, and electricity.

The third fact: It is also a fact that ether as a substance, while remaining as ether, also has various forms and formations, like other kinds of matter.

---

37 *at-Tirmidhi*, "Tafsir Sura 57" 1; Ahmad ibn Hanbal, *al-Musnad*, 2:370. (Tr.)

Just as the same matter has three states, liquid, gaseous, or solid, or can be the origin of three types of formations like water, steam, and ice, there is no logical reason to reject that ether has seven states or levels; there is no rational cause for there to be an objection to this statement.

The fourth fact: A careful observation and study of celestial bodies will reveal that there is some difference between the heavenly levels. For example, the level which contains the huge cloud-like sphere called the Milky Way does not resemble the level of fixed stars. It gives the impression that the fixed stars have ripened, like the fruits of summer, while innumerable new stars constantly appear in the form of a cloud in the Milky Way and begin to ripen. That level of fixed stars appears to one with insight as being different from the level of the solar system. So it may be deduced that there are seven heavenly systems or seven levels that are different from one another.

The fifth fact: It is a fact established by perception, inductive reasoning, observation, and experience that when a material is worked, it changes into new forms, and new materials are produced from it. For example, when a diamond mine begins to be worked, ashes and coal, as well as diamonds are obtained from it. To cite another example, when a fire is lit, it gives rise to flames, as well as to smoke and embers. Also, when hydrogen and oxygen are combined, water, ice, and steam are formed. We know that when a single substance is worked, new formations are created and new forms of matter appear. So when the Creative Power started to work on the matter of ether, He must have created from it the heavens, which *He formed into seven heavens*.

The sixth fact: All the facts mentioned above necessarily indicate both the existence and plurality of the heavens. Since there is more than one heaven, and God, the Ultimate Truth, declares them to be seven in the Qur'an, they are certainly seven.

The seventh fact: As terms like seven, seventy, and seven hundred express multiplicity in Arabic, the universal seven levels may actually comprise multiple levels.

In conclusion: The All-Powerful of Majesty created and formed the seven heavens from ether and organized them into an extremely subtle and wonderful system, sowing the stars in it. Since the Qur'an of miraculous exposition is an eternal address speaking to all levels of understanding among humankind and jinn, surely each level will receive its share from every verse of the Qur'an, and the verses will contain multiple levels of meaning both explicitly and implicitly to satisfy the understanding of all.

Truly, the Qur'anic address is so comprehensive and contains such multiple levels of meaning that it considers all degrees of understanding, from the most uneducated common people to the highest of the elite. This shows that each of its verses has aspects that address every level. It is because of this subtle reality that seven types of people have understood the following seven levels of meaning from the universal meaning of "seven heavens":

From *He formed them into seven heavens*, a short-sighted and narrow-minded person thinks of the atmosphere with all the formations of air. Another type of person, who is dazzled by cosmology, thinks of the stars, popularly known as the Seven Planets, and their orbits. Yet another group thinks of the seven heavenly spheres resembling ours, which are inhabited by living creatures. A further group of people thinks of the solar system being separated into seven levels, and the existence of another seven systems like the solar system. And yet another group of humankind thinks of the matter of ether being formed into seven levels. Another group, with a broader mind, regards all the visible heavens gilded with stars as a heaven, which is the heaven of our world, and understands that there are six more similar heavens. The seventh and highest class of humanity does not consider the seven heavens to be restricted to the corporeal realm. Rather, they understand that there are seven other realms, such as the Realm of the Hereafter, the Realm of the Unseen, and the Realm of Immaterial Representations or Ideal Forms, and that each of these realms has its own heaven encompassing it like an envelope.

And so, the verse in question has many further specific meanings, like the above-mentioned seven levels of meaning inferred by the seven classes of humanity. Everyone receives their share according to their level of understanding and finds their sustenance at that heavenly table.

Since that verse has so many numerous true meanings that confirm it, the unreasoning philosophers and baffled cosmologists who criticize it on the pretext of rejecting the existence of the seven heavens are like silly children throwing stones at the stars to make one fall. If the verse indicates even a single truth with its meanings, or if a single one of the meanings inferred from it is true, then the verse is true in its general meaning. Furthermore, even if among its specific meanings the verse has a meaning that is literally untrue, but which is commonly accepted, this may have been included among the meanings in order to take into consideration and show respect for the public view. We have seen that the verse has numerous particular meanings, all of which are true. Now consider how modern cosmology or the sciences of geography and astronomy err and, by closing their eyes to the comprehensive meaning of the verse, and ignoring its particular meanings all of which are true, infer a fanciful meaning from it according to their imperfect understanding, hurling stones at it. But the stones fall back and break their heads, destroying their beliefs.

In short, the Qur'an was revealed in seven recitations, and with seven aspects of accurate articulation, seven sorts of miraculousness, seven levels of truth, and seven pillars. Since unbelieving ideas or approaches of materialism have the effect of jinn or devils and cannot ascend to the seven levels of the Qur'an's heavens, they cannot realize the stars of the verses and thus give false reports. But the meteors of truth fall from the stars of the verses onto their heads, burning them. It is not possible to ascend to the heavens of the Qur'an with jinn-like ideas of misguided philosophy. The stars of the verses can only be ascended with the ladder of true wisdom and on the wings of belief and with the Islamic way of thought and life.

> O God! Bestow blessings on the Sun of the heaven of Messengership and the full moon of the firmament of Prophethood, and on his Family and Companions, who are the stars of guidance for the rightly-guided.
>
> All-Glorified are You. We have no knowledge save what You have taught us. Surely You are the All-Knowing, the All-Wise.
>
> O God! O Lord of the heavens and the earth! Adorn the hearts of the scribe (and translator) of this treatise and his companions with the stars of the truths of the Qur'an and belief! Amen.

The Thirteenth Gleam

The Thirteenth Gleam

The wisdom in and meaning of seeking refuge in God from Satan

This is about the meaning of *I seek refuge in God from Satan, eternally rejected (from God's Mercy).*

In the Name of God, the All-Merciful, the All-Compassionate.

And say: "My Lord! I seek refuge in You from the promptings and provocations of the satans. I seek refuge in You, my Lord, lest they be present with me." (23:97–98)

This treatise is about the meaning of seeking refuge in God from Satan. The matter will be studied as Thirteen Indications. Since some of the Indications have been convincingly explained in some parts of the *Risale-i Nur*, such as the Twenty-Sixth Word, they will be discussed here only briefly.

First indication

QUESTION: Since satans (devils) have no part at all in creation, and God Almighty supports the followers of truth with His mercy and favor, and the attractive beauties of truth strengthen and encourage the followers of the truth, and the repulsive ugliness of misguidance revolts even the people of misguidance, what is the wisdom in the frequent success of the party of Satan? And why do the followers of truth always feel it necessary to seek refuge in God Almighty from Satan?

THE ANSWER: The wisdom and reason is this: misguidance and evil are, for the most part, negative and destructive, and lead to extinction, while right guidance and good are in the main positive, constructive, formative and reformative, and lead to existence. As is known to all, a single man can destroy in one day a building which it took twenty men twenty days to build. While it is the All-Majestic Creator's Power Which creates and sustains human life, the survival of which He has made dependent on the existence of all the vital parts of the human body and the vital conditions of existence, by cutting off a part of the body a tyrant may prepare the ground for death, which is non-being when considered in relation to life. For this reason, the saying, "Destruction is easy," has become proverbial.

It is because of this reality that the people of misguidance sometimes triumph over the powerful followers of truth with only a weak force. But the followers of truth have such a formidable stronghold that when they take shelter in it, those terrible enemies cannot even approach them and can do them no harm. Even if they cause some temporary harm, as stated in the Divine declaration, *The final outcome is in favor of the God-revering, pious*, (7:128) everlasting reward and profit compensate for that harm. This formidable stronghold in which to seek shelter is the Shari'a of Muhammad, upon him be peace and blessings; it is his Sunna.

Second indication

QUESTION: It seems to be extremely ugly and revolting that satans, who are pure evil, are created and allowed to attack believers, and that many people fall into unbelief and are condemned to Hellfire because of them. How do the Mercy and Grace of the Absolutely All-Beautiful, All-Gracious One, the truly All-Merciful and All-Compassionate One, permit this unlimited ugliness and terrible calamity. Many people have asked about this matter, and it is a question that arises in many minds.

THE ANSWER: There are certainly some minor evils in the existence of Satan, but his existence causes numerous universal good results and allows for human attainment and perfection. However many degrees and ranks there are from a seed to a huge tree, the grades of human innate capacity are more numerous. Indeed, there are as many degrees as the reflections of the sun—from its reflection in a tiny shining object or a bubble on the sea to the sun itself. The development of these capacities or potentials requires action and work. What triggers the mechanism of the development is effort and struggle. This struggle is against satans and other harmful agents and things. Otherwise humans would have had a constant (spiritual) station or rank like those of angels, and there would have been no gradations or differences in spirituality among humankind. It is contrary to wisdom and justice to forsake thousands of instances of good in order to avoid some minor evil.

It is true that the majority of people fall into misguidance because of Satan, but in general something is important and valuable due to its quality, not due to its amount. Consider that if someone who has a thousand and ten seeds lets his seeds germinate under the earth, and ten become trees and a thousand rot, surely, the benefit the ten trees give to that man will reduce to nothing the loss that a thousand rotten seeds cause him. Similarly, through the struggle against the carnal, evil-commanding soul and the satans, the benefit, honor, and value humanity gains thanks to ten perfect people who, like stars, enlighten humanity, certainly reduce to nothing the harm caused by the people of unbelief who are so bad as to be considered rotten. This is why the Divine Mercy, Wisdom, and Justice have permitted the existence of Satan, and allow him to attack humans.

O people of belief! Your armor against those awful enemies is the utmost reverence for God and righteousness woven on the workbench of the Qur'an. Your shield is the elevated Sunna of the noblest Messenger, upon him be peace and blessings. Your weapon is to seek refuge in God's protection and ask Him for forgiveness for your sins.

Third indication

QUESTION: It does not seem to be reasonable in accordance with its perfectly balanced and proper eloquence and styles that the wise Qur'an complains greatly of the people of misguidance, and frequently draws attention to them, threatening them severely. It is as if it were mobilizing armies against a powerless man. It threatens them because of a single minor action, as if they had committed thousands of crimes. Even though they are essentially poor and miserable, with no claim to any of the possession or dominion of existence, the Qur'an deals with them as if they were aggressive partners of

God in His Dominion, and complains of them. What is the reason for this and the wisdom in it?

THE ANSWER: The reason and wisdom is this: since Satan and those following him follow the way of misguidance, they can cause great destruction with a minor action, and they can do many creatures great wrong with a small deed.

Consider that through some minor action or act of neglect of an insignificant duty, a man on a large, royal merchant ship of a king can cause the efforts of all those who have a duty related to the ship to go for nothing. So, the illustrious owner of the ship complains of that rebellious one and severely threatens him on behalf of all his subjects that have some connection with the ship. And he severely punishes him, considering not his insignificant action but its awful consequences, and not in his own illustrious name but in the name of the rights of his subjects.

Similarly, even with their apparently minor faults and rebelliousness, the people of misguidance, who are the party of Satan and exist on the ship of the earth together with the people of right guidance, can violate the rights of many creatures and cause their exalted duties to be fruitless. So it is pure wisdom and completely appropriate and perfectly eloquent that the Eternal Monarch complains greatly of them and severely threatens them, frequently drawing attention to their destruction as if He were mobilizing great forces against them. And it is in accordance with the requirements of the situation, which is the basis of eloquence; rather, it is eloquence itself as eloquence is defined as speaking (or writing) in accordance with the requirements of the situation. Such a reaction is in no way an exaggeration, which would be wastefulness in words.

It is a fact that the one who does not seek refuge in an exceptionally formidable stronghold in the face of awful enemies causing great destruction with a small act will suffer greatly. So, O people of belief! That heavenly stronghold of steel is the Qur'an. Enter it and be saved!

Fourth indication

It has been unanimously accepted by verifying scholars and saints of spiritual discovery that non-existence is pure evil and that existence is pure good. Good, beauty, and excellence or perfection usually have their source in existence and are attributed to it. Even if sometimes they may superficially appear to be destructive and lead to non-existence, they are essentially constructive, positive and serve existence. Yet all instances of ugliness, such as misguidance, sins, and calamities originate and serve non-existence and destruction. Even if they may sometimes seem to be constructive and related to existence, they are essentially negative, destructive, and both originate and lead to non-existence.

Also, it is an observable fact that the existence of something like a building requires the existence of all of its parts, while its destruction or non-existence is possible through the non-existence of one of its main parts. Furthermore, existence requires and is based on a certain cause, which we call its *raison d'être* (reason for being). Whereas non-existence may be based on things that originate in and lead to non-existence.

It is because of these two rules that despite the terrible, destructive actions and varieties of unbelief, misguidance, and evil which they perpetrate, those who can be considered to be devils among the humans and jinn cannot have any part in creation or the Divine authority over existence. They do not commit such evils based on a creative power, but rather commit them by causing good, positive, and constructive things to be neglected and left undone. For anything evil, which is destruction, does not require existence or inventive power. Rather, something originating in non-existence or the ruin of a necessary part causes a great destruction or evil.[38]

Since the Zoroastrians could not grasp this subtle truth, they attributed real existence to evil, which they regarded as unbefitting for God, and invented the doctrine that there is a creator of good, called Yazdan, and a creator of evil, called Ahriman. However, the imaginary god of evil they called Ahriman is Satan, who causes evil by, out of his particular free will, always doing evil, which has and can have no part in the act of creation.

So, O believers! Your most important weapon against this terrible destruction of the devils and the greatest equipment for repair is imploring God for forgiveness and seeking refuge in God by saying, "I seek refuge in God

---

[38] God Almighty always wills and does good either in itself or on account of its results; He manifests all His Attributes and Names to create good. But humanity, either by its essential nature changing from good to evil, or by neglecting to do what should be done in order to be able to receive the good that is sent by God, or doing something which will annul any of the good, positive manifestations of God, makes that good evil for itself. (Tr.)

from Satan, eternally rejected (from God's Mercy)." And your stronghold is the elevated Sunna of the Prophet, upon him be peace and blessings.

Fifth indication

In the Books He sent, God Almighty repeatedly gives the glad tidings of a mighty reward like Paradise and warns of a tremendous punishment like Hellfire. In addition, He frequently gives and calls to guidance and encourages to good and Paradise, and warns against misguidance and threatens with both Hellfire and other kinds of severe punishment. Despite all such means of guidance and following the Straight Path, believers may be defeated in the face of the feeble, repulsive ploys of the party of Satan, which promise no real reward. This preoccupied my mind for a long time. I wondered how a believer could not pay heed to the severe threats of God Almighty despite their belief, and why this heedlessness did not annul belief. And if, as proclaimed in the Qur'an, *the guile of Satan is ever feeble* (4: 76), how could they rebel against God and be defeated by Satan's ever-feeble schemes? Some among my friends, although they had sincerely confirmed the truths which they heard from me many times and despite their extremely good opinion of me and sincere relation to me, were taken in by the hypocritical compliments of a heartless, corrupt man, and assumed a position in his favor and against me. "All glory be to God!" I uttered. "Can a man fall so low? How insincere a man he is!" By talking badly about that poor man, I committed a sin.

Later, the truths mentioned in the previous Indications became clearer in my mind and illuminated many obscure points. Thanks be to God, through that illumination, I came to understand that the Qur'an's emphatic encouragement and advocacy are completely proper, and believers are taken in by the deceit of Satan not due to a lack of belief or weakness in their belief. I also understood that those who commit major sins do not become unbelievers, and that the Mu'tazilites[39] and some Kharijite sects are mistaken in their doctrine that one who commits a major sin becomes an

[39] The *Mu'tazilites* or al-*Mu'tazilah*: The school of the Muslim "rationalists" which accorded creative effect to human will and agency, concluding that it is human beings who create their actions. In addition, it denies God Almighty attributes, claims that God is absolutely obliged to reward those who believe and do good deeds, and punish those who disbelieve. (Tr.)

unbeliever or is in a state between belief and unbelief. Furthermore, I realized that my unfortunate friend had not undergone as contemptible a degeneration and vileness as I had thought, although he had sacrificed numerous instructions in truth for the favor of a villain. I thanked God and was saved from the danger of thinking in this way because, as I explained above, Satan may throw people into perils through a paltry incitement that leads to destruction. Moreover, the human carnal soul always lends an ear to Satan. And the human powers of anger and lust are two instruments that both receive and transmit Satan's suggestions.

It is for this reason that the two Names of God Almighty, the All-Forgiving and the All-Compassionate, face believers with forgiveness and compassion in the most comprehensive and profound fashion. And the Almighty declares in the wise Qur'an that His most important grace for the Prophets is forgiveness and calls on them to implore Him for forgiveness. By repeating the sacred statement, *In the Name of God, the All-Merciful, the All-Compassionate* at the beginning of every *sura* (chapter) and ordering it to be recited at the start of every lawful deed or act, God indicates that His all-encompassing Compassion is a stronghold and a center for refuge. He makes a shield of the phrase *I seek refuge in God from Satan, rejected eternally*, by ordering *Seek refuge in God!*

Sixth indication

One of the most dangerous stratagems of Satan is that he causes some sensitive and simple-minded people to confuse imagining unbelief with confirmation of unbelief. He shows the unintentional perception of misguidance as misguidance itself, and causes some ugly thoughts and concepts to occur to such people. Also, by presenting a possible occurrence as an intentional conviction of its possibility, he leads people to worry about the certainty of their belief. Consequently, such poor, simple people imagine that they have fallen into misguidance or unbelief, and despairing of their belief, they become a plaything for Satan. Satan works both on their despair and these weak spots, and confused by what is imaginary and what is the reality, they either go mad, or actually embrace misguidance in utter despair that there is no longer anything else to do. What follows is a summary of our explanations in some parts of the *Risale-i Nur* about how groundless these stratagems of satans are:

Just as the image of a snake in a mirror does not bite, or the image of fire does not burn, or the reflection of something filthy does not soil, so neither can the unintentional reflections of unbelief and association of partners with God in the mirrors of imagination and thought, or the shadows of misguidance, or the imaginings of blasphemous words corrupt faith, change conviction, or damage respectful courtesy. For it is a well-known principle that neither the imagining of blasphemy or unbelief is blasphemy or unbelief respectively, nor can the unintentional thinking of misguidance be misguidance.

As for the occurrence of doubt among the faithful, something being possible in itself to occur does not negate the certainty of belief or harm it. It is an established principle in the science of religious methodology that something being possible in itself to occur does not negate the certainty that derives from knowledge. For example, we are certain that the Barla Lake continues to exist as a lake full of water. However, it is possible that it has sunk into the ground at this moment or it may sink at any time. But, since this possibility does not arise from any substantial indication or reason, we do not doubt its actual existence. For it is another methodological principle that any probability which does not arise from proven reality is not to be taken into consideration. Despite these truths, the unfortunate one who is exposed to the satanic suggestions mentioned above worries that they have lost their certainty of the truths of belief because of such unsubstantial possibilities. A person may be subjected to many unintentional disapproved occurrences concerning the noblest Prophet, upon him be peace and blessings, on account of his human aspects. But none of these occurrences harm the certainty of belief. If a person thinks that they cause harm, then they themselves are suffering harm.

It even sometimes occurs that Satan whispers bad things about God Almighty through his cable to the heart. That person trembles, thinking that their heart has become very corrupted if Satan can whisper such things. Whereas, their fear and trembling and opposition to the whispering of Satan prove that the bad things in question do not come from their heart; they rather come from the cable of Satan or are directly suggested by Satan.

Among the human inner faculties are one or two that I have not been able to specify; these are uncontrollable by the power of will, and a person is not held accountable for them. Sometimes they take a person under their influence and, without paying heed to the truth, commit wrong things. Satan suggests to the person when they are under their influence, "You have no capacity to believe and obey the truth, so you involuntarily commit such falsehood. This means your fate has condemned you to disobedience and, therefore, wretchedness." The poor person falls into despair and perishes.

So, a believer's stronghold against the above-mentioned schemes of Satan is the unchanging, fundamental principles of the Qur'an, and the truths of faith which have been definitely established by the purified, exacting scholars. And believers should ignore this last scheme of Satan and seek refuge in God from it. For the more importance they attach to it, the more it draws attention to itself and grows and swells. A believer's antidote and remedy for such spiritual wounds is the elevated Sunna of the Prophet, upon him be peace and blessings.

Seventh indication

Question: The authorities of the *Mu'tazila* regard the creation of evil as evil, and therefore do not attribute the creation of unbelief or misguidance to God. By doing so, they think they are holding God free from any kind of defect or wrong action. However, in regarding humanity as the creator of evil deeds, they fall into misguidance.

The *Mu'tazilite* authorities also hold that by committing a major sin, a believer loses their belief, for committing such a grave sin cannot be reconciled with believing in God and the punishment of Hell. Committing major sins means disregarding God's "wrath" and the eternal punishment of Hell. So, if a person, who for fear of imprisonment in the world restrains themselves from doing anything contrary to the law, commits any of those sins, this certainly demonstrates their lack of belief.

The Answer: As explained in the Twenty-Sixth Word, which is concerned with Divine Destiny and Decree, the creation of evil is not evil; doing an evil act is evil. For creation considers all the results to issue from the action carried out. Since the existence of an evil is preliminary to many good results, if one takes these results into consideration, the creation of evil becomes good. For example, fire produces numerous good results. If, through misuse of their free will, some people make fire an evil for themselves, they cannot claim that the creation of fire is evil. Similarly, the creation of satans has numerous wise results like causing human progress in many respects. So, if some are defeated by satans by misusing their free will and doing evil acts, they cannot assert that the creation of Satan is evil. Rather, they do evil to themselves by misusing their free will to do an evil.

A person concentrates only on what they do, without knowing or intending the good results that come from it, and so may cause an evil result to come about. But out of pure grace, God causes numerous good results to come from an evil act, and considers these results while creating any evil which a person does. (If He does not create it at all, this means the annulment of the free will He has given to humanity.) So, since creation is concerned with the good results that issue, the creation of evil is not evil; rather, it is good. Since the *Mu'tazila* could not understand this subtle reality, they asserted that the creation of evil is evil, and the creation of ugliness is an ugly deed. In order to hold God Almighty free of all faults and defects, they did not attribute the creation of evil to Him, and fell into misguidance. They wrongly interpreted one of the six pillars of belief, namely, believing in Divine Destiny and Decree, which requires us to confirm that whether we judge a thing to be good or evil, it is from God.

As for the second part of the question, which is concerned with how someone who commits a major sin can remain a believer, it has convincingly been explained in the foregoing Indications (particularly the fifth one) how a believer can commit a sin. Secondly, just as the human carnal soul prefers an ounce of immediate pleasure to a ton of future pleasure, so, too, it shrinks in fear from an immediate slap more than it would from the thought of a year's future torment.

In addition, when emotions prevail, a person does not heed the judgments of reason. Under the influence of desires and whims, they prefer the slightest immediate delight to a vast, future reward. They keep away from some trivial present distress more than they fear some dreadful postponed torment. For desires, emotions, and whims are blind to the future. When the carnal soul gives them support, the heart, which is the seat of belief, and reason can no longer speak and are defeated. So, committing major sins does not arise from a lack of belief, but from the defeat of the heart and reason through the prevalence of emotions, desires, and whims.

Furthermore, as understood from the previous Indications, as evil is the way of destruction, the way of evil and passions is easy to follow. Human and jinn satans can swiftly drive people towards it. It is an absolutely astonishing fact that although, according to a Prophetic Tradition, a light like a fly's wing from the World of Eternity is, on account of its being eternal, equal to all the pleasures and bounties a person may receive from a whole worldly life,[40] some unfortunate people can prefer the pleasures of this fleeting world to all of the pleasures of the everlasting world, and thus follow in the footsteps of Satan.

It is because of the reasons mentioned that the wise Qur'an, repeatedly and insistently, and with threats and encouragement, restrains believers from sin and urges them to do good.

This powerful, ever-recurring guidance of the wise Qur'an once made me think that such recurrent warnings and cautions show believers to be inconstant and unreliable. It presents them as being in a state irreconcilable with human honor. For, while a single order that an official receives from their superior is sufficient for them to obey, if the superior repeats the same order ten times, the official will truly be offended. He or she will retort, "You are accusing me; I am not a treacherous person." Despite this fact, the wise Qur'an persistently repeats its orders to the most sincere believers.

When this idea drew my attention, I was with two or three of my loyal friends. I frequently warned them against the intrigues of human satans. They did not say I was accusing them or feel offended. But I said to myself, "I am offending them with my recurrent warnings. I am accusing them of disloyalty and inconstancy."

Then, suddenly, the reality explained in the foregoing Indications occurred to me in detail. I came to understand that the persistent warnings of the Qur'an are perfectly apt, in full conformity with the situation, purely eloquent and free of any exaggeration or extraneous words, and that they are full of wisdom. I also perceived why these loyal friends of mine did not feel offended. The summary of this reality is as follows:

Since satans incite people to the way of destruction, they cause much evil with a few actions. For this reason, those who follow the way of truth and guidance need many cautions and repeated warnings and great help. This is why God Almighty offers His help to believers through His one thousand and one Names by way of recurrent warnings, and extends thou-

---

40 al-Qurtubi, *al-Jami' li-Ahkam al-Qur'an*, 13:7. (Tr.)

sands of hands of compassion to help them. He does not wound their honor; rather, He preserves it. He does not diminish the value of the human being, but shows what great evils Satan can cause.

So, O people of truth and right guidance! The way to be saved from the aforementioned intrigues of human and jinn satans is to make your headquarters the school of the Ahl al-Sunna, who are the people of truth, and enter the stronghold of the unchanging, fundamental rules and precepts of the Qur'an of miraculous exposition, and follow the elevated Sunna of the Prophet Muhammad, upon him be peace and blessings, as your guide. Thus will you find salvation.

Eighth indication

QUESTION: You have pointed out in the Indications above that since the way of misguidance is easy and is a way of destruction and unrestraint, many have taken that way. Whereas, in some other parts of the *Risale-i Nur*, you have convincingly explained that the way of unbelief and misguidance is so difficult and troublesome that no one would take it; that it is a way impossible to follow and that the way of belief and right guidance is so easy and clear that everyone should have taken it.

THE ANSWER: There are two types of unbelief and misguidance. One sort pertains to actions and is of a secondary degree, or particular. That is, it negates the articles of faith or is a non-acceptance of the truth. This way of misguidance is easy to take and accordingly has been shown in the *Risale-i Nur* as being easy.

The second sort of unbelief and misguidance is a judgment or conclusion of the heart and mind. It does not only comprise negation of belief but opens up a way opposed to belief. This means acceptance of falsehood and the willful admission of the opposite of the truth. It is not non-acceptance so that it should be easy, but the acceptance of non-existence, and can only be accepted by proving non-existence. According to the rule, "Non-acceptance cannot be proved," it is evidently not easy to prove it.

It is this sort of unbelief and misguidance which is shown in some other parts of the *Risale-i Nur* to be so difficult and troublesome as to be almost impossible to accept and follow. Anyone with the slightest consciousness would not follow such a way. Furthermore, as convincingly explained in the

Risale-i Nur, this way entails such terrible pains and is so full of suffocating darkness that anyone with the least intelligence would not desire or attempt to follow it.

QUESTION: How, then, can the majority of people take such a painful, dark, and troublesome way?

THE ANSWER: They have fallen into it and cannot extricate themselves. In addition, since the vegetable and animal powers in humanity cannot see the final results of their choices and deeds, a lack of reasoning and due consideration dominates over human faculties, so they do not want to get out and console themselves with a temporary, readily available pleasure.

QUESTION: There is such dreadful pain and fright in misguidance that an unbeliever, not only cannot receive pleasure from life but they must even not be able to live. They must be crushed by that pain and nearly die of that fright. For while, because they are human, they have innumerable desires and are deeply attached to life, how can one who, because of unbelief, sees death as an eternal separation and non-existence, and always witnesses living beings perishing and those they love going into everlasting "non-existence" through death, continue to live? How can they receive pleasure from life?

THE ANSWER: They deceive themselves through a very strange satanic sophistry, and continue to live. They suppose that they are receiving pleasure. I will indicate their condition by way of a well-known parable.

It is related that they said to the ostrich, "You've got wings, so fly!" But it folded its wings and said, "I'm a camel," and did not fly. So it fell into the hunter's trap. In order that the hunter would not see it, the ostrich stuck its head into the dust. Having left its huge body in the open, it made itself a target for the hunter. Whereupon, they said to it, "You say you are a camel, so carry loads!" But it chose to unfold its wings and answered, "I'm a bird," and was saved from the trouble of carrying loads. In the end, it was left without both food and protector, and the hunter took it away.

In the same way, in the face of the Qur'an's heavenly proclamations, absolute unbelief has mostly changed to skepticism. So, if they are told, "You think death is eternal non-existence. The gallows, on which you think you will be sent to non-existence, stand before your eyes. How can one who constantly sees them before their eyes receive pleasure from life?" Due to the portion which they have received from the Qur'an's universal mercy and all-encompassing light, they will reply, "Death is not eternal extinction. There may be an everlasting life." Or like an ostrich, they plunge their heads into the sand of heedlessness so that the appointed hour of death may not spot them, nor may the grave stare at them, nor may the decay of things fire arrows at them.

In short, like an ostrich, when due to their skepticism they see death to be eternal non-existence, the decisive proclamations of the Qur'an and other heavenly books that are concerned with the afterlife provide a chance for the unbelievers, and to this they hold fast. This saves them from always feeling the dread of death and eternal non-existence. If it is then said to them, "Since we are bound to go to an everlasting realm, we should bear the difficulties of the religious obligations here so that we may have a good life there," their skepticism causes them to reply, "Maybe there is no such a realm, so why should I work for something which does not exist?" As they feel saved from the pains of eternal extinction thanks to the probability of permanence provided by the Qur'an, they also feel saved from the difficulties of carrying out the religious obligations due to the probability of the non-existence of an eternal life afforded by skeptical unbelief. Thus, from their perspective, unbelievers suppose they receive more pleasure from this life than believers. However, the idea generated by this satanic sophistry is extremely superficial, unbeneficial, and temporary.

Thus, the wise Qur'an contains some sort of mercy for the unbelievers also, as it saves them, to a certain extent, from the life of this world turning into Hell for them. It provides for them a kind of doubt through which they can continue to live. Otherwise, they would suffer a Hellish spiritual suffering in this world, and it would be a living Hell which would eventually drive them to suicide.

So, O people of belief! With full confidence and belief, enter under the protection of the Qur'an, which saves you from the feeling and supposition of eternal extinction, and the hells of this world and the Hereafter. Also, enter the fold of the elevated Sunna with full submission and appreciation, and be saved from misery in this world and punishment in the Hereafter!

Ninth indication

QUESTION: The people of guidance, among whom are the Prophets, particularly the Pride of Creation, as the greatest of them, upon him and other

Prophets be peace and blessings, are the party of God. Although they are usually favored with Divine help and mercy, why are they sometimes defeated by the people of misguidance, who are Satan's party? Also, what was the reason for and the wisdom in the hypocrites of Madina's insistence on misguidance without accepting the Straight Path despite the Prophethood and Messengership of the Seal of the Prophets as bright as the sun, and his efforts of guidance based on and supported by the miraculousness of the Qur'an so effective as if it was the greatest elixir, and the Qur'anic truths more captivating than the universal law of gravitation?

THE ANSWER: In order to solve these awesome questions, a profound principle should be expounded. It is as follows:

The All-Majestic Creator of the universe has two types of Names, those issuing from or related to His Majesty and those issuing from or related to His Grace and Beauty. Each of the Names belonging to either sort demonstrates Itself in manifestations particular to Itself. This causes the existence of opposites in creation to combine with one another. However, since opposites exist to complement and help each other, they are usually in defensive or offensive positions. This is the origin of clashes, changes, and transformations, but serves progress and development. Conflict is especially and more effectively in force in the life of humankind, which is the most comprehensive fruit of the tree of creation. Humankind has always existed with a division into conflicting parties. Although conflict in the life of humankind has caused calamities, it is also the mechanism of human progress. The occasional defeat of the people of guidance has always served to make them wake up from the sleep of heedlessness into which they have frequently fallen and rediscover the essentials of guidance, clinging to them more powerfully than ever before.

A significant reason for the occasional victory of the people of misguidance is as follows:

There is negligence and omission in all kinds of misguidance, including especially unbelief. Negligence and omission are quite easy and do not require any positive, constructive action. Misguidance means destruction, which is extremely easy and possible through minimum action. It also tends to aggression, and, therefore, can cause others much harm. Because of these and because of a tendency to tyranny and the fear this engenders in hearts, the leaders of misguidance in particular hold a position of power in the eyes of the people. In addition to all this, humanity, which by nature is blind to consequences and addicted to readily available pleasures, has certain vegetable and animal powers that pursue pleasures, demand satisfaction, and are difficult to control. They cause human faculties such as the heart and reason to abandon their duties which are required by true humanity and which are related to the final end of humanity.

In contrast, the sacred way of the people of guidance, particularly that of the Beloved of the Lord of the Worlds and all other Prophets, pursues existence, construction, and repair, and requires positive action, the observation of certain bounds, the consideration of consequences, worship and servanthood, and keeping the carnal, evil-commanding soul under strict control, putting an end to its tendency to freely dominate over human beings. It is for this reason that the hypocrites in Madina closed their eyes to that Brightest Sun like bats and, captivated by a satanic force of resistance against that Greatest Power of Attraction, remained in misguidance.

QUESTION: The noblest Messenger, upon him be peace and blessings, is the Beloved of the Lord of the Worlds. What he holds in his hand—the Qur'an—is absolute truth, and whatever he speaks is true. Some of the soldiers in his army are angels. He quenches the thirst of a whole army with one handful of water, and gives a banquet to a thousand people with four handfuls of wheat and the meat of one goat. He throws a handful of dust at the army of unbelievers, and when that dust enters their eyes, they all flee. How is that this most virtuous and godly Commander who worked almost a thousand miracles, like those mentioned, suffered a setback in the second stage of the Battle of Uhud and at the beginning of the Battle of Hunayn?

THE ANSWER: The noblest Messenger, upon him be peace and blessings, was sent to humankind as a guide and leader to be followed so that humankind would learn the rules of social and personal life from him, become accustomed to obeying the laws (of the operation of the universe and life) that issued from the Will of the All-Wise One of Perfection, and act in conformity with the principles of His Wisdom. If the noblest Messenger, upon him be peace and blessings, had always acted in reliance on and been supported by wonders and miracles in his social and personal life, he could not have been a perfect guide or leader.

It is for this reason that he worked miracles only when needed and in order to invalidate the unbelievers' denials and to confirm the truth of his

Message. In the course of his everyday life, he was the first to obey the Divine commands and observe the Divine laws of the operation of the universe and life that issue from or are based on the wisdom of God as the Lord (Creator, Sustainer, and Administrator of the universe) and His Will as the All-Glorified. He sought protection by wearing armor when facing the enemy and ordering his troops to enter their trenches. He received wounds and suffered hardship. Thus, he led his community in obeying and observing God's laws of wisdom and the operation of the universe and life.

Tenth indication

One of the most abstruse deceits of Satan is that he causes his followers to deny his existence. Since those whose minds have been confused by materialistic philosophy in particular hesitate in this evident matter, I will say some things concerning this trick of Satan. They are as follows:

In the same way that there are corporeal evil spirits who function like Satan among human beings, it is also certain that there are incorporeal evil spirits among the jinn. If the latter were clothed in physical bodies, they would be the same as these evil human beings. If, on the other hand, these devils in human form were able to remove their physicality, they would be the same as the jinn-satans. It is because of this extremely close relationship that one false school assumed, "The excessively evil spirits in human form become devils after they die."

As is known, when something of high quality is corrupted, it becomes more corrupt than something of less quality. For example, when milk and yoghurt go bad, they can still be eaten, but when butter goes bad, it can no longer be eaten; it even sometimes becomes like poison. Similarly, if human beings, the noblest, possibly the highest, of creatures, are corrupted, they become more corrupt than any other corrupted creature. Like vermin that receive pleasure from the stink of putrefied flesh and snakes that take pleasure at biting and poisoning, they enjoy and are proud of the evil they commit and their corrupt morals in the marsh of misguidance, as well as the harm and injustices they inflict in the darkness of wrongdoing. It can be said that they take on the nature of Satan. In short, a decisive proof for the existence of jinn-satans is the existence of human-satans.

Secondly, the numerous decisive proofs presented in the Twenty-Ninth Word for the existence of angels or other spiritual beings is also proof of the existence of jinn-satans. We refer this point to that Word.

Thirdly, religions are agreed upon the existence of angels, who represent and supervise the laws that are in effect in good deeds and issues. Likewise, wisdom and reality require that there should be evil spirits or satans (devils) to represent the laws that are effective in evil acts and who have some part in them. It may even be said that the existence of conscious veils before evil is more necessary. For as explained at the beginning of the Twenty-Second Word, everyone cannot see the essential good in everything. So, in order not to object to the All-Majestic Creator because of apparent evils and defects and not to accuse His Mercy and criticize His Wisdom or complain of Him, there must be a screen between God and apparently evil deeds. Any objection, criticism, or complaint should be directed at the screen, and not turned to the All-Munificent Creator and the absolutely All-Wise. Just as He has made illnesses a veil to save the angel of death, *Azra'il*, from the resentment of those who die, so too has He made *Azra'il*, upon him be peace, a veil before His taking souls at death, so that complaints arising from death and similar events, which some may suppose to be mercilessness, should not be directed at God Almighty. Just so, and even more certainly, the wisdom of God as the Lord demands the existence of Satan in order that the objections and criticisms that arise from evil should not be directed to the All-Majestic Creator.

Fourthly, as the human is a micro-universe (a microcosm), so too the universe is a macro-human being. This micro-universe is an index and summarized form of that macro-human. So the macro-originals of models among human beings will necessarily exist in the macro-human. For example, the existence of human memory is a decisive proof of the existence of the Supreme Preserved Tablet. Likewise, everyone experiences that there is a center in one corner of the heart which functions as an instrument for evil suggestions, and a tongue which speaks under the influence of the power of groundless fear and fancy, and that when corrupted, the power of groundless fear and fancy may become like a small Satan, acting contrary to its owner's will and desires. All these are a certain proof of the monstrous satans in the world. Functioning as an ear and tongue respectively, the satanic center in our heart and the power of groundless fear and fancy suggest the existence in the outer world of an evil being that blows in the former and makes the latter speak.

Eleventh indication

The wise Qur'an miraculously states that the universe becomes angry with the evil acts committed by people of misguidance, and the universal elements (like the heavens and earth with its oceans, rivers, and mountains) become enraged, and all other things and beings become furious. That is, by mentioning the attack of the heavens and earth upon the people of Noah who drowned in the Flood, and the wrath of the element of air at the obstinate unbelief of the peoples of Thamud and 'Ad, the peoples of the Prophets Salih and Hud respectively, and the fury of the element of water and the sea at Pharaoh's people, and the rage of the element of earth at Qorah, and as declared in the verse, *Almost bursting with fury* (67: 8), the fury and anger of Hell at the people of unbelief, and the rage of certain other elements and creatures at the people of unbelief and misguidance,[41] the Qur'an restrains the people of misguidance and rebellion in a miraculous and most effective fashion.

QUESTION: Why do the sins of these worthless people, who are absolutely powerless before God, cause the anger of the universe?

THE ANSWER: As demonstrated in some other parts of the *Risale-i Nur* and in the foregoing Indications, unbelief and misguidance is a terrible aggression and crime that concerns the whole of existence. For what is expected of the universe, and of the most important purposes of its creation, is humanity's worship of the Creator and its response to the Divine Lordship with belief and obedience. However, by rejecting the recognition of the Creator, the people of unbelief and misguidance annul that supreme pur-

---

41 God Almighty sent a hurricane of stones upon the tribe of 'Ad, who were destroyed in a sandstorm which lasted seven nights and eight days (7: 72; 11: 58; 23: 27; 26: 120; 69: 7), and overthrew the cities of the people of Lot, upon him be peace, sending upon them an evil rain of stones (7: 84; 11: 82–83; 15: 73–74). An awful blast seized the tribe of Thamud, the people of the Prophet Salih, upon him be peace (7: 78; 11: 67; 15: 83; 69: 6), and the people of Shu'ayb, upon him be peace (7: 91; 11: 94; 26: 189). Qorah was one of Moses' people, but he betrayed and oppressed them by collaborating with Pharaoh against them, and rebelled against God. In the end, the Almighty caused the earth to swallow him and his wealth (28:81). God caused the people of Noah, upon him be peace, to drown in the Flood (7: 64; 11: 42–44), and Pharaoh, Haman, and their hosts in the sea (10: 90; 20: 77–78; 26: 65–66). (Tr.)

pose, which is the ultimate cause of the existence of creatures, and the reason for its continuance. This is a violation of the rights of all existence. Moreover, as they deny the manifestations of the Divine Names that appear on all creatures and, therefore, refuse to give them their true, exalted value due to their being the mirrors of those manifestations, they insult the sacred Names and degrade the value of all creatures and denigrate them. In addition, while all creatures are each an official of the Lord charged with a sublime duty, through unbelief they are debased and reduced to merely being lifeless, transient, and meaningless things; thus unbelievers infringe the rights of the whole of existence.

Thus, since in all its varieties and according to the degree of each, misguidance disdains the wisdom of the Lord in the creation of the universe and the purposes of the All-Glorified One for the continuance of its existence, the universe, with whatever is in it, becomes angry with the people of misguidance and rebellion.

O wretched human, who is physically small but whose guilt and wrongs are grave, and whose sins and shameful acts are tremendous! If you want to be saved from the wrath and hatred of the whole of existence, you should enter the sacred sphere of the wise Qur'an and follow the elevated Sunna of the noblest Messenger, who conveyed the Qur'an to us, upon him be peace and blessings. So enter that sphere and follow the Sunna!

Twelfth indication

This Indication consists of four questions and answers.

FIRST QUESTION: How can eternal punishment in Hell be justice in return for a certain number of sins committed in a limited life?

THE ANSWER: As has been clearly understood in the foregoing Indications, and particularly in the Eleventh, the crime of unbelief and misguidance is a boundless crime, and is a violation of infinite rights.

SECOND QUESTION: The Shari'a judges that the punishment of Hell is in return for one's actions, but Paradise is a pure Divine favor. What is the reason for this?

THE ANSWER: As is clear in the previous Indications, however insignificant and partial a free will they have, and even though their free will and action have no share in creation, humans can cause awful destruction and evils. For destruction and evils are extremely easy and it is possible to bring them about with a slight action. Also, as their evil-commanding soul always inclines towards harm and evil, humans themselves are held responsible for the evils brought about as a result of any insignificant action. For their evil-commanding soul has desired them to do so and they themselves have done them. Since evils mean destruction and are not positive and constructive, humans—as servants—become the ones who commit the act, and since they will and commit them, God, the Ultimate Truth, creates the acts. So in return for that limitless crime, they most definitely deserve infinite punishment.

As for good deeds, since they denote construction and existence and require the Creator to come into existence, human partial free will and action cannot be their creative cause. A human being cannot be their true agent. In addition, the carnal soul never desires good deeds; it is the Divine Mercy Which demands them and drives humans to do them, and the Divine Power brings them into existence. A human being can only claim to own them through belief, wishes, or intentions. Once they have possessed them, these good deeds become thanks for all the limitless Divine bounties accorded to them before, like the bounties of existence and belief. But Paradise, promised by God, will be given purely as a favor of the All-Merciful One. Apparently it is a reward, but in reality it is a pure favor.

In short, the cause of evil is the human evil-commanding soul, so the human deserves the punishment, while as the cause of good deeds originates in God, so also their Creator is God. Humans can only claim ownership through belief; they cannot say, "I demand my reward"; rather, they may appeal to God, "I hope for Your favor."

THIRD QUESTION: As is understood from the foregoing explanations, since evil multiplies through spreading, infection, pervasion, and encroachment, evil should be recorded as one thousand. Whereas, since a good deed denotes construction or existence, and does not multiply, or does not occur by the servant's creation or the carnal soul's desire, it should not be recorded at all or it should be recorded as one. So, why is an evil deed recorded as one and a good deed as anywhere from ten to a thousand?

THE ANSWER: By doing so, God, the Ultimate Truth, demonstrates His infinite Mercy and the grace of His Compassion.

FOURTH QUESTION: The successes of the people of misguidance, and the power they exhibit, and their victories over the people of right guidance show that there is some power and truth by which they are supported. Does this not mean either that the people of right guidance suffer some weakness, or that the people of misguidance possess some truth?

THE ANSWER: No, neither do the people of misguidance have some truth, nor do the people of truth suffer any weakness. But regrettably, some ordinary people who are shortsighted and lacking in sound reasoning waver and doubt, harming their belief. For they say, "If the people of truth had been perfectly true (in their belief and way), they should not have suffered such a degree of defeat and degradation. For the truth has all power, and as stated in the essential principle, *The truth is exalted and always prevails, and it cannot be overcome*, might lies in the truth. So, if the people of misguidance who triumph over the people of truth had not possessed a true power and a point of support, they could not have been triumphant and successful to this extent."

As is demonstrated in the foregoing Indications, neither does the defeat of the people of truth arise from their lacking in power and being without truth, nor is the victory of the people of misguidance due to their power or having a true point of support. So, in their entirety, the previous Indications provide an answer for this question. Here, we will point only to a number of the weapons that the people of misguidance employ to deceive people, as follows:

I have repeatedly observed that the people of dissension and disturbance, who form ten percent of the population, defeat the righteous, who make up the other ninety percent. In great astonishment, I have been preoccupied with the reasons for this and have come to understand that their victory is not due to their power, but due to their causing dissension and unrest, baseness, and destruction, it is due to their taking advantage of the disagreements among the people of guidance, to sowing conflict among them, and working the weak spots in their character and evil potentials that are like mines of corruption in human nature, to provoking the selfish feelings, inclinations, interests, and ambitions, to the hypocritical flattering of the carnal soul's inclination towards despotism, self-pride, fame, and glory, and due to people's fear of their ruthless destruction. Through such satanic devices, they temporarily triumph over the people of truth. But since *the final, happy outcome is in favor of the God-revering, pious* (7: 128), and because of the principle, *The truth is exalted and always prevails, and it cannot be overcome*, in addition to the fact that the benefit this yields is not significant, their temporary victory will be the means of earning Hell for themselves and Paradise for the people of truth.

Thus, since misguidance causes the weak to show themselves as able, and, thus, insignificant people gain fame, self-centered, fame-seeking, and ostentatious people take on a position against the people of truth to be able to show themselves as powerful with a little action and gain status for themselves by intimidating and terrorizing others and causing harm. They seek to gain fame by causing destruction, which comes not from their power or ability, but from their lack of the true power and ability that is necessary for an approvable attainment. It has become proverbial that one such fame-seeker sullied a place of worship so that people might talk about him. His fame-seeking caused him to welcome the curse of people.

O poor human, who has been created for the world of eternity but is enamored of this fleeting world! Lend an ear to the verse, *Neither the heaven nor the earth shed tears over them* (44: 29). It clearly declares that the heavens and the earth, which are connected with humanity, do not weep over the death of anyone from among the people of misguidance; rather, they are happy about it. The verse is alluding to the fact that the heavens and the earth weep over the death of the people of right guidance, and do not desire their separation because the whole universe is sincerely connected with the people of belief and is pleased with them. For, since the people of belief recognize the Creator of the universe through belief, they appreciate the value of the universe, and respect and love it. Unlike the people of misguidance, they do not despise it or cherish enmity towards it.

O human, think over this! You are bound to die. If you follow your carnal soul and Satan, your neighbors, and even your relatives, will be happy with your death, as they will be relieved of your evil acts. But if you seek refuge in God from Satan, who is eternally rejected from God's Mercy, and follow the Qur'an and the All-Merciful's Beloved, the heavens, the earth, and all beings in them will be sorry at your separation and weep according to your rank and the rank of each of them. By giving you a splendid, mournful farewell, they will indicate that according to your rank you will have a good welcome in the realm of eternity where you will enter through the gate of the grave.

Thirteenth indication

This consists of three points.

First point

One of the most deceitful stratagems of Satan is that he deceives shortsighted people with constricted hearts and narrow minds concerning the comprehensiveness and greatness of the truths of belief. He says, "It is said that a single Being executes lordship over and administers all particles and galaxies and other existent things and beings in all their states. How can one believe in such an extraordinarily great, incomprehensible matter? How can one comprehend it within one's heart and mind?" By taking advantage of human weakness and limited understanding, he awakens a feeling of unbelief.

THE ANSWER: The reality which silences this scheme of Satan is *God is the All-Great*. Its true answer is also *God is the All-Great*. One of the purposes for the frequent repetition of *God is the All-Great* among the marks of Islam is to eradicate this stratagem. For the limited power and narrow mind of the human being can see such infinitely great truths in the light of *God is the All-Great* and confirm them. They can sustain these truths on the strength of *God is the All-Great* and situate them within the sphere of this blessed mark. True human beings speak to their hearts, when they begin to doubt, as follows:

It is clearly observed that the universe is administered and directed in the most orderly fashion. In fact, such an extraordinary work requires a wonderful art and an infinitely amazing organization for its existence and maintenance. This can be explained in two ways. Either an All-Powerful, All-Willing Eternally Besought One, to Whose existence all particles of the universe testify, can accomplish this most astonishing affair, or every being, rather, every particle of the universe, should have absolute divinity, all-encompassing knowledge, and limitless power so that the perfectly balanced, extraordinarily ordered, and most distinctively adorned existence and direction of the universe is possible. In the first way this tremendous matter is wonderful but easy to explain, while the second, which is the way of unbelief and associating partners with God, is infinitely unreasonable and inconceivable.

In short, if one does not accept the most reasonable existence of a single, infinitely great, and omnipotent Lordship, then one will feel obliged to follow a most unreasonable, inconceivable way. Even Satan cannot offer the way of impossibility, denying the reality of the infinite Grandeur, Which is absolutely required for the existence and administration of the universe.

Second point

Another of Satan's important schemes is that he calls on human beings not to admit their faults so that he can bar the way of imploring forgiveness and seeking refuge in God for them. He also provokes the egotism of the human carnal soul in order that the soul may defend itself like a lawyer, holding itself exempt from all faults.

An evil-commanding soul which heeds Satan does not want to see its faults. Even if it sees them, it explains them away in various ways. As stated in the adage, *The eye of contentment is blind to faults*, a person who considers their soul in approving terms does not see their faults. Since they do not see their faults, they do not admit them. Consequently, they neither implore God for forgiveness nor seek refuge in Him, and so become the playthings of Satan. If a noble prophet like the Prophet Joseph, upon him be peace, says, *I do not claim myself free of error, for assuredly the human soul always commands evil, except that my Lord has mercy* (12: 53), how can one trust one's carnal, evil-commanding soul?

One who accuses their own soul sees their own faults. One who sees and admits their own faults implores God for forgiveness. One who implores God for forgiveness seeks refuge in God from Satan and committing faults. One who seeks refuge in God is saved from Satan's evils. Not seeing one's faults is a fault greater than the former ones committed. Non-admission of one's faults is a grave defect. If one sees a fault, then it ceases to be a fault. The one who admits their fault deserves forgiveness.

Third point

One of the Satanic plots which corrupts human social life is that Satan causes people to veil all the merits of a believer because of a single evil committed by the believer. The unfair ones who heed this scheme of Satan feel enmity towards that believer. However, when God Almighty weighs up the deeds of the responsible beings with absolute justice on His supreme scales on Judgment Day, He will judge measuring the goods deeds against their evil deeds. Furthermore, since there are many more causes that lead to evil and committing such acts is easier, He may sometimes eliminate many evils because of one single good deed.

So, we should act in this world in accordance with that Divine justice. If a person's good deeds or merits are greater than their evil acts, either in terms of quality or quantity, that person is worthy of love and respect. More than that, we should consider them with an attitude of forgiveness on account of any one single merit they may have. However, due to the innate tendency to injustice in their nature and through the incitement of Satan, the human being can forget a hundred merits of a person because of one single evil, and feel hostility towards their Muslim brother or sister, thus earning a sin. Like a fly's wing which covers the eye, concealing the mountain from it, due to their feeling of hatred and grudge, the human becomes blind and forgets the virtues of other believers, be they as great as a mountain, because of an insignificant evil act, and is hostile towards them, becoming an instrument of corruption and disorder in human social life.

Through another scheme similar to this one, Satan corrupts sound and straightforward thinking, and destroys sound reasoning about the truths of belief. It is as follows:

Satan attempts to destroy a positive judgment based on hundreds of proofs concerning a truth of belief through a minor negative indication. Yet, it is an established principle that a single positive proof demonstrating the existence or truth of something is preferable to a hundred denials. The statement of a witness in favor of the existence or occurrence of something is preferred to a hundred claims of its non-existence or non-occurrence. Consider this truth by means of the following comparison:

There is a palace with hundreds of doors. If one of its doors is opened, people can enter the palace and open the other closed doors. If all of its doors are open with the exception of only a few, no one can claim that that the palace cannot be entered.

Thus, the truths of belief are that palace. Each proof is a key that opens a door. If one of the doors remains closed, the truths of belief cannot be abandoned and denied. Satan, however, presents to the view a door which has remained closed due to some reasons or because of heedlessness or ignorance, and causes all the positive proofs to be disregarded. Saying, "This palace cannot be entered; rather, it is not a palace, and there is nothing in it," he deceives people.

So, O poor human who is afflicted by Satan's schemes! If you desire a healthy religious, personal, and social life, and want sound thinking, correct viewpoints, and a pure, sound heart at rest, weigh up your deeds and whatever occurs to your mind and heart on the scales of the explicit, fundamental principles and precepts of the Qur'an and the elevated Sunna of the Prophet, upon him be peace and blessings. Always take the Qur'an and the elevated Sunna as your guide, and saying, "I seek refuge in God from Satan, eternally rejected (from God's Mercy)," seek refuge in God Almighty.

In conclusion, the above thirteen Indications are thirteen keys. With these keys, open the gate of the fortified stronghold of the following *sura* of the Qur'an of miraculous exposition, which explains, *I seek refuge in God from Satan, eternally rejected (from God's Mercy)*:

> *I seek refuge in God. In the Name of God, the All-Merciful, the All-Compassionate.*
>
> *Say: "I seek refuge in the Lord of humankind, the Sovereign of humankind, the Deity of humankind, from the evil of the sneaking whisperer (the Satan), who whispers into the hearts of humankind, of the jinn and humankind."*

Enter it and find safety.

All-Glorified are You. We have no knowledge save what You have taught us. Surely You are the All-Knowing, the All-Wise.

And say: "My Lord! I seek refuge in You from the promptings and provocations of the satans. I seek refuge in You, my Lord, lest they be present with me."

The
Fourteenth Gleam

The Fourteenth Gleam

The meaning of the hadith, "The earth stands on the ox and the fish." • The People of the Cloak • The meaning, worth and mysteries of the Basmala

This consists of Two Stations. The First Station is an answer to two questions.

First station

In His Name, All-Glorified is He.

There is nothing but it glorifies Him with His praise.

Peace be upon you, and God's mercy and blessings.

My dear and faithful brother, Rafet Bey!

The answer to the question you ask about the earth standing on the ox and fish is to be found in some parts of the *Risale-i Nur*. Concerning such questions, twelve important principles have been explained in the Third Branch of the Twenty-Fourth Word. Those principles are guidelines that allow the perception of various meanings of the Prophetic Traditions and contain important standards by which to dispel doubts about them. Since there are many things preventing me from occupying myself with scholarly matters, I cannot answer your questions adequately. Therefore, I will give a brief answer to your present question.

You say that some *hojas* (religious teachers) claim that the earth stands on an ox and a fish, while geography sees that the earth is a planet traveling in space. There is neither an ox nor a fish holding it up.

THE ANSWER: There is an authentic Prophetic Tradition reportedly narrated by Ibn 'Abbas, may God be pleased with him. They asked God's Messenger, upon him be peace and blessings, "What does the earth stand on?" He declared, "The earth stands on the ox and the fish."[42] It is also narrated that this question was asked twice and in one of his answers, he said that it stands on the ox, and in the other, on the fish. Some scholars of Hadith have explained this Tradition in the light of certain superstitious stories taken from some Israelite sources. In particular, some Israelite scholars who became Muslims narrated the stories about the ox and the fish they had encountered in the earlier Scriptures along with the Prophetic Tradition mentioned, and changed the meaning of the Tradition to something strange. For now, I will write three principles so that we can understand such Traditions correctly and I will approach the Tradition you ask about from three different perspectives.

The first principle

When some of the scholars of the Children of Israel became Muslims, their former knowledge became "Muslim" and came to be attributed to Islam. However, there were errors in their former knowledge, and these errors do not belong to Islam.

The second principle

When passing from the hands of knowledge to the hands of ignorance, with the passage of time, a metaphor comes to be regarded as a reality. For example, once during my childhood the moon was eclipsed. I asked my mother about it. She answered that a snake had swallowed the moon. I asked why it continued to appear. She explained, "The snakes of the sky are like glass, and they show what is inside them."

42 al-Hakim, *al-Mustadrak*, 4:636; at-Tabarani, *Jami' al-Bayan*, 1:153.. (Tr.)

For a long time this memory of my childhood stayed with me. I would say, thinking about it, "How can such a groundless superstition be repeated by sensible people like my mother?" When I later studied astronomy I realized that those who spoke like my mother took a comparison for a reality. For, during a lunar eclipse the moon passes through some portion of the earth's shadow. This can occur only when the moon is full, and when the sun, earth, and moon are exactly in line, or very close to being in line. The shadow is actually composed of two cone-shaped components, one nested inside the other. There is another condition for an eclipse to occur. This is when the moon is near one of the two intersection points of its orbit with the earth. Using a metaphor, classical astronomers called the two components "the two great snakes." They called the two intersecting points "the head" and "the tail." When the moon comes to the head and the sun to the tail, the earth comes between them, and the moon is eclipsed. According to the metaphor above, "the moon has entered the mouth of the snake." Thus, when this fine, scientific metaphor entered the language of the common people, with the passage of time, it gave rise to the idea that a snake existed large enough to swallow the moon.

From the viewpoint of their duties and with a sacred, fine metaphor which indicates an important truth, two great angels were given the names of the Ox (*Thawr*) and the Fish (*Hut*). When this metaphor passed into the language of the common people from the elevated, sacred tongue of Prophethood, it became interpreted as a reality, and the blessed angels changed places with a large ox and an awesome fish.

The third principle

Just as the Qur'an uses allegories and comparisons, and teaches the most subtle and profound matters to ordinary people by means of the parables and similes they contain, so too do the Prophetic Traditions have allegories that contain familiar comparisons by means of which very profound truths are expressed. For example, as we have described in some other places (*The Letters*, "The Nineteenth Letter"), once a loud noise was heard in the Prophet's presence. He said, "This is the noise of a rock that has been rolling downwards for seventy years and which has now reached

Hell's lowest depths."[43] An hour later, news came that a notorious hypocrite, who recently had reached the age of seventy, had died. This report shows what God's Messenger, upon him be peace and blessings, intended by this eloquent parable.

Now, I will explain three aspects of the Tradition you asked about:

THE FIRST: God Almighty has appointed four angels, one of whom is called the Eagle (*Nasir*), to represent and observe His absolute dominion over the heavens. They are called the "the bearers of the Divine Throne and the heavens." He has also appointed two angels to observe and represent His dominion over the earth, which is a small sister of the heavens and a friend of the planets. One of these angels is called the Ox (*Thawr*), and the other, the Fish (*Hut*). The reason He has given these names to them is as follows:

The earth mainly consists of land and water. It is the fish that inhabit the water, while agriculture, which is the basic means of livelihood for humankind, uses the land, resting on the shoulders of oxen. Since the two angels appointed to the earth are both commanders and supervisors over the earthly creatures and life, they must surely have some sort of relation with oxen and fish. It may be that—the true knowledge is with God—these two angels are represented in the Immaterial World of the Manifestations of Divine Commands and the World of Immaterial Representations or Ideal Forms in the forms of an ox and a fish.[44] So, as both a reference to this representation and to the supervising function of these angels, as well as being an allusion to these two important species among the creatures of the earth, the Prophet's language of miraculous expression stated, "The earth stands on the ox and the fish," and expressed in a very fine, concise sentence a page of profound truths.

SECOND ASPECT: If it is asked upon what this government stands, the answer is, "It stands on the sword and the pen." That is, a government rests

---

43 *Muslim*, "Jannah" 31, "Munaiqun" 15; Ibn Hanbal, *al-Musnad*, 2:371. (Tr.)

44 The earth is a ship created by and belonging to the Lord running in the surrounding ocean of space, and according to a *hadith*, is the tillage of the Hereafter, that is, an arable land which we sow to harvest in the Hereafter. So it is clear how fitting are the name of Fish for the angel who steers that huge unconscious ship on that ocean by God's command in a well-ordered and purposeful fashion, and the name of Ox for the angel who supervises that arable land by God's leave. (Tr.)

on the power and courage of the military's sword, and the administrative ability and justice of the bureaucracy. In the same way, the earth is the dwelling place of living beings and the commander of living beings is humanity. The means of livelihood for the majority of people who live by the sea is fishing, and the means of livelihood for the majority of those who do not live by the sea is agriculture, and therefore dependent on oxen while fish are also an important means of trade for them. So, just as it is said that a state stands on the sword and the pen, it can also be claimed that the earth stands on the ox and the fish. For if the ox should cease to work and the fish should stop producing hundreds of thousands of eggs in a single reproductive season, human life would suffer greatly.

Thus, as a highly miraculous, elevated, and wise reply, the noblest Messenger, upon him be peace and blessings, said, "The earth stands on the ox and the fish." He instructed us, in an extraordinarily concise fashion, in a comprehensive truth concerning the extent to which the life of humankind is connected to the life of the animal kingdom.

Third aspect: Ancient astronomy held that the sun traveled through the sky. They called every thirty degrees of its journey a constellation. If hypothetical lines are drawn between the stars in the constellations to connect them with one another, these lines show the shape of a lion on one occasion, the shape of scales on another, the shape of an ox on another, and the shape of a fish on still another. The constellations were called by these shapes. According to modern astronomy, the sun does not travel. Thus, the constellations now are idle and out of work. We have learned that it is not the sun, but the earth that travels. Thus, instead of these idle heavenly constellations, their counterparts should exist along the annual orbit of the earth in smaller sizes. That is to say, the heavenly constellations should be represented along the annual orbit of the earth. This means that each month the earth falls in the shadow of one of these constellations. It is as if the annual orbit of the earth is a mirror in which the heavenly constellations are reflected.

It is reported that as mentioned before, the question about where the earth stands was put to God's noblest Messenger, upon him be peace and blessings, twice. In one of his answers, he said that it was on the ox, and in the other, he said, "It is on the fish." Pointing to a scientific reality which would only be understood many centuries later, he on one occasion said in a way fitting for the miraculous tongue of Prophethood, "It is on the ox," because the earth at that time was under the hypothetical form of the constellation of the Ox (Taurus) when he gave this answer. When the same question was asked a second time and he answered that the earth was on the fish, the earth was at that time in the shadow of the constellation of the Fish (Pisces).

With these answers, God's Messenger, upon him be peace and blessings, indicated a reality which would only be understood in the distant future. In other words, he indicated that the duty of the earth is fulfilled by turning around the sun and the fact that the heavenly constellations are idle and it is rather the constellations along the earth's annual orbit that are at work. God knows best what is right.

The strange, unreasonable stories in some books about Islam concerning this Prophetic Tradition are either borrowings from earlier Israelite books or allegories or interpretations of some scholars of Hadith, which certain careless people took for *hadiths* and attributed to God's noblest Messenger, upon him be peace and blessings.

Our Lord, take us not to task if we forget or make mistakes!

All-Glorified are You. We have no knowledge save what You have taught us. Surely You are the All-Knowing, the All-Wise.

THE SECOND QUESTION: This is about the People of the Cloak.

My brother! God's noblest Messenger, upon him be peace and blessings, covered 'Ali, 'Ali's wife and the Messenger's daughter Fatima, and their sons Hasan and Husayn, may God be pleased with them, with the blessed cloak he was wearing, and prayed for them reciting the verse, *God only wills to remove from you, O members of the (Prophet's) Family, all that may be loathsome, and to purify you to the utmost of purity* (33: 33).[45]

With respect to your question about the People of the Cloak, which has remained unanswered, omitting the subtle truths and meanings that this event contains, only one out of many of the instances of wisdom relating to the mission of Messengership will be explained. It is as follows:

---

45 *Muslim*, "Fadail as-Sahaba" 61; *at-Tirmidhi*, "Tafsir Sura 33" 7. (Tr.)

God's noblest Messenger, upon him be peace and blessings, saw with his eye of Prophethood, which penetrated the Unseen and the future, that thirty or so years later serious strife and dissent would break out among the Companions and the generation to succeed them, and that blood would be shed. He also saw that the most distinguished and illustrious among them would be the three—'Ali, Hasan, and Husayn—whom he covered with his cloak. In order to declare 'Ali's innocence and acquit him in the view of the Muslim Community, and to offer condolences to Husayn, and to congratulate Hasan on the treaty he would make with Mu'awiya in order to remove the serious dissent among the Muslims that disrupted their unity, and to proclaim the honor Hasan would earn and the great benefit he would give to the Muslim Community, and in order also to declare that the descendants of Fatima would be purified and honored and deserve the elevated title of the People of the Prophet's Family or Household, he covered them in the cloak, thus giving himself and these four the title of the Five People of the Cloak.

Certainly 'Ali, may God be pleased with him, was the rightful caliph. However, the blood shed during his caliphate was of great importance and, therefore, the mission of Messengership required that the Messenger should declare his innocence in the sight of the Muslim Community for the blood shed and the events of dissent that occurred during his caliphate. Thus, with this Tradition, God's Messenger, upon him be peace and blessings, declared 'Ali's innocence and bade the Kharijites, who wrongfully accused him of error and heresy, and the aggressive partisans of the Umayyads, to be silent. The fanatical partisans of the Umayyads and Kharijites, who went to extremes concerning 'Ali and accused him of misguidance, and the Shi'a, who went to the opposite extreme due to the truly heartrending martyrdom of Husayn, introducing innovations to the Religion, and declaring themselves to be free of the two Elders of Islam, Abu Bakr and 'Umar, may God be pleased with them, have caused great harm to the people of Islam.

Thus, through the event of the Cloak and the related prayer, God's noblest Messenger, upon him be peace and blessings, absolved 'Ali and Husayn, may God be pleased with them, of the accusations that would be leveled against them, and saved his Community from having an ill-opinion of them. He, on account of his mission of Messengership, also congratulated Hasan, may God be pleased with him, on the good he did with the Muslim Community by signing the treaty with Mu'awiya, and announced that the blessed descendants of Fatima, may God be pleased with her, known as the Prophet's Family, would be highly honored, and like Mary's mother, who said, "*I commend her [Mary] and her offspring to You for protection from Satan eternally rejected from God's Mercy*," (3: 36), Fatima herself would earn great, extra honors by virtue of her descendants.

> O God! Bestow blessings on our master Muhammad, and on his pure, righteous, pious, and virtuous Family, and on His Companions, strivers in God's cause, noble and favored and good. Amen.

Second station

I expound upon six of the innumerable mysteries of the *Basmala*: In the Name of God, the All-Merciful, the All-Compassionate. A bright light from the *Basmala* concerning Divine Mercy touched my dimmed mind from afar. I wanted to capture and record it as notes in twenty to thirty sections of "Mysteries." Alas, I have not been able to do this yet, and my twenty to thirty have been brought down to six. Even though addressed particularly to myself, I refer it for the approval of my exacting brothers with the hope that it may benefit those with whom I am associated spiritually and whose souls are wiser than mine. The argument addresses the heart rather than the mind, and regards the inner experience and pleasure rather than consisting of rational proofs.

In the Name of God, the All-Merciful, the All-Compassionate.

> *[The Queen] said: "Chieftains, here delivered to me is a letter worthy of respect. It is from Solomon, and is: In the Name of God, the All-Merciful, the All-Compassionate."* (27:29–30)

First mystery

Three stamps of Lordship are impressed upon the face of the universe, the earth, and humanity. They are one within the other, and each carries a pattern of the others:

Divinity: We see this in how all entities in the universe help and cooperate with one another, and how they have a general interconnectedness and reciprocity. The referent is *In the Name of God.*

Divine Mercifulness: We see this in the resemblance, proportion, orderliness, harmony, grace and mercy in the disposition, raising, and administering of plants and animals. The referent is the All-Merciful, in *In the Name of God, the All-Merciful.*

Divine Compassion: We see this in the subtleties of kindness, fine points of affection, and rays of compassion on the face of the human comprehensive nature. The referent is the All-Compassionate, in *In the Name of God, the All-Merciful, the All-Compassionate.*

Thus, the *Basmala* is the sacred title of the three seals of the Divine Absolute Oneness, which form a luminous line on the page of the universe, and a powerful ray and golden thread of that Oneness. Revealed from above us, the tip rests upon humanity, a miniature of the universe and its fruit. The *Basmala* links the world to the Divine Throne, and is a stairway for us to rise to the throne of true humanity.

Second mystery

Divine Unity (which demonstrates Itself through the manifestation of the Divine Names throughout the universe) is evident in the boundless multiplicity of individualized creatures. So as not to overwhelm our minds in the all-encompassing manifestation of these Names, the Qur'an, being a miracle of exposition, constantly reiterates the manifestation of Divine Absolute Oneness within Unity—the concentrated manifestation of certain Divine Names on beings individually.

Consider this analogy: The sun encompasses innumerable things in its light. But to hold the totality of its light in our minds, we would need a vast conceptual and perceptual power. So lest the sun be forgotten, all shining objects reflect its properties (light and heat) as best they can and so manifest themselves as the sun, and those properties (heat, light, and the color spectrum) encompass the objects that the sun faces.

Similarly—*to God applies the most sublime attribute*[46]—just as God's Oneness, His being Eternally Besought, and His Divine Names are manifested in everything, particularly in living things and especially in our mirror-like nature, each Divine Name related to creatures encompasses all creatures through Divine Unity. Thus, the Qur'an constantly draws our attention to the seal of Divine Oneness within Divine Unity, lest our minds be overwhelmed by Unity and our hearts become heedless of the Pure and Holy Essence. So, it is the *Basmala* which indicates the three important aspects of the stamp of Divine Absolute Oneness or Uniqueness.

Third mystery

Divine Mercy causes the universe to rejoice. It gives the spark of light and life to dark entities, and nurtures and raises up creatures struggling to attain their endless needs. It causes the universe to be directed towards humanity, just as a tree is directed towards its fruit, and to hasten to our assistance. It fills and lights up boundless space, an otherwise void and empty world, making it rejoice. For transient humanity, Divine Mercy also appoints eternity and the rank of the creature addressed and beloved of the One, Eternal before and after eternity. Since Divine Mercy is so powerful a truth, so inviting, mild, helpful, and worthy of love, say: *In the Name of God, the All-Merciful, the All-Compassionate*, and cling to this truth, and be saved from endless desolation and need. Draw near to the Eternal Monarch, and become the one He addresses, befriends, and loves through the rays and intercession of that Mercy.

Why do all entities gather around humanity with purpose and foresight, and hasten to meet our needs with perfect orderliness and grace? Do they recognize us and so run to help us—as irrational as it is, in many respects, impossible, for it requires that we, who have no power, should have the power of the mightiest, absolute sovereign? Or does this help reach us via the recognition of One Absolutely Powerful behind the veil of the visible universe? In other words, the One, All-Knowing and All-Compassionate, knows and has mercy on us, and puts all the entities of the universe at our service.

---

46 The Qur'an, 16: 60. This verse is mentioned although we sometimes need comparisons to explain abstract truths for the Divine Being, He is, in fact, beyond all comparisons. In addition, the most sublime comparisons should be made to explain Divine truths. (Tr.)

Consider this: How could the All-Majestic One, Who causes all entities to turn towards you with their hands outstretched to help you, not know and see you? He knows you and teaches you through His Mercy that He knows you. So know Him, and reverently show that you do. Understand with conviction that Divine Mercy, which exists together with Wisdom, Knowledge, Grace, and Power, subjects the universe to your service, even though you are a slight, transient, wholly feeble, powerless, and needy creature. Most certainly, such Mercy requires total and sincere gratitude as well as honest and ardent reverence. So say, *In the Name of God, the All-Merciful, the All-Compassionate*, as this expresses and interprets such feelings. Make it the means of admission to His Mercy, and an intercessor at the Court of the All-Merciful.

The presence and actuality of Divine Mercy is as obvious as the sun. Just as a center-patterned tapestry is woven by positioning and sequencing the warp and weft to the center, so also the luminous threads extending from the manifestations of Divine Names throughout the universe weave a seal of such compassion, a tapestry of such kindness, a pattern of such grace within the stamp of Mercy, being impressed upon the mind more brilliantly than the sun.

The Gracious All-Merciful One, Who causes everything to serve life; Who demonstrates His Compassion in self-sacrifice, the extraordinary sweetness of this compassion, of motherhood in plants and animals; He Who subjects animate life to humanity and thereby displays our importance and status as the finest and loveliest weave of the Divine Lordship as well as the brilliance of His Mercy—this One has, due to His absolute lack of need, made His Mercy an acceptable intercessor for His animate creatures and humanity. So, if you are truly human, say, *In the Name of God, the All-Merciful, the All-Compassionate*, and find this intercessor.

Nothing but Divine Mercy brings to life, nurtures, or administers all plant and animal species. Divine Mercy neither overlooks nor confuses one with another, but raises each at the right time and with perfect order, wisdom, and grace. It impresses the seal of Divine Oneness upon the earth's surface. In the same way that the existence of this Mercy is as certain as the existence of the creatures of the earth, so too are the creatures proofs of the actual manifestations or reality of this Mercy.

The seal of Mercy and Divine Oneness is impressed upon the earth and upon humanity's nature. The mercy stamped upon us is not less than the compassion and mercy stamped upon the universe. Our nature is comprehensive, as we are at the center of the weave and we are the focal point of the Divine Names.

How could the One Who gives you this face, Who impresses upon it the stamp of Mercy and the seal of Oneness, leave you to your own devices? How could He consider you of no account, have no regard for your actions, and so make all of creation, which is directed towards you, futile and wasteful? How could He make the Tree of Creation worthless and rotten with decayed fruit? Would He cause His perfect, indisputable Mercy to be denied when it is as obvious as the sun, and His Wisdom, which is as clear as light?

You can ascend to the throne of that Mercy by *In the Name of God, the All-Merciful, the All-Compassionate*. Grasp its importance by looking at the beginning of each Qur'anic *sura*, all worthwhile books and good actions. A most decisive argument for this phrase's worth is the comment of leading Islamic scholars, like Imam Shafi'i[47]: "Although the *Basmala* is a single verse, it was revealed 114 times in the Qur'an."

Fourth mystery

In the face of Divine Unity that is manifested within the boundless multiplicity of individualized creatures, declaring, *You alone do we worship* (1:5) is not enough for everyone—our minds wander from reality. We would have to possess a heart as comprehensive as the earth to observe the One in His Oneness behind the unity that lies within the totality of individualized entities so that we could say, *You alone do We worship, and from You alone do We seek help* (1:5). Thus, the seal of Divine Oneness must be apparent on each individualized entity and species, and a seal of Divine Oneness should exist within the stamp of Divine Mercy, so that everyone at every level can turn to the Pure and Holy One and, by say-

47 Al-Shafi'i, Muhammad ibn Idris (d. 820): Muslim legal scholar, founder of the Shafi'i legal school. He developed a new synthesis of Islamic legal thought. He mainly dealt with what the sources of Islamic law were and how they could be applied by the law to contemporary events. His *ar-Risala* entitles him to be called the "father of Muslim jurisprudence." (Tr.)

ing, *You alone do we worship, and from You alone do we seek help* (1:5), address Him directly.

It is because of this mighty truth that the wise Qur'an abruptly juxtaposes the individual detail with the totality, the small with the large, the particular with the general. To prevent the mind from wandering and the heart from drowning, to allow the spirit to find its True Object of Worship directly, the Qur'an mentions our creation and speech, and the fine details of the favors and wisdom in our features, while mentioning the creation of the heavens and the earth. This truth is miraculously shown in *And among His signs is the creation of the heavens and the earth, and the varieties in your languages and in your colors* (30:22).

There are stamps of various kinds and degrees in the universe that show that it is God Almighty Who has created, sustains, and directs us. Although these stamps, existing in concentric circles of different sizes, display a unity behind the multiplicity of innumerable creatures, it is still a unity within multiplicity and, therefore, cannot enable worshippers to address God directly. Thus the stamp of Divine Oneness must be on everything; that is, through the concentrated manifestation of God's Names on it, each thing and species should display that it is God Who has created, sustains, and directs it, so that multiplicity may not detract minds from seeing the Pure and Holy One in everything in the universe, and so that a way can be opened up to the hearts to enable them to turn to and address Him directly.

Also, a most entrancing design, a radiant light, an agreeable sweetness, a pleasing beauty, and a powerful truth have been placed upon the stamp of Divine Oneness to draw our attention and hearts to it. Mercy's vigor and power draw sentient beings' attention to It, and enable them to attain the seal of Oneness, to concentrate on the One of Absolute Oneness, and thereby to address Him directly, declaring, *You alone do we worship, and from You alone do We seek help* (1:5).

Thus, *In the Name of God, the All-Merciful, the All-Compassionate*, being the index of the Chapter of Opening (*Surat al-Fatiha*) and an epitome of the Qur'an, is the sign and interpreter of this mighty truth. Whoever equips himself or herself with this can travel through the levels of Divine Mercy; whoever causes it to speak can learn the mysteries of Divine Mercy and see the lights of Divine Compassion and Pity.

Fifth mystery

There is a Tradition to the effect that God has created humanity in the form of the All-Merciful One. Its extravagant interpretation by some Sufis does not accord with the fundamentals of belief. Some ecstatic Sufis assert that our spiritual nature is "in the form of the All-Merciful." Immersed in their contemplative and spiritual trances, they might be excused for expressing mistaken views. If others consider such views acceptable, they are in error.

The Pure and Holy God, Who orders and administers the universe as easily as if it were a palace or a house, Who treats galaxies as if they were particles and sends them traveling through space with wisdom and grace, Who dispatches the minutest particles as if they were obedient officials, has no equal or match, no partner or opposite. According to, *There is nothing like to Him, and He is the All-Hearing, the All-Seeing* (42:11), He has no form, like, or peer. Nothing resembles Him or is similar to Him. On the other hand, according to, *And to Him applies the most sublime attribute in the heavens and the earth, and He is Exalted in Might, the All-Wise* (30:27), humanity can conceive of His acts, Attributes, and Names via allegory and comparison. Thus, the Tradition's intended meaning is, "Humanity's form, in its totality, reflects the Divine Name the All-Merciful."

This Divine Name is evident via the lights of all the Names manifested in the universe and on the earth through innumerable proofs of God's absolute Lordship. In the same way, the All-Merciful is also manifested fully in our comprehensive form, which is a miniature form of the universe.

A further indication may be derived from the following analogy: Animate creation and humanity are loci of evidence of the Necessarily Existent One, proofs and mirrors to the All-Merciful, All-Compassionate. These proofs are so certain, clear, and evident that just as we might say that a mirror reflecting the sun "has the form of (or is like) the sun" (emphasizing the brilliant evidence of the sun's light), we also might say, "Humanity has the All-Merciful One's form," stressing our being a clear evidence of, and perfect connection with, the All-Merciful. Therefore, the more moderate and balanced believers in the Unity of Being said, "There is no existent but He," expressing the evidence's clarity and the connection's perfection.

> O God, O All-Merciful, All-Compassionate. Through the truth of *In the Name of God, the All-Merciful, the All-Compassionate*, have mercy

> on us as befits Your being the All-Compassionate. Open to our understanding the mysteries of this phrase, as befits Your being the All-Merciful. Amen.

Sixth mystery

O unhappy humanity, laboring under infinite impotence and never-ending need! Understand the value of Mercy as a means and an intercessor. It is the means to a Majestic Sovereign in Whose army vast galaxies and minute particles serve together in perfect obedience and harmony. That Majestic Sovereign of Eternity is the Absolutely Wealthy and Self-Sufficient One, having no need and being in need of nothing and no one at all. Everything is under His authority and direction, obedient before His Glory and Grandeur, awed and prostrate before His Majesty. O human! Mercy uplifts you to the Presence of that Absolutely Wealthy, Independent, and Eternal Sovereign Who befriends you and addresses you as His beloved servant.

Yet, just as the light of the sun provides you with its reflection through your mirror although you cannot draw close to it, so too does the Light of His Mercy make the Pure and Holy One, the Sun of Eternity, close to us, although we are infinitely far from Him. So, O human! Whoever finds this Mercy finds an eternal treasure of unfailing light. This Mercy can be reached through the Sunna of the noblest Prophet, its most brilliant exemplar and representative, its most eloquent voice and herald, whom the Qur'an hails as *a mercy for all the worlds*, He can be reached by calling the blessings of God upon him, for the intent of this prayer is mercy. As a prayer of mercy for the living embodiment of Divine Mercy, it reaches the *mercy for all the worlds*. So use this prayer to reach him, and make him the means by which you can reach the Mercy of the All-Merciful. All Muslims repeatedly say this prayer for the *mercy for all the worlds*, which is synonymous with Mercy. Doing so is a dazzling demonstration of how precious is the gift of Mercy, and how broad is its sphere.

In conclusion, the Prophet Muhammad, upon him be peace and blessings, is both the most precious jewel in Mercy's treasury and Its doorkeeper. The first and foremost key to Mercy is *In the Name of God, the All-Merciful, the All-Compassionate*, and the easiest key to use is praying for or calling for God's blessings and peace to be bestowed on the Prophet.

O God! For the sake of the mysteries of *In the Name of God, the All-Merciful, the All-Compassionate*, bestow blessings and peace on the one You sent as a mercy for all the worlds as befits Your Mercy and the honor due to him, and on his Family and Companions. Grant us mercy so that we are free of the need for mercy from any among your creatures, other than You. Amen.

All-Glorified are You! We have no knowledge save what You have taught us. Surely You are the All-Knowing, the All-Wise.

The Fifteenth Gleam

This consists of the Contents of *The Words*, *The Letters*, and *The Gleams* from the First to the Fourteenth. Since they have been included in the relevant volumes, they have not been included here separately.

The Sixteenth Gleam

The Sixteenth Gleam

- *The conditions for the saintly predictions to come true*
- *The most immediate matter confronting Muslims at the present*
- *Deliverance and success are and should be expected from God Almighty*
- *Visiting the hairs attributed to the beard of God's Messenger*
- *The sun's setting in a spring of hot and black muddy water*
- *The barrier Dhul-Qarnayn built and Gog and Magog*
- *Five things of the Unseen*

In His Name, All-Glorified is He.

There is nothing but it glorifies Him with His praise.

Peace be upon you eternally, and God's mercy and blessings!

My dear and faithful brothers Hoja Sabri, Hafiz Ali, Mesut, the Mustafas, Husrev, Rafet, Bekir Bey, Rüştü, the Lütfüs, Hafiz Ahmed, Shaykh Mustafa, and others!

I feel I should write to you briefly about four matters which have been discussed by many.

The first curious question

Some from among our brothers, like the honorable Çaprazzade Abdullah, asked, "Some saints of spiritual discovery predicted that the Ahl al-Sunna would enjoy relief and success last Ramadan, but it did not happen. Why do such saintly people of spiritual discovery make wrong predictions?

What follows is a summary of the answer I gave them:

A Prophetic Tradition says that sometimes a calamity is judged to come upon (those who deserve them), but if some alms are given in the meantime, they can confront and repel it.[48] This Tradition shows that a Divine judgment given in return for an act can be canceled due to certain conditions. So, the judgments of which the saintly people of spiritual discovery have become aware are dependent on certain conditions, and if those conditions are not present, the judgment is not put into practice. Like the judgment about the time of a person's death which is not final but made dependent on certain conditions, the judgments in question are given and written on the Tablet of Effacement and Confirmation, which is a sort of notebook of the Supreme Preserved Tablet, (on which all the final, decisive judgments of Destiny are kept recorded). It is extremely rare that spiritual discoveries can penetrate the Supreme Preserved Tablet; most of them cannot rise that far.

This reality explains that the predictions based on spiritual discoveries concerning last Ramadan or the Religious Festival of Sacrifice or certain other times did not come true because the conditions required for their occurrence were not fulfilled. Those who made them did not tell lies, nor were they mistaken in their discoveries, for they had been decided but did not come about because the conditions on which their occurrence was dependent were not present.

It is a reality that the sincere prayers of the majority of Ahl al-Sunna could have formed a reason for the removal of religious heresies and innovations. But since some other innovations were practiced in the mosques in the blessed month of Ramadan, they formed an obstacle to the acceptance of the prayers, and the expected relief did not come. Like almsgiving that repels calamities, as declared in the above-mentioned Prophetic Tradition, the sincere prayer of the majority attracts general relief. But since the necessary power of attraction was not formed due to innovations in the mosques, the expected relief and success were not bestowed.

---

48 *at-Tirmidhi*, "Zakah" 28; al-Bayhaqi, *Shu'ab al-Iman*, 3:245; al-Ajluni, *Kashf al-Khafa'*, 2:30. (Tr.)

The second curious question

In the propitious political conditions of the last two months, an attempt should probably have been made to alleviate conditions both for myself and the brothers with whom I have close connections. However, without giving any attention to that situation, I offered an idea in favor of the worldly people who oppress me. Some were astonished and said, "What do you think about the policies followed by those hypocritical and heretical top officials who oppress you; why do you do nothing concerning them?" What follows is a summary of my answer:

The greatest danger facing the Muslims at this time is the corruption of their hearts and the damage to their belief through misguidance caused by modern scientific approaches and philosophy. The sole solution for this is light. We should present light so that the hearts can be reformed and belief saved. If we act with the mace of politics and prevail over them, those unbelievers turn into hypocrites. Hypocrites are worse than unbelievers. So a mace does not serve to reform hearts at this time; it causes unbelief to hide itself in the heart and turn into hypocrisy. At this time, a powerless one like me cannot use the mace and light together. This is why I am obliged to cling to the light with all my strength; I must not consider the mace of politics in any form whatever. As for what the physical *jihad* demands, we are not charged with it at the moment. A mace is necessary for one who must and can use it in order to form a barrier against the assaults of the unbelievers and apostates. As for us, we only have two hands. Even if we had a hundred hands, they would be sufficient only to use the light. We have no hands to hold the mace.

The third curious question

The hostilities of the foreign forces like the British and Italians to the present government should have excited the Islamic zeal which was the true point of support and the source of the moral strength of this country's government for centuries, and become a means for the revival to some extent of the public symbols and marks of Islam and the removal of heretical innovations. Although this was possible, why did you sternly oppose war, pray for a peaceful settlement and give great support to the government of those innovators? Does this not imply an indirect support of innovations?

THE ANSWER: We desire relief, deliverance, exhilaration, and success, but not with the sword of the unbelievers. Let the sword of the unbelievers boomerang on themselves; we do not need what may come from their swords. In fact, it is those Western refractory enemies of Islam and Muslims who have set those hypocrites against the people of belief, and raised the heretics against us.

In addition, the calamity of war is totally harmful to our service of the Qur'an. It would be a great cost if our hundreds of valuable brothers were to abandon the service of the Qur'an and take the mace of physical *jihad* in their hands. Just as the All-Powerful One clears the atmosphere of clouds in a minute and displays the shining sun on the clear face of the sky, He may also dispel these dark and merciless clouds and show the truths of the Islamic life like the sun. He may bestow them on us without expense or trouble. We expect from His Mercy that He will not sell them to us at great expense. May He give insight and sound judgment to the heads of those at the top of this country's government, and belief to their hearts. That would be enough.

The fourth curious question

They ask, "Since what you hold in your hands is light, not a mace, and light should not be opposed nor fled, nor does harm come from displaying it, why do you advise precaution to your friends, and prevent them from showing certain parts of the *Risale-i Nur* to people?"

A brief answer to this question is: Most of those at the top are "drunk"; they do not read the *Risale-i Nur*, including indeed those parts; even if they read them, they cannot understand them. They interpret them wrongly and attack them. In order for the *Risale-i Nur* to be able to remain free from such attacks, those people should not see such works until they have come to their senses. Also, there are many unscrupulous people, who, out of spite or ambition (for some worldly advantages) or fear, deny the light or close their eyes to it. It is for this reason that I advise my brothers to be careful and cautious and not to give the truths into the hands of those who are undeserving of them, nor to do things which will provoke the suspicions of worldly people.

Conclusion

Today I received a letter from Rafet Bey. Concerning his question about the hairs of the Prophet's beard kept in various places, I say as follows:

As understood from the relevant Prophetic Traditions, there is a limited number of hairs from the blessed beard of the noblest Messenger, upon him be peace and blessings, which fell and were collected by the Companions. Despite their numbering only between forty and sixty, the fact that there are hairs attributed to his blessed beard in thousands of places caused me to think much about them at one time. It occurred to me that these are not only the hairs from his blessed beard, but also the hairs which fell from his blessed head whenever he had it shaved; the Companions, who did not lose anything from him, preserved these. These could number in their thousands and may be equal to the hairs that exist in thousands of places.

I also wondered at that time whether it had been authentically established that the hairs found in all the mosques belonged to the Messenger, upon him be peace and blessings, therefore making it acceptable to visit them. It suddenly occurred to me that visiting such strands of hair is a means of calling God's blessings and peace upon the noble Messenger, and of expressing one's love and veneration for him. Something functioning as a means does not require a consideration of its essential nature. If a strand of hair is visited as that of the noble Messenger but it did not actually belong to the Messenger, upon him be peace and blessings, if it is commonly accepted as having belonged to him and functions as a means of expressing veneration, regard, and calling God's blessing and peace upon the Prophet, then it is not necessary to authentically establish whether the strand really belonged to the Messenger. So long as there is no evidence to the contrary, this is enough. For the general acceptance of Muslim people counts as a sort of proof.

If some of the righteous, meticulous people raise objections to such matters on grounds of approved piety, or precaution, or preference for the best and the indubitable, their objections are restricted to themselves. Even if they regard visiting these hairs as an innovation in the Religion, it is included among acceptable innovations, because it is a means of calling God's blessings and peace upon God's noblest Messenger, upon him be peace and blessings. In his letter, Rafet Bey says that this matter caused dispute among the brothers. I advise my brothers that they should avoid arguments that cause conflict and discord. They should become accustomed to discussing matters in the form of exchanging ideas without disputing.

* * *

In His Name, All-Glorified is He.

There is nothing but it glorifies Him with His praise.

Peace be upon you eternally, and God's mercy and blessings!

My dear, faithful brothers from Senirkent, Ibrahim, Şükrü, Hafız Bekir, Hafız Hüseyin, and the honorable Hafız Recep!

Heretical people have long raised objections to the three matters you conveyed through Hafız Tevfik.

The first is the apparent meaning of the verse, *Until, when he (Dhul-Qarnayn)*[49] *reached the setting-place of the sun, he saw it setting in a spring of hot and black muddy water* (18: 86).

The second is: Where is the barrier of Dhul-Qarnayn?

The third is about Jesus' promised coming towards the end of time and killing the *Dajjal* (the Anti-Christ).

These questions require lengthy answers. However, I will answer them briefly.

Your first question

Since the Qur'an considers the level of understanding of the common people, who constitute the majority, and speaks in a way which everyone can understand, it frequently uses metaphors, similes, allegories, and parables. So the sentence, *he saw it setting in a spring of hot and black muddy water*, expresses that Dhul-Qarnayn saw the sun setting in the shores of the Atlantic Ocean, which appeared as if it were a boiling, muddy spring from where he was standing, or he saw it setting in the fiery, smoking crater of a volcano. That is to say, Dhul-Qarnayn advanced to such a point from where he saw a swamp along the shore of the Atlantic Ocean vaporizing in the intense heat of summer, and he witnessed the apparent setting of the sun in the ocean, which seemed to him to be a large pool behind that swamp. Or he saw the sun, the eye of the sky, hiding in a new, fiery crater at the peak of a volcano, which was spewing out rocks, earth, and lava.

With this sentence, the miraculously eloquent expression of the wise Qur'an teaches us many matters. First of all, it tells us that Dhul-Qarnayn

49 For Dhul-Qarnayn, see the Qur'an, 18:83–98.

advanced in northern Africa towards the Atlantic Ocean during an extremely hot summer and then he saw that the ocean was like a boiling pool. During his advance, he also witnessed the eruption of a volcano.

It is well known that the sun's movement is apparent and indicates the movement of the earth. So its setting is also apparent but this is not what the verse above is speaking of. The word spring is a metaphor. A vast sea appears like a small pool from afar. A sea which appears beyond swamps and from which mist and vapors rise because of the heat can be likened to a hot, muddy spring. The use of *'ayn* for the spring, which in Arabic also means the sun or an eye, is highly meaningful and apt regarding eloquence.[50] This is the description of what appeared to the eyes of Dhul-Qarnayn from afar, and it is fitting for the grandeur and exaltedness of the heavenly address of the Qur'an, which comes from the Supreme Divine Throne and commands the heavenly bodies, that it states that the subjugated sun, which performs the duty of a lamp in the guesthouse of the All-Merciful One, is hidden in a spring of the Lord like the Atlantic Ocean. With its miraculous style, the Qur'an presents the sea as a hot spring and a steaming eye. And that is how the sea appears to heavenly eyes.

In short, Dhul-Qarnayn saw the vast Atlantic Ocean as a muddy spring from afar. However, the Qur'an's eyes are very close to everything and, therefore, do not see it as Dhul-Qarnayn saw it, which was affected by the distance. While it tells us how the ocean appeared to the eyes of Dhul-Qarnayn, the Qur'an also suggests that it belongs to, and has come from, the "heavens," and this is why it sees the earth sometimes as a palace, sometimes as a cradle, and sometimes as a page. Thus, calling the vast, vaporizing Atlantic Ocean a spring shows the grandeur and exaltedness of the Qur'an.

Your second question

Where is the barrier of Dhul-Qarnayn? Who were Gog and Magog?

The Answer: Long ago I wrote a treatise about these matters. It silenced the heretics at that time. But now I do not have it with me, nor does my

---

50 The word "spring" (*'ayn*) in *in a hot, muddy spring*, suggests a subtle meaning from the viewpoint of eloquence as follows: after the sky gazes upon the Divine beauty and grace on the face of the earth with its eye of the sun, and the earth watches the Divine grandeur above with its eye of the sea, these two eyes close, one within the other, and cause the eyes on the face of the earth to close. With a single word, the Qur'an miraculously reminds us of these facts and points to the end of the daily duties of the eyes.

memory work to help me. Also, a brief explanation of these matters is to be found in the Third Branch of the Twenty-Fourth Word. I will therefore briefly touch on only a few points, as follows:

According to verifying scholars, the very name of Dhul-Qarnayn, which has the affix *Dhu*, meaning having or possessing, shows that he was not Alexander the Great. Such titles were used by the kings of Yemen, so he might have been one of the kings of Yemen who lived at the time of Prophet Abraham, and who was taught by Khadr.[51] Alexander the Macedonian, however, lived approximately three centuries before Christ, and was taught by Aristotle.

The established, known history of humanity stretches back approximately four thousand years. This deficient, short view of history cannot give accurate knowledge about the times before the Prophet Abraham, upon him be peace. It either gives superstitious information, or denies some facts, or can provide only very brief knowledge. The reason Dhul-Qarnayn became known from early times in Qur'anic commentaries by the name of Alexander was either because he was also known as Alexander, so he was the Alexander of ancient times, or because the particular events mentioned in the Qur'an are the tips of universal facts, and several powerful kings and conquerors lived who were like Alexander the Macedonian and who acted like Dhul-Qarnayn. Dhul-Qarnayn, whose guidance resembled the guidance of the Prophets, built a barrier between the oppressing and oppressed peoples, preventing raids by cruel tribes. Like Dhul-Qarnayn, some other powerful world-conquerors and kings, guided by either the Prophets or spiritual masters, who are the kings of the spiritual realm of humanity, constructed barriers between mountains and strongholds on mountain tops that were important means of saving the oppressed from the oppressors. They built them either with their own material power or gave guidance and instruction for their construction. They then built walls around towns and citadels inside them, and later made artillery and battleships. The most famous of these barriers or walls, the Great Wall of China, which covers a distance of thousands of miles, was built to halt the attacks of savage tribes that are mentioned in the Qur'an as *Ya'juj* and *Ma'juj* (Gog and Magog) and

---

51 For al-Khadr, see the Qur'an, 18:60–82. The Prophet Moses, upon him be peace, made a mysterious journey with him during which he learned the mysteries of Divine Destiny and the inner meanings and real causes of events. (Tr.)

several times raided and destroyed the civilized world of humanity from east to west. Like this wall, which for centuries prevented the assaults of those savage peoples, some other barriers were also constructed through the efforts of certain Dhul-Qarnayn-like Persian kings in the mountains of Caucasia, in the region of Darband, to halt the assaults of some northern pillaging peoples. There are many barriers of this kind. Since the wise Qur'an addresses the whole of humanity, by mentioning a particular incident exemplary of its sort, it is referring to all similar incidents. It is for this reason that the narrations and the views of the Qur'anic commentators about Dhul-Qarnayn and the tribes of Gog and Magog differ.

In addition, the wise Qur'an sometimes moves from one incident to another distant one because of the close relationships between them. One unaware of this relationship thinks that the two incidents were close in time. Thus, the Qur'an mentions the final destruction of the world in relationship to the destruction of the Barrier not because of the proximity between them in time, but because of the relationship of the subjects. That is to say, just as the Barrier was or will be destroyed, so too will the world be destroyed. Also, just as mountains, firm barriers set by God, will be destroyed with the destruction of the world, so too is the Barrier, firm as a mountain, bound to crumble to dust at the world's destruction. Even though it suffers damages from convulsions through time, for the most part it can remain intact. For instance, being one of the examples of the Barrier of Dhul-Qarnayn, the Great Wall of China has survived for thousands of years. It is interpreted as a long meaningful, petrified line from ancient history written by the human hand on the page of the earth.

Your third question

There are brief but sufficient answers in the First and Fifteenth Letters to your question about Jesus, upon him be peace, killing the *Dajjal* (the Anti-Christ).

* * *

In His Name, All-Glorified is He.

There is nothing but it glorifies Him with His praise.

Peace be upon you eternally, and God's mercy and blessings!

My dear, self-sacrificing, faithful brothers, Hoja Sabri and Hafız Ali!

Although you ask for a detailed reply to your question about the five things of the Unseen of which God alone has exact knowledge and which are mentioned at the end of *Sura Luqman*,[52] unfortunately neither my mood nor physical conditions allow such an answer. I can only touch on a few points concerning the matter. As can be understood from your question, some heretics have criticized the Qur'an's declaration that only God knows when rain will come and what is in the wombs; these are among the five things of the Unseen the exact knowledge of which belongs to God alone. They say that observatories can discover the time of rain, and the sex of embryos can be known through X-rays. According to their assertion, it is possible to have knowledge about the five things in question.

THE ANSWER: The exact time of rain does not depend on any specific rule. It exclusively depends on the Divine absolute Will, and comes from the treasury of Mercy. One of the many instances of wisdom behind this fact is as follows:

The most important and valuable realities in the universe are light, existence, life, and mercy. These four things are directly and exclusively dependent on the Divine Power and Will. In other things and events, apparent causes and means, and regular "laws" function as veils before the acts and executions of the Divine Power and Will to a certain extent. However, there are no such veils functioning with respect to existence, life, light, and mercy. For the purpose for giving a part to these veils in creation is not in force in the five things of the Unseen under discussion. Since the most important realities in existence are mercy and life, and since rain is a means for life and mercy, indeed it is pure mercy, then there can be no intermediaries between it and the Divine Will, and no laws and regularity can hide that Will. Thus, everyone in every situation and at all times should feel thankfulness to God and the necessity to worship Him, and should pray to Him for rain. If rain had come dependent on an exclusive law, people would have relied on that law and the door of thanksgiving and prayer would have been closed.

---

52 The verse in question is: *With God alone rests the knowledge of the Last Hour (when it will come). He sends down rain (just at the time and place He alone knows), and He alone knows what is in the wombs. No soul knows what it will reap tomorrow, and no soul knows in what place it will die. Surely God is All-Knowing, All-Aware* (31:34). (Tr.)

The rise of the sun clearly has many benefits for humankind. But since it is bound to a regular law, we neither pray nor offer thanks for its rising. And since humans know the time of its rising every morning, it is not regarded as being among the things of the Unseen known to God alone. But since the exact time of every rain does not follow a certain, regular law, people feel obliged to take refuge at the Divine Court with prayers and pleadings, and give thanks for it because they regard it as a special bounty coming from the treasury of Mercy.

It is because of this that the Qur'an includes the exact time of rain among the five things of the Unseen the exact knowledge of which belongs to God alone. Guessing it from its signs that have already appeared does not mean knowing the Unseen, but it means guessing it from its preliminary signs when it has emerged from the world of the Unseen and drawn close to the corporeal world. Through some sort of presentiment, we can have some knowledge about even some of the most secret events that belong to the Unseen when they are about to occur, but this does not mean knowing the Unseen; rather, it means knowing something which is about to happen. This is so normal that, for example, through the sensitivity of my nervous system I can sometimes feel the rain even twenty-four hours before it comes. This means that rain has preliminary signs which show themselves through some sort of humidity, and indicate that rain will follow. Functioning like a law, this feeling or perception becomes a means for people to have pre-knowledge of some matters that have left the world of the Unseen, that are no longer absolutely unknown, but have not yet entered the sphere of human accurate knowledge or the manifest world. However, knowing the exact time of the rain which the Divine Will has not yet judged to come out of His treasury of special mercy and, therefore, has no signs, is particular to the All-Knowing of the Unseen exclusively.

The second matter

Knowing through X-rays whether the fetus in the mother's womb is male or female is not contrary to the meaning of the above-mentioned verse's part, *He knows what is in the wombs*. For what the verse means by "what is in the wombs" is not restricted to the fetus' sex; it also refers to the character of the future baby, its potentials and particular features which will have a part of their own in its future life, and even the amazing stamp of the Eternally-Besought-of-All on its face, (which symbolizes the fate or general outline of its future life). This knowledge belongs to the All-Knowing of the Unseen exclusively. Even if hundreds of thousands of X-ray-like minds of humanity came together, they still could not discover the meanings on the face that distinguish it from all other human beings. So how can they discover the basic distinctive identity, nature, character, and innate capacity of the child, which are hundreds of times more amazing than the meanings of its physical features?

As we said at the beginning, existence, life, light, and mercy are the most important realities in the universe, and they have been given the most prominent rank in creation. So, one reason for the comprehensive reality of life being dependent with all its subtleties on the Divine Will and Mercy exclusively is this:

With all its faculties and aspects, life is a means of thankfulness, worship, and glorification. For this reason, the Divine Being, Who alone deserves and must be given thanks, worshipped, and glorified, has not placed veils of laws or material causes between life and His Will and Mercy. God Almighty has two distinctive manifestations in the physical and non-physical features of unborn children. One displays His Unity, absolute Oneness or Uniqueness, and being the Eternally-Besought-of-All. That is, by being in agreement with other human beings in respect of bodily structure and members and human faculties, the child bears witness to the Unity of the Creator. In the language of this reality, the fetus announces, "Whoever has given me this structure and these members is also the Maker of all human beings who resemble me in bodily composition. He is also the Maker of all living creatures."

This language of the fetus does not pertain to the Unseen (the exact knowledge of which belongs to God exclusively); since it follows a certain law and is common to its species, it can be known by humanity. It is a language which has entered the observable realm from the realm of the Unseen.

The other distinctive manifestation of God in the physical and non-physical features of unborn children is that with the language of its particular character and innate capacity and particular facial features, a fetus articulates the absolutely free choice and independence and the particular mercy of the Maker. This language comes from the absolutely Unseen, which none other than timeless Knowledge can perceive before it comes into existence. A minuscule part of it which can be detected in the mother's womb is not enough for the whole of it to be known.

In short, in the features of the fetus' innate capacity and in its facial features, there is evidence of God's Unity and proofs of His Will and absolute independence. If God wills and enables me, some other points concerning the Five Things of the Unseen will be written. But for now I have no more time and my condition does not allow it, so I conclude here.

The Everlasting, He is the Everlasting.

Said Nursi

All-Glorified are You. We have no knowledge save what You have taught us. Surely You are the All-Knowing, the All-Wise.

The Seventeenth Gleam

The Seventeenth Gleam

Important notes concerning Islamic thought, belief, worldview, and action

This Gleam consists of Fifteen Notes taken from The Flower (from the Garden of the Qur'an, included in *al-Mathnawi al-Nuri* ["Seedbed of the Light"]). It was thought that it would comprise seventeen Notes, with the Sixteenth Note being included in this book as the Twenty-Third Gleam under the title of the Treatise of Nature, and the Seventeenth One as the Twentieth and Twenty-First Gleams under the title of the Treatises of Sincerity.

In the Name of God, the All-Merciful, the All-Compassionate.

Introduction

Twelve years before this Gleam was written (1921), I wrote down in *Notes* in Arabic, in such treatises as the Flower, the Light, the Grain, the Whiff, the Spark, and the Drop,[53] a number of gleams concerning the Divine Unity that dawned on me by Divine Grace during a period of mental activity, traveling in mind, and spiritual expansion in Divine knowledge. Since they were written in a way that shows one tip of an immense truth and only one ray of a bright light,

[53] These treatises were later translated into Turkish, and collected in and published in a summarized form as *Mesnevî-i Nuriye*. They were translated into English in their totality and published as *al-Mathnawi al-Nuri* – Seedbed of the Light by The Light in 2007. (Tr.)

and as each was in the form of a reminder addressing myself, their benefit for others was limited. The great majority of my most distinguished and sincere brothers do not study Arabic. Their insistent requests have obliged me to write them in Turkish, some briefly and some in detail. Since the Notes in question comprise the initial, manifest experiences from the knowledge of the truth of New Said, they have been translated without making any essential changes. For this reason, some of them are also to be found in some other parts of the *Risale-i Nur*, and some have been left in their original brevity, so that the original refinement should not be lost.

First note

I addressed myself, saying, O heedless Said! Do not set your heart on what will abandon you when this world is destroyed. How can you set your heart on what will leave you when you die, on what will not accompany you on your journey to the intermediate world of the grave? How can you count on what will abandon you in one or two years, debiting your account with its sins, and on what forsakes you at the very moment you have obtained it?

If you are a sensible one, have no care for what perishes during the revolutions of the Hereafter, the continuously changing conditions of the intermediate world of the grave, or the world's tumults and convulsions, or what will not be able to accompany you on your journey to eternity. Do not grieve at their decay and departure. Consider your own nature; among your subtle faculties there is one, which being pleased only with eternity and the Eternal, turns only to Him and lowers itself only before Him. If you gave it the whole world, it would not satisfy that inborn need. It is the king of your senses and faculties. Obey that king, which is obedient to the command of the All-Wise Originator, and find salvation.

Second note

I saw myself in a true dream telling people, "O human! It is a Qur'anic principle that you must not consider anything other than God Almighty as greater than you to the degree that you worship it. Nor must you consider yourself greater than anything and thus claim greatness before and dominion over it. For, just as all creatures are equally far from being the Object of Worship, they are also equal in being creatures."

Third note

Know, O heedless Said! Under an illusion, you see the exceedingly temporary world as undying and permanent. You look around and, believing the world to be stable and perpetual, think you are stable and perpetual. Therefore, only the world's final destruction frightens you, as if you would live until that destruction. Come to your senses! For you and your own world are decaying every moment. Due to this illusion, you are like one who holds a mirror reflecting a mansion, a town, or a garden. The least movement or change of the mirror causes a tumult in that reflected image with which the person is so content. The fact that the originals of the reflected mansion, town, or garden are constant does not benefit you, for your share is only what the mirror reflects.

Your life is the mirror, and the support of your mirror is your life. So consider your mirror and how both it and the reflection can perish at any moment. Since this is the reality, do not burden your life, your own world, with what it cannot bear.

Fourth note

Know that the All-Wise Originator usually restores to life that which is of great value. That is, He does not let valuable things perish permanently through the changes of seasons, years, and centuries; rather, He continually returns them to life. When you look at the types of resurrection occurring daily, yearly, and every century, you see this established, regular practice of God.

Thus, based on this regular practice or law, we say: since sciences agree that humanity is the most perfect fruit of the Tree of Creation and has the greatest importance and value, and since each person is like a species of other living beings, then each person will be resurrected on Judgment Day with his or her exact identity and body, title and form.

Fifth note

Since Western science and civilization had some degree of influence on Old Said's thought, when New Said began journeying in the mind and heart, they caused disease of the heart and great difficulties. For this reason, when New Said wanted to shake off that erroneous philosophy and degenerate civilization from his mind, in order to silence the suggestions and whisperings of his evil-commanding soul, which testified in favor of Europe, he felt compelled to hold the following discussion, which in one respect is very brief and in another is long, with the collective personality of Europe.

It should not be misunderstood; Europe is two. One is that which, benefiting from the religion of Jesus and Islamic civilization, serves human social life and justice through its scientific and technological inventions, the other is that which is based on naturalistic and materialistic philosophy and, supposing the evils of civilization to be virtues, has driven humankind to vice and misguidance. While journeying in spirit at that time, I said to this second collective personality of Europe, which holds in its hand useless, harmful philosophy and dissolute civilization in the place of beneficial sciences and the virtues of civilization:

Know, O second Europe! You have taken in your right hand dark, deviating philosophy and in your left hand corrupt, harmful civilization. Then you claim that humanity's happiness lies in them. I wish your hands would be broken and that your two offerings would cause you to die.

O you wretched spirit, which spreads unbelief and ingratitude! Can one with a corrupt conscience and suffering from mental or spiritual illnesses be happy with rich clothes, superficial, deceptive glitter, and worldly possessions? Do you not see that for one who is disappointed or disillusioned by the non-fulfillment of every expectation, sweetness turns sour, pleasure changes into pain, and the world becomes narrow? How can one exposed to your evil, whose heart and spirit have been stricken with your misguidance and left frustrated and distressed, find happiness with what you offer? Can one be described as happy when their body is in a deceiving, fleeting paradisiacal state or while their spirit and heart are in hellish torment? See, you have led astray wretched humanity in this way, and caused them hellish sufferings in a false paradise.

O evil-commanding soul of humankind! Consider the following parable and see where you have driven humankind. There are two roads before us. We choose one and begin to walk. At every step helpless people are attacked by thugs who rob them of everything, destroy their houses, and beat them so savagely that even heaven weeps for them. Wherever we look we see the same scene, filled with the shouts of the oppressors and the cries and lamentations of the oppressed. Since we feel pain when others are in pain, our conscience cannot bear such injustice or laments. So, those who see such events will either abandon all human feelings and, no longer concerned with the destruction of others as long as they themselves remain safe, surrender to the utmost degree of savagery, or utterly ignore the demands of the heart and reason.

O Europe, corrupted with vice and misguidance and taken far from the religion of Jesus! You have used your genius which, like the *Dajjal*, has only a single eye, to bring humanity to this hellish state as a "gift" and then, seeing that this illness is so incurable that it casts humankind from the highest of the high to the lowest of the low, reducing them to the basest level of bestiality, you offer people charming amusements and fancies as a cure to anaesthetize them. However, your cure will kill you. The road you have opened up for humankind and the happiness you have given them resemble the first road in the parable.

The other road, which the wise Qur'an has bestowed on humankind, is this: We see that at every station, place, and town, the soldiers of a just sovereign perform their duties. Now and then the sovereign's officials come, take the weapons and other belongings lent to them by the government, and give them their discharge papers. The soldiers are pleased, although outwardly they look sad because the horses and weapons which they love have been taken back; but now they can visit the sovereign and return to the capital of his country. If the demobilization officials meet a recruit who does not know them and they ask him to surrender his weapons, that recruit tells them, "I am the sovereign's soldier and in his service. My final destination is with him. If he has sent you here, welcome. If not, stay away, for no matter how many of you there are, I will fight with you—not for myself, because I do not own myself, I belong to my sovereign: both my self and my weapons are in trust from my owner. So I shall not submit to you but shall preserve my sovereign's trust and protect his royal dignity and honor."

This is only one of the thousands of instances of joy and happiness on the second road. Throughout the journey, we constantly see new troops gathered or mobilized with joy and celebrations under the name of birth, while many others are discharged with cheers and military bands under the name of death. The wise Qur'an has offered humanity this road as a gift. If people respect it and use it as a guide, they will enter this second road. *Then no fear shall come upon them, neither shall they grieve* (10:62).

O second, corrupted Europe! A number of your rotten and baseless foundations are as follows. You say, "All living creatures, from the greatest angel to the tiniest fish, are their own lords; they work in their own name, and strive for their own pleasure. They have the right to life, and their only aim in life is to survive." Do you not see the universal mutual helping among them, established by their All-Munificent Creator as a principle of munificence which is perfectly obeyed in all the spheres of the universe? Plants help animals, and animals help humanity. But, supposing that the compassionate, munificent manifestations of this universal law of mutual assistance are conflict and contention, you preach that life consists of conflict. How can this be true? Can you not see that the particles or atoms of all food help to nourish the body's cells? This mutual assistance results from everything obeying the order of a Munificent Lord, and proves that no living creature is the lord of itself. But another rotten foundation of yours is that you say, "Everything owns itself or is its own lord." Another clear proof that nothing owns itself is this: Among all living agents, the most honorable, and the one endowed with the most extensive will and the widest field of activity is humanity. Despite this, our part even in our daily acts, like thinking, speaking, and eating, which we do by our will and power, is minuscule. So how can those who do not own even one hundredth of their most ordinary acts such as these, claim ownership and lordship over themselves?

If this most honorable creature, one endowed with the widest scope of free will, has so little part in its own ownership and lordship, to what degree can other animate and lifeless things claim lordship over themselves?

O Europe! You have fallen into such error because your genius has caused you to forget your Lord—the Creator of everything. As a result, this illusion about your true nature has caused you to attribute all things and acts to (material) causes, and to share what belongs to God with false "claimants" to divinity. This compels all living beings to struggle with innumerable aversions and hostilities to satisfy their endless needs through an atom's weight of power, the capacity of will of a strand of hair, a single gleam's light of consciousness, and a tiny sparkle of life. Whatever they have (in the name of power and will, consciousness and life) cannot satisfy even one of their needs. When misfortune visits them, they seek help from deaf and blind causes. *But the appeals of unbelievers are but destined to go to waste* (13:14).

Your dark and darkening genius has changed humanity's day into a night illuminated by false, illusory lights. Those lights do not smile with joy in the face of humankind rather they mock their idiotic rejoicings in their pitiful and lamentable state.

Students of your genius see every living being as a wretched one attacked by darkness from all sides. They see the world as an abode of lamentation, and all voices in it are wailings over death and suffering. Students completely educated by your genius become pharaohs and tyrants, but such pharaohs and tyrants that they adore the meanest things and are attached to every beneficial means as if these means were their lords. They are apparently refractory, but so humble themselves for the sake of pleasures that they even kiss Satan's feet for the meanest benefit. They appear to be very powerful, but as they have no point of support (in their inner worlds), they are in reality infinitely weak. Your students seek only to satisfy their carnal appetites, pursuing their own personal benefits under the screen of patriotism and self-sacrifice, and working to satisfy their greed and conceit. They love only their own self and sacrifice everything for it.

The sincere students of the Qur'an, however, are worshipping servants of God, but they are such esteemed servants that they do not lower themselves even before the greatest creature or interest, and do not make even the supreme benefit of Paradise the aim of their worship. They are mild and gentle, but only humble themselves before their Creator and with His permission, and they exert themselves for the well-being of all humanity in both worlds. They are poor, but independent of all through what their Munificent Lord has stored in them; they are weak, but the strongest of all through their Master's strength, Whose power is infinite. Let alone seeking this fleeting world as their aim in life, they do not seek even to enter Paradise, and are not pleased with it. Would the Qur'an allow its true students to take this fleeting world as their aim in life while it does not allow them to take even eternal Paradise as their final goal? (Their aim is to obtain the good pleasure of their Lord alone, and Paradise is only a reward.) Thus you can understand what different aims these two kinds of students pursue in their efforts.

You can further compare the zeal and self-sacrifice of the students of the wise Qur'an with the pupils of your corrupt philosophy as follows:

The pupils of your corrupt philosophy flee from even their own family members to pursue their own interests, and even file a lawsuit against them. Whereas, the students of the Qur'an regard all righteous inhabitants of the heavens and earth as family members, and feel so strong and sincere a relationship with them that they pray for them, saying, "O God, forgive all believing men and women!" Their happiness makes the Qur'an's students happy. They see even the greatest things, such as the Supreme Throne of God and the sun, as God's dutiful and subjugated officials and as servants and creatures like themselves.

The Qur'an imparts such joy and elation to the spirits of its students that in place of the string of ninety-nine prayer beads, it gives all the atoms of the ninety-nine worlds that display the manifestations of the ninety-nine Divine Names to its students as prayer beads. It says to them, "Recite your glorifications and supplications with these!" Look at such saintly students of the Qur'an as 'Abdul-Qadir al-Jilani, ar-Rufa'i,[54] and ash-Shadhili,[55] and see how they used everything in the universe, down to the chains of atoms, raindrops, and breaths of all creatures to glorify, mention, and praise God.

Thus, look at the miraculous instruction of the Qur'an of miraculous exposition and see how humans are elevated by it—although defeated by a microbe and driven to distress and despair by the least grief and anxiety, see to what exalted ranks they rise, to what extent their faculties are developed by the Qur'an's enlightening guidance. Such people regard the world and its contents as insufficient to say their beads, for their daily recitations, and they belittle Paradise as the aim of their invocations, glorifications, and praises. Despite this, they do not consider themselves greater or more virtuous than the least of God's creatures. They combine the utmost dignity with the utmost modesty and humility. You can see from this how abject the students of corrupt philosophy are.

So, concerning the truths which the one-eyed genius of corrupt Western philosophy perceives wrongly, the guidance of the Qur'an—which considers the two worlds, which looks at them with its two shining eyes,

---

54 Ahmad ibn 'Ali ibn Yahya ar-Rufa'i (1120-1184), founder of the Rufa'iya Sufi order, is one of the most renowned and celebrated saints of Islam. (Tr.)

55 Shaykh Hasan ash-Shadhili (d. 1258): One of the leading, most celebrated saints of Islam. He founded the Shadhiliyah, one of the most important Sufi brotherhoods. (Tr.)

penetrating the Unseen, and points with its two hands to the happiness of humankind in both worlds—says:

> O humanity! The selfhood and property which you hold in your hand is not yours; it is in trust to you. It belongs to the Owner (of all things); He is an All-Compassionate and All-Munificent One, Who has power over and knows everything. He wants to buy from you His property that He entrusted to you, to preserve it on your behalf so that you will not lose it. He will give you a very great price in return. Like a soldier, you have responsibilities and certain duties, so act in His Name and for His sake. He provides you with whatever you need and protects you against whatever you cannot overcome.
>
> The purpose of your life is to reflect the manifestations of His Names and Essential Qualities. When misfortune visits, you say, "*Surely we are God's and in His service, and surely to Him we are bound to return* (2: 156). So, O misfortune, if you have come with His permission, welcome. We are returning unto Him and desire a vision of Him. He will free us from life's duties and difficulties whenever He wills. If, O misfortune, this is to happen through your hand, it is alright. However, if He has allowed you to come to test my truthfulness to His trust, but has not allowed me to submit myself to you, so long as I have the power I will never submit His trust to one not entitled to receive it."

This is one of the numerous examples of being able to see the reality of the two ways. But people vary in guidance and misguidance, and heedlessness has many degrees. Everyone cannot perceive completely this truth in all its degrees. For heedlessness numbs the senses. Especially in the present age, it has numbed the senses to such an extent that the "civilized" are insensible to this acute pain. However, increased sensitivity owing to developments in the sciences, and the warnings of tens of thousands of deaths every day may yet tear this veil of heedlessness asunder. But how regrettable it is that many people in Muslim lands imitate Westerners blindly and take the way of misguidance under the influence of their irreligious trends of thought and scientific materialism.

O young people, especially those in Muslim lands! Do not try to imitate Westerners blindly! After you have suffered such misfortune at the hands of this second Europe, how can you still trust in and follow its debauched fallacies? Those who imitate them in their dissipation join their ranks unconsciously and condemn to death both themselves and their brothers and sisters. Be aware that the more you follow them in immorality, the more you contradict your claims of patriotism! Does your following them in this way mean despising devotion to "national" values and ridiculing the nation? May God guide us, and you, to the Straight Path.

Sixth note

O you unhappy person who is alarmed at the great numbers of unbelievers and their shared denial of some of the truths of belief, and who has consequently been shaken in your faith! Know that value and importance are not judged by quantity. If men or women cannot remain human, they turn into devilish animals. As they advance in animalistic greed and appetites, like many of those who deny the Religion, they increase in bestiality. You see that although this world contains far more (real) animals than human beings, human beings have been given supremacy over all animal species as God's vicegerents on earth.

What is an unbeliever? They are people who do not believe in the Religion. They are those who are created for the prosperity of the world. They may also serve as a means of comparison in understanding the degrees of the Almighty's blessings upon believers. Finally, He will consign them to Hell, which they deserve.

So, the agreement of the unbelievers and the misguided on denying and negating a truth of belief has no weight, for denial, even if in the form of affirmation, is negation or repudiation; therefore, their agreement on denial has no power. A thousand deniers are equal to one denier. For example, if all but two people in Istanbul rejected the sighting of the crescent moon (at the beginning of Ramadan), and those two state that they have seen it, the testimony of these two would invalidate the negation and agreement of that great multitude. So, since in reality unbelief and misguidance are negation, denial, ignorance, and acceptance of non-existence, even the agreement of unbelievers in great numbers would have no significance. In matters of belief, which have been proven and established to be true, the affirmation of two believers based on observation and experience is preferable and prevails over the agreement of multitudes of people of misguidance.

Another reason for this is as follows:

Affirmation relates to the reality or fact itself, whereas negation depends on the one who negates. So those who believe and affirm are agreed on a reality or fact, and their affirmations support one another. But since denial issues from many different excuses and depends on those who deny, the agreement of deniers has no power or validity. If a thick cloud makes it impossible for all people, except a few, to see the sun, can we say that the sun is not there? Of course not, for those who cannot see it will say, "I cannot see the sun," not, "The sun does not exist."

This is because, as in the example of the new moon, one who does not see it in the sky says, "In my view, there is no moon. It does not appear so that I can affirm that it has risen." Another says, "I cannot see the moon, so it has not appeared yet." Every person has a reason, and every reason may come from a different cause. Since the view of each is different, and the causes that prevent them seeing the object may also be different, their claims are all different as well; each claim cannot reinforce the other claims. But those who affirm the appearance of the moon do not say, "In my view, the new moon is there," but, "The fact is that the new moon has appeared in the sky." Those who see it all make the same claim based on a fact. Yet, since the views of those who negate and deny are all different, their assertions and the causes leading them to these assertions also are different. They are not based on the reality or the fact itself. No negation can be proved because such a proof requires an all-encompassing knowledge.

It is an established rule that "the non-existence of something cannot be proved without extreme difficulty." If you claim the existence of something, it is enough to merely point it out. But if you claim its non-existence, the whole world has to be sifted through so that you will be able to prove its non-existence. As a result, the unbelievers who deny a truth are like people coming together to go through a narrow hole or jumping over a ditch; it is useless and has no weight or value if a thousand people try to do the same thing. They cannot help one another. But those who affirm point to a fact and come together around something that is real in itself. So their affirmations corroborate one another. Affirmation by many people is like coming together to lift a great boulder: the more hands that are stretched out, the more strength they receive, and the easier it becomes.

Seventh note

O you unfortunate one who claims patriotism and urges Muslims to strive for worldly life, forcing them to imitate Western material progress. Be careful that the ropes by which some of them are connected to the Religion are not broken. For if some break their ties with the Religion under such foolish coercion, they will then cause great harm to our social life, as if they are a fatal poison. For apostates go completely bad and become like poison to social life. For this reason, unlike followers of other revealed religions living among Muslims, people who commit major sins openly and without shame are treated like traitors. Their testimony is not accepted in court, for their consciences are guilty and corrupt.

O unfortunate sinner! Do not be deceived by the great numbers of such transgressors, and do not claim that the majority of people share your views. For transgressors are not pleased with their transgression. Without seeking transgression, they find themselves in it. Almost all transgressors want to be pious and devout Muslims, to see their superiors as pious and righteous, only except those—May God save us from such corruption!—whose consciences have been corrupted through apostasy and receive pleasure from poisoning, like snakes.

Do you think that Muslims never love the world or that they need awakening to awareness of their poverty so that they do not forget their share of the world? It is not so; rather, greed has intensified and caused believers to lose. The saying, "The greedy are subject to loss and disappointment," has become proverbial.

Also, many factors invite people to the world—one's carnal soul, needs, passions, desires, Satan, the superficial sweetness of the world, bad friends, and the like—while those inviting to the Hereafter and eternal life are few. Patriotic feelings and efforts should add to this few. If you act otherwise and silence them and help the many, you will be a companion of Satan.

Do you think that our poverty comes from our ascetic tendencies because of attachment to the Religion, and laziness arising from renunciation of the world? No! Do you not see that the Magians, Buddhists, and others subjected to Europe's assaults and domination are poorer than us? Do you not see that the Muslims have more than they need to make ends meet and live well enough, but that it has been usurped and swindled from them by Westerners?

If you expect that following their civilization with its corrupt aspects will lead to better rule and security in the country, you are mistaken, for controlling and governing a hundred transgressors with bad morals and weak, shaken beliefs is harder than doing the same with thousands of pious believers. Muslims do not need to be urged to strive greedily for the world. What they need is good organization of labor and arrangement of working hours, profitable cooperation, and internal security and mutual trust. These are only possible through awareness of God and piety.

Eighth note

Know, O friend, who does not know the pleasure and happiness in labor and giving service, that out of His perfect Mercy, God the Ultimate Truth has included part of the reward for service in serving, and part of the reward for action in acting. Thus even lifeless creatures obey God's commands of creation and the operation of the universe with perfect zeal and pleasure. Everything, from bees, flies, and chickens, to the sun and the moon carries out its duties with perfect pleasure. This means that they receive pleasure from their work so that they perform it perfectly, even though unconsciously and without considering the consequences.

QUESTION: Living creatures can receive pleasure, but how can inanimate beings have zeal and derive pleasure?

THE ANSWER: Inanimate beings seek honor, position, perfection, beauty, and order, not on their own accounts, but on account of the Divine Names manifested in them. They become mirrors to the Names of the Light of Lights by carrying out their natural duties, and are illumined, refined, and developed.

For example, a drop of water or a piece of glass, which is unimportant and without light in and by itself, turns to the sun with its pure heart and, by making its heart the throne of the sun, smiles on our faces. Similarly, by serving as mirrors through their duties to the Names of the All-Majestic One with absolute grace and perfection, like that drop of water or piece of glass, minute particles and compounds of existence develop from being simple objects to a very high rank of manifestation, refinement, and illumination. They take pleasure from receiving and reflecting the manifestations of the Names of the One of absolute Majesty, Beauty, and Perfection, and thereby realize great development by obeying the Creator's commands. Since they attain a very high, refined rank due to their duties, it can be said that if they have the capacity to receive pleasure, that is, if they can enjoy being a part of the general life of the universe, then they carry out their duties with absolute pleasure.

As the greatest evidence of the pleasure in the performance of duties, look at how your senses and organs enable you and humanity as a whole to survive. They take so much pleasure in serving that they are tormented if they can no longer serve. See how much pleasure animals get from fulfilling their duties. Do you not see that the rooster puts the hens before himself and calls them to eat the food he finds? It can be understood from his manner that he does so with great zeal, pleasure, and pride. The pleasure he receives from fulfilling this task is greater than that he derives from eating. Also, look at the hen leading her chicks. She will sacrifice her life for their sake, throwing herself at a dog. She will remain hungry to be able to feed them. She receives such pleasure in serving her chicks that such service causes hunger pangs and fear of death to be preferable.

Animal mothers try to protect their young, and attain pleasure in motherly duty, so long as the young need help and protection. When the young have grown enough to take care of themselves, this duty ceases and so does the pleasure. But the duties of human mothers continue to some extent. For with respect to their innate weakness and helplessness, humans continue to be children in one respect and are in continuous need of compassion.

So, consider the males and females of the animal species, like the rooster and the mother hen, and understand that they fulfill their duties not for their own sake or perfection, but for the sake of the All-Munificent Bestower of bounties, the All-Majestic Originator, Who employs them and, out of His Mercy, includes pleasure in the fulfillment of their tasks.

Another proof that the wage of natural duties is included in the duty itself is this: Look at the plants and trees that obey their Creator's commands. Their adornment and scent, which attract those who will benefit from them, display their zeal, and their sacrifice of themselves for their blossoms and fruit is an indication to the attentive that the pleasure they receive in obeying those commands causes them finally to rot and sacrifice themselves. Look at fruit-bearing trees, like the coconut and fig, which bear cans of milk and sweets on their heads, and see how they ask for the purest sustenance like milk from the treasury of Mercy with the tongue of their disposition, and how they feed their fruits with it. They feed on mud but supply their fruit with the purest of sustenance. A pomegranate tree contents itself with muddy water but offers in its fruit pure sherbet given to it by its Lord. Look at the seeds in the ground and see how, like a prisoner in a very narrow dungeon earnestly desiring to go out into a garden or open space, they are zealous to grow and send shoots into the air.

This Divine law that is prevalent throughout the universe shows that inactive things become more tired than active, ever-renewing ones, for while the former complain about the slowness of time and their lives and want to pass them quickly through indulging in amusements, the latter are full of thanks and do not want their lives to pass quickly. It is a universal principle that the one who lives in idleness complains of their life, while the one who strives and works is thankful. It is also for this reason that the saying, "Comfort lies in hardships and difficulties, while hardship lies in ease," has become proverbial.

When you look at lifeless things, you see that they have the potential ready to be realized. The above-mentioned Divine law displays itself in the development of potentials into actual abilities through great effort and exertion. This shows that zeal and pleasure lie in that movement. If the inanimate creature has a part in the general life of the universe, the zeal originates in itself; otherwise it pertains to the thing which represents it. Do you not see how delicate water freezes enthusiastically when its Originator commands it to do so? Despite its weakness and tenderness, when the water in a closed iron container hears its Lord's command, "Turn into ice and expand!" carried by the language of freezing sub-zero temperatures, it "feels" such intense zeal that it turns into ice and cracks hard iron.

From the rotations of the "suns" and their journeys to the turning of atoms like Mawlawi dervishes, all movement and effort in the universe, without exception, depend on the law of Divine Destiny and are determined and controlled by Divine Power. They manifest themselves by the Divine command of creation and administration that proceeds from the Hand of Divine Power and contains Knowledge, Will, and Command. Each particle or atom, compound, and living creature is like a soldier who is connected with all appropriate military spheres and duties. For example, an atom in one cell of your eye is connected to your eye, your facial nerves, the veins of your body, and so on, as necessary. So everything testifies to the necessary Existence of the All-Powerful One in two respects:

The first is that despite its essential powerlessness, everything performs duties that require great power and capacity.

The other is that despite its absolute ignorance, everything acts in utmost conformity with the principles that form the order of the universe and the laws that are operative in the maintenance of the universal balance. Lifeless things like atoms and tiny creatures like bees cannot know the universal order and balance, which are among the most important matters of the "Manifest Book of the Universe." How can a lifeless atom or a tiny creature like a bee know or understand the basic principles and laws of the Book of the Universe, which is in the Hand of the All-Majestic One Who opens and closes the levels of the heavens as though they were only the sheets of a notebook? If you absurdly suppose that an atom has eyes and a mind to be able to read and understand the fine writing of that Book, then you should attempt to reject the testimony of that atom.

The All-Wise Originator has made the principles of the Book of the Universe become embodied in a particular pleasure and a special need in an extraordinarily beautiful form and concise fashion. Everything that acts out of a special need and with a particular pleasure acts unwittingly in compliance with the laws of that Book. For example, when a gnat comes to the world, it immediately attacks a person's face; it strikes it with its long staff to attain the water of life for itself, and it drinks it. It displays the skill of a veteran fighter in evading attacks to kill it. Who taught that tiny, inexperienced, newborn creature these arts of fighting and extracting water? If I were in its place, I would have been able to learn such skills only after a long period of instruction and many trials.

You can compare animals like the bee, favored with inspiration, the spider, and the nightingale, which weaves its nest like a stocking, with the gnat. You can make the same comparison for plants. For the absolutely Munificent One, Whose Majesty is exalted, has given each living creature a "guidebook" written in the ink of pleasure and need. He has included in this "guidebook" the program of His commands for the creation and operation of the universe, and a brief description of the duties of each creature.

See how the All-Wise One of Majesty has inscribed the part of these commands and contents that are particular to the bee in a "treasure chest," inserting it into the bee's head. The key to this chest is the pleasure that is particular to the industrious bee. With this, the bees open the chest, read the program, understand the command, and act accordingly, announcing the meaning of the verse, *And your Lord inspired the (female) bee* (16: 68).

Based on what has been said already, you can draw a significant message, one of many, through belief from, *My Mercy embraces all things* (7: 156); *There is nothing but it glorifies Him with His praise, but you do not understand their praising* (17:44); and *When He wills a thing, His command is but to say to it: "Be!" and it is. Glory be to Him in Whose Hand is the dominion of all things, and unto Him you are returning* (36:82–83).

Ninth note

Know that Prophethood is the epitome of perfection and good that is shared by humanity. The True Religion is the most perfect expression of absolute happiness and pure beauty. Belief is pure, transcendent good. Since a radiant beauty, an extensive, exalted good, an articulate truth, and superior perfection are apparent in creation, then right and truth are evidently found on the side of Prophethood and in the hands of the Prophets, while misguidance, evil, and ruin are on the opposite side.

Out of the countless beauties and virtues of servanthood to God, consider only the following: Through servanthood and worship, the Prophet, upon him be peace and blessings, unites the hearts of all believers in God's Unity on many occasions, such as the five daily Prayers and the Friday Congregational and *'Iyd* (Religious Festive Day) Prayers. And he brings their tongues together on the same, single word (the Word of Belief in God's Unity). At these times, each believer responds to the illustrious and majestic address of the Eternal Object of Worship with the sound of the hearts of all believers and their supplications and recitations. This vast agreement and encompassing solidarity in worshipping the Eternal Object of Worship are as if the entire earth is making these recitations, saying these prayers, performing the Prayer in all the regions, fulfilling the order, "Perform the Prayer correctly!" issued in all its awe from above the seven heavens.

By executing this order and participating in the huge congregation of praying believers, weak and helpless human beings, despite being like a minute particle in the universe, become servants loved by the Creator of the earth and the heavens. They are honored with rule on the earth in His Name, and become the leader of all animate beings, as well as the final purpose for the universe's creation. If, as in the Unseen world, the countless proclamations of "God is the All-Great" uttered during and after the five daily Prayers, and particularly during and after the *'Iyd* Congregational Prayers, unite in this corporeal world, it would be exaltation of God by the entire earth.

It would be as if the earth shook mightily through the recitations and glorifications of the entire Muslim world on the *'Iyd* Prayers, exalting God with all its spheres and mountains, saying, "God is the All-Great," with its tongue of Mount Arafat in the mouth of Makka, and with the sincere intention of its heart of the *qibla*—the Ka'ba. This phrase of exaltation of God assumes a form in the air of the caves—the mouths of believers scattered throughout it—echoing in the heavens, and resounding in the Intermediate Realms (between this world and the worlds of the Unseen).

And so, we praise and glorify and exalt to the number of the particles of the earth the All-Majestic One, Who has made the earth a prostrating worshipper of Him such that it glorifies and exalts Him, and has made it a place of worship for His servants, and a cradle for many of His creatures. We offer thanks to Him to the number of His creatures that He has made us the community of the noblest Messenger, upon him be peace and blessings, who taught us worship of this sort.

Tenth note

In order to reach the light of knowledge of the Ultimate Truth, and to see His manifestations in the mirrors of His signs and witnesses, and to "observe" Him through arguments and evidence, you should not touch every ray of that light that passes over you or occurs to your heart or appears to your mind with the fingers of objection or criticism, or with the hand of suspicion. Nor should you extend your hands in order to seize the ray that appears to you. Only isolate yourself from the conditions of heedlessness, open yourself to those lights that come, and turn to, them wholeheartedly.

It is my experience that there are three sorts or categories of witnesses and evidence of knowledge of God. Some of them are like water. You can feel and see them, but cannot hold them with your hands. Free yourself from random thoughts, and be absorbed in them with all your being. Do not examine them with the fingers of criticism; if you do so, they flow away and are lost. That water of life cannot remain between fingers.

Those of the second category are like air. You can feel them, but cannot see or seize them. Expose your face, mouth, and spirit to those breezes of Mercy. Breathe them in with your spirit rather than responding to them with your hands of criticism stretched out to seize them. Discard your criticism and suspicion, otherwise they will disappear. These witnesses and evidence cannot be held in our hands.

Those of the third category are like light. You can see them, but cannot touch or receive them. Turn to them with the eyes of your heart and with the sight of your spirit. Wait for them to come by themselves. Light cannot be held in the hand nor sought out with the fingers. It can be hunted only with the light of insight. If you extend your hand to it ambitiously, or measure it with material tools, this will cause it to hide, even if it is not extinguished. Light is not pleased with material or physical confinement, restriction, or physical possession.

Eleventh note

Know that the styles of the Qur'an of miraculous exposition bear great mercy and affection. For the majority of its audience are ordinary people. Their minds are simple, and since they cannot understand subtle things, the Qur'an reiterates the clear signs inscribed on the foreheads of the heavens and earth so that they can be understood. It presents to their view visible signs inscribed in large letters, such as the creation of the heavens and earth, sending down rain from heaven, and the reviving of the soil (each spring). It rarely draws attention to the signs that are written in small, delicate letters, so that ordinary people will not suffer difficulty in reading them.

Also, the expressions of the Qur'an are so fluent and natural that it is as if the Qur'an itself were a reciter. It recites the verses written on the sheets of the universe with the pen of Power. More than that, it is as if the Qur'an were a recitation of the book of the universe and a verbal expression of its order. It reads the Essential Qualities of the Eternal Designer and inscribes His acts and deeds. If you would like to see this eloquence of expression, listen with a wakeful and attentive heart to such *suras* as The Tiding (78) and verses like, *Say: "O God! Absolute Master of all dominion..."* (3:26).

Twelfth note

O my friends who are listening to these Notes!

Although they should be kept secret, I sometimes write my heart's entreaties and supplications to my Lord. This is because I most humbly expect the Almighty, out of His Mercy, to accept the speech of my book after death silences my tongue. The words of repentance and regret of my short-lived tongue are not sufficient to atone for my countless sins. The language of books, which is relatively more lasting, is more effectual. Thirteen years before (this treatise was written in 1920), when as the result of a stormy transformation in spirit, the laughter of Old Said changed into the weeping of New Said—at a time when I awoke from the sleep of youthful heedlessness in the morning of old age—the following supplication was written in Arabic. The translation of a part of it is as follows:

> O All-Compassionate Lord, All-Munificent Creator! My life and youth have passed in the misuse of my willpower. What is left in my hands of the fruits of that life and youth is only painful sin, humiliating pain, and misguided anxiety and suspicion. With this heavy burden, diseased heart, and ashamed face, I am approaching the grave. Like my friends, beloved ones, and relatives who have died, with utmost speed, out of my free will, without deviating to the left or the right, I am apparently drawing closer to the door of the grave.
>
> The grave is the first mansion or door established on the way to eternity through eternal separation from this fleeting realm. I have come to understand, with absolute certainty, that the world, to which I am attached and which I love so much, is bound to perish, and so heads to extinction. All the creatures in it also observably emigrate and disappear in convoys. This world is particularly pitiless and deceitful to those who, like me, follow their carnal, evil-commanding souls. If it gives a single pleasure, it causes a thousand pains in return. For a single grape, it deals a hundred slaps.

O All-Compassionate Lord, All-Munificent Creator! Since whatever is bound to come is near to hand, I see that I have donned my shroud, lain down in my coffin, and bid farewell to my friends. While I am heading for my grave, I am crying at the Court of Your Mercy with the mute tongue of my dead body and the articulate tongue of my spirit, "Help! Help! I seek refuge in You, O All-Affectionate, All-Bounteous One! Save me from the shame of my sins!"

Now I have reached my grave, and I am standing on my body that lies beside my grave, with my shroud wrapped around my neck. Raising my head towards the Court of Your Mercy, I cry out with all my strength, "Help! Help! I seek refuge in You, O All-Affectionate, All-Bounteous One! Save me from the heavy burden of my sins!"

Now I have entered my grave. Those who saw me off have left me. I am expecting Your forgiveness and mercy, seeing that there is no shelter and refuge except in You. In the face of the ugliness of sins, the monstrosity of rebellion, and the narrowness of this place, I am crying, "Help! Help! I seek refuge in You, O All-Merciful, All-Affectionate, All-Bounteous, All-Requiter (of good and evil)! Save me from the company of my ugly sins. Broaden my place! O God! " O God! Your Mercy is my refuge, and Your Beloved, the Mercy for All the Worlds, is my means to reach Your Mercy. I complain unto You, not of You, but of my soul and of my state.

O my All-Munificent Creator and All-Compassionate Lord and Sustainer! Your creature and servant called Said is both rebellious, and powerless, and heedless, and ignorant, and diseased, and abject, and sinful, and old, and wretched, and like a fugitive slave; but after forty years he has repented and wants to return to Your Court. He seeks refuge in Your Mercy, acknowledging his innumerable sins and errors, his addiction to illusion and ailments, and supplicates to You in the utmost humility. If out of Your perfect Mercy You admit him, forgive and have mercy on him, that is what is expected of You. For you are the Most Compassionate of the compassionate. Otherwise, what other door is there to be sought save Yours? There is no Lord other than You Whose Court may be sheltered in. There is no True Object of Worship other than You in Whom one can seek refuge!

There is no deity but You; You are One, You have no partner. The last word to be pronounced in this world, which is the first word in the Hereafter and in the grave is: I bear witness that there is no deity but God, and I also bear witness that Muhammad is God's Messenger, may God Almighty bestow blessings and peace on him.

Thirteenth note

This consists of Five Matters which cause confusion.

The first matter

Although those who strive on the way of the Ultimate Truth should consider only their own duties, they take into consideration how God will act and respond to them, and so fall into error. It is narrated in *Kitab Adabu'-Din wa'd-Dunya* ("The Book on the Standards of Manners in the Affairs of the Religion and the World")[56] that Satan attempted to tempt Prophet Jesus, upon him be peace, by saying, "Since everything has an unchanging, appointed end and depends on Divine Destiny, throw yourself down from this high place, and see whether you will die." Jesus, upon him be peace, replied, "It is the right of God to try His servant, while the servant has no right to try Him." That is, God Almighty tries His servants, saying to them, "If you do that, I will do this with you; let Me see whether you will do it." But His servants have no right, nor are they allowed to try God Almighty and say to Him, "If I do that, will You do this?" Doing so, testing God's Lordship, is bad conduct, and contrary to servanthood. So, humans should perform their own duties, and not interfere in God's business.

It is well known that when Jalalu'd-Din Khawarzmshah,[57] one of the heroes of Islam, was going to war, his ministers said to him, "You will be victorious; God Almighty will make you victorious." He replied, "I am charged with striving in God's cause. I cannot interfere in God's judgment or way of acting. It is His judgment whether He will make me victorious or not." Due to his understanding of the true meaning of submission to God, he was wonderfully and unexpectedly victorious on many occasions.

---

56 This book is by Abu'l-Hasan Ali ibn Muhammad al-Mawardi (972–1058 CE). He is known in Latin as Alboacen. He was a Muslim jurist belonging to the Shafi'i school. He also wrote on matters concerning Qur'anic interpretation, philology, ethics, and literature. His book on Islamic government titled *al-Ahkam as-Sultaniyya wa'l-Wilayat ad-Diniyya* ("The Principles of Government and Religious Authority") is recognized as a classic in the field. (Tr.)

57 Jalalu'd-Din Khawarzmshah (d. 1231) the last emperor of the State of Khawarzmshahs. He fought successfully against the attacks of the founder of the Mongol Empire Genghis Khan (Temujin) between 1220 and 1231. However, when he attacked the Seljuk State in the present Turkey, he was defeated and killed by some nomads. (Tr.)

Humans should not consider how God will conclude their acts which they do out of their free will. (Instead, they should try to do their own duties in the best way possible.) For example, the people who newly join the *Risale-i Nur* fire the enthusiasm of some brothers and sisters and lead them to further efforts. But when people do not heed them, this disheartens the weak among them and causes them to lose their enthusiasm to some extent. However, God's noblest Messenger, upon him be peace and blessings, who is the greatest and most universal master and leader and the perfect guide, strictly followed the Divine decree, *Nothing rests with the Messenger but to convey the Message fully* (5: 99), and conveyed the Message with greater effort and seriousness when people did not heed him. For in accordance with the verse, *You cannot guide to truth whomever you love, but God guides whomever He wills* (28: 56), he perfectly understood that causing people to heed the Message and be guided is absolutely in God's hand. Thus, the Prophet Muhammad, upon him be peace and blessings, never tried to interfere in God's business or judgment.

And so, O my brothers and sisters! Neither should you interfere in what does not pertain to you by basing your actions on it, nor should you assume a position from which to test your Creator.

The second matter

Worship is carried out only as a Divine command and only to please Him. The Divine command requires worship and its result is Divine good pleasure. The fruit and benefit expected of it pertain to the Hereafter. However, provided that this is not the intention or the ultimate reason, the fruit and benefits accorded in the world, without expecting them, do not damage worship or the spirit of servanthood. They may even serve to encourage the weak. But if these worldly benefits are what is intended and what is expected in return for worship, this in part invalidates worship. It may even render any act of worship completely fruitless.

Those who do not understand this subtle truth recite, for example, the well-known daily recitation of Shah Naqshband,[58] which has hundreds of merits, or *al-Jawshan al-Kabir* ("The Great Shield"), which has thousands of

---

[58] Muhammad Bahau'd-din Shah al-Naqshband (d. 1389): One of the most prominent Islamic spiritual masters and founder of the Sufi Naqshbandiyyah order. Among his books are *Risalatu'l-Warida, Al-Awradu'l-Baha'iyya, Hayatnama,* and *Tanbihu'l-Ghafilin.* (Tr.)

merits, intending some of the worldly benefits they may bring. As a result, they do not receive the intended benefits, and shall not receive them, nor do they have the right to receive them. For those benefits cannot be the primary reason for reciting such prayers. If God wills, He may grant those benefits purely as a grace, without the reciter having desired them. If they are desired, this damages the sincerity to some extent, and causes the recitation to be no more than an act of worship. However, weak people usually need encouragement to recite such meritorious invocations. If they recite them purely for God's sake but also consider their worldly benefits, this is harmless and even acceptable. Since this instance of wisdom cannot be understood properly, many doubt, even deny, the value of such recitations when they do not receive their benefits as narrated by the leading spiritual masters and our righteous predecessors.

The third matter

"Happy is the person who knows their limits and does not exceed them." The sun is reflected in a piece of glass, and drop of water, and a pool, and a sea, and the moon, and all other planets. Each of these contains the sun's image according to its capacity, and each knows its limits. In accordance with its capacity, a drop of water says, "I have an image of the sun," but it cannot say, "I am a sea-like mirror to the sun." In just the same way, saints have different ranks according to the capacity of each to reflect the manifestations of the Divine Names. Each of the Divine Names has manifestations like those of the sun, from each person's heart to the Divine Supreme Throne. Every heart is a throne, but it cannot say, "I too am the Divine Supreme Throne."

Those who, instead of knowing their essential powerlessness, destitution, faults, and defects, which form the basis of worship and servanthood, and so prostrating before the Divine Court in entreaty, but who rather attempt to proceed on the way to God with great expectations from God and pride in their acts of worship hold their tiny hearts equal to the Divine Throne. They confuse their drop-like stations with the ocean-like stations of saints. In order to show themselves fitting for those high stations, they stoop to artificiality, affectation, and meaningless self-promotion, causing themselves many difficulties.

In short, a Prophetic Tradition says, "All may perish except the knowledgeable, and the knowledgeable may perish except those who practice, and those who practice may perish except the sincere, and the sincere are in grave danger."[59] So, the only means of salvation is sincerity. It is of great importance to attain sincerity. A minute sincere act is preferable to masses of insincere ones. What will cause us to attain sincerity is that we must do our religious duties only because they are God's commands and in order to please God. We must never interfere in God's business.

Everything requires sincerity and everything can be done with sincerity. At the very least, even a small amount of sincere love is superior to tons of dutiful love for which some return is expected. Someone has described this sincere love as follows: "I do not demand return or reward for love, for love demanding a price is weak and transient."[60] Sincere love has been included in human nature and, especially, in all mothers. The compassion of mothers contains this sincere love to the utmost degree. Their sacrifice of their lives, including even their eternal lives, for their children, clearly demonstrates that mothers demand no return for the love of their children. While the whole capital of a hen is its life, it sacrifices its own head in order to save the head of its chick from the jaws of a dog.

The fourth matter

We should not receive the bounties that come to us at the hands of some worldly means or agents as if these means or agents were providing these bounties for us. If any means or agent is something without consciousness and free will, like an animal or a tree for example, it gives the bounty directly on behalf of God Almighty. Since it gives in the Name of God, you should receive it, saying *In the Name of God*. If the agent has consciousness and free will, they should say while giving, *In the Name of God*; then receive it, otherwise do not receive it. For apart from its explicit meaning, the verse, *Do not eat of that over which God's Name has not been pronounced* (6: 121), has also an implicit meaning, which is this: "Do not eat of any bounty which does not recall the True Bestower of bounties, and is not given in His Name."

59 al-Ajluni, *Kashf al-Khafa'*, 2:415; Abu Hamid Muhammad al-Ghazzali, *Ihya'u 'Ulum ad-Din*, 3:414. (Tr.)

60 This couplet is by Abu Tayyib Ahmad ibn Husayn al-Mutanabbi (915–965): see adh-Dhahabi, *Tarikh al-Islam*, p. 103. Al-Mutanabbi was an Iraqi-born Arab poet. (Tr.)

Since this is so, both the one who gives and the one who receives should say, *In the Name of God*. If the one who gives does not say, *In the Name of God*, and you are in need, then say, *In the Name of God* while receiving it. See the Hand of Divine Mercy over their head, kiss that Hand in thankfulness, and receive it from them. That is to say, see the act of bestowing in the bounty, and consider the True Bestower of bounties in the act of bestowing. This consideration is an act of thanksgiving. Then if you wish, pray for the agent or means, as the bounty has been sent to you by their hand.

What deceives those who attribute everything to apparent means or agents or causes are two things—the bounty and the means or agent in our example—coming together; this is called "accompaniment." They suppose that as the two things exist together, they cause one another. Also, since the non-existence of a part may be the cause of the non-existence of the whole, the non-existence of one thing is the cause of the other thing being non-existent, and thus they suppose that a single part is the cause of the existence of a whole, or that one thing's existence is the real agent or essential cause of the other thing. This incorrect supposition causes people to attribute the bounty that comes to them to apparent, material causes, or to its apparent agent, and thus they feel ingratitude and offer thanks to them. However, the existence of a bounty depends on the existence of many other things, while its non-existence is possible through the non-existence of one of those things. For example, one who does not open the irrigation channels to water a garden becomes the cause of the garden drying up and the non-existence of the bounties that come through the garden. But the existence of those bounties depends on the existence of many other requirements, and the main cause for their existence, as well as that of everything else, is the Divine Will and Power. So understand just how manifest is the error of supposing the two things being together to be the real cause of each other's existence, and know how mistaken are those who attribute everything to material causes or agents in heedlessness of their Creator or real Agent.

"Accompaniment" is one thing, and the ultimate cause for the existence of something is another. A bounty comes to you; the intention of a person to do you some good accompanies the bounty, but it is not the real cause of its coming to you. The real cause is the Divine Mercy. It is true that if the person had not intended to do you some good, that bounty would not have come to you; the absence of their intention would have been the cause of the bounty not reaching you. But the person's intention is never the ultimate cause of the bounty's existence or coming to you. It can only be one of the conditions or requirements for its existence. For example, some of the students of the *Risale-i Nur*, such as Husrev and Rafet, who are honored with many Divine favors, confuse "accompaniment" with the real or ultimate cause, and show great gratitude to their teacher. However, God Almighty has caused the favor of benefiting from the Qur'an lessons which He has bestowed on them to accompany or concur with the favor of explaining the meanings of the Qur'an which He has bestowed on their teacher. They say, "If our teacher had not come here, we would not have been able to receive these lessons, so his teaching is the ultimate cause of our benefit." However, I say:

My brothers! God Almighty's favors on me and you have concurred; the ultimate cause of both is Divine Mercy. Like you, I too confused accompaniment or concurrence with the real cause, and felt great indebtedness to hundreds of *Risale-i Nur* students like you who have "diamond-like" pens. I would say, "Had it not been for them, how could a poor, semi-literate one like me have done this service?" But later I came to understand that God Almighty has made the favor of serving His cause that He has bestowed on you to accompany the favor of causing me to serve His cause. Therefore, my and your activities cannot be the ultimate cause of one another. Rather than thanking you, I congratulate you on His favor to you; and you, instead of feeling indebted to me, should pray for me.

Unfortunately, there are many degrees of heedlessness in this matter.

The fifth matter

Just as giving the property of a community to one person is a wrong, and one who lays hands on the property of a charitable foundation commits a wrong, so too, attributing the product of a community's labor or the honor and merits resulting from the good deeds of all its members to the leader or teacher of the community is a wrong committed against both the community and the leader or teacher. For doing so flatters the leader's or teacher's ego and encourages their arrogance. While only a doorkeeper, it causes them to suppose that they are kings. Furthermore, it may even lead them to wronging themselves by stirring up ostentation or hypocrisy in them, which is a kind of concealed association of partners with God.

Indeed, the commander cannot claim the booty, victory, or glory that belongs to the battalion that has conquered a castle. In the same way, a guide or teacher should not be considered to be the source or origin (of the favors coming to their pupils). Guides or teachers should be known only as mirrors reflecting these favors. For example, if you attribute the heat and light of the sun coming to you through a mirror to the mirror itself, in heedlessness of the sun, and are grateful to the mirror instead of the sun, this would be foolishness, even lunacy. The mirror should be preserved, because it receives and reflects the favor. The spirit and heart of the guide is a mirror; it receives the lights or effusions that emanate from God Almighty and is the means of their being reflected to the pupils. So, such a teacher should not be ascribed a higher rank than that of being a means for spiritual or intellectual illumination. It sometimes may even happen that a teacher or guide who is considered to be a source is neither a source nor a mirror. Pupils suppose the illumination or effusions they receive due to the purity of their intention, sincerity, and the strength of their loyalty to and concentration on their teacher as having come from the mirror of the teacher's spirit. It is as if by magnetism a window onto the World of Immaterial Representations or Ideal Forms has been opened in the mind of one who gazes attentively at a mirror. They observe many strange things in it. However, it is not the mirror in which they observe these strange things, but rather they observe them in the window that has opened in their mind because of their attentive gaze at the mirror. Similarly, it sometimes occurs that a sincere pupil of a deficient *shaykh* may be more advanced than the *shaykh*. The pupil then guides the *shaykh* and so becomes the *shaykh*.

Fourteenth note

This consists of four short remarks concerning Divine Oneness.

The first remark

O one who ascribes creativity to causes!

Imagine that you see a wonderful palace being built of different marvelous jewels. But some can be found only in China, others only in Spain, and others in Yemen, while others are found nowhere but in Siberia. If you see that suddenly these precious jewels have been easily procured and carried from the east, north, west, and south all on the same day that the palace is being built, would you doubt that the master builder who builds it is a miracle-working ruler who dominates the entire earth?

And so, each living being is a Divine palace. Particularly a human being is the most beautiful and wonderful of palaces. Some of the jewels of this palace called humanity are gathered from the World of Spirits, some from the World of Immaterial Representations or Ideal Forms and the Supreme Preserved Tablet, and others from the worlds of air, light, and elements. Human needs are infinite, and human desires encompass the heavens and the earth.

And so, O human being! Since you are such a being, the One Who has made you can only be the One in relation to Whom the world and the Hereafter are just two dwellings for His creatures; the earth and the skies are each a page for His inscriptions, and He controls all time as though it were a single day. In this case, it is only He Who dominates the earth and the heavens and holds the reins of the world and the Hereafter, Who has the right to be worshipped by humans, and is the One in Whom humans must seek refuge, and to Whom they must turn as the only Savior.

The second remark

There are some foolish people who, because they do not recognize the sun, start to love it when they see its image in a mirror. They try to preserve the mirror with intense attachment to it so that the sun's image in it may not be lost. But if they understand that the sun does not perish or disappear when the mirror does, they will direct their love only to the sun itself. The image in the mirror does not depend on the mirror for its permanence; rather, the mirror's permanence depends on it. The permanence of the mirror's "liveliness" and its shining (with the sun in it) are possible only through the permanence of the sun's manifestation and the mirror's facing the sun.

O human being! With your nature, identity, and heart you are like that mirror, and the love of permanence implanted in your nature is, in essence, not for the mirror. Rather, it is felt for the manifestation of the Everlasting One of Majesty, which is reflected in the mirror according to its capacity.

However, due to your foolishness, you direct the mirror to other objects. This being the case, say, "O Everlasting One, You are the Everlasting One!" That is to say, "Since You exist and are everlasting, those who are transient and mortal may do what they want to do with us; let them do it, for I do not mind whatever befalls us."

The third remark

O human being! The All-Wise Originator has implanted within your nature a strange characteristic: Since the world cannot contain you, you frequently utter, as if in a suffocating dungeon, a sound of disgust. Yet something as small as a mustard seed, a cell, a memory, or a minute of time so absorbs you that you are lost in it and are passionately attracted to it. Your mind and heart, which cannot be contained by the huge world, are contained by that smallest thing.

Also, the All-Originating One has equipped your nature with such faculties that some of them would not be satisfied even if they could swallow the world. Some others cannot tolerate even a microscopic particle. Like the eye that is unable to bear the weight of a single hair while the head carries a heavy stone, these faculties cannot endure the weight of even a hair, that is, an insignificant state that arises from heedlessness and misguidance. They are sometimes even extinguished and die.

So be alert and careful, always act with caution and in fear of sinking. Do not drown in a morsel, a word, a grain, a glance, a beckoning, a kiss! Do not cause your faculties that are so extensive that they can contain the whole world to drown in such a thing. For there are some small things which can in one respect swallow many large things. See how the sky and its stars are contained in a piece of glass, and most of the pages of your life history and actions are inserted in your memory, which is as small as a mustard seed. Thus, there are minute things which in one respect contain and swallow larger ones.

The fourth remark

O one addicted to the world! Your private world, which you think to be very spacious, is a grave-like, narrow place. But since its "walls" are made of "glass," with reflection it can expand as far as the eye can see. While being narrow like a grave, it appears to be as large as a town. It is as follows:

With respect to this worldly life's material dimensions, the past, which is represented by the right wall of your private world, has finished and the future, which is represented by the left wall, does not exist. However, as your world's two mirror-like walls face each other, they are reflected one within the other and come together at the point of your present time, making it difficult for you to distinguish between what is real and what is reflected. The "line" of your present extends into your past and future and becomes a spacious area. So reality is lost in what is imaginary, and you suppose a non-existent world to be existent.

In the same way that a tiny dot at the end of a stick spun round at high speed appears to be a broad circle, despite actually being a tiny dot, your private world too appears to you to be spacious because of your heedlessness and delusions. If, moved by a calamity, you stir that narrow world, you will strike your head against a wall, which you supposed to be distant. You will suffer disappointment and lose sleep. Then you will see that your world, which you supposed to be spacious, is narrower than a grave, and more difficult to move along than a decaying, narrow bridge. Your life passes more quickly than lightning, and it flows away faster than a river.

This being the nature of the worldly, animal life and corporeal existence, be freed from animality, restrict your carnal appetites, and enter the level of the life of the heart and spirit! You will find a broader sphere of life than your imagined world and a realm of light. The key to that sphere and realm is to awaken the heart and spirit with the sacred pronouncement, *There is no deity but God*, which is the expression of Divine Oneness that uncovers the mysteries of knowledge of God and makes them work.

Fifteenth note

This is about the verses, *And so, whoever does an atom's weight of good will see it; and whoever does an atom's weight of evil will see it* (99: 7–8), which indicates the most universal manifestation of the Divine Name, the All-Recording and Preserving.

If you look at the pages of the Book of the Universe inscribed on the pattern of the Manifest Book—the Qur'an—you can see the most comprehensive manifestation of the Divine Name, the All-Recording and Preserving, and the examples of the truth expressed in the verses above.

For instance, take a handful of seeds from various trees, flowers, and plants. Then bury these things, each of which is like a small coffer of a tree or a flower or a plant, and which vary in kind and many other aspects, in the darkness of the simple and solid earth. Then water them with simple water, which lacks perception and cannot discriminate between things, and runs wherever you send it.

Now come back in the spring, the arena of the annual resurrection, and look! Notice the time when the *Israfil*-like[61] Angel of Thunder calls out to the rain, as if blowing the Trumpet and giving the glad tidings of life being breathed into the seeds buried under earth; you will see that, through the manifestation of the Divine Name, the All-Recording and Preserving, those seeds that resembled one another in appearance and were all mixed up, follow perfectly the commands of growth issued by the All-Wise Originator. They act in such conformity with those commands that their actions display consciousness, perception, purpose, will, knowledge, and wisdom. For you see that those seeds which were apparently similar to one another have separated out and become distinct from one another.

For example, that tiny seed has become a fig tree, and has started to spread the All-Wise Originator's bounties over our heads. It stretches them to us on its branches, which are its hands. And those two seeds, which resembled it in appearance, have grown into a sunflower and a pansy. They have adorned themselves for us; they smile before us and make themselves loved by us. Each of the other seeds has become a different tree or plant or flower, and yields the fruit particular to each. Stimulating our appetites with their forms, scents, and tastes, they invite us to themselves and sacrifice themselves for their customers so that they may rise from the level of vegetable life to that of animal life. You can derive further lessons for yourselves.

The seeds develop in such a way that a single handful of seeds become a garden filled with various trees, flowers, and plants. There is no fault or error. They demonstrate the fact expressed in the Qur'anic statements, *You*

61 Israfil is one of the four great angels. He will blow the Trumpet twice, the first time as a sign and apparent cause of the overall destruction of the world and the second time restoring all the dead to life in the other world. (Tr.)

do not see any fault or incongruity in the creation of the All-Merciful. Look yet again: can you see any rifts? (67: 3) Through the manifestation and favoring of the Divine Name, the All-Recording and Preserving, each of the seeds preserves and displays without confusion or error the legacy inherited from its parentage. This certainly indicates that the All-Recording and Preserving Being Who does this wonderful act of recording and preserving will display the more comprehensive manifestations of His preservation during the Resurrection. Such faultless and clear instances of recording and preservation in insignificant and temporary things and events is decisive proof that all the good and evil deeds, words, and works of humanity, who are the vicegerents on the earth and who bear the Supreme Trust—the deeds, words, and works of which have eternal effects and great importance—are precisely recorded and preserved, and will be subject to account.

So, is humanity to be left to its own devices? God forbid! Rather, humans are destined for eternity, and will certainly be met with either eternal happiness or perpetual misery. Whether small or great, they will be called to account for all deeds, and either be rewarded or punished.

In short, witnesses to the most comprehensive manifestation of the Divine recording and preserving and to the truth of the verses mentioned at the beginning are beyond number. The witness we give in this matter is a mere drop from the ocean, or an atom from a mountain.

All-Glorified are You! We have no knowledge save what You have taught us. Surely You are the All-Knowing, the All-Wise.

The Eighteenth Gleam

This has been published in *Lema'at* ("The Flashes," which is included at the end of *Sözler* ["The Words"]) and *Sikke-i Tasdik-i Gaybî* ("The Stamp of Confirmation of the Tidings of the Future").

The Nineteenth Gleam

The Nineteenth Gleam

On frugality

This treatise is about frugality and contentment, and wastefulness and extravagance.

In the Name of God, the All-Merciful, the All-Compassionate.

Eat and drink, but do not be wasteful! (7:31)

This verse presents a very important lesson in wisdom by decisively ordering frugality and forbidding wastefulness. This matter contains seven points:

First point

The All-Compassionate Creator demands thankfulness in return for the bounties He has bestowed on humankind. Wastefulness is contrary to thankfulness and implies a slighting of the bounty in a manner that will cause loss. Frugality, however, means worthwhile respect for the bounty.

Truly, frugality is both a form of thankfulness and respect for the Divine mercy that comes in the form of bounties, as well as being a certain cause of abundance, an abstinence-like means of health for the body, a source of honor that rescues one from the disgrace of what is nothing more than begging, and an effective means of feeling the pleasure in bounties and tasting the pleasure in bounties that some may not find delectable. As for wastefulness, since it means running counter to these instances of wisdom, it has grave consequences.

Second point

The All-Wise Originator has created the human body in the form of a wonderful palace or a well-ordered city. The sense of taste in the mouth is like the doorkeeper, and the nerves and blood vessel are the telephone or telegraph wires by which the sense of taste communicates with the stomach, which is in the center of the body. When something enters the mouth, the body or the stomach becomes aware of it by means of the sense of taste. If what has entered is of no use to the body, or if it is bitter or harmful, the taste buds say, "No entrance!" and the mouth spits it out immediately.

Thus, the sense of taste is only a doorkeeper, while in respect to the maintenance of the body the stomach is in the position of manager or governor. So, when a gift worth, for example, a hundred dollars comes to the palace or the city to be given to the manager or governor, only five dollars is appropriate for the doorkeeper in the form of a tip, lest he becomes conceited or spoiled and, forgetting his duty, he lets mutineers into the palace who will give him a greater tip.

Based upon this truth, suppose there are two morsels, one consisting of nutritious food like cheese or eggs, costing only one dollar, while the other is of the choicest baklava and costs ten dollars. The morsels are of no difference to the body for utilization, either before or after entering. Indeed, the one dollar's worth of cheese or egg may be more nutritious. There is only half a minute's difference from the viewpoint of affecting the sense of taste in the mouth. How meaningless and harmful an extravagance it is to increase the cost from a dollar to ten dollars just for the sake of thirty seconds' pleasure.

Now, while the gift to be offered to the palace's manager or city's governor is worth one dollar, giving the doorkeeper a tip nine times greater will only corrupt him. He will claim rule over the palace or city. Anyone who offers a greater tip or pleasure will be admitted and cause disorder or damage. He will compel the owner of the body to cry out, "Oh! Call a doctor, and have him bring my temperature down or put out this fire!"

Thus, frugality and contentment mean acting in conformity with Divine wisdom in the creation and life of humanity. The sense of taste is in the position of a doorkeeper, so it must be given only its due. Wastefulness means acting in opposition to wisdom, and therefore causes punishment. It upsets the stomach, causing a loss in appetite, and harm to the health. It encourages eating with a false or artificial appetite which arises from variety of foods. It also causes indigestion and illness.

Third point

In the Second Point above, we said that the sense of taste is a doorkeeper. Truly, it is a doorkeeper for the people of heedlessness and for those who have not been able to advance in spirituality or thankfulness. We should not squander our health for the sake of satisfying the sense of taste.

However, the sense of taste of those who are really the people of truth, thankfulness, and spirituality is, as explained in the Sixth Word, a supervisor and inspector in the kitchens of Divine Mercy. It serves to recognize and weigh the varieties of Divine bounties with minute scales, each designed for the number of food and drinks, which in turn inform the stomach as a form of gratitude. In respect of this duty, the sense of taste does not serve only the body as a mere material entity, but it also serves the heart, spirit, and intellect. So its position is superior to that of the stomach.

Provided that one does not squander, but rather fulfills the duty of thanksgiving, and recognizes and perceives the varieties of Divine bounty, and eats and drinks lawfully, and provided that one does not cause one's own humiliation, a person can pursue pleasure in consumption. They can choose tasty food and drink in order to employ their sense of taste in gratitude. The following wonder of 'Abdul-Qadir al-Jilani is an enlightening example of this:

Once, Shaykh 'Abdul-Qadir al-Jilani, one of the greatest poles of spirituality, may God sanctify his holiness, had a pupil who was the only child of an old, anxious woman. That respected woman went to visit her son only to find him eating a piece of dry, black bread. His physical weakness that was a result of this asceticism aroused his mother's compassion. Pitying his condition, the woman went to al-Jilani to complain, and saw that the respected Shaykh was eating fried chicken. She said to him, "O master! My son is nearly dying of hunger, but you are eating chicken!" Whereupon, the renowned Spiritual Pole said to the chicken, "Rise up, by God's leave!" Many truthful, trustworthy, and reliable people narrated that the bones of the chicken brought themselves together and jumped off the dish as a live chicken. The holy Spiritual Pole responded to the woman, "When your son reaches this level, then he too can eat chicken!"[62]

With this act, the holy Pole meant, "Whenever your son's spirit prevails over his body, and his heart over his carnal soul, and his intellect over his stomach, and he demands pleasure for the sake of thankfulness, then he can eat delicious things."

Fourth point

God's Messenger, upon him be peace and blessings, declares, "One who observes economy does not suffer shortage in livelihood for their family."[63]

There are innumerable, decisive proofs of frugality as a means of abundance and good living. If I were to provide examples from my own life, I say, supported by the testimony of those who have accompanied me, that I have observed much abundance due to frugality. Even nine years ago (in 1926), a number of tribal leaders who were exiled to Burdur with me tried their hardest to make me accept their *Zakah* (religiously obligatory alms) so that I might not suffer privation or humiliation. I said to them, "Although I have little money, I am economical, and accustomed to contentment with a little. So I am richer than you." I rejected their insistent and repeated offers. It is extremely interesting that two years later some of those who had offered their *Zakah* to me were in debt because they were uneconomical. Thanks be to God, seven years on from then, the little money I had was still sufficient for me, due to the abundance that arose from economy. It saved me from being forced to borrow from people or deviate from my way of remaining independent of others, which was one of the principles of my life.

One who does not observe economy is certain to be humiliated and begging from others. Today, people lend money only at increased returns.

---

62 'Abdul-Qadir al-Jilani, *Ghunyat at-Talibin*, 502; an-Nabhani, *Jami'u Karamat al-Awliya*, 2:203. (Tr.)

63 Ahmad ibn Hanbal, *al-Musnad*, 1:447. (Tr.)

Sometimes in return they receive honor, sometimes bribes, and sometimes religious sacred values. A dollar costs "one thousand dollars."

If people observe economy and are content with the satisfaction of the essential needs of life, as declared in the verses, *Surely God—it is He Who is the All-Providing, Lord of all might, and the All-Forceful* (51: 58), and *No living creature is there moving on the earth but its provision depends on God* (11: 6), they will be provided with enough sustenance to live in a way that they do not expect. There are two sorts of sustenance.

One is the sustenance that is absolutely essential to life. The verse above (11: 6) proclaims that God has guaranteed this for every living being. Unless people interfere with this sustenance by the misuse of their free will, their essential sustenance will find them. They will not feel compelled to sacrifice either their religion or their honor.

The second sort is sustenance that is superfluous. Through the abuse of our willpower, faculties, and neediness, inessential needs have become essential ones, and because of invented customs, we have become addicted to them. As this sort of sustenance is not guaranteed by the Lord, it is also extremely expensive to obtain at our time. Many can only procure such inauspicious goods either by sacrificing their honor and accepting humiliation, or by stooping to assuming a manner as if begging or kissing the feet of some vile person, or by sacrificing the religious, sacred values which are the light of eternal life.

Also, at this time of poverty and deprivation, fair people suffer the pangs of conscience out of awareness of the pains of the hungry and needy; this sours any pleasure that comes from unlawful income. During such bizarre times such as these, we should be able to manage only with what is absolutely necessary of these doubtful goods. For according to the rule, "Necessity is determined according to its extent," when forced, unlawful goods may be consumed to the minimum degree necessary, not more. Only in dire necessity can a Muslim eat of, for example, forbidden carrion, and only until they have staved off starvation; they can only eat enough not to die of hunger. Also, one cannot eat with full appetite and pleasure in the presence of several hungry, deprived people.

What follows is an episode from history showing that frugality is the cause of honor and excellence:

Khatam at-Tayi,[64] who was world-famous for his generosity, once gave a large banquet. Having given plenty of gifts to his guests, he went out for a walk in the desert. He saw a poor old man who was carrying a load of thorny bushes that pierced his skin and caused him to bleed. Khatam said to him, "Khatam at-Tayi is giving a large banquet and distributing gifts. Go there and you will receive five-hundred *dirhams* in return for your load of five *dirhams*." The thrifty old man answered, "I carry this thorny load in my honor and dignity; I do not like to feel obliged to Khatam at-Tayi." Later, they asked Khatam, "Have you come across anyone more magnanimous and estimable than yourself?" He answered, "I found an old thrifty man, whom I came across in the desert, who was more estimable, honorable, and magnanimous than me."

Fifth point

Out of His perfect Munificence, God Almighty makes a poor person aware of the pleasure of His bounty the same as a rich one, and a deprived one the same as a king. Indeed, the pleasure a poor person receives from a dry piece of black bread due to satisfaction and frugality is greater than that a rich one receives from the choicest baklava he eats with a lack of appetite that comes from excess and frequent eating.

It is really surprising that some extravagant, self-indulgent people accuse the thrifty of being stingy. God forbid! Frugality is dignity and true generosity. Stinginess and meanness are the hidden, true side of the apparent nobility of the people of extravagance and self-indulgence. The following incident, which took place in my room in Isparta in the year when this treatise was written (1935), confirms this:

One of my students constantly tried to make me accept—against my principle of not accepting gifts—a gift of about three kilos of honey. However much I excused myself because of my principle, I could not persuade him. I told the three brothers staying with me to take it so that they might eat of it during the holy months of Sha'ban and Ramadan and not to

---

64 Khatam at-Tayi lived in the period of *Jahiliyya* just before the revelation of Islam. He was very rich and, in addition to certain other virtues, extremely generous. His son 'Adiyy ibn Khatam became Muslim towards the final years of the Prophet Muhammad, upon him be peace and blessings. (Tr.)

be left without something sweet to eat, and so that the student who brought it might earn reward. I myself had more than one kilo of honey as well. Those three brothers were modest and appreciative of frugality. But they preferred altruism, which is in fact a virtue, and ate up about three kilos of honey in three nights by each one offering it to the others, preferring the others over themselves. Smiling, I said, "I would have made you enjoy the taste of that honey for thirty to forty days, but you have reduced the thirty days to three. I hope you have enjoyed it!" But I used my more than one kilo of honey economically. During both Sha'ban and Ramadan I ate of it, and, all praise be to God, I offered to each of those brothers a fairly large teaspoonful of honey every evening while breaking the fast. It became the means of significant reward.

Those who saw this conduct of mine might have thought it to be stinginess, while thinking the behavior of my three brothers to be generosity. But there is a sublime dignity and a great abundance and reward lying under that apparent stinginess. If those brothers had not abandoned their way of action, which was apparently generosity, it would have given a result much more embarrassing than stinginess, such as having to beg from others or being dependent on others for their living.

Sixth point

There is a great difference between frugality and stinginess. Just as modesty or humility is a praiseworthy quality which superficially resembles self-degradation or humiliation, but which is completely different, and dignity is another praiseworthy quality that is apparently similar to haughtiness, but utterly different, frugality, which was among the exalted virtues of the Prophets and indeed is one of the foundations of the universal order based on Divine wisdom, has nothing to do with stinginess, which is a mixture of baseness, meanness, greediness, and avarice. What follows is an incident corroborating this:

'Abdullah ibn 'Umar, the eldest and most renowned son of Caliph 'Umar, may God be pleased with him, and who was one of the most distinguished scholars among the Prophet's Companions and one of the famous seven among them called 'Abdullah, once had a heated dispute in the marketplace over something worth only a few *dirhams* for the sake of economy and trustworthiness, which is one of the pillars of commercial life. A

Companion saw him, and thought the manner of the son of the illustrious Caliph who had ruled over half of the old world was an odd sort of stinginess. He followed 'Abdullah to his house. He witnessed that the illustrious Imam stayed for some time with a poor man who was standing at his door. Then he saw him again sitting for a while with another poor man whom he encountered at another door of his house. Curious now, the Companion, who was watching from afar, advanced and asked the two poor men, "The Imam halted for a while with you. What did he do?" Each of them replied, "He gave me a gold piece." The Companion thought to himself, "All-Glorified is God! How is it that he heatedly argued over a few *dirhams* in the marketplace and gave away coins worth hundreds of *dirhams* in complete happiness and contentment without letting anyone know?"

He left and found 'Abdullah ibn 'Umar, and said, "O Imam! Explain it to me! In the market you did that, but in your house you did this!" The Imam replied, "In the marketplace it was what is required by economy, good sense, and the preservation of reliability and truthfulness, upon which commercial life is based. It was not stinginess. And what I did in my house was due to compassion, magnanimity, and the duty of brotherhood. The former was not stinginess, nor was the latter excessiveness."

The following words of Imam Abu Hanifa are an explanation of this fact: "There can be no excess in doing good (to the needy or those worthy of it), as there is no good in wastefulness."[65]

Seventh point

Wastefulness causes greed, and greed has three results:

The first is discontent. Discontent destroys enthusiasm for work and endeavor, and causes complaints instead of thankfulness, and leads to laziness. It also causes the discontent person to pursue easy gain, even though this is unlawful, instead of a lesser gain that is legitimate. Such a person loses his credit, and even his honor.

The second result of greed is disappointment and loss. Greedy people miss their target, subject themselves to disregard, and are deprived of assis-

---

65 al-Ghazzali, *Ihya'u 'Ulum ad-Din*, 1:262; al-Qurtubi, *al-Jami' li-Akham al-Qur'an*, 7:110. (Tr.)

tance. They are a confirmation of the proverb, "The greedy person is condemned to disappointment and loss."[66]

An encompassing law in the world of living beings displays the results of greed and contentment. For example, the "natural" contentment of trees causes their food to hasten to them and thus shows the great advantage of contentment. Yet, animals pursue their food in greed, but suffer great difficulty in procuring it and are not always able to find it in sufficiency. This demonstrates how harmful greed is.

The contentment of the helpless young manifested by their inability and weakness causes a pleasant sustenance like milk to flow out to them from an unexpected place, while wild animals greedily pursue their food, but usually find it to be deficient and a dirty sustenance. This also proves our thesis clearly.

Also, their contented attitude is the means for fat fish to find sufficient food, while more intelligent animals like foxes and monkeys pursue their food greedily, but are usually thin because they cannot find sufficient sustenance. This again shows to what extent greed is the cause of hardship and contentment is the cause of ease.

Those among people who greedily resort to usury or deception to earn their living can only find unlawful and insufficient food at the cost of humiliation, while nomadic, desert people who prefer contentment, live with dignity and without suffering any deprivation. This also proves our claim.

Many scholars, scientists, and literary people suffer neediness and poverty because of the greed that arises from their intelligence, while many stupid, incapable persons become rich due to their "natural" contentment.[67]

---

66 Wastefulness causes more consumers and a decrease in producers. Everyone fixes their eyes on the government's door. Then industry, craftsmanship, trade, and agriculture, upon which social life depends, lessen and decline. Consequently, the country decays and is impoverished. (Tr.)

67 They asked Bozorgmahr, the intelligent minister of the famous Persian Shah Anushirvan (Khosrau 1) (531–579 CE), why the learned were seen at the doors of rulers and the rulers were not seen at the doors of the learned, even though knowledge was superior to rulership. The minister answered, "This is because of the knowledge of the learned and the ignorance of the rulers." That is to say, because of their ignorance, rulers do not know the value of knowledge; otherwise they would go to the doors of the learned to seek it. But because of the knowledge of the learned, they know the value of money and merchandise as well, and seek them at the door of rulers. Bozorgmahr gave a witty answer, referring to the greed of the learned that arises from their cleverness and causes their poverty and humiliation.
Signed: Husrev (one of the leading students of Said Nursi).

This decisively proves that unlawful sustenance comes in parallel with neediness and helplessness, not with the ability or the power of will. For the older and stronger a child grows, the less their sustenance becomes and the more difficulty they suffer in obtaining it. As declared in the *hadith*, "Contentment is an inexhaustible treasure,"[68] contentment is a treasury of good living and ease of life, while greed is a mine of loss and misery.

The third result of greed is that it damages sincerity and injures the deeds done for the sake of the Hereafter. For if a pious, righteous person is greedy, they will seek the acceptance and respect of people. One who considers the acceptance and respect of people cannot have complete sincerity or purity of intention. This result is worthy of great attention.

In short, wastefulness leads to a lack of contentment. A lack of contentment gives rise to despair, which destroys enthusiasm for work, causing laziness, and opening doors to continuous complaints.[69] Lack of contentment also damages sincerity and opens the door to ostentation and hypocrisy. It also destroys dignity and directs one to beggary.

However, economy leads to contentment. As declared in the *hadith*, "Whoever is content is honored, and whoever is avaricious suffers debasement,"[70] contentment brings honor, and encourages work and endeavor. It increases zeal, and urges one to work. A content person who receives their wage in the evening, however small it is, works again the next day with the same zeal. But a greedy one does not wish to work; even if they work, they do so reluctantly.

Contentment arising from economy also opens the door to thankfulness and closes the door of complaint. A content person is thankful throughout their life. Also, because of the contentment and independence, which arises from contentment, they do not seek the acceptance or respect of others. Therefore, the door to sincerity in their religious acts opens to them, while the door to ostentation and hypocrisy closes.

I have observed the great harm of wastefulness on a broad scale. This occurred as follows:

---

68 at-Tabarani, *al-Majma' al-Awsat*, 7:84. (Tr.)

69 Whenever you meet a wasteful, discontented one, you hear complaints. However rich they are, their tongue still complains. But when you meet even the poorest but most content person, you will hear only thanks.

70 Ibn al-Athir, *an-Nihaya fi Gharib al-Hadith*, 4:114.

I visited a blessed town nine years ago. Since it was winter, I could not see its sources of wealth. The late mufti[71] of the town, may God have mercy on him, said several times to me, "Our people are poor." This touched me very much. I felt continuous pity for those people for several years. Eight years later in the summer, I visited that town for a second time. I looked at the fields and vineyards, and remembered the mufti's words. "All-Glorified is God!" I said, for the crops of the fields and vineyards were far greater than the needs of the town. Its people should have been very rich. I was amazed. Then I understood why they were poor through a fact that has never deceived me and guides me to understanding the truth: the Divine gift of abundance had disappeared because of wastefulness. It was for this reason that, despite such abundant sources of wealth, the late mufti spoke of the poverty of the people.

Indeed, just as paying the *Zakah* and frugality have been proven through experience to be the cause of Divine gifts of abundance, so too are there innumerable incidents that show that wastefulness and not giving the *Zakah* cause this abundance to disappear.

The Plato of Muslim sages and the master of physicians and Muslim philosophers, the famous genius Abu 'Ali ibn Sina[72] interpreted the verse, *Eat and drink, but do not be wasteful!* (7: 31), from the viewpoint of medicine as follows:

I summarize the science of medicine in two couplets,
And the beauty of words lies in their conciseness:
Eat little when you eat, and after eating
Do not eat again for a certain period of time; health lies in digestion.
There is nothing heavier for the body to tolerate
Than putting food after food in the stomach.

All-Glorified are You. We have no knowledge save what You have taught us. Surely You are the All-Knowing, the All-Wise.

---

71 A *mufti* is the religious authority officially charged in towns to explain religious matters and direct religious affairs. (Tr.)

72 Abu 'Ali Ibn Sina (Avicenna) (980–1037): One of the foremost philosophers, mathematicians, and physicians of the golden age of Islamic tradition. In the west he is also known as the "Prince of Physicians" for his famous medical text *al-Qanun* "Canon." In Latin translations, his works influenced many Christian philosophers, most notably Thomas Aquinas. (Tr.)

The
Twentieth Gleam

The Twentieth Gleam

On sincerity or purity of intention

In the Name of God, the All-Merciful, the All-Compassionate.

> *We have sent down to you the Book with the truth (embodying it, and with nothing false in it); so worship God, sincere in your faith in Him, and practicing the Religion purely for His sake. Be aware that it is to God alone that all sincere faith, worship, and obedience are due.* (39: 2–3)

> All may perish except the knowledgeable, and the knowledgeable may perish except those who practice, and those who practice may perish except the sincere, and the sincere are in grave danger.[73]

The Qur'anic verses and the *hadith* quoted above show how essential sincerity is in Islam.

A very significant question

Why is it that while worldly people who are heedless of Divine guidance, and even misguided and hypocritical ones, can cooperate without rivalry, religious people and scholars, and followers of Sufi ways differ in rivalry. Agreement should naturally be on the side of the followers of truth, and discord and conflict are the natural consequences of hypocrisy and following divergent ways; how is it that they have changed places?

---

73 al-Ajluni, *Kashf al-Khafa'*, 2:415; al-Ghazzali, *Ihya'u 'Ulum ad-Din*, 3:414. (Tr.)

The answer

I will set forth seven of the many causes for this painful, tragic, and heart-rending situation.

The first

Just as the disagreement of the people of truth does not come from their lack of the truth, so too the agreement of the worldly people who are heedless of Divine guidance is not based on following the truth. Rather, modern social life demands a division of labor and has caused the formation of social classes, professional groups, and political parties, each of which has its own particular duties, wages, renown, and popular respect.[74] So, there is almost no point of rivalry, conflict, and dissension. It is for this reason that however evil the way that each follows may be, they can come together for their interests.

However, as for religious people, particularly scholarly ones, and those following Sufi ways, their duties are concerned with the whole people, and there are no worldly wages determined for them, nor do they have a specified place, or share of fame or popular acceptance. Many may demand the same position, and many hands may be stretched out for the same material and immaterial reward. This may cause conflict and rivalry, and discord and disagreement may take the place of concord and agreement.

The cure for this dreadful disease is sincerity. That is, by preferring attachment to the truth to self-love, always holding the truth over selfish motives, following the Prophetic rule, *My wage is only due from God* (10: 72), remaining indifferent to any material or immaterial wage that comes from people;[75] and in accordance with the principle, *What rests with the*

---

74 A *Reminder*: Public attention and respect cannot be demanded, but may be given by people themselves. If it is given, one should not be pleased with it. If one admits it with pleasure, one loses sincerity and ostentation takes its place. If public attention and respect come in return for seeking fame and public honor, it is not a reward but a reproach and punishment for a lack of sincerity. Harmful to sincerity, which is the life of all good deeds, fame and public attention are only a temporary, slight pleasure that lasts until the door of the grave, but takes on the form of torment in the grave. Therefore, one should not seek public attention or respect, but be wary of it and flee from it. Be warned, all you who are fame-seekers and who pursue public attention and respect!

75 One should take as a principle the altruism of the Companions or the quality of preferring others to one's own self, which the Qur'an praises. One should prefer others to one's own self in receiving gifts and alms, and not seek any worldly return for religious service. If it comes

Messenger is only conveying the Message (24: 54), knowing that it is God Who will bestow popular respect and acceptance if He wills, and that obtaining popular respect and acceptance is not included in religious duties, one can attain sincerity. Otherwise, sincerity will vanish.

Second cause

The misguided people agree and cooperate because of their abasement, while the rightly-guided people disagree because of their dignity. That is to say, since the worldly people of heedlessness and misguidance do not base themselves on the truth, they are weak and abased. Because of their abasement, they need to find strength and power. This need leads them to hold fast to alliance with and help from others. However erroneous their way, they can preserve agreement. It is as if they find some sort of partisanship of truth in wrongfulness, sincerity in misguidance, a religious fanaticism in irreligion, and concord in hypocrisy and dissension, which makes them successful in their cause. For sincerity is never fruitless, even if it is for the sake of evil. Whatever one seeks with sincerity, God will grant it to him or her.[76]

However, religious or rightly-guided people, including in particular scholarly ones and those who follow the Sufi ways, base themselves on the truth and each among them considers only their Lord on their way and relies on His assistance. Therefore, they are dignified, and when they feel they are in need, turn towards their Lord for help instead of towards people. Because of certain differences on the paths they follow, they do not feel in need of any help that comes from these other paths or alliance with their followers. If, in addition, they have a certain degree of egotism or self-cen-

---

without demanding, it should be considered as a Divine favor, and one should not place oneself under any obligation towards people. No wages should be demanded or received in return for religious service. Demanding any worldly return for religious service causes a loss of sincerity. The community should provide for people of religious service, who also have the right to receive a share from the *Zakah*. But they should not demand it. If it is given without having been asked for, it should not be regarded as a reward for the service done. Rather, one should act in perfect contentment, and prefer others who are qualified for the same service and who are more deserving of the reward to one's self. By acting so as to be able to be included among those whom the Qur'an praises, *Indeed, they prefer them over themselves, even though poverty be their own lot* (59: 9), one can attain sincerity.

76 "Whoever seeks and strives earnestly shall find," is a true principle.

teredness, supposing themselves to be right and their opponents wrong, discord and rivalry will take the place of concord and love. This causes a loss of sincerity and utter failure in the fulfillment of duties.

The cure for blindness to the critical consequences of this dreadful state lies in following nine principles:

- We should always act positively. That is, we should act out of love for our own way, and not allow enmity towards or criticisms of other true ways to interfere in the fulfillment of our duties or to play a part in our thoughts and actions.
- We should consider that, irrespective of the particular paths within the general sphere of Islam, that there are certainly numerous points of agreement and bonds of unity in Islam that generate and require love, brotherhood, and concord.
- On the condition that they do not criticize the paths of others, everyone who follows a true path has the right to say, "My path is true and more beautiful," but they cannot imply the falsity or ugliness of the paths of others by saying, "Only my path is true," or "The beautiful path belongs only to me." We should adopt this just rule of conduct.
- We should consider that agreement with the people of truth attracts Divine help and success, and is a means of dignity in religious life.
- Realizing that even the most powerful individual resistance is subject to failure, and indeed fails, in the face of the attacks of the collective force of the people of misguidance and wrong, due to their solidarity, the people of truth should form a collective force through agreement in order to preserve right and justice against that dreadful collective force of misguidance.
- We must save the truth from the assault of falsehood. Therefore,
- We should renounce self-centeredness and egotism, and
- Abandon the mistaken concept of honor and self-esteem, and
- Give up worthless feelings of rivalry.

By following these nine principles, we can attain sincerity and fulfill our duties completely.[77]

Third cause

The disagreement among the people of truth does not emanate from a lack of zeal or aspiration, nor does the agreement of misguided people arise from having lofty ideals or great endeavors for the same. Rather, the disagreement of the rightly-guided arises from the misuse of the endeavor for their lofty cause, while the agreement of the misguided comes from weakness and impotence that arises from not having an elevated cause and endeavoring for the same.

What causes the rightly-guided to misuse their endeavors for their cause and therefore leads to discord and rivalry among them is their extreme aspiration for eternal reward and the fulfillment of the duties pertaining to the Hereafter, which is regarded as a praiseworthy quality from the viewpoint of the eternal life. With the thought of "I will gain this reward; let me guide these people; let them listen to me," they take up a position of rivalry to their true brothers and sisters who are in real need of their love, assistance, and brotherhood. The egotism of scholarly people, which engenders in them the feelings, "Why do my pupils go to him for learning and guidance? Why do I not have as many pupils as he has?", makes them incline to taking up a place in people's opinions or a love of position, which is an evil quality, and causes them to lose sincerity, opening to them the door of ostentation.

The cure for this error, this wound, this appalling spiritual disease, is as follows:

One can gain God's good pleasure through sincerity, not through a multiplicity of followers or great success. For it is God Who will or will not confer these latter, and they cannot be demanded. It even sometimes happens that a single word may result in one's salvation and obtaining God's

---

77 A *hadith* informs us that towards the end of time, the true followers of Jesus' religion will cooperate with the people of the Qur'an and be able to resist their common enemies, namely materialists and heretics. So, at this time, the people of truth and religion need to agree and cooperate sincerely not only with their brothers and sisters in religion, but also with the true, sincere followers of Jesus' religion, especially with the spiritual leaders among them, temporarily refraining from disputing controversial matters among themselves to struggle against their common enemies—the aggressive enemies of religion.

good pleasure. Therefore, quantity should not be given much importance. For the guidance of a single person may sometimes be as pleasing to God as the guidance of a thousand. In addition, sincerity and attachment to the truth require that we should earnestly desire Muslims to benefit from anyone or any school or path of guidance they can. Thinking, "Let them take lessons from me and cause me to gain reward!" is a trick of the carnal soul and egotism.

O human, greedy for eternal reward and feeling discontent with what you have done pertaining to the Hereafter! There were several Prophets who had only a limited number of followers but received the limitless reward of the sacred mission of Prophethood. So, the true success is not having a vast following but rather is gaining God's good pleasure. What do you imagine yourself to be that by thinking, "Let everyone listen to me," you forget your own duty and interfere in God's Will? It is only God Who, if He wills, will make people accept you and gather around you. So mind your own duty, and do not interfere in God's Will.

Furthermore, it is not only human beings who listen to the preaching of the truth and earn reward for those who preach it. God Almighty has innumerable other conscious beings like angels and other spirit beings that inhabit every corner of the universe. Therefore, if you desire much reward, take sincerity as the foundation of your actions and consider only gaining God's good pleasure so that all the reflections in the air of the blessed words that issue forth from your mouth may gain life through your sincerity and purity of intention, and reach the ears of countless conscious beings, illuminating them and earning you reward. For when, for example, you say, "All praise and gratitude are for God," millions of multiplied reflections of this statement are inscribed in the air by God's leave. The All-Wise Inscriber, Who wastes not and does nothing useless or in vain, has created many ears to listen to those blessed words. If they gain life through sincerity and purity of intention, these words enter the ears of spirit beings like some tasty fruit. If there is no sincerity and God's good pleasure does not give them life, they are not heard, and their reward becomes limited to the single, original utterance made by the mouth. This fact should particularly be considered by those who memorize the Qur'an but feel uncomfortable because their voices are not beautiful enough and few people listen to them.

Fourth cause

Just as contentious disagreement among the rightly-guided does not arise from their shortsightedness and failure to foresee consequences, so the sincere agreement among the misguided people does not result from their farsightedness and ability to take consequences into due consideration. Rather, although guided by the truth and right and not being dragged by the blind impulses of the carnal soul the people of right guidance follow the farsighted inclinations of the heart and the intellect, they fail to preserve sincerity and straightforwardness and thus fall into disagreement.

As for the people of misguidance, under the influence of the carnal soul and lusts and driven by desires and impulses which are blind to consequences and prefer an ounce of immediate pleasure to a ton of future pleasure, they can come together in powerful, sincere alliances for the sake of instant benefits and immediate pleasures. Indeed, lowly and heartless worshippers of the carnal soul can sincerely come together around immediate worldly pleasures and benefits. The people of right guidance are in fact expected to preserve straightforwardness and perfect sincerity to form a powerful, selfless unity because they follow lofty intellectual and spiritual principles and aim at human perfections and the fruits of the Hereafter. But since they cannot be fully freed from egotism and self-centeredness or liberate themselves from going to extremes, they lose their agreement, which is a sublime source of power, and their sincerity is shattered. Thus, their duty concerning the Hereafter is harmed. This also makes gaining God's good pleasure truly difficult.

The cure for this grave disease is, with the guidance of the principle of *loving for God's sake*, proudly accompanying those who follow the Straight Path, deferring leadership to them, renouncing egotism with the thought that whoever is following the Straight Path may be better than oneself, and thus gaining sincerity, knowing that an ounce of deeds done with sincerity is preferable to tons of deeds done without sincerity, and preferring being a follower to leadership, which brings responsibility and therefore is risky. By doing so, one can be saved from the disease of egotism, going to extremes, and insincerity, which was mentioned above; one is able to gain sincerity and properly fulfill one's duties pertaining to the Hereafter.

Fifth cause

The disagreement of the rightly-guided people does not arise from their weakness, nor does the powerful agreement of the misguided people arise from their strength. Rather, the lack of agreement among the rightly-guided people is due to their strength which results from the point of support that is provided by perfect belief, while the agreement of the people of heedlessness and misguidance comes from their weakness and impotence that results from the fact that they can find no point of support in their hearts. The weak form powerful unities because they desperately need alliance and agreement. But since the powerful do not feel this need much, their unity is weak. Lions do not need union, nor do foxes, and therefore they live as individuals, whereas wild goats (and oxen) form herds to protect themselves against wolves and lions. This means that the community and collective personality of the weak is strong, while the community and collective personality of the powerful is weak.[78] The Qur'an makes a subtle allusion to this fact. Although the feminine form of the verb should have been used for the community of women where there are two instances of femininity (women is a feminine noun, and as a plural subject requires the feminine form of the verb in Arabic), it uses the masculine form of the verb in, *And women in the city said* (12: 30). While in *The desert Arabs said* (49: 14) the feminine form of the verb for the community of men is used. This usage delicately implies that the community of weak, feeble, and tender women gains strength, toughness, and sternness with togetherness, and so acquires some sort of manliness. As it therefore appropriates the masculine form of the verb, the Qur'anic use of this form is the best suited. By contrast, since strong men, particularly those of the desert Arabs, rely on their own individual strength, their community suffers from weakness, to which cautiousness and the feeling of a lack support only add. This is why their community takes on a kind of femininity and requires the feminine form of verb; again, the Qur'an has used this form most appropriately.

---

[78] Among the most powerful and influential organizations in the West is the American Organization for Women's Rights and Liberty, even though women form the fair and weak sex among humankind. Likewise, despite being the weakest and least populous among nations, the Armenian committees display the greatest sacrifice and commitment. These two facts provide another proof for our thesis.

Thus, due to their submission to and trust in God, which is provided by belief in God, and which is a most powerful point of reliance, the people of truth do not display neediness before others or ask for their help. Even if they sometimes feel needy, they do not need to hold fast to this help. But since the worldly people are neglectful of the true source of support for humanity in worldly affairs, they suffer weakness and impotence, and therefore cooperate sincerely and even with self-sacrifice in dire need of external help and support.

In short, the people of truth, who do not consider or seek the rightful power that lies in agreement, fall into disagreement as an evil and harmful result of this lack of consideration. But the people of misguidance, who follow false ways, perceive the power of agreement due to their weakness, and attain agreement, and this is an extremely important means for the attainment of goals.

The cure for this disease of the people of truth is to adopt as guidance in life the powerful Divine prohibition in, *Do not dispute with one another, or else you may lose heart and your power and energy desert you* (8: 46), and the wise Divine command for social life in, *Help one another in virtue and goodness, and righteousness and piety* (5: 2). We should also consider how harmful to Islam disagreement is, and how it facilitates the triumph of the misguided people over the people of truth, and join the caravan of the people of truth sincerely and self-sacrificingly in awareness of our innate powerlessness. Also, renouncing self-centeredness and forgetting individual selfish interests, we should be freed from ostentation and pretension, and thus acquire sincerity.

Sixth cause

The disagreement of the people of truth does not come from a lack of courage, lack of aspiration to a lofty goal, or lack of endeavor for its realization. Nor does the sincere cooperation of the heedless people of worldliness and misguidance in their worldly affairs arise from their courage, or from possessing a lofty ideal, or from endeavor for the realization of the same. Rather, as the people of truth mostly concentrate on the benefits that pertain to the Hereafter, they distribute their courage, aspirations, and endeavors among numerous important matters. Since they do not also devote their time, which is the most fundamental capital of humanity, to one single concern, their cooperation with others cannot be strong. They have numerous concerns over a broad sphere of duties.

As for the worldly people of heedlessness, since their only concern is the worldly life, they devote all their energy to the matters that are concerned with the worldly life and concentrate on them with all their feelings and faculties. They firmly cling to whatever may help them with their worldly concerns. Like a crazy diamond merchant who pays hundreds of dollars for a few cents' worth of glass, they spend all their time, which is everyone's greatest capital, on those matters, which are actually worth five cents and to which the people of truth may pay ten cents at the most. But as this sort of attachment and concentration, even if for the sake of falsehood, has the effect of sincerity, the worldly people succeed in those matters and triumph over the people of truth. This triumph of the worldly people drives the people of truth to humiliation, subjection, pretension, and ostentation, causing them to lose sincerity. They feel constrained to flatter and toady to certain despicable, selfish, and cowardly people of the world.

O people of truth! O truth-loving followers of the Divine way of life and true spiritual paths! Counter this awful disease of discord and disagreement by overlooking each other's faults and closing your eyes to each other's shortcomings. Act with the good manner described in the holy Criterion's verse, *When they happen to pass by anything vain and useless, they pass by it with dignity* (25: 72). Abandoning internal disputes while you are subject to external attacks and regarding the deliverance of the people of truth from decline and humiliation as your primary, most urgent and important duty that pertains to your afterlife, realize among you brother/sisterhood, love, and cooperation, which are insistently enjoined by hundreds of Qur'anic verses and Prophetic Traditions. Establish with all your powers a much stronger unity with your fellows and brothers and sisters in religion than that which exists between the worldly people, and allow no disagreement or discord among you! Never think, "Rather than spending my valuable time on such insignificant matters, I would be better to spend it on valuable things such as religious recitals, invocations, and reflection," drawing aside and weakening unity! For something you may regard as insignificant may be very important for this spiritual *jihad*. In just the same way that under certain important and special conditions one hour's watch kept by a private may be equal to a whole year's worship, a valuable day you spend on a minor matter pertaining to religion at this time of the defeat of the people of truth may be worth a thousand days. Since whatever is done is for God's sake, it is not considered small or great, valuable or valueless. An atom expended for God's sake with sincerity becomes like a star. Besides, what is of importance is not the nature of the means employed, but the result it yields. So long as the result intended is God's good pleasure, and whatever is done is religiously lawful and done with sincerity, that is, purely for God's sake, it is not small, but great.

Seventh cause

The disagreement and rivalry among the people of truth does not come from jealousy or greed for the world; nor does the agreement of the worldly and heedless people arise from magnanimity or nobility. Rather, the people of truth are unable to maintain magnanimity and zeal for endeavor, both of which originate in the truth and the praiseworthy form of competition in doing good on the way of the truth. Both because of this and because of the infiltration of some who are unqualified to work for the truth, they misuse that praiseworthy form of competition to a certain degree, and fall into rivalry and disagreement, thus doing great harm to both themselves and the community of Muslims.

As for the people of worldliness and heedlessness, in order not to lose the benefits to which they are so attached and not to offend the leaders and companions they adore for the sake of their benefits, in their humiliation, cowardliness, and due to the lack of a sublime goal or endeavor for the same, they form unity at all costs with their fellows, however abased, treacherous, and harmful they be, and sincerely come together with their partners in whatever way may be for their common interest. They benefit from this cooperation due to their sincerity.

So, O disunited, calamity-stricken people of truth! Since at this time of calamity you have lost sincerity and been unable to make God's good pleasure your sole aim, you have caused all the people of truth to suffer the present humiliation and defeat. In matters relating to the Religion and the afterlife there should be no rivalry or jealousy, and indeed there cannot be either from the viewpoint of the truth. For jealousy and the ensuing rivalry arise from the conflict, dispute and competition that are caused by many hands being stretched out to obtain the same object or many eyes being fixed on the same position, or many stomachs demanding the same food. Since in the world many desire and apply for the same thing, and the world is too narrow and temporary to satisfy the limitless desires of humanity, people fall into rivalry. However, there is no cause for rivalry in the Hereafter, where each individual will be given a Garden across which they can walk for five hundred years, with seventy thousand palaces, and where every one of the people of Paradise will be fully satisfied with his or her share.[79]

Therefore, there can be no rivalry or jealousy about good deeds done to gain eternal happiness in the Hereafter. One who shows jealousy is either a person of ostentation, who is pursuing worldly results in the fulfillment of good deeds, or an ignorant devotee who does not know the reason good deeds should be done, or perceive that the spirit or essence of good deeds is sincerity. By feeling some sort of enmity towards God's beloved servants because of this rivalry, such a person takes up a position by which they deny

---

79 A *significant question:* It is related from God's Messenger, upon him be peace and blessings, that in Paradise a person will be given a garden across which they can walk for five hundred years (*at-Tirmidhi*, "Janna" 8). How can we explain this in a way people can understand?
The Answer: In this world everyone has a private, temporary world as spacious as the world itself. Everyone's life is the pillar of their private world, from which they benefit with all their external and internal senses and faculties. Each person can say, "The sun is my lamp, and the stars are my candles." All other creatures do not prevent them from privately owning and benefiting from these; rather, they add to the beauty and comfort of everyone's private world. Similarly, in addition to the private garden that contains thousands of palaces and *houris*, one incomparably richer and more beautiful than that in the world, every believer will have an area of benefit as spacious as a walk of five hundred years. Through their senses, which will develop to the utmost degree of each, they will have as great enjoyment as Paradise and eternity will allow them. The enjoyment of others will not harm another's share in the general enjoyment of Paradise; rather it will add to it, making his or her private Garden and share in Paradise more enjoyable. A person benefits in this world from a garden that is large enough to walk through in an hour, from an excursion area in which one can walk for a day, or from countryside that has enough room for a month's walk, or from a continent that can take a year to cross, with their mouth, ears, eyes, sense of taste, and all other senses and faculties. So too, in the realm of eternity, a person's senses of smell and taste, which can benefit in this world from a garden only as large as an hour's walk, will benefit in Paradise from a Garden as spacious as a year's walk. The faculties of sight and hearing, which can have limited benefit in this world, will benefit in Paradise from a Garden that is spacious enough to walk for five hundred years. Every believer's enjoyment will be in proportion to the developmental degree of their senses, feelings, and faculties through the rewards they earned in the world.

the limitless vastness of God's Mercy. What follows is an event that corroborates this reality:

One of our former companions cherished enmity towards a man. When that man was praised for his good deeds and even saintliness in the presence of our companion, he showed no signs of jealousy or discomfort. When, however, another one said to him, "That enemy of yours is courageous and strong," we saw a strong feeling of jealousy and rivalry provoked in him. We said to him:

> Sainthood and righteousness are as valuable as a diamond with respect to eternal life, yet you felt no jealousy of your enemy on account of them. But worldly strength is to be found in oxen, and courage in wild wolves, and compared with saintliness and righteousness, they are like a piece of glass compared to a diamond.

The man answered:

> We have both fixed our eyes in this world on a single thing, a single position. The steps by which we will reach it are things such as strength and courage. This is why I was jealous of him. But there are countless positions in the Hereafter. Although he is my enemy here, there he may be a sincere, beloved brother of mine.

O people of truth and followers of spiritual paths! Serving the truth is like carrying and preserving a great, heavy treasure. The greater the number of powerful hands that rush to the aid of those who carry it on their shoulders are, the happier and more pleased they will be. Far from being jealous, though, one should proudly and lovingly applaud the superior strength, effectiveness and assistance of these true brothers and self-sacrificing helpers who come forward to offer their help; why then do we respond to them with rivalry, thus losing sincerity? Why in the eyes of the worldly, misguided people, who themselves are a hundred times lower than you, as their way is lower than yours, do you expose yourselves to appalling accusations such as earning the world by misuse of the Religion, exploiting the knowledge of truth to earn your livelihood, and ambitiously and greedily competing for worldly interests?

The sole remedy for this disease is condemning one's own soul and taking the side of the fellows against one's soul. One should also follow the following principle adopted and established by scholars in the art of debate:

"A person who desires, in debate on a subject, his own thesis to be true and is happy with its turning out to be right and the opposing side to be wrong and mistaken, is an unfair one." Such a person is also in loss, for when they win the debate, they have learned nothing new; rather, their probable pride may cause them further loss. But if the truth turns out to be on the opposing side, they will have learned something previously unknown to them and thereby acquired something beneficial, as well as having been saved from probable pride. Therefore, a fair, truth-loving one wounds the pride of their carnal soul for the sake of the truth. When they see the truth in the hand of their opponent, they willingly accept it and support it.

If the people of the Religion, the truth, and knowledge, and the followers of spiritual paths take this principle as a guide, they will attain sincerity, and succeed in their duties pertaining to the Hereafter. They will also be saved through God's Mercy from the present tragic decline and wretchedness.

All-Glorified are You. We have no knowledge save what You have taught us. Surely You are the All-Knowing, the All-Wise.

The Twenty-First Gleam

The Twenty-First Gleam

On sincerity or purity of intention

This Gleam should be read at least once a fortnight.

In the Name of God, the All-Merciful, the All-Compassionate.

Stand in the presence of God in utmost devotion and obedience (2: 238). *Do not dispute with one another, or else you may lose heart and your power and energy desert you* (8: 46). *He is indeed prosperous who has grown it in purity. And he is indeed lost who has corrupted it* (91: 9–10). *Do not sell My Revelations for a trifling price* (2: 41).

O my brothers and sisters of the Hereafter, and companions in the service of the Qur'an! You should know—indeed you know—that in this world, and particularly in the services done for the afterlife, a most important foundation, and a greatest power, and a most acceptable intercessor, and a firmest point of reliance, and a shortest way to the truth, and a most answerable prayer, and a most blessed and marvelous means of achieving one's goal, and a most sublime virtue, and a purest form of worship is sincerity, or doing something good or any religious deed purely for God's sake. Since sincerity has many varieties of power and light, such as those mentioned, and since at this terrible time, in the face of dreadful hostilities, under severe pressure, and amidst the forceful heretical innovations in the Religion and many forms of misguidance, an extremely heavy, important, comprehensive, and sacred duty of serving belief and the Qur'an has been placed on our shoulders by the Divine Grace despite our powerlessness, deprivations, and being few in number; we are certainly compelled more than everyone else to gain sincerity with all our strength and are in dire need of inculcating it in ourselves. Otherwise, our attainments in our sacred service will in part be lost and we will no longer be able to continue it; we will be held responsible. Furthermore, we will be a target of the severe threat contained in the Divine prohibition, *Do not sell My Revelations for a trifling price* (2: 41), and by damaging sincerity to the detriment of eternal happiness and for the sake of some harmful, depressing, egotistic, repulsive, hypocritical base feelings or insignificant benefits, we will violate the rights of our brothers and sisters in this service and transgress against the duty of serving the Qur'an, desecrating the truths of belief.

O my brothers and sisters! Numerous harmful obstacles appear before works of great good. Satans strive very much against those who try to do these works. We should rely on the strength of sincerity against these obstacles and satans. We must avoid things that harm sincerity to the same degree that we avoid snakes and scorpions. As declared by the Prophet Joseph, upon him be peace, "*Yet I do not claim myself free of error, for assuredly the human carnal soul always commands evil, except that my Lord has mercy*," (12: 53) the carnal, evil-commanding soul should not be trusted. Do not let egotism or the evil-commanding soul deceive you! In order to remove the obstacles before sincerity so that we gain and preserve sincerity, let the following principles be a guide for you:

Your first principle

You should pursue God's good pleasure in your actions. If He is pleased with you, even if the whole world is displeased, it is of no consequence. If He approves, it has no effect even if all others reject your ideas and actions. When He is pleased and approves, even if you do not seek the approval of others, should He will it to be so and His Wisdom requires it, He will make others accept it and be pleased with you. For this reason, it is absolutely necessary to aim at God Almighty's good pleasure in the service of the Qur'an and belief.

Your second principle

You should not criticize your brothers and sisters in their service of the Qur'an or belief, and do not provoke their envy by making a display of your attributes. For a person's hands do not compete with each other, nor do their eyes criticize one another, nor does their tongue oppose their ears, nor does their heart see the faults of the spirit. Rather, their members complete the deficiencies of one another, veil one another's shortcomings, assist one another in meeting their needs, and help one another with their duties. Otherwise, the life of that person's body would be extinguished, their spirit would go away, and their body would decompose.

Similarly, the components of a factory are not in rivalry with one another, nor do they attempt to take precedence over or dominate one another. Nor do they find faults with or criticize one another, destroying each other's enthusiasm for work or condemning the others to idleness. Rather they help one another to work with all their capacities for the achievement of a common goal, and proceed towards the realization of the purpose of their existence in true solidarity and unity. Should even the slightest encroachment or domination interfere, it would cause confusion in the working of the factory, making it dysfunctional. In consequence, the owner of the factory would demolish it completely.

And so, O students of the *Risale-i Nur* who serve the Qur'an! We are the members of a collective personality worthy of the title of "the perfect or universal human." We are like the components of a factory working for eternal happiness in the eternal life. We are also the crew of a blessed ship aiming to carry the Community of Muhammad, upon him be peace and blessings, to the shore of salvation, which is the shore of the Abode of Peace and Happiness. Therefore, we need and are compelled to realize true solidarity and unity, which can only be attained through sincerity and which can gain for four people the power of one thousand one hundred and eleven.[80]

If three 1's do not unite or come together, they will have only the value of 3. But if they unite or come together, they will gain the value of 111. Four separate 4's make 16. But if they come together in true brotherhood, along the same line for the fulfillment of the same duty, they will have the value of the power of 4444. History records numerous events which bear witness to the fact that 16 self-sacrificing people in true brotherhood have obtained

[80] Four 1's put side by side make 1111. (Tr.)

the moral strength of more than 4000 people.[81] This is because each individual in a true, sincere union can also see with the eyes of the other brothers and sisters, and hear with their ears. It is as if each of the ten persons in true solidarity and unity has the value and power of seeing with twenty eyes, thinking with ten intellects, hearing with twenty ears, and working with twenty hands.

Your third principle

You should know that all your power lies in sincerity and truth. Indeed, power lies in truth and sincerity. Even those who are wrong may have power through sincerity despite being wrong.

The service of the Qur'an and belief are evidence of the fact that power lies in truth and sincerity. What we have been trying to do here for seven or eight years of service has been a hundred times greater than my twenty years of service to learning and the Religion in my native region and in Istanbul. Moreover, while in my region and Istanbul I had hundreds more assistants than my brothers and sisters who work with me now, here I am alone, a stranger, and under the surveillance of unjust officials and am persecuted by them. Therefore, I have no doubt that the power which makes our seven or eight years of service here a hundred times more successful than my former twenty years of service comes from your sincerity. I also confess that through your profound sincerity you have saved me to an extent from the ostentation that results from the fame and renown which flattered my soul. I hope God will enable you to attain perfect sincerity and cause me to gain it as well.

You know that all heroes of spirituality support you due to your sincerity. If you want to receive their constant support, you should attain perfect

81 In addition to being the means to innumerable advantages and benefits, solidarity and unity based on sincerity is the strongest shield and point of support against fear, and even death. For when death comes, it takes one soul. A person who strives in true unity with their fellows on the way of God's good pleasure for the realization of the purposes related to the Hereafter, has as many souls as their brothers and sisters. Therefore, such a person meets death with a smile and says, "Even though only one of my souls dies, my other souls will continue to live and cause me to gain as many rewards as they do. So by means of these souls, I will continue to live in respect of reward; I am only dying in respect of sin."

sincerity as described in, *they prefer them (their brothers and sisters in religion) over themselves* (59: 9).

Prefer the souls of your brothers and sisters to your own in honor, position, public approval, and even in things like the material benefits of which the carnal soul is enamored. Be so magnanimous that you are pleased that a friend of yours, not yourself, conveys a most subtle and fine truth of belief to those who are in need of it, thus saving you from feeling conceited. If you desire to gain a reward by conveying such truths, it is harmless and does not incur a sin, but the spirit of sincerity and magnanimity, which should always exist among you, may be damaged.

Your fourth principle

As if it were you who possess the merits and virtues of your brothers and sisters, take pride in them and be thankful to God for them.

The Sufis circulate among themselves such terms as "annihilation in the guide," and "annihilation in the Messenger." I am not a Sufi, but we should have this principle among ourselves as "annihilation in the brothers and sisters." This is called among the brothers and sisters "mutual annihilation." It means the brothers and sisters being annihilated in one another. That is to say, oblivious of their own merits and the pride which may arise from them, each person lives with the merits and feelings of their brothers and sisters in their mind. The basis of our way is brotherhood. My relation with you is not like that between a father and children or a Sufi guide and his pupils. It is rather a relation between brothers and sisters. At the very most, my position of teaching may have some part in it.

Our way is also the closest friendship. Friendship requires being the closest, most self-sacrificing friend, the most appreciative companion, and the most magnanimous brother or sister. The very basis of this form of friendship is heartfelt sincerity. One who destroys this sincerity falls from the pinnacle of friendship. They may possibly fall to the bottom of a very deep pit. They cannot find anything in between to cling on to.

There are two ways. It is possible that those who leave this way of ours now, which is the great highway of the Qur'an, unwittingly help the force of heresy, which is hostile to us. I hope that God will enable those who enter the sacred sphere of the Qur'an of miraculous exposition by way of the

Risale-i Nur always to give support to light, sincerity, and belief, and never to fall into such pits.

O my friends in the service of the Qur'an! One of the most influential means of attaining sincerity and preserving it is "contemplation of death." While long-term worldly ambitions damage sincerity and cause ostentation and worldliness, the "contemplation of death" leads one to abhor ostentation and gain sincerity. By never forgetting death and always considering the transient nature of this worldly life, one can be saved from the tricks of the carnal soul. Followers of Sufi paths and the people of truth who follow the Qur'anic declarations, *Every soul is bound to taste death* (3: 185), and *You will surely die, and surely they (too) will die* (39: 30), have adopted contemplation of death as a principle in their spiritual journeying and have done away with the illusion of remaining in the world eternally. They imagine themselves to be dying, being washed, and buried in the grave. Influenced by this way of prolonged contemplation of death, to an extent they are able to give up long-term worldly ambitions. There are numerous advantages to such contemplation. The Prophetic saying, "Frequently remember that which dispels pleasures and makes them bitter,"[82] urges us to such contemplation. However, since our way is not a Sufi one, but rather the way of journeying directly to the truth, it is not necessary for us to do this in an imaginary or hypothetical form like the Sufis. Rather than concentrating on the future to bring it to the present, we should go to the future in the mind, and contemplate it.

Without the need for imagination or supposition, one can look at one's own corpse, which is the single fruit on the tree of life. Not only will you see your own death, one can also see the death of one's era at some distance. If one goes a bit further, one can observe the death of the world, and this opens the way to perfect sincerity.

Another important means of attaining sincerity is that, based on certain, verified belief and the lights of belief-guided reflective thought on God's works of art—the whole creation—which leads to knowledge of the Maker, we can experience the omnipresence of the All-Compassionate Creator, and without seeking the acceptance or attention of any other than Him, and understanding that by looking to others for help in His presence is not

---

82 *at-Tirmidhi*, "Qiyama" 86; *an-Nasa'i*, "Jana'iz" 3. (Tr.)

right conduct in His presence, we can be saved from ostentation and attain sincerity. This kind of attainment has numerous degrees and stages. To whatever degree a person can benefit from their share, this much is beneficial. Many other truths are mentioned in the *Risale-i Nur* which can save a person from ostentation and gain them sincerity, so we will cut the discussion short here.

Things destroying sincerity

Out of numerous things which destroy sincerity and drive one to ostentation, I will briefly mention two or three as follows:

THE FIRST is that rivalry in material benefits gradually destroys sincerity. It also harms the results of any service done, and causes the loss of the desired material advantage.

Our people have always cherished respect for those who strive for the truth and the Hereafter and have helped them. With the intention of having a share in the service they do sincerely and devotedly, our people have tried to provide for them so that such people would not be preoccupied with earning their livelihood and thus wasting their time. However, help and respect should not be sought or demanded; they should be given willingly. Nor should they be expected or sought by giving the impression of being in need of them. Such support should come without expectations. Otherwise sincerity will be damaged, and one may be a target of the Qur'anic prohibition, *Do not sell My Revelations for a trifling price* (2: 41), with the result that one's good deeds may not be acceptable to God.

Thus, the carnal soul, first desiring and expecting material benefit, then not wanting it to go to others, provokes a feeling of rivalry towards a true brother or sister or a companion in the same service. This damages sincerity, and is sacrilegious to the service done; the person becomes unlovable and disagreeable in the sight of the people of truth and discernment. It also causes the loss of the material benefit intended. This matter requires much elaboration. Therefore, I will cut it short here and relate two examples which will reinforce the sincerity of my true brothers and sisters and the unity between them.

The first example is that in order to have great wealth and power, the worldly people, and even some politicians, committees, and certain manipulators of social life, have adopted the principle of participation in or corporate ownership of wealth. Despite all the disadvantages and misuses such a practice can cause, they can also obtain an amazing power and benefit. However, participation in wealth has many disadvantages and does not change the nature of property. Although each participant enjoys theoretical ownership, they cannot benefit from it. But if believers adopt this principle in deeds pertaining to the Hereafter, it will bring much benefit with no loss. For every partner will enjoy the full reward of the whole of those deeds.

For example, supposing four or five people own a single oil lamp. One brings oil, another a wick, another a mantle, another matches; they light the lamp. Each of them owns the lamp. If each has a mirror on a wall, he will own both a separate, reflected room included in their shared room, and a separate lamp reflected in it.

Similarly, as accepted by the people of truth and required by the comprehensiveness of Divine Mercy and Munificence, the whole of the reward and light that emanates from sincere participation in the wealth to be spent for the afterlife, and brotherly and sisterly solidarity and cooperation, and joint enterprise in full unity will be added to the record of each participant. Therefore, O my brothers and sisters! I hope that God will save you from rivalry in material benefits. However, it is possible that, like some followers of the Sufi paths, you might be deceived in respect of the benefits that pertain to the Hereafter. But you should understand that some personal, minor reward can never be compared with the reward and light to be brought by good deeds done by a group that supports one another, as in the example above.

Second example: In order to attain great results or products from their work, craftsmen join their skills and labor and obtain great wealth. It is narrated that once ten men tried to make needles, each working on their own. As a result of their individual labor, each was able to make three needles a day. Then, adopting the principle of joint enterprise, they came together, one bringing iron, and another lighting the furnace, and another piercing the needles, and another placing them in the furnace, and another sharpening the point, and so on. Each was occupied only with the part of the work assigned to him, wasting no time and also acquiring a specific skill in the art of needle-making. Then they shared among themselves the result of their joint enterprises and division of labor. They saw that instead of three, each had three hundred needles a day as his share. This event was widely circulated among the craftsmen in order to urge them to join their efforts.

So, O my brothers and sisters! If unity and agreement in worldly affairs yield such great results, you can correlate this with how profitable it would be to join efforts in deeds that pertain to the Hereafter, the reward of which is not divided and is given to each participant wholly by Divine Grace. This huge profit should not be lost out of rivalry and insincerity.

The second thing which destroys sincerity is flattering the ego and giving a lofty position to the evil-commanding soul by pursuing public attention and acceptance in the name of fame, renown, or status in people's eyes. This is the most perilous of spiritual diseases, one that leads to ostentation and self-centeredness, which is regarded as a hidden association of partners with God.

O my brothers and sisters! Our way which we try to follow in the service of the wise Qur'an is based on truth and requires true brotherhood. Brotherhood requires self-annihilation among the brothers and sisters and preferring them to oneself.[83] Therefore, there should not be rivalry among us that arises from seeking status in people's eyes. This is totally contrary to our way. Since every individual can enjoy the total honor of all brothers and sisters, I hope that the students of the *Risale-i Nur* are distanced from sacrificing that great collective honor for personal, selfish, competitive, and minor fame and renown. They should be rational and spiritually mature enough not to stoop to such lowly, harmful things. But everyone has an evil-commanding soul, and sometimes selfish impulses and desires can control a person to such extents, despite their heart, mind, and spirit. I never think of accusing your hearts, minds, or spirits. But the carnal soul, impulses, desires, and fancies sometimes deceive. For this reason, you are sometimes warned severely. The severity in the warnings is because of these impulses, desires, and fancies. Therefore, act cautiously.

If our way had been based on submission to a *shaykh*, there would have been a single position or a limited number of inferior positions. Numerous capacities would have been candidates for these positions, and this would have provoked envy and selfishness. But our way is based on brotherhood. No brother or sister can be another's parent or assume the position of spiritual guide. Brotherhood entails a broad range of positions, and allows no

---

83 Happy is the one who, in order to have a large pool of sweet water flowing from the heavenly spring of the Qur'an, casts their ego, which is like a block of ice, into the pool and melts it.

rivalry or contest. Brothers and sisters are helpers and supporters of one another, each completing another's service. This demonstrates how harmful it would be to cherish greed for personal reward; competing for personal reward in ways that are based on a fatherly position or that of a spiritual guide, despite whatever personal excellence or spiritual attainments they may possess, causes followers on some Sufi paths to suffer greatly from rivalry and disagreements among themselves. Their vast, sacred power cannot withstand the gales of heresies.

THE THIRD OBSTACLE to gaining sincerity is fear and avarice. Referring you to the Six Human and Satanic Intrigues (The Fourth Section of the Twenty-Ninth Letter in *The Letters*), where this obstacle has been explained together with some others, I make all His All-Beautiful Names our intercessor with Him, and entreat the Most Compassionate of the compassionate that He will enable us to attain perfect sincerity.

> O God! For the sake of Surat al-Ikhlas (the Qur'anic Chapter of Sincerity), include us among Your servants sincere and endowed with sincerity. Amen. Amen.

All-Glorified are You. We have no knowledge save what You have taught us. Surely You are the All-Knowing, the All-Wise.

A confidential letter to some of my brothers

I will mention an aspect of two *hadiths* to my brothers who appear bored and reluctant to serve the Qur'an and belief by writing and making multiple copies of the *Risale-i Nur*'s parts, and prefer certain supererogatory acts of worship in these three months, namely Rajab, Sha'ban and Ramadan, which are the months of concentration on worship more than other times. Serving the Qur'an and belief is actually a sort of worship in five respects.[84]

---

[84] We asked our teacher about these five respects. The answer we received is below:

- Such efforts strive to defend the Qur'an and belief against the people of misguidance and heresy, which is the most important *jihad* at the present.
- They serve our teacher by helping him to communicate the truths of belief.
- They serve Muslims in respect of belief.
- They provide religious education and knowledge through writing.
- They ensure worship in the form of reflective thought, one hour of which may sometimes be equal to a year's supererogatory worship.

Signed: Rüşdü, Husrev, Rafet

The first *hadith* is, "(At the Last Judgment,) the ink spent by true scholars of the Religion is equal in weight to the blood of the martyrs."[85]

The second *hadith* is, "Whoever follows my Sunna when my Community is corrupted, there is for him (or her) the reward of a hundred martyrs."[86]

O brothers and sisters who show boredom and reluctance. These two *hadiths* together show that a drop of the black light—ink, which is like the water of life—that flows from the blessed pens serving the truths of belief, the essentials of the Islamic life, and the elevated Sunna of the Prophet, upon him be peace and blessings, at this time may be of use to you on Judgment Day as being equal to a hundred drops of the blood of martyrs. Therefore, try to gain this!

If you say: The *hadith* mentions the scholars, but some of us are only scribes.

The Answer: One who carefully studies these treatises for a year to understand them fully can be an important, eminent scholar of this time. Even if they do not understand them fully, the students of the *Risale-i Nur* have a collective personality, and this is surely a scholar of this time. Your pens are the fingers of that collective personality. Although, in my view, I am not entitled to be regarded as such, due to your good opinion of me you have regarded me as your teacher and as a religious scholar. Since I have difficulty in writing, your pens may be regarded as mine, and you will receive the reward indicated in the *hadith*.

Said Nursi

---

85 al-Ghazzali, *Ihya'u 'Ulum ad-Din*, 1:6, 8; Ibn Hajar al-Asqalani, *Lisan al-Mizan*, 5:225; al-Munawi, *Fayd al-Qadir*, 6:466. (Tr.)

86 at-Tabarani, *al-Mu'jam al-Awsat*, 5:315; al-Bayhaki, *Sunan*, "Zuhd" 118. (Tr.)

The Twenty-Second Gleam

The Twenty-Second Gleam

Why the worldly people continuously interfere with Said Nursi's afterlife • Does Said Nursi aim to secure power and social position for himself? • Answers to cruel treatment by certain local authorities

In His Name, All-Glorified is He.

I present this brief treatise, which I wrote twenty-two years ago to my most sincere and trusted brothers while in the village of Barla in the province of Isparta, to the governor of Isparta and the Justice and Security Departments, so that those who have been keeping me under strict surveillance for twenty-five to thirty years may understand that we have no secrets. They should know that our greatest secret is this treatise.

Said Nursi

Three indications

> *Whoever puts his trust in God, He is sufficient for him (for all his needs). God surely executes what He decrees; assuredly God has appointed a measure for everything.* (65: 3)

This matter consists of three indications.

First indication

AN IMPORTANT QUESTION ABOUT MY PERSON AND THE *RISALE-I NUR*: Many people ask me, "Although you do not interfere with the world of the worldly people, why do they interfere with your afterlife at every opportunity, and yet the law of no country interferes with those who live a reclusive life?"

THE ANSWER: The answer of the New Said to this question is to remain silent. He says, "Let Divine Destiny provide the answer for me." But the head of the Old or Former Said, which the New Said has temporarily borrowed, feels compelled to say as follows:

Those who should answer this question are the local government of the province of Isparta and its people. For this question concerns them more than me. As the local government, which consists of hundreds of people, and a population composed of hundreds of thousands of people, are obliged to think about the matter on my behalf and defend me, why should I speak to the prosecutors unnecessarily and defend myself? For I have been in this province for almost nine years, and I am turning my back more and more on their world. I have nothing which has remained hidden. Even my most confidential treatises are circulating in the hands of government authorities and some members of parliament. If I had had an idea and made an attempt to interfere in worldly affairs, which would have been something to cause alarm and anxiety, the local authorities of this province would have known about it. Although they have been keeping me under surveillance for nearly nine years, and I have unhesitatingly told everything about me to those who have visited me, they have been unable to find anything contrary to law on my part so that they could arrest and punish me. If I have committed a blameworthy act that could harm this country's happiness and future, all the members of the local authorities, from the governor to the village police chief, should be held responsible for it, and in order to be absolved of it, they should be obliged to defend me by making a mountain out of a molehill against those who do so in order to be able to accuse me. Therefore, I refer the answer of this question to them.

As for why the people of this province are obliged to defend me more than myself; for nine years I have been trying to serve both the worldly and eternal happiness of these dear, friendly and brotherly people and to strengthen their belief by means of nearly one hundred treatises, which have demonstrated their influence. Neither have they suffered any harm because of these works, nor has any sign of purposeful political inclination been provoked in them. Rather, all praise be to God, due to the strength of the belief of the people and their firmness in attachment to the Religion, which they have acquired by means of the *Risale-i Nur*, this province of Isparta has gained some sort of sanctity resembling that of Damascus of former times and the University of al-Azhar in Egypt. In addition, the *Risale-i Nur* has brought this province greater piety than that of all other provinces, as it has caused the people's strength of belief to prevail over heedlessness in their zeal for worship, and over a carefree, dissipated life. Therefore, these people, including even the irreligious among them—if there are any—must feel obliged to defend me and the *Risale-i Nur* for their own benefit. It is totally their right to defend me, so my insignificant right does not drive me to defend myself at a time when I, a powerless one, have already completed my duty and, thanks be to God, thousands of students have worked and are still working in my place. A man who has so many thousands of advocates does not need to defend his own case.

Second indication

This is an answer to a criticizing question.

The worldly people ask, "Why are you resentful towards us? You have not applied to us even once, and have remained silent. You complain about us bitterly and say that we are persecuting you. But we have our own principles; we have some particular rules, as demanded by this age. You reject their applicability to you. One who applies the law is not an oppressor, and one who does not accept the law is rebellious. In this age of freedom and in this new republican era, the principles of egalitarianism and the abolition of despotism are our basic laws. But your former life and present lifestyle show that you are trying to secure power and social position beyond the government's power and influence by drawing public attention and gaining public acceptance through the position of religious teacher and appearing as an ascetic. This may be tolerated under a bourgeois government, but we prefer to adopt the principles of socialism and Bolshevism, which have emerged with the awakening of our common people. Therefore, your position opposes our principles and is disagreeable to us. For this reason, you have no right to complain or be resentful about the distress we cause you."

THE ANSWER: If those who launch a new way in human social life do not act in conformity with the Divine laws of the creation and the operation of the universe, they cannot be successful in their attempts at progress and in doing good things. Rather, their actions only serve evil and destruction. Therefore, one can be successful in realizing absolute equality among human beings only by changing the basic nature of humanity and abolishing the Divine wisdom in its creation. I belong to the class of common people both by birth and lifestyle, and sincerely adopt the principle of the equality of rights before the law in my way of thinking and action. And due to my innate compassion and the justice ordered by Islam, I am one of those who have opposed the despotism and oppression of the elite known as the bourgeoisie for a long time. I therefore support absolute justice and oppose wrongdoing, despotism, and oppression with all my strength.

However, basic human nature and the wisdom in the creation of humanity are not in conformity with absolute egalitarianism. For the All-Wise Originator, Who in order to show the perfection of His Power and Wisdom makes a single thing yield a great result or fulfill numerous duties, and Who has numerous books written on a single page, causes humankind to carry out the duties of thousands of species. It is for this significant reason that God Almighty has created humankind with a nature that would divide it into as many "classes" as there are animal species. He has not restricted by birth the powers, faculties and feelings of humanity as He has restricted those of animals, but has equipped it with the capacity to rise to the limitless ranks of progress and accomplishment. Because of this, while being a single species, humanity has become like thousands of species and has been appointed as the ruler of the earth—the species which should work for the prosperity of the world in accordance with the Divine laws—and become the fruit of the universe or the final result of creation and the monarch of living beings.

Thus, the most important mechanism of variety in humankind is competition in virtue which, in turn, arises from belief. Virtue can be removed from humanity only by changing human nature, extinguishing the power of reason, killing the heart, and destroying the spirit. Although they should have been flung in the face of this age, which has brought an awful tyranny under the veil of freedom, the following lines were wrongfully flung in the face of a very important person:

> How can it be possible to destroy freedom through tyranny and injustice?
> Try and remove consciousness, if you are able to, from humankind!

In place of these lines, I would like to say what follows, flinging it in the face of this age:

> How can it be possible to destroy truth through tyranny and injustice?
> Try and remove the heart, if you are able to, from humankind!

Or,

> How can it be possible to destroy virtue through tyranny and injustice?
> Try and remove conscience, if you are able to, from humankind!

Virtue arising from belief can be the cause of neither oppression nor despotism. Oppression and despotism mean a lack of virtue. The people of virtue prefer participating in human social life through the admission of human innate powerlessness, poverty, and humility. All praise be to God, I have always followed and am following this same way in my life. I have never claimed virtue on my part, but I say in thankfulness to God Almighty for His favor that He has favored me with the virtue of understanding and serving the branches of knowledge of belief and the Qur'an. All praise be to God, I have always used this Divine favor for the benefit and happiness of this Muslim nation with His help. I have never intended to make it a means of domination over others and have always hated and avoided public attention and acceptance, which is sought by the majority of the people of heedlessness.

And so, O worldly people! Although I have never participated, nor have any intention to participate, as testified by my life during these nine years of captivity, in your world nor have had anything to do with your principles, according to what law and with the purpose of what benefit have you inflicted all this surveillance and oppression on me? No government in the world allows such lawless treatment and no one can approve of it. Therefore, it is not only I who am resentful of such a degree of ill-treatment; if they knew of it, the whole of humanity, and even the universe, would find it completely repugnant and strongly resent it.

Third indication

A demagogic, crazy question:

Some authorities say: Since you live in this country, you must obey the laws of the Republic. But why do you evade these laws under the guise of seclusion? For example, it is contrary to the laws and the principle of equality adopted by the Republic to assume some merit or virtue which does not arise from one's duty, or to exercise power and influence through it. Why do you have your hands kissed, although you have no official job, and why do you assume an attitude of self-advertising so that people may lend an ear to you?

The Answer: Those who apply the laws should apply them first to themselves and then to others. By not applying a principle to yourself which you impose on others, you are first of all violating and opposing your own principles and laws. For you demand to apply the principle of absolute equality to me. Therefore I say as follows:

Whenever a private shares the same social status and public respect and attention as a marshal, or whenever a marshal lowers himself to the status of a private and has no value whatsoever outside his duty, or whenever a brilliant, victorious chief of military staff receives from people the same degree of attention and respect that the simplest private does, then you can talk about absolute equality and say to me accordingly, "Do not call yourself a religious teacher! Do not accept any respect! Deny whatever virtue you have! Serve your own servant! Be a companion of beggars!"

You say: "Respect and public position and attention are enjoyed in office and are particular to those who have official duties. You are a man without a job, so you cannot accept public respect like those who have official jobs."

The Answer: If humans consisted of only a body and were immortal in the world, and if the door of the grave were to be eternally closed and death were eliminated, and if duties were then to be restricted only to the military and government officials, your words would have some meaning. But since humans do not consist only of a body, then the heart, tongue, and mind cannot be plucked out to feed the body. They too require sustenance.

Further, since the door of the grave cannot be closed, and everyone first and foremost worries about the future beyond the grave, then the duties that require public obedience and respect are not restricted only to political and military positions that relate to the worldly life. As it is a duty to give passports to those who travel abroad, so it is a duty to give passports to those who travel towards eternity and to give them light to illuminate their dark way; no other duty can be more important than this. One can deny such a duty only by denying death and contradicting the testimony of tens of thousands of witnesses who every day sign the signatures of their corpses to the truth, "Death is a reality."

Since there are moral and religious duties required to meet the essential, immaterial needs of people, the most important of those duties involves providing passports for the journey towards eternity, pocket torches of the heart in the darkness of the intermediate realm of the grave, belief as the key to eternal happiness, and instruction in belief and its strengthening. Surely, the learned who fulfill these duties will not deny in ingratitude the blessing of knowledge and the virtue of belief bestowed on them by God, nor lower themselves to the level of the dissolute and sinners. They will not contaminate themselves with the heresies and vices of the base. For this reason they prefer solitude, which you do not like and suppose to be inequality.

Despite this being the truth, I say the following, not to those arrogant ones like you who persecute me and go farther in egotism and violation of the law of equality than Pharaoh—because the arrogant suppose humility to be abasement, so one should not be humble before them—but rather, I say this to the fair-minded, the humble, and the just:

> All praise be to God, I am aware of my faults and innate powerlessness as a human being. Far from arrogantly demanding a respected status of superiority over Muslims, I would always prefer to see my endless faults and insignificance, find consolation in imploring God for forgiveness, and ask people for prayers rather than respect. I think all my companions know this state of mine. However, while serving the wise Qur'an and teaching the truths of belief, in order to preserve the dignity of learning that is required by that position, on account of those truths and in honor of the Qur'an, and in order not to bow before the people of misguidance, I temporarily take on that attitude of dignity. I think it is not the right of the worldly people's laws to oppose this!

An astonishing kind of treatment: It is well known that everywhere the learned and authorities of education make judgments according to knowledge and learning. They feel respect and friendship towards all those in whom they see knowledge and learning, wherever they may find them, on account of their profession. Even when a professor from a hostile country comes to this country, the learned and university lecturers visit him out of respect for his learning, and pay respect to him.

However, when (during the days of the invasion of Istanbul) the highest council of the British clergy asked for a six-hundred-word answer to the six questions put to the Office of the Shaykhul-Islam, a man of learning, one who has been subjected to the disrespect of the native authorities of education, provided a six-word answer and this had wide approval. That same man of learning has opposed the most basic principles and thoughts of certain irreligious philosophers of the West with the true knowledge he received from the Qur'an, and has triumphed in his way of thought and belief. Also, six months before the declaration of the Second Constitution, he challenged both the religious scholars and scholars of modern sciences to a debate, and himself asking no questions, gave completely correct answers to their questions.[87] Having devoted all of his life to the happiness of this nation, he has published almost a hundred treatises in their language to illuminate them. But how unfortunate it is that those who have caused that man—a fellow-citizen, co-religionist, friend, and brother—the greatest trouble, those who have been nurturing enmity towards him, and indeed showing him disrespect, are certain members of the departments of formal education and religious affairs.

Now, what do you have to say about this? Is this civilization? Is this devotion to education? Is this patriotism? Is this nationalism? Is this republicanism? God forbid! It is none of these. It is Divine Destiny allowing a man of learning to receive enmity instead of the friendship that he had hoped for, or the respect he should have received, so that he should not contaminate his purity of intention to serve the Qur'an and belief with a show of knowledge.

Conclusion

AN ASTONISHING ASSAULT WHICH IN FACT WAS THE MEANS TO THANKFULNESS

Those extremely arrogant worldly people are so sensitive in their egotism that if their most recent treatment of me had been conscious, it would have

87 This way of address does not belong to the New Said. It belongs to the Old or Former Said and is directed at the arrogant persecutors among the worldly.

been regarded as some sort of wonder-working or one of great genius. It is as follows:

As if perceiving in me some degree of ostentatious egotism through their sensitive balance of egotism, they violently counter my egotism, which I have not perceived. For these last eight or nine years, I have experienced eight or nine times that after being treated unjustly by them, I have contemplated Divine Destiny and searched out the tricks of my soul, thinking, "Why has Destiny set them to trouble me?" Each time I have come to understand that my soul showed a natural, unconscious tendency to egotism, or it deceived me knowingly. So, I have concluded that Divine Destiny did justice to me through the wrongdoing of these tyrants.

For example, this summer my friends brought a fine horse for me to mount. I rode to an excursion area. Since a selfish desire for recreation appeared in me without my being aware of it, the worldly people countered that desire of mine so fiercely that they destroyed not only that hidden desire, but also my appetite for many other things. It even occurred that after Ramadan, on discovering an appreciative allusion to our service of a great, holy, saintly scholar from the distant past, which meant a wonder-working of his penetrating the Unseen, my soul attempted to assume, under the guise of thankfulness, an ostentatious egotism due to the sincerity and piety of my brothers and sisters and the respect shown towards me by visitors and their good opinion of us. Suddenly, with their boundless sensitivity and as if perceiving even the smallest traces of ostentation, the worldly people attacked me. I thank God Almighty that their wrongdoing became a means of rediscovering sincerity for me.

> *And say: "My Lord! I seek refuge in You from the promptings and provocations of the satans. I seek refuge in You, my Lord, lest they be present with me."* (23:97–98)

> O God! O All-Protecting! O Best of Protectors! Protect me and protect my friends from the evil of the evil-commanding soul and Satan, and from the evil of the jinn and humans, and from the evil of the people of misguidance and the people of rebellion. Amen. Amen. Amen.

All-Glorified are You. We have no knowledge save what You have taught us. Surely You are the All-Knowing, the All-Wise.

The
Twenty-Third Gleam

The Twenty-Third Gleam

On nature or refuting naturalistic atheism

A reminder

The way of disbelieving naturalists is extremely irrational and based on superstitious beliefs. But why are such famous, intelligent naturalist philosophers able to accept such an obviously superstitious way of thought? The fact is that they cannot discern the reality of their way, which cannot help but yield such superstitious beliefs, although it is impossible to arrive at them reasonably or to accept them. They violently attack the Qur'an and the truths and essentials of belief, condemning whatever they cannot grasp as superstitious, and base their unbelief on nature. The Qur'anic verse, *Their Messengers said: "Can there be any doubt about God, the Originator of the heavens and the earth?"* (14: 10), which declares the existence and Oneness of God, is in fact too obvious to require discussion. Therefore, I will try to show why this is so and why it is impossible reasonably to infer the results the naturalist philosophers have arrived at with their methods. However, since numerous proofs for the existence and Oneness of God have been elaborated in certain parts of the *Risale-i Nur*, I will offer here some other proofs and make a brief mention of some different proofs where necessary.

Introduction

O human! There are certain monstrous phrases uttered by people that imply unbelief. Some believers also use them without realizing what they actually mean. I will explain three of the most important of these.

THE FIRST: "The causes have brought it about."

THE SECOND: "Things have formed by themselves."

THE THIRD: "It is natural; nature necessitates and creates it."

Indeed, since things undeniably exist, and, as clearly observed, each thing comes into existence with great artistry and many wise purposes, and since nothing is eternal or without beginning, and everything comes into existence within time, then, O unbeliever, either things, for example, that animal, have been invented by lifeless, unconscious, deaf, and blind material causes coming together in a way requiring universal knowledge, consciousness, and will, or they form by themselves, or nature, or what you call natural powers, caused it to exist. There is a fourth alternative that combined with absolute Knowledge and Will, the Power of an All-Powerful One of Majesty has invented it. Since there is no other way to explain the existence of things other than these four, if the first three can decisively be proven to be impossible, the fourth way, which is the way of Divine Oneness, will necessarily and undoubtedly be proven true.

The first way

This is the theory that things come into existence by the coming together of material causes. Out of numerous arguments that show the falsity and impossibility of such a stance, I will mention only three.

THE FIRST IMPOSSIBILITY

Suppose there are hundreds of jars full of quite different substances in a pharmacy. We want to make some sort of liquid medicine or ointment out of them. So we go to the pharmacy and find out what the necessary ingredients are and what amount of each we should use. We see that an extremely precise amount should be taken from every ingredient. If the minutest amount more or less is taken, both medicine and ointment will lose their special properties and be of no use.

Is it at all possible or conceivable that those jars could be knocked over by a storm and exactly the required amount from each ingredient should come together to form the medicine and ointment demanded? Can there be something more superstitious or absurd than seeing such a coincidental formation as possible?

In this example we should think of each thing, particularly each living thing, as an animate ointment and each plant a living medicine. They are composed of numerous substances taken from a great variety of things in extremely precise amounts. Their attribution to the coincidental coming together of physical causes is much more impossible and inconceivable than the formation of any ointment or medicine as a result of the accidental coming together of substances in precisely required amounts, pouring from the jars as in the example.

In short, it is only by an all-comprehensive, limitless Wisdom, an infinite Knowledge, and an all-encompassing Will that any living thing in this vast pharmacy of the universe can be formed from the ingredients taken from substances in extremely precise amounts and measured on the scales of Divine Destiny or Determining and Decree. One who claims that they are the work of blind, deaf, and ignorant "natural causes and powers," or elements like floods, is more stupid than the one who asserts that the medicine in the example is self-formed as the result of the jars being knocked over.

The second impossibility

If everything is attributed to "natural causes," not to the All-Powerful One of Majesty, the One and Unique, this means that many of the physical elements and causes should be present and work in the body of every living thing or being. However, that so many different and conflicting causes and elements come together of their own accord in perfect order and extremely precise measurements in the body of even the smallest of creatures, like a tiny fly, is so obviously inconceivable that one with even the smallest bit of consciousness could say, "This is inconceivable; it cannot occur." Indeed, the tiny body of a fly has a relationship and connection with most of the elements and causes in the universe; in fact, it is a summary or index of them. If it is not attributed to the Eternal, Powerful One, those elements and physical causes should be present and operate in it of their own accord. It is even required that they should be present and work in each of the cells of its eyes, which are tiny samples of its body. For if the causes or agents responsible for something's existence are of a physical nature, they should be present in the immediate vicinity of, rather, inside their result. Therefore, attributing a fly to "natural" causes and elements requires that those causes and elements should be present and work in each of its cells. Even the most foolish of the people of sophistry would be ashamed of such an assumption.

THE THIRD IMPOSSIBILITY

It is an established rule that "a single, unique thing of particular individuality can only have issued from a single, unique source." If, in particular, a thing is a living one with a perfectly ordered and most sensitively balanced life, it will self-evidently display that it has not issued from numerous, different hands, which would be certain to cause great confusion and conflict, but rather it has issued from the Hand of a single All-Powerful, All-Wise One. Furthermore, the random coming together of innumerable inanimate, ignorant, unrestricted, unconscious, blind, and deaf "natural" causes and elements for the existence of something would only cause the increase of their blindness and deafness amidst the limitless probabilities. Therefore, attributing any being, which has a unique, particular individuality formed of innumerable elements in perfect order and a most sensitively balanced way, to such causes would be as unreasonable as accepting numberless impossibilities all at once.

Ignoring these impossibilities, physical causes or agents or powers affect something through direct contact. However, they have contact only with the exteriors of things or beings. But we see that the interiors of living beings in particular, where the hands of physical or "natural" causes or agents have no contact, are ten times better ordered, more delicate, and artistic than their exteriors. The tiniest living things, the minutest creatures, which the hands of physical or "natural" causes and agents cannot reach and with which they do not have direct contact, not even with their exteriors, are more strange and wonderful in art and more amazing in creation than the largest creatures. This being the case, only one who is a hundred times more deaf and blind than the inanimate, ignorant, crude, distant, and conflicting causes and elements can attribute these creatures to those causes and elements.

The second way

This is the claim that things are formed by themselves. This is equally inconceivable and impossible in numerous ways. As examples, we will explain three of them.

The first impossibility

O denier of the Creator! You can accept something that is impossible as possible in numerous ways. For you exist and are not a simple, inanimate, or unchanging substance. Rather, you are like a perfectly well-ordered and continuously renewed factory or like a wonderful palace that undergoes continuous change and renewal. Innumerable particles are ceaselessly working in your body, which has connections and mutual relations with the universe, particularly in respect of the provision and permanence of your species. The particles in your body are careful not to destroy those connections and relations. It is as if they consider the entire universe from the perspective of your relations with it and assume their positions accordingly. Therefore, if you do not accept that the particles in your body are not tiny officials moving in accordance with the law of the Eternal, All-Powerful One, or the soldiers of one of His hosts, or the nibs of the Pen of Divine Destiny, or the points of the Pen of the Divine Power, then each particle working in your eye would have to have an eye capable of seeing the whole of your body together with the whole of the universe, with which your body is connected and related. You would also have to ascribe to each particle an intelligence equivalent to that of a hundred geniuses; it would have to have the capacity to know your whole past and future, your ancestors and descendants, the origins of the elements that form your body, and the sources of your sustenance. Attributing the consciousness and knowledge of a thousand Platos to an unintelligent particle is obviously misguided.

The second impossibility

Your body also resembles a wonderful palace that has a thousand domes kept in suspense with the stones all supporting one another. Rather, your body is a thousand times more wonderful than any palace. For that palace of your body is constantly renewed in perfect order. Even if we ignore your spirit, your heart, and other immaterial faculties, each of which is extremely wonderful, each member of your body is like a domed mansion. Supporting one another in perfect order and balance, your atoms form miracles of Art and Power, such as the eyes and the tongue. If those atoms were not officials working in perfect obedience to the orders of the Builder of that universe, then each of them would have to both dominate and be dominated by all the other atoms of the body, and be the origin of many Attributes that belong to the Necessarily Existent One exclusively, yet be both absolutely independent and dependent at the same time. Therefore, attributing any existent being, which has a unique individuality because of being a work of the Single One of Unity and Uniqueness, to the innumerable atoms that form it, is an obvious, hundred-fold impossibility.

THE THIRD IMPOSSIBILITY

If your body had not been "written" by the Pen of the Eternal All-Powerful One, Who is One and Unique, and were rather a work of nature or "natural" causes, then there would have to be as many printing-blocks or molds of nature as the number of its cells and the compounds they form in your body contained one within the other. For example, this book in your hand has either been written by a single scribe based on his knowledge, or if you claim that it has been formed by itself or nature, then there would have to be as many keys as the number of its letters. There are as many iron letters in a printing press as the number of the letters in the alphabet. They have to be arranged one by one in order to write a word, and therefore it can be said that as many iron letters as there are letters of a book are required for a book to produce itself. Furthermore, there is a kind of calligraphy consisting of only one large letter, yet, in which, for example, a whole Qur'anic *sura* of five or six pages can be written. This means that in order to write a single letter in a printing press, we need thousands of iron letters. Similarly, each living thing or being is like such a letter. It contains almost everything that exists in the universe. So, just as the attribution of a book to itself or to its iron letters requires those letters to come together by themselves in a conscious, meaningful way in a printing press, if we attribute a living thing or being to itself, then we would have to accept that all of the atoms or innumerable samples of the universe have come together consciously to form it. Even if we were to accept this ridiculous idea, which involves as many impossibilities as the particles of a living being, even of the universe, it is infinitely far from explaining life and its origin, or the many immaterial faculties of a conscious living being, such as reason, consciousness, and willpower.

The third way

This is the claim that "it is natural; nature necessitates it and has created it." This claim also involves numerous impossibilities, only three of which follow:

The first impossibility

If the art and creativity observed in living beings that display infinite knowledge, wisdom, and willpower are attributed not to the Pen of Determining and the Power of the Eternal Sun but to blind, deaf, and unconscious nature and "natural powers," this means that we accept that either nature should have present innumerable machines or printing presses in every being to invent it or nature should include in every being enough knowledge, will, power, and wisdom to create and administer the universe.

Consider that we see a reflection of the sun in every transparent thing, in every piece of glass or bubble of water. If we do not attribute the suns appearing in every transparent thing to the one and single sun in the sky, then we have to accept that in all things, even in those that are so small that they cannot contain a match head, there is a miniature sun that possesses all the qualities of the sun in the sky. In addition, we would also have to accept that there are as many suns as there are reflections of the sun in every piece of glass or every bubble in the oceans, rivers, or lakes, and so on.

In exactly the same way, if all existent things, animate or inanimate, are not attributed to the manifestations of the Names of the Eternal Sun, then we would have to accept that everything, particularly every living thing or being, has in itself a nature or a power or, quite simply, a deity, that possesses infinite knowledge, will, power, and wisdom. Such an idea is the most false and superstitious of the impossibilities in the universe. One who ascribes the Art of the Creator of the universe to unconscious nature or certain nominal powers lacks consciousness more than any other being.

The second impossibility

If all those perfectly ordered, and most artistically and wisely fashioned things and beings were attributed not to an infinitely Powerful and Wise One, but to nature, this would mean that nature should have in every bit of soil as many factories and printing presses as exist in Europe so that each bit of soil can be the means for the formation and growth of the flowers and fruit-bearing trees which grow there. For a pot of soil displays the actual capacity to give shape and form to the many different flowers whose seeds are buried in it. So, if those flowers are not attributed to the All-Powerful One of Majesty, then there would have to be a different machine for each flower in the soil.

Like sperms and eggs, all seeds are formed of the same elements. Each is a composition of oxygen, hydrogen, carbon and nitrogen, and is exposed to the effects of such unconscious things as air, water, heat, and light. But we see that each flower has a particular shape, smell, and color, and is completely different from others. Therefore, this requires that in that soil there should be as many factories as there are in Europe so that all those different living fabrics, thousands of various embroidered textiles, could be woven.

Thus, you can see how unreasonable are the naturalists' and materialists' claims, and how unscientific and superstitious is attributing creativity to nature or causes or to things themselves.

If you ask: How do the difficulties that arise from the attribution of existence to nature disappear when existence is attributed to the Unique, Eternally Besought-of-All? How does existence, which is inconceivable when attributed to nature, become easy and necessary when attributed to God, the One and Unique?

The Answer: We have seen when explaining the existence of a sun in every transparent thing on the earth, including every drop or bubble of water in the oceans that it is inconceivable and impossible for there to be as many suns as there appears to be. But if we attribute those (reflected) suns to the single sun in the sky, it is extremely easy to explain their existence. (It can even be said that the existence of the sun makes the existence of innumerable reflected suns necessary and inevitable.) Likewise, attributing all existent things to a Unique, Eternally Besought-of-All makes their existence so easy that we cannot help but think that their existence is necessary and inevitable. A connection between them and that Unique One is enough for their existence. But if this connection is cut off, with each thing being left to nature or to itself, then we would have to accept that in order to create a tiny creature like a fly, which is a miniature sample of the universe, blind and deaf nature should have enough knowledge, power, and wisdom to create and govern the entire universe. This is a thousand-fold impossibility.

In short, just as it is inconceivable and impossible that the Necessarily-Existent One should have any partner or like in His Divine Essence, so too is the participation or interference of others in His creation and Lordship over His creation inconceivable and impossible.

As for the second part of the question, as stated in many other parts of the *Risale-i Nur*, when existence is attributed to the Single One of Uniqueness, then the being of all things becomes as easy as that of a single thing. But if it is attributed to "natural" causes or nature, it becomes as difficult for each thing to exist as it is for all things.

When a person joins the military or is connected to the state as an official, that person can be the means for the fulfillment of duties that exceed their own individual power and influence by a hundred thousand times. They can even take a king captive in the name of the state. Yet this person does not, nor are they compelled to, carry the equipment and power necessary to fulfill all the duties in which they play a part. By reason of their connection, the army, which is their point of support, carries such necessities. Therefore, any duties this one person carries out may be as great as those of the army or state. It is just like an ant as an official of God being able to destroy the palace of the Pharaoh, or a fly killing Nimrod, or a pine seed, the size of a grain of wheat, producing all the parts of a huge pine tree.[88] If the connection of the person with the army is severed, leaving them to their own devices, then either their power will be restricted to themselves, or

[88] Due to its connection with the Creator, that seed works under the command of Divine Destiny or Determining and is the means for the fulfillment of many extraordinary duties. If that connection is cut off, the creation of the seed requires more capacity, equipment, and skill than it takes to create a huge pine tree. For all the parts of the pine tree, which is a work of Divine Power, would be present in the potential tree—the seed, which is a work of Divine Destiny. The factory that produces a tree is a seed. The tree encapsulated in the seed by Destiny grows into a tree with that Power.

they will have to carry all the equipment belonging to the army and possess its power if they are required to carry out the same duties as they do as a member of the army. Even the clowns who invent stories and fantasies to make people laugh would be too ashamed to relate the second case.

To cut it short, when attributed to the Necessarily Existent One, the existence of all things is so easy as to be regarded as necessary and inevitable. But when attributed to nature, the existence of all things is unreasonable, impossible, and inconceivable.

The third impossibility

The following two comparisons, which are mentioned in some other parts of the *Risale-i Nur*, explain this impossibility:

The First Comparison: A wild, uneducated man enters a palace which has been built in a vast desert and decorated with all the fruits of civilization. Having examined all the thousands of marvelous, artistically made objects, as there is no one in the palace and due to his ignorance and lack of sufficient intelligence, he thinks that one of the objects in the palace must have made the palace with whatever there is in it. But whichever object he examines, he cannot convince even his crude and uneducated intellect that that object has built the palace.

Later, he finds a notebook in which there is written the detailed plan of the palace, a list of its contents, and the rules of its management. It is also impossible for the notebook, which has no hands, eyes, or tools, to have built and decorated the palace. However, having not encountered anything visible to which he can attribute the existence of the palace, and since in comparison with the other objects the notebook, which contains the rules of the palace's construction, decoration, and management, seems to be more able to explain its existence, the man feels obliged to say, "It is this notebook which designed and built the palace, and decorated it with all those objects, which it had made and set in this palace." Is this not sheer stupidity and nonsense?

As in this comparison, a naturalist who denies God enters this palace of the universe, which is infinitely more well-ordered and more perfect than the palace in the above-mentioned comparison, and which is decorated with miracles of Wisdom throughout. Not thinking that it is the work of the

Necessarily Existent Being's Art, Who is beyond the sphere of contingency, and evading that thought, he focuses on what they wrongly call "nature." Nature is, in fact, a board of Divine Destiny or Determining in the sphere of contingency. Divine Destiny or Determining uses it for inscribing and erasing Its judgments. From another perspective, nature is an ever-changing notebook of the titles or laws of the Divine Power's regular acts, and an index of the works of His Art as the Lord of the worlds. However, the naturalist who enters the palace of the universe says, "All these things require a cause for their existence. There is nothing visible that is more apt than this 'notebook' to attribute it to. Even though it is completely unreasonable to accept this blind, unconscious, ignorant, and powerless 'notebook' as the creator of the palace of the universe, which clearly requires an infinite knowledge and power for its existence, since I do not admit the existence of the Eternal Maker, I had better say that this 'notebook' has made this palace." To which we reply:

> O foolish one! Lift your head out of the swamp of naturalism, and turn round! You will see the Maker of Majesty, to Whom all things, from atoms to galaxies, testify, each with its own tongue, and at Whom they point, each with its own finger. Behold the manifestation of the Eternal Designer, Who has made that palace and written its program in that "notebook"! Lend an ear to His Book—the Qur'an—and be saved from your nonsensical words!

The Second Comparison: An extremely rough, uneducated man enters a magnificent barracks. He watches the disciplined actions of a marvelously ordered army carrying out its drill. A regiment, a battalion, and an army corps sit down, stand up, march, and take up and put down arms as though they were a single private. Since his crude mind cannot understand this and thus denies that the army is working under the orders of a commander acting according to the laws of the state, he imagines that all the soldiers are tied to one another with strings. He thinks what a wonderful string this must be and is astonished.

Later, on Friday, he goes and enters a magnificent mosque, for example Ayasofya (Haghia Sophia). He observes that the congregation of Muslims performing the Friday congregational Prayer rises, bows, prostrates, and sits at the voice of one man. Since he does not know the Shari'a, which is the collection of sacred Divine laws and principles that guide the lives and worship of Muslims, he imagines that the members of the congregation are bound to one another with strings which control them and make them move like puppets. With this most ridiculous idea in his mind, he leaves the mosque.

Like this comparison, a naturalist denier of God enters this world, which is, in one respect, a splendid barracks of the Sovereign of eternity for His numerous hosts, and, in another respect, a well-ordered mosque of the Eternal, All-Worshipped One for His servants. He fancies that the laws which the Eternal Sovereign's Wisdom has established for the order and operation of the universe—the laws which have only nominal existence and are in fact the titles of His acts in the administration of the universe—have a physical existence and have enough knowledge and power to govern the entire universe. Instead of attributing these to the Divine Power, he attributes the existence and operation of the universe to these laws of nominal existence which he calls "nature"—and which have no power, knowledge, wisdom, consciousness, and will—and to what he calls "natural forces," which are in truth a manifestation of Divine Power. He regards these forces as an independent power that is able to direct the universe. This is a thousand times greater abasing ignorance than the ignorance of the man in the above-mentioned comparison.

In short, if the thing which naturalists call "nature" has an external reality, it can, at the very most, be a work of art, not an artist; it can be a design, not a designer; a set of decrees, not an issuer of decrees; a set of the laws of the creation and operation of the universe, not a lawgiver; a created veil before God's Dignity, not a creator; something originated according to God's way of acting, not an originator; only a law, not an independent, conscious power or a powerful one; and a set of lines to inscribe on, not a source or origin or an author.

To conclude, since things and beings exist and, as stated in the introduction of this treatise, there can be no other way to explain their existence than the four mentioned above, and since the first three of these ways have been proven to be invalid because of the impossibilities elucidated, then necessarily and self-evidently, the fourth way is clearly the only valid way. It is the way of Divine Existence and Unity. It is indicated by the verse quoted at the beginning, *Can there be any doubt about God, the Originator of the heavens and the earth?* (14: 10), which clearly and undoubtedly states that there can be no doubt about the Existence or Unity of God, and that everything issues directly from His Hand of Power, and the heavens and the earth are under His Grasp of supreme control and direction.

O one who attributes creativity to "nature" and "natural" causes! The nature of everything, like the things themselves, is created, for it is full of art, original, and particular to itself. In addition, like everything itself, which is the result of a cause, its apparent cause is also created. In addition, the existence of everything depends on the existence of numerous "instruments." Therefore, there must be an Absolutely Powerful One Who creates both the things and their nature and causes, and the instruments required. And what need does that All-Powerful One have to share impotent causes in His creativity and Lordship over existence? God forbid such a thought! Rather, He creates things together with their causes so that He displays the manifestations of His Names and His Wisdom. By so doing, He establishes an apparent, ordered cause-and-effect relationship, and makes the apparent causes a veil in people's sight between His Dignity and what people may see as being defective or incompatible with mercy in things and events.

Which is easier and more reasonable for a watchmaker? Making the cogs of a clock and then arranging them to form the clock, or inserting a wonderful machine inside the cogs and then leaving the making of the watch to the lifeless hands of the machine? Is the second alternative easier and more reasonable or inconceivable and impossible? Use your reason to be the judge!

Or a scribe readies a pen, a piece of paper, and ink to write a book. Is it easier and more reasonable for him to write the book by himself, or to invent a machine inside the pen, the piece of paper, and the ink, more artistic and more troublesome than the book itself, and then tell that unconscious machine to write the book, while he does not interfere? Is not the second alternative a hundred times more difficult than the first?

If you say: It is true that inventing a machine to write a book is a hundred times more difficult than writing it, but there is also an ease in this because numerous copies of the same book can be produced with that machine.

THE ANSWER: By ever renewing the limitless manifestations and effects of His Names through His boundless Power in order to exhibit them in ever differing fashions, the Eternal Designer and Inscriber creates things with such particular identities and features that none of the missives of the Eternally Besought-of-All and the books of the Lord are the same as others.

In order to display different meanings, each thing must have a different identity and features particular to itself.

If you have eyes, look at the human countenance: you will see that although from the time of Adam all human faces have had the same structure and organs, each has particular features distinguishing it from all others. Therefore, each human face is a different, particular book. Creating each with its particular features requires a different writing set and a different composition. In order to collect the necessary materials for each and establish each exactly in its place, there must be a completely different workshop. Even if we, supposing what is impossible to be possible, think of nature as a printing press, in addition to making a new arrangement of the iron keys of letters for every piece of writing, all the particles required for the existence of each body must be collected from all corners of "nature" in exact amounts and specific proportions and arranged in it in perfect order; this is a hundred times more difficult than arranging the iron keys of letters for every piece of writing. In order to do all these things, there is still an absolute need for the all-encompassing Knowledge, Will and Power of the absolutely Powerful One. Therefore, this hypothesis of a machine is a totally meaningless fantasy.

Like these comparisons of the watch and book, the Maker of Majesty, the All-Powerful One creates both the causes and their effects together, and out of His Wisdom makes the existence of the effects dependent on their causes. He has an assembly of laws for the creation and operation of the universe, which are in fact the titles of His acts of creation and direction. By His Will, He has appointed a nature for each thing as a mirror to those acts or laws, and by His Power He creates each thing according to its nature. Therefore, is it easier to accept this truth, which, being completely reasonable and the conclusion of innumerable rational proofs, leaves us no other alternative but to accept it, or to assume that what you call nature and natural causes, which are blind, unconscious, contained in time and space, mortal, and devoid of any knowledge or will, have the limitless equipment required for the existence of each and every thing, and are able to carry out such deeds as the creation and direction of a whole universe, which require infinite knowledge, wisdom and discernment? Is this second alternative not beyond all possibility, even inconceivable?

The disbelieving naturalist replies: Even if in the light of your explanations I admit that the way of thought I have adopted to date is beyond reason and unacceptable, and believe in the 'Necessarily Existent One' as the Creator of all things, saying 'All praise be to God for belief,' still I have one doubt. Although we accept that God is the Creator, what harm can there be in some insignificant causes playing a certain role in the creation of some things in respect to the sovereignty of God's Lordship? Does this imply a defect on the part of His Sovereignty?

THE ANSWER: As clearly explained in some parts of the *Risale-i Nur*, by its very nature, sovereignty rejects interference. Even an insignificant director or official does not tolerate the interference of even his own child with his authority. The fact that in history some religious rulers have killed their innocent sons in fear that the sons might attempt to interfere in their rule demonstrates how fundamental this "law of rejection of interference" is in rulership. The "law of prevention of others' participation," which the independence of sovereignty demands, rejects the existence of two sovereigns at the same time in the same place, whether it be a country or town. This has shown its great force through upheavals in human history.

Thus, if the sense of relative and transient rulership and sovereignty in humanity, which is powerless and in need of help, rejects the interference and participation of others, and seeks to preserve its independence in its position so jealously, then, if you can, compare how indispensable the rejection of interference and prevention of participation is to the All-Majestic One, Whose absolute sovereignty is based on or arises from His absolute Lordship over creation, Whose absolute rulership arises from His Divinity, Whose absolute independence arises from His absolute Oneness and Uniqueness, and Whose absolute self-sufficiency arises from His absolute Power.

As for the second part of your doubt, which is: If certain parts in the creation and control of some insignificant things is attributed to some insignificant causes, and those things assign some part of their worship to those causes, what harm does this cause in the worship of all beings from particles to galaxies, which is dedicated to the Necessarily Existent Being, Who is the Absolute Object of Worship?

THE ANSWER: The All-Wise Creator of the universe has made the universe like a tree with conscious beings as its most perfect fruit, and humanity as the most comprehensive fruit among conscious beings. Should that

Absolute Sovereign and All-Independent Ruler, that Single One of Uniqueness, Who has created the universe so that He could be known and loved, allow others to own humanity, the fruit of the whole universe? Would He also allow humanity's thanks and worship, for which it has been created, and which are therefore its most elevated fruit, to be dedicated to others? Would He, totally contrary to His Wisdom, make the result of creation and the fruit of the universe futile and in vain? God forbid such a thought!

Also, would He give consent to the worship of creatures being dedicated to others, which would mean a denial of His Wisdom and Lordship? While He demonstrates through His acts that He wills to be known and loved to a boundless degree, would He cause Himself to be forgotten and His most elevated purposes for the existence of the universe to be denied by allowing the thankfulness, love, and worship of all creatures to be directed towards anything else other than Him?

O friend who has given up naturalism! Now it is your turn to speak! He replies:

> All praise be to God, these two doubts of mine have been resolved. You have convincingly explained God's absolute Oneness and why He is only the True Object of Worship, and that nothing else other than Him has the right to be worshipped and is not worthy of worship. Therefore, the denial of this truth would mean arrogance to the extent of denying the sun and the daytime.

Conclusion

The person who has renounced naturalism and accepted belief in God said, "All praise be to God; I no longer have any doubts concerning God's existence and Oneness, but still I have a few questions."

The first question

We hear many people who are idle in performing the daily Prayers ask: What need does God Almighty have for our worship? Why in the Qur'an does He severely reprimand those who do not worship and threaten them with such a terrible punishment as Hell? How does it behoove the moderate, mild, and balanced style of the Qur'an to display such severity in the face of an insignificant fault?

THE ANSWER: Truly, God Almighty has no need at all for your worship, nor indeed for anything else. But you need to worship, for in truth you are spiritually ill. We have indicated in many parts of the *Risale-i Nur* that worship is a cure for many spiritual wounds of humanity. If a patient responds to a compassionate doctor who insists that he should take the medicines prescribed for his illness, saying, "What need do you have for the medicine? Why are you insisting in this way?", you can understand how foolish this would be.

As for the severe threats of the Qur'an against the non-fulfillment of the duty of worship with terrible punishments, it is like this: In order to protect his subjects' rights, a monarch punishes an ordinary man to the extent that he violates those rights. Likewise, one who does not worship, including in particular the Prayer, is seriously violating the rights of the creatures who are like subjects of the Absolute Sovereign of eternity. For the perfection of creatures displays itself through glorification and other kinds of worship manifested by their relationship with the Maker. One who does not worship does not, indeed cannot, see their worship, and even denies it. By reducing the creatures from their position of each being a missive of the Eternally Besought-of-All and a mirror to His Names by reason of their worship to the degree of being insignificant, inanimate, meaningless, aimless, and randomly existent things, this person has insulted them, and denies their perfections.

Indeed, everyone sees the universe in their own mirror. God Almighty has created humanity as a measure and scale for the universe. He has given each person a particular, private world out of the universe. The particular world of each person takes on the color of his or her heart. For example, a desperate, weeping person sees creatures as weeping and in despair, while a cheerful, optimistic one sees them as also cheerful and smiling. One who worships God Almighty in a serious, reflective manner can discern to certain degree the actual worship and glorifications of creatures, while a person who does not worship, due to either heedlessness or denial, thinks of creatures in a manner devoid of any truth and completely contrary to their actual perfections, and thus violates their rights.

Furthermore, no one is their own creator and owner; everyone is a servant of God Almighty. Therefore, those who do not perform the prescribed Prayers, defeated by their carnal, evil-commanding soul, wrong themselves, although they are servants of their Master and Owner. So, their Owner makes severe threats in order to protect His servant's rights against the evil-commanding soul, and to restore them. In addition, one who does not worship, which is God's purpose for His creation or the ultimate reason for a person's existence, is transgressing the Divine Will and Wisdom, and therefore deserves punishment.

In short, those who do not worship both wrong themselves, the servants of God Almighty owned by Him, and wrong and transgress the rights of creatures that arise from the perfections they share as worshipping servants of God. Just as unbelief is an insult to creatures, so too is the non-fulfillment of the duty of worship a denial of the perfections shared by creatures. Likewise, it is a transgression against Divine Wisdom and this deserves severe threats and punishment. It is in order to express this truth that the Qur'an of miraculous expression has chosen the severe style under discussion, which, in complete conformity with eloquence, corresponds to the requirements of the situation.

The second question

The person who has renounced naturalism and has come to believe next asks: It is astonishing that with whatever it has and whatever it does, and in every aspect, everything totally depends on Divine Will and Power. The infinite abundance which we clearly see in existence, and the limitless ease in the creation of things that arise from their being created by One God, and which is demonstrated by such Qur'anic verses as

> *Your creation and your resurrection are but as (the creation and resurrection) of a single soul* (31: 28), and *The matter of the Hour (of Doom) is (in relation with the Divine Power) but the twinkling of an eye, or even quicker* (16: 77),

show that this supreme, astonishing fact is completely acceptable and rational. However, we cannot comprehend this supreme, astonishing fact. How do you explain this ease?"

THE ANSWER: It was explained clearly and in a convincing way while commenting on, *He is powerful over all things*, which is the Tenth Phrase of the Twentieth Letter. In particular, it was explained even more clearly in the Addendum to that Letter that when all things are attributed to One, Single Maker, their existence becomes as easy as the existence of a single thing. If they are not attributed to a Single One of Uniqueness, the existence of a single thing becomes as difficult as the existence of all things; indeed, the existence of a seed becomes as difficult as the existence of a tree. But if all things are attributed to their true Maker, the existence of the universe becomes as easy as the existence of a tree, and the existence of a tree as that of a seed, and the existence of Paradise as that of spring, and the existence of spring as that of a flower. In some parts of the *Risale-i Nur*, we have mentioned many reasons for and several instances of wisdom behind the limitless value of things despite the infinite abundance in existence, and the perfect artistry in everything despite the infinite facility and speed in things coming into existence. We will briefly point out only a few of them as follows:

For example, if the command of a hundred privates is given to one officer, their command will be a hundred times easier than the command of a single private by a hundred officers. Likewise, the equipping of an army by a single center or factory or government is as easy as the equipping of a single soldier, while the equipping of a single soldier by many different centers of command or factories is as difficult as that of a whole army. For there would have to be as many factories as there is equipment for an army.

It is observed that by reason of growing from a single seed and on one root and of growing and feeding through a single law, the growth of a tree that yields thousands of fruits is as easy as a single fruit. But if a tree were dependent on multiple sources for its growth, with the result that all the necessities vital for each fruit were to be provided from different places, then each fruit would become as difficult to produce as a tree. To produce even a single seed, which is a sample and index of the tree, would be as difficult as the production of the tree. For all the substances for the growth and life of a tree are also necessary for the seed.

Thus, there are hundreds of examples like these which show that it is easier for thousands of things that are dependent on a single source to come into existence than for a single thing depending on multiple sources to come into existence. Referring you to some other parts of the *Risale-i Nur* for a detailed explanation of this fact, we will here explain only a significant aspect of it that is related to Divine Knowledge, Power, and Destiny. It is as follows:

You are an existent being. If you attribute yourself to the Eternal, All-Powerful One, you will understand how He has created you with a single command out of nothing, like striking a match. However, if you do not attribute yourself to Him, but rather to physical causes and nature, then since you are a well-ordered summary, a fruit, and a miniature index of the universe, in order to make you, all the substances necessary for the formation of your body would have to be finely sieved from the universe and collected from all its corners in precise measures. For material substances are only used for formation or composition, and physical causes may serve only as means for their collection. Every sensible person knows and admits that they cannot create out of nothing what they themselves do not have. Therefore, they would have to collect all the particles of substances necessary for the body of even a minute living being from all corners of the universe.

Now understand what ease there is in Divine Unity and attributing everything to Him, and what difficulties lie in misguidance, in associating partners with God!

Secondly, when everything is attributed to a Single Creator, existence is infinitely easy from the perspective of there being Divine Knowledge as well. It is as follows:

Destiny is identical with Knowledge in one respect. It appoints a certain measure for each thing, which can be regarded as its particular, immaterial mold. That measure or mold appointed by Destiny serves as a model for its existence. When Divine Power creates, It does so with extreme ease according to that appointed measure. Now, if that being is not attributed to the All-Powerful One of Majesty with an unlimited, all-encompassing, eternal Knowledge, not only do thousands of difficulties appear, but its existence would be a hundred times more inconceivable. For if it were not for the measure appointed by Divine Destiny or Knowledge, thousands of material molds made in the physical world would have to be used in the body of a minute organism.

So, understand why there is infinite ease in attributing everything to a single Source, and why there are endless difficulties in accepting multiple sources or associating partners with God. Also, realize what an objective, undeniable, clear, and elevated truth is stated by the verse, *The matter of the Hour (of Doom) is (in relation with the Divine Power) but the twinkling of an eye, or even quicker* (16: 77).

The third question

The friend who has found the right guidance asks: Those most renowned among philosophers claim that nothing is invented out of nothing, and nothing goes into absolute extinction. The factory of the universe runs on the cycle of composition and decomposition. Is this so?

The Answer: Those most renowned among the philosophers who do not view creation in the light of the Qur'an see the formation and existence of creatures by nature and physical causes as inconceivably difficult and they are divided into two groups. One group is the Sophists. Abdicating reason, which is exclusive to humanity, they find it easier to deny the existence of the universe, including their own, than to follow the way of misguidance which attributes creativity to nature and physical causes. Denying, therefore, both their own and the universe's existence, they descend into absolute ignorance.

The second group is aware of the fact that ascribing creativity to nature and physical causes incurs endless difficulties even for the existence of so tiny a creature as a fly or a seed, and is therefore irrational. This leads them to deny the act of creation, and claim that nothing can exist out of nothing, and annihilation is impossible. They fancy that everything consists in the cycle of composition, decomposition, and re-composition, dependent on the random motion of atoms and the winds of coincidence.

Now, see the ignorance of those who consider themselves to be the most intelligent of all, and understand to what points of intellectual poverty misguidance can drag people!

Consider an Eternal Power Which created the universe in six days, and shows Itself in the simultaneous creation and re-creation of hundreds of thousands of species on the earth every year, and replaces the world every spring in six weeks with a new one more full of art and wisdom than the former! Like applying a chemical to invisible writing to make it visible, this Power gives external existence to the archetypes of things and beings already determined and identified in Divine Knowledge by Divine Destiny. Therefore, it would be more foolish and ignorant than the Sophists to deny this Power the capacity of creation and reject the act of creation. Since both these two groups of unfortunate ones, who are absolutely impotent in themselves and have nothing more than a partial willpower at their disposal, yet are more proud and refractory than Pharaoh, and nature and physical causes, on which they rely, are unable to make something out of nothing and annihilate it utterly, they claim that nothing exists out of nothing, and something existent does not go into non-existence, thus denying the Absolutely All-Powerful One creation and sending into non-existence.

The All-Powerful One of Majesty has two kinds of creating. One is origination and invention. That is to say, He brings a being into existence out of nothing together with whatever is necessary for it. The other is making and composing. That is, in order to demonstrate the perfection of His Wisdom and numerous subtle instances of It, such as displaying manifestations of many of His Names, He makes certain things out of the elements of the universe. Being the All-Providing, He also dispatches to them atoms and substances subservient to His command, and makes them operate within.

Thus, bringing into existence out of non-existence and sending into non-existence are two constant, infinitely easy practices of the Absolutely All-Powerful One, Who both invents or originates and makes or composes. One who makes the claim that a Power Which each spring creates out of nothing the forms and attributes of hundreds of thousands of living species together with all their conditions and states cannot give existence to what does not exist deserves non-existence.

The one who abandons naturalism and accepts the truth concludes: Praise and thanks be to God Almighty, I have attained perfect belief to the number of the particles of existence, and have been saved from groundless suppositions and misguidance. And not one of my doubts remains.

All praise be to God for the Religion of Islam and perfection in belief!

All-Glorified are You. We have no knowledge save what You have
taught us. Surely You are the All-Knowing, the All-Wise.

The Twenty-Fourth Gleam

The Twenty-Fourth Gleam

• On Islamic dress for women
• A "conversation" with Muslim women

In the Name of God, the All-Merciful, the All-Compassionate.

O Prophet! Tell your wives and your daughters, as well as the women (wives and daughters) of the believers, to draw over themselves some part of their outer garments (when outside their homes and when before men whom they are not forbidden to marry because of blood relation). (33: 59)

This verse orders the veiling of women. However, modern, dissolute civilization opposes this order of the Qur'an; it does not consider the veiling of women to be natural for them, and regards it as a form of slavery.[89]

The answer

I will explain only four of the instances of wisdom in this order of the Qur'an, which shows that veiling is entirely natural for women, and that any assertion contrary to it opposes the innate disposition of women.

89 Part of my defense for the Court of Appeal, which silenced the (Eskişehir) Court: "I say to this court of law: If there is justice on the face of the earth, it will surely quash the decision which has convicted a person who, based on the unanimous agreement of around three hundred and fifty thousand commentaries of the Qur'an and the common belief of all our forefathers during over one thousand, three hundred and fifty years, discussed a sacred, true Divine principle, which every century, hundreds of millions of people have followed in their social life during those one thousand, three hundred and fifty years."

The first instance of wisdom

Veiling is natural for women and their innate disposition demands it. For women are weak, gentle and delicate in nature, and feel in need of protection and help for both themselves and their children, whom they love more than their own lives. Therefore, they have an inborn tendency to make themselves loved and not to be rebuffed.

Also, six or seven out of every ten women are either advancing in age or unattractive. They do not want to show their age and be known to be unattractive. Many among them do not, out of jealousy, want to appear unattractive in relation to others who are more beautiful. In addition, they are afraid of being subjected to aggression or aspersion, and do not want to be accused of unfaithfulness by their husbands. All these and similar other factors naturally lead them to cover themselves. If noted carefully, it is the elderly among women who hide themselves most. Out of ten women, there are only two or three who are both young and beautiful and do not feel uneasy about displaying themselves.

It is a fact that people are made uncomfortable at and hurt by the gaze of those whom they do not like, often finding it unbearable. Indeed, if a beautiful, immodestly dressed woman takes pleasure at the gaze of two or three out of the ten men who can canonically marry her, she cannot bear the gaze of the remaining seven or eight. Also, since a beautiful woman who is not morally corrupt is sensitive and easily affected, she will certainly be distressed at indecent, dirty looks that experiences have proven to have a harmful effect, and which are, indeed, poisonous. We even hear that in Europe, where women do not cover themselves, many women are disturbed by gazes and complain to the police, saying, "These scoundrels keep staring at us and disturb us." This means that the unveiling of women by modern civilization is contrary to their natures, while the order in the Qur'an for veiling is not only in conformity with women's natures, but it also saves these mines of compassion who may be worthy companions for all eternity from degeneration, abasement, and from what is, in effect, slavery and wretchedness.

Furthermore, women are by nature fearful of men who are strangers. Fear naturally demands protection. For in addition to having to bear the heavy burden of carrying a child for eight or nine months, which will certainly embitter eight or nine minutes' pleasure, there is also the possibility of suffering the calamity of bringing up the child for eight or nine years in return for the eight or nine minutes' illicit pleasure. As it frequently happens, a woman has a natural fear of men who are strangers, and her disposition causes her to keep away from them. Her natural weakness forces her not to stir up the appetites of strange men and cause their assault, showing that her cloak is her shield and stronghold. I was told that a shoe-shiner had beset the bare-legged wife of a high-ranking man in the capital city, in the market-place, in broad daylight in front of people. This deals a slap in the shameless faces of those who oppose the veiling of women.

The second instance of wisdom

The substantial and strong relationship, and the love and interest between men and women do not arise only from the needs of the worldly life. Indeed, a woman is not a companion of her husband only in the world; she is his companion also in the eternal life and he is hers. As she is so, she certainly should not attract the looks of others besides her husband, her everlasting companion, to her beauty, and should not offend him and arouse his jealousy. As, from belief, her believing husband's relationship with her is not restricted to this worldly life, he does not feel merely animal love towards her during her years while she has beauty, but rather he should both love and respect her sincerely not only when she is young and beautiful but also during her old age, as she will be his companion in also the other, eternal life; for sure, humanity requires that she should in return present her beauties to his view alone and restrict her love to him. Otherwise she would gain very little but lose much.

Islam demands that the husband and wife should be a good match each for the other. This should be so particularly in the matter of religion. How happy is the husband who sees his wife's good religious life and follows her, becoming a pious one in order not to lose her companionship in the eternal life. How happy is the wife who sees her husband's good religious life and becomes a pious, righteous one in order not to lose her eternal friend. Alas for the man who indulges in dissipation, which will lose him his righteous wife forever. How unfortunate is the woman who does not follow her God-revering, pious husband and loses her eternal, blessed friend. And thousands of woes on the unhappy husband and wife who imitate each other in transgression and dissipation, and help each other to enter Hellfire!

The third instance of wisdom

Happiness in family life is possible and continuous through mutual confidence, sincere respect, and love between the husband and wife. Immodest dress and indecency destroy this mutual confidence, respect, and love. For many out of the women who prefer immodest dress wish to be found beautiful and attractive by others. (Most husbands think that their wives who prefer immodest dress want to make themselves loved by other men whom they find more handsome than them.) There can always be men who are more handsome than the husband of any wife. Nine out of ten of them will find men who are more handsome than their husbands. And only one out of twenty men does not find women who are more beautiful than his wife. Then, in addition to the evaporation of the mutual love and respect between the couples, extremely ugly and base feelings may arise, as follows:

By nature, men do not feel any lust towards the women who are within the forbidden degrees of relationship for marriage, like for example, their sisters, because the faces of such relatives suggest affection and licit love due to their close kinship, and thus do not arouse any sexual inclinations. But leaving uncovered the parts of the body which the Shari‘a has forbidden to be exposed to close relatives, like the legs, might arouse extremely nasty feelings in some base souls. For the face of a close relative suggests close kinship and does not resemble the faces of others outside the degrees of kinship. However, a bare leg is the same as that of a canonical stranger in the feelings it may arouse. Since it does not have any distinguishing mark to recall the close kinship of its owner, it may attract lusty looks from some men of close kinship who have a low character. Such looks mean a degeneration that makes one's hair stand on end.

The fourth instance of wisdom

Everyone wants to have children. There is no nation or government which does not support an increase in the population. In fact, the noblest Messenger, upon him be peace and blessings, declared, "Marry and increase, for on the Resurrection Day I will take pride in your large numbers in comparison to other communities."[90] However, immodest dress causes the number of marriages to decrease. For even the most dissolute and modern young man wants his wife to be chaste. Since he does not want her to be immodest like himself, he prefers remaining single, and even falls into illicit relationships.

Women cannot restrict their husbands' behavior to the extent that men can restrict theirs. For being the director of the internal affairs in the home, and therefore charged with all her husband's property, possessions, and children, the most essential characteristic of women is loyalty and confidence. Immodest dress may cause the husband to lose his confidence in her and suffer pangs of suspicion. In fact, courage and generosity, two praiseworthy qualities when found in men, are not regarded (in traditional communities) to be so in women as they are in men, as they may suggest a lack of trust and loyalty. The primary duties of men are to protect, provide maintenance, be kind, and respect, but the loyalty expected from women is greater. It is more difficult for women to restrict their husbands' behavior. While a woman cannot be shared and be married to more than one man at the same time, a man can have more than one woman in wedlock.

Our country cannot be compared with Europe because honor can be preserved there to a certain extent by violent means such as the duel, despite immodest dress. One who makes eyes at the wife of an honorable, self-respecting man does so only after he has taken his life in his own hand.[91] Furthermore, the people of Europe with the exception of those of the Mediterranean countries are mostly cold and frigid, like its climate. However, compared to Europe, the Muslim lands are torrid. It is a well-known fact that the environment has an effect on people's morality. In those cold countries, immodest dress excites the carnal appetites and desires of those cold people only relatively, and does not lead to much abuse. But immodest dress continually incites the carnal desires of the easily influenced and sensitive people of hot countries, and causes much abuse, waste, the weakening of young generations, and a loss of strength. Instead of satisfying natural needs once a month or every twenty days, people feel forced

[90] Abdur-Razzaq, *al-Musannaf*, 6:173; al-Ajluni, *Kashf al-Khafa'*, 1:380. (Tr.)

[91] This was so historically. (Tr.)

to do so every few days. Since they are obliged to avoid their wives for one to two weeks in every month because of contingencies like their monthly period, they are defeated by their carnal appetites, and will become inclined to illicit relationships.

Urban people cannot attempt to unveil women on the pretext of how rural women dress. For rural women have to work outside and do heavy work for the livelihood of themselves and their families, which usually makes them worn-out and somewhat coarse. Therefore, their being partially unveiled neither attracts as much attention like urban women nor incites carnal desires. Furthermore, since there are also only a few dissolute, idle men in villages, even one tenth of the vice witnessed in cities is not found there. So such a comparison cannot be made.

In His Name, All-Glorified is He.

A "conversation" with the women who are my believing sisters of the Hereafter

I have observed the sincere and enthusiastic interest of some women in the *Risale-i Nur* in some provinces, and realized that their confidence in my instructions far exceeds my due. When, for the third time I returned to blessed Isparta, which bears the meaning of the *Medresetu'z-Zehra*,[92] I was told that these women, who are my blessed sisters of the Hereafter, were waiting to receive a lecture from me in the form of the sermons preached in the mosques. But I am ill with four or five different illnesses and in a miserable state, almost unable to think and speak. However, it occurred to me last night that fifteen years ago, I wrote *A Guide for Youth* at the request of some young people, and many have benefited from it. Women are in even greater need of a guide at this time. Therefore, despite my miserable state and ill health, I am presenting concisely certain useful matters in three concise points for the notice of these blessed sisters and young brothers of mine, whom I see as my offspring.

[92] *Medresetü's-Zehra* is the name of the university which Said Nursi enthusiastically desired and tried to establish in Van throughout his whole life, and in which he suggested that both physical and religious sciences should be taught. (Tr.)

The first point

Since one of the most essential principles of the *Risale-i* Nur is compassion and women are heroes of compassion, they are by nature more closely connected with the *Risale-i Nur* than others. All praise be to God, this natural connection displays itself in many places. And since the self-sacrifice contained in this compassion means true sincerity and demands nothing in return, it is of great importance, particularly at this time.

The fact that as demanded by her nature, a mother sacrifices her life in order to save her child from danger without demanding anything in return shows that women are capable of great heroism. By developing this heroism, they can save both their worldly and other-worldly life. However, this powerful and valuable characteristic may not develop or may be misused because of some evil trends. A minor example out of hundreds is as follows:

A compassionate mother accepts the risk of every sort of self-sacrifice and brings up her child so that her child should not meet any danger and should receive every sort of benefit and advantage. She spends all her wealth so that her son can be an official of high position; (considering only his worldly happiness,) she takes him from the Qur'an school and sends him to Europe. Without considering that her child's eternal life is at risk, she tries to save him from any worldly "prison," and does not take into consideration that he may be sentenced to the prison of Hell. Completely opposite to her inherent compassion, she makes her innocent child a claimant against her in the Hereafter, while he should be her intercessor. The child will complain about her, saying, "Why did you not strengthen my belief, and thus you caused my perdition here?" Furthermore, since he did not receive a proper Islamic education, he cannot respond to his mother's wonderful compassion in the way it deserves in the world; in fact, he does so very deficiently.

If she does not misuse her compassion and works to save her child from dying while in misguidance and from eternal loss in the everlasting prison of Hell, since the equivalent of the rewards to come from all the good deeds of the child will be recorded in the book of his mother's good deeds, he will continuously send lights to her spirit after her death, and will wholeheartedly be an intercessor for her in the Hereafter, not a claimant against her. Thus, he will be her blessed child for all eternity.

It is a fact that the first master and most effective teacher of any person is their mother. Regarding this fact, listen to what follows from me, which I have always felt strongly within my own self:

I am eighty years old and have received lessons from a great many people. Yet I swear that the most persistent and established of these lessons are the religious advice and instructions which I received from my late mother and they have always remained fresh for me. They have been implanted in my nature as though they were seeds planted in my physical being. I observe that other lessons have been constructed upon those seeds. That is to say, I see the advice and instructions which my late mother implanted in my nature and spirit when I was a child to be each essential seeds amidst the great truths that I now observe at the age of eighty.

For example, compassion or affection is the most important of the four principles of my way and the greatest truth upon which the *Risale-i Nur* is based and which it propagates. I observe with certainty that I received it from the compassionate conduct and religious teachings of my mother. Therefore, it means the misuse of the sincere and self-sacrificing compassion of motherhood if a mother turns the face of her child from the Hereafter, which is a treasury of diamonds for her innocent child, to the world, which is like temporary fragments of glass.

It is a proof of women's heroism in regard to compassion, which demands nothing in return and leads them to sacrifice their very lives without considering any personal advantage or show, that a hen, which is a tiny sample of that compassion, attacks a lion and sacrifices its life in order to save its chicks.

The most precious and most essential principle in Islamic education and the deeds pertaining to the Hereafter is sincerity. The compassion of women has true sincerity like this. Therefore, if these two virtues—compassion and sincerity—properly develop in women and are used in the proper way, it will be the means of a great triumph and prosperity for Islam and Muslims. The heroism of men cannot be without the demand for return; they always demand recompense in many ways. At the very least they demand glory and renown. But regrettably, unfortunate women feel obliged to display some other kind of ostentation arising from weakness and impotence in order to be saved from the evil and oppression of tyrannical men.

The second point

While I have been in seclusion this year and long withdrawn from the social life, I took a glance at the affairs of the world for the sake of some of my brothers and sisters who are the students of the *Risale-i Nur*. I have heard complaints from many of the friends about their own family lives. "What a pity!" I uttered. The special stronghold of people, and particularly of Muslims, and a sort of Paradise for them, and a small, private world for them is family life. "Has this begun to break up as well?" I said to myself. I sought the reason, and I came to know that some corruption-spreading committees were working to harm the social life of Islam, and thereby the Religion of Islam, by misleading youth and driving them to dissipation by means of their animal desires. I also realized that some other similar committees were working secretly and effectively to drive careless, imprudent women to wrong ways. I understood that a terrible blow has come to this Muslim nation from that quarter. And so I tell you my sisters and brothers or children-in-religion what follows with utmost conviction:

There is no means other than the Islamic religious education that will secure our happiness in the Hereafter, as well as in this world, and save our innate elevated qualities from corruption. You hear about the situation they have fallen into in communist Russia. It is said somewhere in the *Risale-i Nur* that a sensible man does not build his love for his companion for life on her physical, brief beauty, which will last only five to ten years. Rather, he should build it on her compassion and good conduct that is particular to womanhood, which are the best and most permanent of beauties, so that when that helpless one gets older, her husband's love for her may persist. For his wife is not merely his temporary helper or companion in this worldly life, but an eternal, lovable companion of life for all eternity. Therefore, as they grow older, they should increasingly love, respect, and show compassion to each other. Modern family life, which is subject to an eternal separation after a temporary, animal companionship under the veil of civilization, is being destroyed at its very foundations.

It is also said elsewhere in the *Risale-i Nur* how happy the husband is who sees his wife's good, religious life and follows her, himself becoming a pious one in order not to lose her companionship in the eternal life. How happy is the wife who sees her husband's good religious life and becomes a pious, righteous one in order not to lose her eternal friend. She earns the eternal happiness of the Hereafter in her life in this world. Unfortunate is the man who follows his wife living a dissipated life, and instead of trying to make her give it up, joins her. Unfortunate is the woman who sees her husband's sinful life, and imitates him in another manner. And woe to the husband and wife who help each other to enter the Hellfire! That is, they encourage each other to the evils of civilization.

All such statements in the *Risale-i Nur* as these mean that a happy family life and happiness in both worlds, as well as the development of women's innate, elevated qualities, are possible only through following the Islamic precepts.

The most important point in family life is as follows:

If a woman sees bad conduct and faithlessness in her husband, and just to spite her husband, breaks her loyalty to him and destroys his confidence in her, like the discipline in the army becoming spoiled, the factory of that family is utterly destroyed. The woman should rather try her hardest to reform her husband's faults so that she can save her friend for eternity. If she unveils herself in an attempt to show herself to others and make herself attractive to them, she will harm herself in every respect. For the one who abandons faithfulness suffers its recompense in the world too, because, by nature, she is afraid of and distressed by the looks of those who are strangers to her. She cannot bear the looks of eighteen out of twenty strangers. As for men, they feel uncomfortable and distressed by the looks of only one out of a hundred women outside the forbidden degrees of relationship for marriage. In addition to suffering torment in that respect, women may also be accused of unfaithfulness, and because of their weakness, they cannot protect their rights.

In short, just as women are not like men in their heroism of compassion and sincerity, and men cannot be equal to them in this respect, so too innocent women are absolutely not able to compete with men in vice. For this reason and due to their weakness and very nature, they are afraid of and avoid strangers and feel compelled to conceal themselves under their outer garments, because if a man commits indecency for the sake of eight minutes' pleasure, he will suffer little loss. But the consequence of the eight minutes' pleasure of indecency for a woman is that she may have to bear in this world a heavy load for eight months and suffer the difficulty of bringing up that unprotected child for his first eight years. She therefore cannot compete with men in vice and pays a penalty a hundred times greater.

Incidents of this kind show that women have an innate capability for lofty virtues and morals but not for worldly pleasure in vice and dissipation. Essentially, they are blessed humans with a natural tendency towards a happy family life that is based on Islamic education and precepts. God damn those corruption-spreading committees which try to divert them! And may God save those sisters of mine from the evil of such dissolute wretches. Amen!

My sisters! I say to you truthfully: rather than accepting the domination of a dissolute, immoral husband neglectful of Islamic precepts for the sake of an easy life, deriving help from contentment and frugality in your nature, try to economize and obtain your livelihood like innocent peasant women; do not attempt to sell yourselves. If it is your fate to have to get along with a husband not suitable for you, resign yourself to your fate. God willing, he will be reformed through your resignation. Otherwise, you will apply to the courts for a divorce, which I have heard of recently, but this is not in keeping with the honor of Islam and the good name of our nation.

The third point

My dear sisters! Know with certainty that in pleasures and enjoyment that are outside the bounds of Islamic law, there are pains and distress ten times greater. This is convincingly explained in parts of the *Risale-i Nur* such as the Sixth, Seventh, and Eighth Words in *The Words* and *A Guide for Youth*. Therefore, be content with the pleasures that Islam permits. Your innocent conversations with your innocent children in your home are more pleasurable than a hundred movies.

Know also with certainty that the true pleasure in worldly life lies in belief and within the fold of belief. And there is a particular, spiritual pleasure in every one of your good deeds. As convincingly demonstrated in the *Risale-i Nur*, misguidance and vice cause extremely bitter and grievous suffering, even in the world. I myself have experienced and observed on many occasions that belief contains a seed of Paradise, while in misguidance and vice there is a seed of Hell. This reality is repeatedly stated in the *Risale-i Nur*. Even those who oppose the *Risale-i Nur* most obstinately, as well as the courts and the authorities chosen by them, have been unable to refute this. Now, in my place, let primarily The Treatise on Islamic Dress for Women, and A Guide for Youth, and The Short Words (the Words 1–9, included in *The Words*), teach you, my blessed, innocent sisters, and the younger ones among you, who are like my children in faith.

I have heard that you want me to teach you in the mosque. But my ill health and many other reasons do not allow it. I have decided to include all my sisters who read and accept this instruction which I have written for you in my prayers and all my spiritual gains, like the students of the *Risale-i Nur*. If you obtain and read the *Risale-i Nur* at least partly in my place, then according to our rule, you will also have a share in the prayers and spiritual gains of all the students of the *Risale-i Nur*, who are your brothers.

I was going to write more, but since I am very ill, weak, and old, and have many duties like correcting the manuscripts of the *Risale-i Nur*, for now let this much suffice.

The Everlasting, He is the Everlasting.

Your brother in need of your prayers
Said Nursi

The Twenty-Fifth Gleam

The Twenty-Fifth Gleam

Twenty-five remedies for those who are ill

This treatise was written as a medicine, a solace, a spiritual prescription, and as a visit wishing recovery for those who are ill.

A reminder and an apology

This spiritual prescription, which was written at great speed, has not been revised and has been left as it occurred to my heart. Therefore, I request the readers, and particularly the unwell, not to feel offended by any disagreeable expressions that may be contained within. I also request them to pray for me.

Those who, when a disaster befalls them, say, "Surely we belong to God (as His creatures and servants), and surely to Him we are bound to return." (2: 156)

"And He it is Who gives me food and drink; And Who, when I fall ill, heals me." (26: 79–80)

In this Gleam, we explain the twenty-five remedies which may offer true consolation for those who are ill or struck by misfortune, who make up one tenth of humankind.

The first remedy

You who are unhappy in your sickness! Do not be anxious, persevere instead. Your illness is not a loss for you, but a gain, a sort of cure. For life departs like capital. If it yields no fruits, it is wasted. And if it passes in ease and heedlessness, it is short, bringing almost no profit. Illness makes that capital of yours yield huge profits. Moreover, it prevents your life from being short; it holds it back, lengthening or expanding it, so that it may depart after yielding its fruits. Indicating the fact that life lengthens through illness, this proverb is much renowned and widely circulated: "The time of disaster is very long; the time of enjoyment, very short."

The second remedy

You who are ill and lacking in perseverance! Do indeed persevere and offer thanks. Your illness may transform each of the minutes of your life that pass in illness into one hour's worship. For worship is of two sorts. One is that which is performed, the other is the sort which is not actually performed, but is suffered and thus leads to sincere supplication. Illnesses and disasters are examples of this sort. By means of these, those afflicted deeply feel their innate impotence and weakness; they take refuge in their All-Compassionate Creator and entreat, thus being able to perform sincere worship. There are authenticated narrations from God's noble Messenger, upon him be peace and blessings, that the times of believers which pass in illness are counted as worship, provided they do not complain about God.[93] It is also reliably narrated from the Messenger and there are reports from saints of spiritual discovery that one minute's illness of some patients who show perseverance with thankfulness equals one hour's worship, and a minute's illness of certain spiritually perfected individuals, equals the worship of a day. Therefore, rather than complaining, be thankful for the illness, which makes one minute of your life the equivalent of a thousand minutes and gains for you a long life.

The third remedy

You who are impatient in your illness! The fact that all those who come to this world inevitably depart, that the young grow old, and that the world is perpetually turning amidst death and separation, testifies that humankind has not come to this world for enjoyment or pleasure. In addition, although humankind is the most perfect of living beings, the richest of beings in the

93 *al-Bukhari*, "Jihad" 134; Ahmad ibn Hanbal, *al-Musnad*, 4:410. (Tr.)

equipment of life, and can virtually be regarded as their king, because of dwelling on past pleasures and worrying about future troubles, human beings lead a grievous, troublesome life, much lower than the animals. This shows that humankind has not come to this world to live in ease and pleasure. Rather, possessing vast capital, it has come here to work for an eternal life by doing the required trade. The capital given to it is its lifetime.

Were it not for illness, good health and ease would cause heedlessness, presenting the world as pleasant and making people oblivious of the Hereafter. By distracting them from the thought of death and the grave, good health and ease cause them to waste the capital of life on trifles. But illness suddenly gives them awareness, and says to the body: "You are not immortal, and have not been left to your own devices. You have a duty. Give up haughtiness; think of the One Who has created you; know that you will enter the grave, and make the necessary preparation!" Thus, from this perspective, illness is an advisor that never deceives; and it is an admonishing guide. For this reason, rather than complaining about illness, we should be thankful for it. If it gives much trouble and pain, we should show patience.

The fourth remedy

You who are ill and complaining! It is better for you not to complain, but to give thanks and show patience. For your body, with all its members and your faculties, is not your property. You have not made them, nor have you bought any of your bodily components from any workshop. They are the property of someone else. Their Owner has disposal over His property as He wills.

As stated in The Twenty-Sixth Word (included in *The Words*), a very rich and infinitely skilled clothes designer uses an ordinary man as a model to display his works of art and invaluable wealth in return for wages. For a brief hour, he clothes the model in a jeweled and artistically fashioned garment that he has made. He continues to modify the garment while the model wears it. In order to display his wonderful varieties of art, he cuts the garment, alters it, lengthening it here and shortening it there. Does the model employed for a wage have any right to say, "Your orders to bow and stand up are causing me trouble. Your cutting and shortening of this garment, which must make me more beautiful, spoils my beauty." Can the model accuse the designer of treating him unkindly and unfairly?

You who are ill! As in that simile, the All-Majestic Maker—in order to display the embroideries of His All-Beautiful Names and indeed make you more and more "beautiful"—causes you to undergo numerous, different states and situations in the garment of your body in which He has clothed you, bejeweled as it is with luminous faculties like seeing, hearing, reasoning, and feeling. Just as, through hunger, you learn of His Name, The All-Providing, so too through your illness, you come to know His Name, The All-Healing. Since suffering and disasters manifest the decrees and operations of some of His Names, there are in them gleams of wisdom, and rays of mercy, within which are numerous beauties. If the veil between us and His decrees and acts were to be lifted, you would find many agreeable and beautiful meanings behind the veil of illness, which you are frightened of and dislike.

The fifth remedy

You who are afflicted with illness! I have become convinced through experience at this time that illness is a Divine favor for some people, a gift of mercy. Although I am not worthy of it, for these last eight or nine years, a number of young people have visited me to pray for them because of their illnesses. I have noticed that compared to those of the same age, any unwell young person I have met has begun to think of the Hereafter. They are no longer in the typical intoxication of youth, and have saved themselves to a degree from the animal desires that are embedded in heedlessness. Based on this observation, I would remind them that their bearable illnesses are a Divine favor. I would say, "Brother, I am not opposed to this illness of yours. I do not feel compassion for you due to your illness, so that I should pray for you. Try to show good patience until illness awakens you completely, and after it has completed its duty, God willing, the All-Compassionate Creator will cure you."

I would also say to them as follows:

> Because of the calamity of good health, some of your equals in age become heedless, and do not perform the five daily Prayers; they do not think of the grave, forget God, and damage, even destroy, the eternal life for the sake of the superficial pleasure of an hour's worldly life. But with the eye of illness, you see your grave, which you will in any case enter, and the mansions of the Hereafter beyond it, and

act accordingly. This means that illness is good health for you, while the good health of some of your peers is in fact an illness for them.

The sixth remedy

You who are sick and complain of your suffering, I say to you: Think of your past life and remember the pleasurable, happy days and the distressing, troubled times. For sure, you will either say, "Oh!" or, "Ah!" That is, your heart and tongue will either say, "All praise and thanks be to God!" or, "Alas, alas!"

Notice that what makes you utter a sigh of relief and say, "All praise and thanks be to God!" is that your thinking of the sufferings and calamities that befell you in the past stirs up a kind of spiritual pleasure and causes your heart to be thankful. For the disappearance of suffering is a pleasure. The passing of sufferings and calamities left a lasting pleasure in the spirit. When it is stirred up through thinking, a pleasure pours forth from the spirit with thanks.

What makes you exclaim, "Alas, alas!" is the pleasurable and happy times you enjoyed in the past. Through cessation, they have left an unending pain in your spirit so that whenever you think of them, that pain is aroused and causes sorrow and regret to pour forth.

Since one day's illicit pleasure sometimes causes a year's spiritual suffering, while the pain of one day's temporary illness brings the pleasure of many days' rewards together with the pleasure of its cessation, think of the result of this temporary illness you are suffering now and the rewards it potentially bears. Say, "This too will pass, God willing!" and, instead of complaining, offer thanks.

Another sixth remedy

You, brother or sister in faith, who think of the pleasures of this world and are distressed by illness! If this world were eternal, and if on our way to eternity there were no death, and if the winds of separation and death did not blow, and if there were no "winters" of the spirit in the calamitous and stormy future, I would have pitied you along with you. But since the world will one day say to us, "Now, it is the time of departure!" and close its ears to our cries, warned by these illness, we must give up our love of it before it drives us out. Before it abandons us, we must try to abandon it in our hearts.

Illness reminds us of this reality and says, "Your body is not composed of stone and iron; rather it has been composed of various materials that are subject to partition and dissolution. Give up conceit, be aware of your innate impotence, recognize your Master, know your duties, and learn why you came to the world!" Illness says this secretly in the ear of the heart.

Also, since the pleasure and enjoyment of this world do not last and, particularly if they are licit, this is distressing and painful, do not weep over their disappearance because of illness. On the contrary, think of the worship you are performing by enduring the illness and the rewards that pertain to the Hereafter, and try to be content.

The seventh remedy

You who are ill and have lost the pleasures of health! Your illness does not ruin the contentment of the Divine blessing in health; rather, it causes you to taste it more deeply, and increases it. For if something continues uninterruptedly, it loses its effect. The people of truth agree that "things are known through their opposites." For example, were it not for darkness, light would not be known and it would give no pleasure. Without cold, heat would not be recognized, and would remain unpleasant. If there were no hunger, food would offer no delight. If there were no thirst, drinking water would give no satisfaction. Without illness, health and appetite would be without pleasure.

By endowing humans with numerous senses, organs, and faculties that they may taste and recognize the uncountable varieties of His bounties in the universe, the All-Wise Originator shows that He wills that humans may experience all the varieties of His bounties and give continual thanks. Therefore, as He grants good health and appetite, He will certainly give illnesses and pains. I ask you: If you were not suffering this discomfort in your head or hands or stomach, would you be mindful of the pleasure of the Divine favor of the good health in your head or hands or stomach, and offer thanks? Certainly, not only would you not have offered thanks, you would not have even considered it! You would have expended that good health unconsciously and heedlessly, and perhaps even wantonly.

The eighth remedy

You who are sick and now reflecting on the Hereafter! Like soap, sickness washes away the dirt of sins and cleanses. It is established in an authenticated *hadith* that illnesses are expiation for sins. It says, "As ripe fruits fall from the tree when it is shaken, so the sins of a believer fall away with the shaking during illness."[94]

Sins are perpetual illnesses in the eternal life. They are also illnesses for the heart, conscience, and spirit in this worldly life. If you persevere and do not complain, you are being saved from numerous perpetual illnesses through that temporary illness. But if you do not worry about sins, or are not aware of the afterlife, or do not recognize God, you have such an illness that it is a million times worse than your present illness. Cry out at it, for your heart, spirit, and soul have relations with all the beings in the world. Your connections with them are continually severed through decay, death, and separation, causing innumerable wounds to open up in you. Particularly since you are not aware of the Hereafter and imagine death to be eternal extinction, it is as if you had a body afflicted with uncountable wounds and illnesses. Therefore, what you must do first is to search for belief as the cure for these innumerable spiritual wounds and illnesses of the ailing body. You must correct your creed, and the shortest, most direct way to such a cure is to recognize the Power and Mercy of an All-Powerful One of Majesty through the window of your innate impotence and weakness, which your physical illness shows you beneath the veil of heedlessness that it has rent.

Indeed, one who does not recognize God is afflicted with a worldful of tribulations, while the world of one who recognizes God is full of light and spiritual joy. Everyone is aware of this according to the strength of their belief. The pain of physical illnesses melts away under the spiritual joy, healing, and pleasure that come from belief.

The ninth remedy

You who are ill and acknowledge your Creator! People fear and are distressed by illness because it sometimes leads to death. Since death is frightening to the superficial, heedless view, illnesses that may lead to it cause fear and worry.

So, first of all, know and believe with certainty that the appointed hour of death is certain and does not change. It has many times occurred that the healthy ones weeping beside the seriously ill have died, while the seriously ill have been cured and continue to live.

---

94 *al-Bukhari*, "Marda'" 1, 2, 13; *Muslim*, "Birr" 14. (Tr.)

Secondly, death is not frightening; it is not as it appears to be. Based on the light provided by the wise Qur'an, we have convincingly explained in many parts of the *Risale-i Nur* that for people of belief, death is a discharge from the hardship of the duties of this life. It is also a respite from worship, which is a drill and training in the arena of trials in this world. Moreover, it is a means of reunion with ninety-nine relatives and beloved ones who have already emigrated to the other world. It is also a means of entering the true homeland and eternal abode of happiness. In addition, it is an invitation from the prison of the world to the spacious gardens of Paradise. And it is the time when one receives a wage from the grace of the All-Compassionate Creator in return for a service. Since this is the reality of death, we should view death not as something terrifying, but as the prelude to mercy and happiness.

Moreover, for some of the people of God, the fear of death is not terror of death itself, but rather on account of their hope, through the continuation of the duties of life, that they will gain more merit by performing more good works.

For the people of belief, death is the door to Divine mercy, while for the people of misguidance it is the pit of eternal darkness.

The tenth remedy

You who are ill and worrying needlessly! Your worry is because of the severity of your illness, but your worries make your illness more severe. If you want your illness to be less severe, try not to worry about it. That is, think about the benefits of your illness, the spiritual rewards it brings, and that it will pass quickly. Give up worrying, and cut off the illness at the root.

Indeed, worry doubles the burden of illness; in addition to your physical illness, it causes an immaterial illness in your heart, upon which the physical illness depends and through which it persists. If that worry vanishes through submission, resignation, and thinking of the wisdom inherent in the illness, one of the important roots of the illness will be severed. It becomes less severe and in part disappears. Sometimes a minor physical illness becomes tenfold just through worries and apprehension. When worries and apprehension cease, nine tenths of the illness disappears. In addition to increasing an illness, since worry is an accusation against Divine wisdom, a criticism of Divine Mercy, and a complaint about the All-Compassionate Creator, it causes counter-suffering, and increases illness.

Indeed, just as thankfulness increases favor, so too do complaints increase illnesses and suffering. Furthermore, worry is itself an illness. The cure for it is knowing the wisdom inherent in illness. Since you are now aware of the wisdom in illness and its benefits, apply that ointment to the worry and be relieved. Say, "Oh!" instead of, "Ah!" and "All praise be to God for every state!" instead of, "Alas!" and "Oh dear!"

The eleventh remedy

You, brother or sister in faith! You who are sick and impatient! Although your present illness causes you some suffering, all your former illnesses have produced an immaterial contentment for your spirit resulting in your recovery from them, and a spiritual pleasure arising from the reward received for enduring them. There may be no more illnesses from today on, even from this hour, so no pain can come from something that does not exist. And if there is no pain, there is no grief. But since you imagine otherwise, you are showing impatience. For all the times of illness before today have disappeared together with the pains they have caused, leaving the rewards the illness has brought and the pleasure their departure gives. So, when they should give you the feeling of profit and happiness, it is crazy to think of them and feel grieved, or to be impatient. The future days have not come yet. Thinking of them now and feeling grieved and showing impatience with thoughts about a day that does not exist, or an illness that does not exist, or a suffering that does not exist, and thus giving the color of existence to three degrees of non-existence—if that is not crazy, what is?

Since the times of illness before now have given happiness, and since the times subsequent to it and the illnesses and sufferings (you imagine they may bring) are non-existent, do not scatter the power of the patience God Almighty has given you to the right and left, but mobilize it against the pain of the present hour. Say, "O All-Patient One!" and endure it.

The twelfth remedy

You who on account of illness cannot perform your regular worship or invocations, and regret this! Know that it is stated in a *hadith*, "A pious, God-revering believer who, due to illness, cannot do the invocations he does normally and regularly, receives an equal reward."[95] Illness substitutes for the supererogatory Prayers of the ill person who does their obligatory worship as much as possible and shows patience in submissive reliance on God.

Furthermore, illness reminds people of their innate impotence and weakness, and causes them to pray both verbally and through the tongue of their state. God Almighty has created human beings with boundless impotence and weakness so that they continually seek refuge in the Divine Court and pray and supplicate. Since, according to the verse, *Say: "My Lord would not care for you were it not for your prayer,"* (25:77) the wisdom in the creation of humanity and the reason for its value are sincere prayer, and as illness leads people to such prayers, rather than complaining about illness, we should thank God, and should not turn off the fountain of prayer that has been caused to flow by illnesses.

The thirteenth remedy

You who are unhappy and complain of your illness! Illness is an important treasure and a very valuable Divine gift for some people. Every ill person can consider their illness from this perspective.

Our appointed hour of death is unknown to us. So, in order to save people from absolute despair and heedlessness and to keep them between fear and hope and in a position from which they may lose neither in the world nor in the Hereafter, God Almighty has concealed the appointed hour of death. Since death can come at any time, if it captures the human being in heedlessness, it may cause great harm to their eternal life. But illness dispels heedlessness, makes people think of their afterlife and reminds them of death and thus prepares them for the Hereafter. They sometimes make such great profit that in twenty days they can gain a rank that they could not otherwise have gained in twenty years.

For instance, from among my friends there were two youths, may God have mercy on them, Sabri from the village of Ilema, and Vezirzade Mustafa from Islamköy. I used to note with amazement that although these two were illiterate and could not serve by copying the *Risale-i Nur*, they were among the foremost in sincerity and the service of belief. I did not know why that

95 *Abu Dawud*, "Jana'iz" 1; Ahmad ibn Hanbal, *al-Musnad*, 4:418.

was so. After their deaths I understood that both had suffered from a serious illness. Guided by that illness, unlike other heedless youths who did not carry out the obligatory worship, they had great reverence for God, and performed the most valuable services, attaining a state beneficial to the Hereafter. God willing, the trouble of two years' illness was the means to the bliss of millions of years of eternal life. I now understand that the prayers I sometimes offered for their health were maledictions in respect to this world. I hope that my prayers were accepted for their well-being in the Hereafter.

Thus, it is my belief that these two gained a profit equal to that which can be gained through ten years' piety and righteousness (*taqwa*). If, like some young people, they had trusted in their youth and good health and let themselves fall into heedlessness and dissipation, and if death, which is always on the watch, had grasped them right in the midst of the filth of their sins, their graves would have been the lairs of scorpions and snakes, instead of that treasury of lights.

Since there are such benefits in illness, we should not complain about it, but bear it with patient reliance on God, indeed, with gratitude to Him and confidence in His Mercy.

The fourteenth remedy

You who are sick in that your eyes are afflicted with cataracts! If you knew what a light and spiritual seeing there is beneath the cataracts that may cover a believer's eyes, you would exclaim, "A hundred thousand thanks to my All-Compassionate Lord." I will relate an incident to you to explain this ointment. It is as follows:

One time, the aunt of Süleyman from Barla, who served me for eight years with perfect loyalty and without causing any resentment, became blind. Thinking well of me a hundred times more than was my due, that righteous woman caught me by the door of the mosque and asked me to pray for the recovery of her eyes. I therefore made that blessed woman's righteousness the intercessor for my prayer, and entreated, "O Lord! Restore her sight due to her righteousness." Two days later, an eye specialist from Burdur came and removed the cataracts. But forty days later she again lost her sight. I was much grieved and prayed for her earnestly. I hope that the prayer was accepted for her afterlife, or else my prayer was the most mistaken malediction for her. For there remained only another forty days until her death; forty days later she died—May God have mercy on her.

Thus, rather than looking sorrowfully at the pathetic gardens of Barla with the eye of old age, she profited by being able to gaze on the gardens of Paradise from her grave for forty thousand days, for she had a firm belief and was earnestly righteous.

If a believer loses their sight and enters the grave blind, they may, in accordance with their degree, gaze on the world of light to a much greater extent than the other people of the grave. Just as in this world we see many things that blind believers do not see, if they go from this world with belief, they see to a greater extent than the other people of the grave. As if looking through the most powerful telescopes, they can, in accordance with their degree, see and gaze on the gardens of Paradise as on a movie screen.

Thus, through thanks and patience you can find under the veil that exists on your present eye an eye that is light-filled and light-diffusing and with which you can see and gaze on Paradise above the heavens while under the soil. The eye specialist which will remove the veil from your present eye and enable you to look with that eye is the wise Qur'an.

The fifteenth remedy

You who are sick and sighing and lamenting! Do not consider the outward aspect of illness and sigh; consider its meaning and be content. If the meaning of illness was not good, the All-Compassionate Creator would not have given illness to His most-beloved servants. A *hadith* says, "Those afflicted with the severest trials are the Prophets, then those resembling them, and then those resembling the latter."[96] That is, those most afflicted with suffering and hardship are the best of people, the most perfect of them. The Prophets, including in particular the Prophet Job, upon him be peace, then the saints, and then those foremost in righteousness after the Prophets and saints have regarded the illnesses they have suffered as sincere worship and gifts from the All-Merciful. They have offered thanks in patience. They have seen these illnesses as surgical operations performed by the compassion of the All-Compassionate Creator.

96 *at-Tirmidhi*, "Zuhd" 57; *Ibn Maja*, "Fitan" 23. (Tr.)

O you who cry out and lament! If you want to join this light-diffusing caravan, offer thanks in patience. For if you complain, they will not admit you among them. You will fall into the pits of the people of misguidance, and go along a dark road.

Indeed, there are some illnesses which, if they lead to death, are like a sort of martyrdom. They cause one to gain some certain degree of sainthood. For example, like the believing women who die during or because of childbirth,[97] those who die from pains in the abdomen, and by drowning, burning, or the plague, are considered as martyrs.[98] There are also other such blessed illnesses which help to gain a degree of sainthood for those who die from them. Furthermore, since illness lessens the love of the world and attachment to it, it lightens the pain of parting from the world, which is extremely grievous for worldly people. Sometimes it makes such a departure desirable.

The sixteenth remedy

You who are sick and complain of your distress! Illness induces respect and compassion, which are most important and good for human social life. This saves people from conceited feelings of self-sufficiency, which drives them to unfriendliness and unkindness. For according to the reality stated in, *No indeed, but the human is unruly and rebels, in that he sees himself as self-sufficient* (96: 6–7), a carnal, evil-commanding soul which feels self-sufficient due to good health and well-being does not regard the many causes which are deserving of brotherhood. And they do not feel compassion towards the misfortune-stricken or ill, who should be shown kindness and pity. Yet, whenever they become ill, they are aware of their own innate impotence and neediness, and feel respect towards their sisters and brothers who are worthy of it. They pay respect to their believing brothers and sisters who visit or help them. And they feel human kindness, which originates in fellow-feeling and compassion for the disaster-stricken—a most important Islamic characteristic. Comparing others to themselves, they empathize with them, feel affection for them, and do whatever they can to help them.

---

97 A child-bearing woman may gain some sort of martyrdom if she dies within forty days after giving birth.

98 *al-Buhari*, "Jihad" 30; *Muslim*, "'Imara" 164. (Tr.)

At the very least they pray for others and pay them a visit of consolation, which is a *Sunna* act according to the Shari'a,[99] thus earning reward.

The seventeenth remedy

You who are sick and complain of not being able to do good works due to illness! Offer thanks! It is illness that opens to you the door of the most sincere of good works. Illness is a most important means of continuously gaining reward for the sick person and for those who are looking after them for the sake of God; it is, in addition, a means for supplications to be accepted.

Certainly, there is significant reward for believers who look after the sick. Asking after the health of those who are ill and visiting them—provided it does not tax them—is a *sunna* act, an act highly recommended by our Prophet, upon him be peace and blessings.[100] It is also expiation for sins. There is a *hadith* which says, "Receive the prayers of the ill, for their prayers are acceptable."[101]

Especially if the person who is ill is a relative, in particular parents, looking after them is an important form of worship which yields significant rewards. To please an invalid's heart and to console them is like giving alms. Fortunate is the one who pleases the easily-touched hearts of their father and mother when they are ill, and receives their prayer. Indeed, even the angels applaud saying, "How good, how blessed that is! May God reward them abundantly!" before faithful scenes of those good offspring who respond to the compassion and care of their parents—those most worthy of respect in the life of society—during their illness with perfect respect and filial kindness, showing the exaltedness of humanity.

There is great happiness and joy during an illness which arises from the kindness, pity, and compassion of those around the one who is sick; they reduce the pains of the illness to nothing. The acceptability of the prayers of the sick is of great importance. For the past thirty or forty years, I myself have prayed to be cured of the lumbago from which I suffer. However, I understood that the illness was given to me as an encouragement to prayer. Since prayer cannot be removed through prayer, that is, since prayer cannot

---

99 *Muslim*, "Birr" 40; *Abu Dawud*, "Jana'iz" 7; *at-Tirmidhi*, "Jana'iz" 2. (Tr.)

100 *al-Bukhari*, "Marda'" 4, 5; *Muslim*, "Salam" 47.

101 *Ibn Maja* "Jana'iz" 1; al-Bayhaqi, *Shu'ab al-Iman*, 6:541. (Tr.)

remove itself,[102] I understood that the answer to prayers will be obtained in the Hereafter, and that illness is itself a kind of worship, for through illness one realizes one's innate impotence and seeks refuge in the Divine Court. Therefore, although I have prayed for thirty years to be healed and apparently my prayer has not been accepted, it has never occurred to me to abandon the prayer. Because illness is the occasion or reason for prayer; to be cured is not the effect of the prayer. If the All-Wise and Compassionate One bestows healing, He bestows it out of His pure grace.

Furthermore, if prayers are not accepted in the form we desire, it should not be said that they have not been answered. The All-Wise Creator knows better than us; He gives whatever is good for us. Sometimes in our interest He accepts our prayers for our worldly life in the name of our afterlife. In any event, a prayer that acquires sincerity due to an illness and which arises from our innate weakness, impotence, humility and need in particular, is very close to being acceptable. Illness is the means to the prayer that is sincere in this way. Both the sick who are religious and believers who look after the sick should make the most of this prayer.

The eighteenth remedy

You who are ill and have abandoned offering thanks and have now taken up complaining! Complaints arise from a right to complain. You have no rights violated, nor have you lost anything which would allow you to complain. Rather, there are numerous thanks that are obligatory for you, but you have not fulfilled them. Without performing your duties towards God Almighty, which are His rights over you, you are complaining as if you are demanding rights in a manner that is not righteous. You cannot look at others who are better off than you in health and complain. You are rather charged with looking at those who are worse than you in health, and offering thanks. If your hand is broken, look at those whose hands have been severed. If you have only one eye, look at those blind, lacking both eyes. And offer thanks to God!

---

102 Certain illnesses encourage and are the reason for prayer. Therefore, if a prayer causes the termination of the illness, then prayer would annul the reason for it. This cannot be admitted.

Certainly, no one has the right to consider others as more advantaged than themselves in regard to bounties and to complain. And in tribulations, it is the right of all to consider those who are worse off than themselves, and thus offer thanks. This truth has been explained in a number of places in the *Risale-i Nur* with a simile, a summary of which is as follows:

A person conducts a poor wretch to the top of a minaret. At every step he gives the wretch a different gift, a different bounty. Right at the top of the minaret he gives him the largest gift. Although he deserves thanks and gratitude in return for all those various gifts, the churlish wretch forgets the gifts he has received at each step, or considers them of no importance, and without offering thanks, looks above him and begins to complain, saying: "If only this minaret had been higher, I could have climbed even further. Why isn't it as tall as that mountain over there or that other minaret?" If he begins to complain like this, what great ingratitude this is, what a great wrong!

In the same way, every human being comes into existence from nothing, and without being a rock or a tree or an animal, becomes human. Furthermore, being a Muslim is another great bounty. Most of the time, we enjoy good health and are honored with a great number of bounties. Despite all this, to complain and show impatience because we are not worthy of some bounties due to certain deficiencies pertaining to ourselves, or because we lose them through wrong choices or abuses, or because we were unable to obtain them, and thus to criticize the Divine Lordship, saying, "What have I done to cause this to happen to me?" is a spiritual sickness more disastrous than the physical one. Like fighting with a broken hand, complaint makes illness worse. The sensible person is the one who is proclaimed as,

> *Those who, when a disaster befalls them, say, "Surely we belong to God (as His creatures and servants), and surely to Him we are bound to return." (And they act accordingly)* (2: 156),

and shows patience in submission to God Almighty, so that the illness may complete its duty and depart.

The nineteenth remedy

As a term signifying God's being the Eternally Besought-of-All, while He Himself is in need of nothing, "the All-Beautiful Names" show that all the Names of the All-Gracious One of Majesty are beautiful. Among created beings, the most subtle, the most beautiful, the most comprehensive mirror that reflects God's being the Eternally Besought-of-All is life. The mirror to the beautiful is beautiful. The mirror that shows the beauties of the beautiful becomes beautiful. Just as whatever befalls the mirror through such beauty is good and beautiful, so also whatever befalls life, from the viewpoint of truth, is good, because it exhibits the beautiful imprints of the All-Beautiful Names, which are all good and beautiful.

If life passes monotonously with permanent health and appetite, it becomes a deficient mirror. Indeed, in one respect, it suggests non-existence and nothingness, and causes weariness. It reduces the value of life, and changes the pleasure of life into distress. With the intention of passing their time quickly, out of boredom people let themselves fall into either dissipation or into distractions. They become hostile to their valuable life as if it were a prison sentence, and want to kill it, and make it pass quickly. By contrast, a life that revolves in change and action and different states makes its value felt, and enables us to recognize its importance and pleasure. Even if it is a life of troubles and misfortune, one with such a life does not want life to pass quickly. They make no complaints out of boredom; they do not utter, "Alas! The sun hasn't set yet," or, "It is still night time."

Ask a rich and idle gentleman who is living in the lap of luxury with nothing lacking, "How are you?" You will certainly hear a pathetic reply like, "Time never passes. Let's have a game of backgammon. Or let's find some other distraction to make time pass." Or else you will hear complaints arising from long-term worldly ambitions, like, "I haven't attained this; if only I had done that activity."

Then ask someone struck by disaster or a laborer or a poor man who is in hardship, "How are you?" If they are sensible, they will reply, "All thanks be to my Lord, I am well and working. If only the evening did not come so quickly, I could have finished this task! Time passes so quickly, and life goes on without stopping. Certainly, I have troubles and difficulties, but they will pass too. Everything passes quickly." In effect, such a person is saying how valuable life is and how they regret its passing. This means that they understand the pleasure and value of life which comes with hardship and labor, while ease and health make life bitter and make one desire for it to pass.

You, brother or sister Muslim, who are sick! As is explained convincingly and in detail in some other parts of the *Risale-i Nur*, know that the origin and culture of calamities and evils, and even of sins, is non-existence. As for non-existence, it is evil and darkness. It is because states like continuous ease, silence, inertia, and being sedentary are close to non-existence and nothingness that they make felt the darkness of non-existence and cause distress. As for action and change, they are existence and make existence felt. And existence is pure good, and it is light.

Since this is a reality, your illness has been sent to your body as a guest so that it will carry out many duties like purifying your valuable life, and strengthening and developing it, as well as making other members and faculties of your body turn in assistance towards the part of you that is unwell, and displaying the imprints of various Names of the All-Wise Maker. God willing, the illness will carry out its duties quickly and depart. And it will say to good health, "Now you come, and stay permanently in my place, and carry out your duties. This house is yours. Remain here in a good condition."

The twentieth remedy

You who are sick and seeking a remedy for your ills! Illness is of two kinds. One kind is real; the other is imaginary. As for the real kind, the All-Wise Healer of Majesty has stored up in His mighty pharmacy of the earth a remedy for every illness. Without illness, how can those remedies be known and enjoyed? The Religion requires that medicines should be used in treatment, but we should know that their effect and the cure are from God Almighty. It is He Who gives the cure, and it is He Who provides the medicine.

Following the recommendations of skilful, God-conscious doctors is an important form of treatment. For most illnesses arise from abuses, a lack of abstinence, extravagance, vice, dissipation, and indifference and a lack of care. A God-conscious doctor will certainly give advice and orders that are not contrary to Islamic precepts. They will forbid abuses and extravagance, and give consolation. The sick person has confidence in their recommendations and consolation, and the illness wanes, giving a feeling of relief in place of distress.

But when it comes to illnesses that are imaginary, the most effective medicine of all is to give it no importance. The more importance is given to it, the more it grows and swells. If no importance is given, the illness lessens and fades away. The more bees are disturbed, the more they swarm around a person's head, while if they are paid no attention, they disperse. Also, the more attention one pays to a piece of string waving in front of one's eyes in the darkness, the more it disturbs one and causes one to flee from it like a madman. While if you pay it no attention, you can see that it is an ordinary bit of string and not a snake, and you will laugh at your fear and anxiety.

If the groundless worry about one's health continues for a long time, it is transformed into reality. It is an evil ailment for the nervous and those given to groundless fears and worries; such people make a mountain out of a molehill and their morale is destroyed. In particular, if they encounter unkind and unfair "half" doctors, their worries are provoked and increase. If they are rich, they lose their wealth, or else they lose their wits, or their health.

The twenty-first remedy

You, brother or sister in faith, who are sick! You are suffering physical pain because of your illness, but a significant spiritual pleasure which will remove the effect of your physical pain surrounds you. For if you have a father, mother, or relatives, their most pleasurable compassion towards you, which you have long forgotten, will be awakened and you will see again their kind looks which you received in childhood. In addition, the friends around you who have remained veiled and hidden will look again towards you with love through the attraction of illness. In the face of these, your physical pain is infinitesimal. Also, those whom you serve proudly and from whom you try to receive appreciation now serve you kindly due to your illness, and thus you have become a master of your masters. Furthermore, since you have attracted towards yourself the fellow feeling and human tenderness of people, you have found many helpful friends and kind companions who expect nothing in return. Again, you have received from your illness the order to rest from many exhausting duties, and you are taking a rest. Certainly, in the face of these spiritual pleasures, your minor pain should lead you to thanks, not to complaint.

The twenty-second remedy

You, brother or sister in faith, who suffer a severe illness such as paralysis! Firstly, I give you the good news that for believers paralysis is regarded as blessed. I have long heard this from saintly people, but I did not know the reason. Now, one reason occurs to me as follows:

In order to obtain the approval and good pleasure of God Almighty, and to be saved from the great dangers that this world poses to the spiritual life, and to attain eternal happiness, the people of God have chosen to follow two principles:

The first is contemplation of death. Thinking of the world as transitory and realizing that they too are transient guests in the world who have many duties, they work for the eternal life in this way.

The second: In order to be saved from the dangers of the carnal, evil-commanding soul and blind passions, they have tried to kill the evil-commanding soul through austerity, religious exercises, and asceticism.

And you, my brother or sister, who have lost the health of half your body! Without choosing to do so, you have been given these two principles, which are the cause of happiness, so that your body continually warns you against the fleeting nature of the world and reminds you that humans are mortal. The world cannot drown you anymore, nor can heedlessness close your eyes. And certainly, the carnal, evil-commanding soul cannot deceive someone in the state of half a person by vile lusts and animal appetites; that person is quickly saved from the trials of the evil-commanding soul.

Thus, through belief in and submission to God and reliance on Him, a believer can benefit in a short time from a severe illness like paralysis, rather than undergoing the severe trials of the saints. Thus an illness that is so severe becomes an exceedingly modest exchange for these gains.

The twenty-third remedy

You who are ill and unhappy, alone and a stranger! While your isolation and exile together with your illness arouse sympathy in the hardest hearts and attract kindness and compassion to you, certainly they will also attract the All-Compassionate Creator's compassion towards you, which is certain to be a substitute for the sympathy and compassion of everything else. It is He Who presents Himself to us at the start of all but one of the *suras* of the Qur'an with the Attributes of "All-Merciful and All-Compassionate." Through one gleam of His Compassion, He causes all mothers to nurture their young with wonderful tenderness, and through one manifestation of His Mercy every spring, He fills the face of the earth with bounties. Also, with all its wonders, Paradise, which is the abode of eternal happiness, constitutes a single manifestation of His Mercy. Thus, your relation to Him through belief, your recognition of Him and entreating Him through the voice of helplessness that is found in your illness, and your loneliness in exile will surely attract His mercy towards you.

Since He exists and He looks to you, everything exists for you. Those who are truly alone and in exile are those who have no relation to Him through belief and submission, or who attach no importance to that relation.

The twenty-fourth remedy

You who tend innocent, sick children or the elderly who are like innocent children! Before you is an important commodity for the Hereafter. Carry out these tasks with zeal and endeavor! In the illnesses of innocent children there are many instances of wisdom pertaining to their worldly life. For instance, their illnesses are like exercises and drills for their delicate bodies, and the inoculations and training of the Lord, so that they may be able to withstand the tumults and upheavals of the world in the future. As is accepted by verifying scholars, like expiations for sins in adults, the illnesses of innocent children are also inoculations which will serve their spiritual life, their spiritual purification and development in the future or in the Hereafter. In addition, the merits ensuing from such illnesses are recorded in the notebook of the good deeds of the parents, and particularly of the mother who, out of compassion, prefers the health of her child to her own.

As for looking after the elderly, it is accurately reported from our Prophet, upon him be peace and blessings, and has been established by many historical events, that in addition to bringing mighty rewards, receiving the prayers of the elderly, and especially that of parents, and making their hearts happy and serving them faithfully is the means to happiness both in this world and in the Hereafter.[103] And there are many experiences that establish that a child who perfectly obeys his elderly parents will receive the same treatment from his or her children, and that a child who wounds his or her parents will not only be punished in the Hereafter, but will also be subject to many disasters in this world. Not only looking after relatives who are elderly or innocent children, but also serving willingly any

103 *al-Bukhari*, "Adab" 1–6,; *Muslim*, "Birr" 1–6, 9, 10; *at-Tirmidhi*, "Da'awat" 110.

believing sick person, especially if that one is in need of us—since there is true brotherhood coming from belief—is a requirement of being a Muslim.

The twenty-fifth remedy

You, brother and sister Muslims, who are ill! If you desire a most beneficial, truly pleasurable, and sacred medicine, which is the cure for every illness, develop your belief! That is, through repentance and seeking God's forgiveness for your sins, and the five daily Prayers, and other duties of worship, apply to your illnesses belief—that sacred cure—and the medicine it provides.

Indeed, due to the love of this world and attachment to it, it is as if the worldly people have a sick worldly existence as big as the world. We have convincingly explained in many parts of the *Risale-i Nur* that belief immediately heals that sick existence, which, like the world itself, is subject to the blows of death and separation and "riddled" with wounds and bruises. I cut short the discussion here not to weary you.

As for the medicine of belief, it shows its effect when you carry out your religious obligations as far as is possible. Heedlessness, dissipation, carnal desires, and religiously forbidden amusements prevent the effectiveness of that remedy. Since illness removes heedlessness, reduces the appetites, and prevents one from partaking in religiously unlawful pleasures, take advantage of it. Apply the sacred medicines and lights of true belief through repentance, seeking God's forgiveness, and prayers, and supplications.

May Almighty God restore you to health and make your illnesses expiation for your sins. Amen. Amen. Amen.

> *They say: "All praise and gratitude are for God, Who has guided us to this. If God had not guided us, we would certainly not have found the right way. The Messengers of our Lord did indeed come with the truth."* (7: 43)
>
> All-Glorified are You. We have no knowledge save what You have taught us. Surely You are the All-Knowing, the All-Wise.
>
> O God! Bestow blessings on our master Muhammad, the medicine for hearts and their cure, the good health of bodies and their healing, the light of eyes and their light, and on his Family and Companions, and bestow on them peace.

The Twenty-Sixth Gleam

The Twenty-Sixth Gleam

Hope and solace for the elderly

[NOTE] The reason why, at the beginning of each Hope, I have written of my sorrows and afflictions in a way that may sadden you is to show the extraordinary efficacy of the remedies proceeding from the All-Wise Qur'an.

This Gleam, which is about the elderly, may have been unable to attain fluency due to certain reasons, such as those that follow:

The first: Since it has been generally based on my own experiences and written in a mood that arises from recalling those former times, it was not possible to attain a sequence in expression.

The second: Since it was written rapidly after the early morning Prayer, when I felt fatigued, there is some confusion in expression.

The third: There was not always somebody with me to write, and the scribe who accompanied me had four or five other duties concerning the *Risale-i Nur*. Since we therefore could not find enough time to revise it thoroughly, there is a certain disorder.

The fourth: Both the scribe and I were exhausted after its completion, and felt compelled to be content with a superficial revision of the wording without considering the expression adequately. Because of this, there may naturally be errors of expression. We request that the magnanimous elderly will overlook my errors of expression and as Divine Mercy does not leave empty the hands of the blessed elderly which are opened towards It,[104] we hope that they will include us in their prayers when they open their hands towards the Divine Court.

---

104 at-Tabarani, *al-Majma' al-Awsat*, 5:270; al-Haythami, *Majma' az-Zawa'id*, 10: 149. (Tr.)

In the Name of God, the All-Merciful, the All-Compassionate.

Kaf. Ha. Ya. 'Ayn. Sad. A mention of your Lord's mercy to His servant Zachariah: When he invoked his Lord with a call in secret, saying: "My Lord! My bones have grown feeble and my head glistens with gray hair from old age, and, my Lord, I have never been unblessed in my prayer to You." (19: 1–4)

This Gleam contains twenty-six Hopes.

The first hope

Respected elderly brothers and sisters who have reached the age of maturity: Like you, I am elderly. Out of the desire to share with you the lights of consolation they contain, I will write the Hopes which I have, from time to time, found in my old age and some of my experiences. Of course, the lights I have seen and the doors of hope I have encountered have been seen and opened according to my defective and confused capacity. God willing, your pure and sincere dispositions will make the lights I have seen shine more brightly and strengthen the hopes I have found.

The source, spring, and fount of the hopes and lights to follow is belief (in God and the other pillars of faith).

The second hope

One autumn day when old age was upon me, at about the time of the afternoon Prayer, I was looking at the world from a high mountain and I became overwhelmed by a piteous, mournful and, in some sense, dark mood or state of mind. I saw that I had become old. The day also had grown old, and so had the year; and so too had the world. All those instances of old age made me feel that the time of departure from the world and separation from those I loved had drawn close, and my own old age shook me severely. Suddenly Divine Mercy unfolded in such a way that it changed that piteous sadness and separation into a powerful hope and radiant light of solace. I affirm to you who are elderly like me: the All-Compassionate Creator presents Himself to us in a hundred places in the wise Qur'an as "the All-Merciful and the All-Compassionate." He is always sending His mercy to the aid of the living creatures on the earth which seek it. Every year He sends the spring, which He fills with innumerable bounties and gifts from the Unseen, to us, who are needy of provision, and manifests His mercy abundantly proportionate to our innate weakness and impotence. Thus, the Mercy[105] of our All-Compassionate Creator is the greatest hope and most powerful light in our old age. We can find this Mercy by forming a connection with and adhering to the All-Merciful through belief and by obeying Him by performing the daily Prayers.

The third hope

When I awoke in the morning of old age from the sleep of the night of youth, I looked at myself and saw that my life was hurrying towards the grave as though speeding down a slope. As Niyazi Misri[106] said,

> Each day a stone from the building of my life falls to the ground;
> The soul slumbers in heedlessness and is unaware that its building is in ruins!

my body, the dwelling of my spirit, was decaying, with a stone of it crumbling every day. Having felt this, the hopes and ambitions that had bound me strongly to the world began to be broken off. I felt that the time of separation from my many friends and those I loved was drawing near. I searched for an ointment for that very deep and apparently incurable spiritual wound, but I could find none. Again like Niyazi Misri I said:

> While my heart desired permanence, God, the Truth,
> judged the mortality of my body;
> I am afflicted with an incurable ill; how pitiful it is that
> Luqman is unaware of it!

Then suddenly the light and intercession of the glorious Prophet, upon him be peace and blessings, who is the voice, model, embodiment, herald,

---

105 The things concerning or belonging to God Almighty are sometimes initiated with capital letters and sometimes with small ones. For example, in this paragraph "mercy" is initiated either with a capital letter or with a small one. If it refers to God's Name or Attribute, it is initiated with a capital letter, but if it refers to a manifestation of that Name or Attribute, it is initiated with a small letter. (Tr.)

106 Mehmet Niyazi Misri (1617–1694). He was born in Malatya, Turkey, and died in the island of Limni in the Agean Sea. He was a Sufi *shaykh*, poet, and scholar. *Ilmihali Tariqat* ("The Principles of the Sufi Way"), *Mawadi al-'Irfan* ("The Tables of Esoteric Knowledge"), and *Tevhid Risalesi* (A Treatise of God's Oneness") are among his most famous works. (Tr.)

and representative of Divine Mercy, and the gift of guidance he had brought to humankind became a good ointment for that wound which I had supposed to be incurable.

Respected elderly men and women who feel their old age as I do! We are leaving; there is no use in deceiving ourselves. Even if we close our eyes to it, we will not be allowed to remain here. There is mobilization. The land of the Intermediate Realm of the grave, which appears to us as dark and as the land of eternal separation because of the delusions that arise from heedlessness and in part from the people of misguidance, is the meeting place of friends. It is the realm where we will meet with, foremost, God's Beloved, upon him be peace and blessings, and with all our friends.

We are going to the world of the one who for one thousand three hundred and fifty years, has been the ruler of hundreds of millions of people, and the trainer of their spirits, the teacher of their minds, and the beloved of their hearts. According to the rule, "The cause is like the doer," the equivalent of the merit that his whole Community gains every day through its good deeds is added to his notebook of good deeds. He is the means for the realization of the exalted Divine purposes in the universe and the increase of the value of beings. As recorded in authentic Traditions and discovered by saints of spiritual discovery, when he came into the world, he exclaimed, "My Community! My Community!"[107] He will also hasten to the aid of his Community with the loftiest self-sacrifice and through his intercession when everyone will consider only themselves in the Place of Supreme Gathering in the other world, and again he will exclaim, "My Community! My Community!"[108] We are going to a world that is illuminated by this sun and by the stars of countless saints and purified scholars.

The means of being entitled to that person's intercession, profiting from his light, and being saved from the darkness of the Intermediate Realm is to follow his noble example or way (Sunna).

The fourth hope

When I stepped into old age, my physical health, which perpetuates heedlessness, was broken. Old age and illness attacked me together in unison.

---

107 as-Suyuti, *al-Khasa'is al-Kubra*, 1:80, 85. (Tr.)

108 *al-Bukhari*, "Tawhid" 36; *Muslim*, "Iman" 326. (Tr.)

They continuously disturbed me, causing unceasing trouble. I had nothing binding me to the world, no family, children, or possessions. I saw the fruit of my life's capital, which I had wasted through the giddiness of youth, to be only sins and errors. Crying out like Niyazi Misri, I said:

I had concluded no trade; the capital of life was all wasted away;
I found the road only to find the caravan had moved on
while I had been unaware.
Lamenting, I too set off, all alone, a stranger
With eyes weeping, heart in anguish, mind bewildered and unaware.

I was in exile at the time. I felt a despairing sorrow, a deep regret, a longing for assistance. All at once, the Qur'an of miraculous expression came to my aid. It opened for me such a powerful door of hope and offered me such a light of true consolation that it could have removed any despair and darkness that was a hundred times more intense than mine.

Respected elderly men and women whose interests in the world have begun to cease when the ties that bind them to this world are gradually broken! Is it possible that the Maker of Majesty, Who has created this world as a most perfectly ordered city or palace, would not meet or speak to His most important guests and friends in that palace? Since He knowingly made this palace and ordered and decorated it purposefully, certainly—just as the one who makes something knows—the One Who knows will speak. And since He has made this palace and city as a fine guesthouse and place of trade for us, He will certainly have a book that demonstrates His relations for us and what He desires from us.

The most perfect of such sacred Books is the Qur'an of miraculous expression. It is a miracle in forty respects and at every instant is on the tongues of at least a hundred million people. It diffuses light, and every letter of it provides at least ten merits and rewards, and sometimes ten thousand fruits of Paradise and lights in the Intermediate Realm, and sometimes—due to the meaning and importance of the Night of Destiny and Power—thirty thousand. It also provides the fruit of Paradise and light for the Intermediate Realm of the grave. There is no book in the universe to compete with it in these respects and no one can put one forward. As this Qur'an we hold is the Word of the All-Majestic Creator of the heavens and earth, having issued from His absolute Lordship, supreme Divinity, and all-encompassing Mercy, and is His decree and a source of His mercy—adhere to it. In it is a cure for every ill, a light for every veil and kind of darkness, and a hope for every instance of despair.

The key to this eternal treasury is belief and submission to God, listening to the Qur'an and accepting and reciting it.

The fifth hope

Once, at the onset of my old age, my spirit sought ease in solitude on Mount Joshua (Yusha Tepesi) up the Bosphorus in Istanbul. One day on that high hill, I looked around at the broad horizon, and saw an extremely pathetic scene of decay and separation through the warning of old age. I took a look from the high position of the forty-fifth branch, that is, the forty-fifth year, of the tree of my life to my life's lower levels. I saw that down on each of the lower branches, in each year, there were numerous corpses of those I knew and loved, and to whom I was somehow related. Thinking of the friends who had left, with truly pitiful sorrow that arose from separation, I groaned like Fuzuli of Baghdad:[109]

As I recall your company I weep,
So long as there is breath in this dry body of mine, I cry out...

So saying, I sought solace, a light, a door of hope. All at once, the light of belief in the Hereafter came to my aid, offering an inextinguishable light, an indestructible hope. It is as follows:

Brothers and sisters who are elderly like me! As there is the Hereafter and it is everlasting, and it is a realm much better than this world, and as the One Who has created us is both All-Wise and All-Compassionate, we should not complain of or regret our old age. On the contrary, since old age is a sign of reaching the age of maturity in belief and worship, and signals a discharge from the duties of life and departure for the world of mercy in order to rest, we should be pleased with it.

---

109 Mehmed Fuzuli (1490–1556). One of the greatest poets of Turkish literature. He lived in Iraq and wrote many works both in verse and in prose. His *Divan* ("Collection of Poems"), which he wrote in Turkish, Persian, and Arabic is the most famous among his works. *Layla wu Majnun* ("Layla and Majnun"), *Tarjuma-i Hadith-i Arbain* ("The Translation of the Forty Hadiths"), and *Hadiqat as-Su'ada'* ("The Garden of the Holy Ones") are among his most famous works. (Tr.)

A *hadith* says that one hundred and twenty-four thousand Prophets, who are the most eminent and distinguished among humanity, have been sent.[110] All of these Prophets, based on Divine Revelation and their own spiritual observation, unanimously and in complete agreement gave news that the Hereafter does exist, that human beings will be sent there, and that the Creator will bring it as He promised. In addition, one hundred and twenty-four million saints, with spiritual illumination, discovery, and observation have confirmed the reports of the Prophets with the degree of certainty arising from knowledge, and testified to the existence of the Hereafter. Also, all the Names of the All-Wise Maker, through their manifestations in this world, show the absolutely necessary existence of and necessitate an everlasting realm. For example, the Eternal Power, Which every spring restores to life innumerable corpses of dead trees on the face of the earth with the command of "*Be!*" *and it is*, and Which revives hundreds of thousands of species of plants and animals as samples of the resurrection of the dead, most clearly necessitates the existence of the Hereafter. Likewise, the infinite, Eternal Wisdom, Which allows nothing to be in vain or purposeless, and the Eternal Mercy and Perpetual Favor, Which, with perfect compassion and in an extremely wonderful fashion, provides the sustenance of all living beings that are in need of it, and for a brief time in spring allow them to display their manifold varieties of adornment and decoration, require the Hereafter. Furthermore, the human being is the most perfect fruit of the universe and its Creator's most beloved creature, and of all beings the human is the most closely and deeply connected and concerned with the other beings in the universe. The intense, unshakeable, and constant love of eternity and ambition for permanence that are innate in human nature prove the existence of a permanent realm, an everlasting abode of happiness that will follow this transient world, so decisively that they necessitate the acceptance of the Hereafter with the same certainty that we accept the existence of this world.[111]

---

110 Ahmad ibn Hanbal, *al-Musnad*, 5:265; Ibn Hibban, *as-Sahih*, 2:77. (Tr.)

111 The ease of reporting something which definitely exists and the extreme difficulty in denying it may be seen in the following comparison: if one person says, "There is a wonderful garden on earth, the trees of which have fruits that are cans of milk," and another says, "There isn't," the one claiming it proves his or her claim only by pointing out its place or some of its fruits or a single member of it. Whereas, the one denying it has to scan and show the whole face of the earth. In just the same way, even if we ignore the hundreds of

Since one of the most important things the wise Qur'an teaches us is belief in the Hereafter, and since this belief is so powerful and it provides such hope and solace that if a single person were overwhelmed by old age a hundred thousand times over, the consolation arising from this belief would be sufficient to face it, then surely we who are elderly should say, "All praise be to God for perfect belief," and love our old age.

The sixth hope

Once during my distressing surveillance, having preferred seclusion, I was alone on the top of Pine Mountain (Çam Dağı) in the Barla plateau (in the province of Isparta). I was in need of a light in my isolation. Alone one night on the small platform at the top of a tall pine on the summit of that high mountain, old age recalled to me three or four separations, one within another. As described in The Sixth Letter (included in *The Letters*), the melancholy sound of the rustling trees on that lonely, silent, remote night burdened me greatly in my exile in old age. Old age prompted the following thought: Just as the daylight has changed into this sepulchral black and the world has put on its black shroud, so too the daytime of your life will turn into night, and the daytime of the world turn into the night of the Intermediate Realm of the grave, and the summertime of life into the winter nighttime of death. It whispered this in my heart's ear. My soul was then obliged to respond:

True, I am far from my native land, but being separated from and mourning all those who are now dead, whom I loved during my fifty years of life, is a far more grievous and sorrowful separation than exile from my country. Furthermore, I am drawing close to a much more sorrowful and painful exile than the melancholy exile of the night and the mountain: old age informs me that I am approaching the time of separation from the world altogether.

I then sought a light, a hope, from these sorrowful separations, one within the other. Suddenly belief in God came to my aid and offered such com-

---

thousands of signs, fruits, and marks of Paradise which those who report its existence have pointed out, the testimony of two truthful witnesses to the truth of their report is sufficient. But in order to prove his denial, the one who denies it has to scan the limitless universe and infinite, unending time, and demonstrate its non-existence. And so, my elderly brothers and sisters, understand just how powerful is belief in the Hereafter.

panionship that even if the layered desolation in which I found myself had increased a thousand times, its consolation would have been sufficient.

Elderly men and women! Since we have a Compassionate Creator, there can be no exile for us. Since He exists, everything exists for us. Since He exists and has angels, the world is not empty. Lonely mountains and empty deserts are full of God Almighty's servants. Apart from His conscious servants, His stones and trees also become like familiar friends when viewed through His light and on His account. They may converse with us and give us contentment.

Evidence and testimonies to the number of beings in the universe and to the number of the letters of this vast book of the universe affirm the existence of our All-Compassionate, All-Munificent, All-Intimate, and All-Loving Creator, Maker, and Protector. They show us His Mercy to the number of the members of the living creatures' members, and of the provision and favors they enjoy, all of which are the instruments of His Compassion, Mercy, and Grace, and point the way to His Court. The most acceptable intercessor at His Court is impotence, weakness, and neediness. And the greatest time of impotence, weakness, and neediness is old age. So we should not resent old age, which is an acceptable intercessor at this Court, but welcome it.

The seventh hope

Once at the onset of old age when the laughter of the Old or Former Said was changing into the weeping of the New Said, some worldly-minded people in Ankara, supposing me to be still the Old Said, invited me there, and I went. At the close of autumn I climbed to the top of the city fort, which was dilapidated, and far more aged than me. It seemed to me as if it were formed by petrified historical events. The old age of the season of the year together with my old age, the fort's old age, humankind's old age, the old age of the glorious Ottoman State, and the demise of the sultanate representing caliphate, and the world's old age all caused me to look in the most sorrowful, piteous, and melancholy state from that lofty fort to the valleys of the past and the mountains of the future. I found myself in an utterly dark state of mind in Ankara, encompassed by four or five layers of the darknesses of old age, one within the other, and I sought a light, a solace, a hope.

As I looked to the right, that is, to the past, to find solace, it appeared to me in the form of the vast graveyard of my father and forefathers and the human race, causing me gloom rather than consolation. Seeking a cure I looked to the future on the left. It appeared as a huge, dark graveyard for myself, my contemporaries, and future generations, giving horror in place of relief and solace. Frightened in the face of what was to the left and right, I looked to the present time. To my heedless and historical eye it appeared as a coffin bearing my half-dead, suffering corpse, which was desperately struggling as if dying. Then, despairing from that direction as well, I raised my head and looked to the top of the tree of my life, and there was my corpse: it rested at the top of the tree and was watching me. Feeling horror from this direction too, I lowered my head, looking to the foot of the tree of my life, to its roots. I saw that the dust of my bones underfoot had mixed with the dust of my creation. That too provided no cure; it doubled my pain.

Then I felt forced to look behind me. I saw that this temporary world, which has no foundation, was revolving through the valleys of nothingness and the darkness of non-existence. I had been seeking a medicine for my pain, but this view only aggravated it. Seeing no good in that direction, I looked in front of me, I cast my eye ahead. I saw the entrance of a grave plain to view, right in my path, open and staring at me, its mouth wide open. The highway behind it led to eternity and the convoys traveling it caught my eye. And all that I have as my support and defense in the face of the horrors that come from these six directions is only a limited, insignificant willpower. Since that willpower, which is the sole human defense against those innumerable enemies and harmful things, is defective, short-range, and feeble, with no power to create, it is capable of nothing apart from being something receptive and committing. It can neither turn back and enter the past so that it can silence the sorrows that arise from there nor can it penetrate the future so that it can prevent the fears that come from there. I saw that my pains and ambitions concerning the past and future were to no avail.

Even as I was struggling with the horror, isolation, darkness and despair coming from these six directions, the lights of belief which shine in the heaven of the Qur'an of miraculous expression suddenly came to my aid. They lit up and illuminated those six directions to such a degree that if the horrors and darkness I had seen increased a hundredfold, the lights would still have been sufficient to dispel them. One by one they changed all these horrors into comfort and isolation into companionship. It was as follows:

Belief rent asunder the desolate view of the past as a vast graveyard and showed it with utter certainty to be a familiar and enlightened gathering of friends.

Belief showed the future, which appears in the form of a huge graveyard to heedless eyes, certainly to be a banquet of the All-Merciful in delightful palaces of happiness.

Belief rent the view of the present time as a coffin, as it appears to heedless eyes, and showed it with certainty to be a place of trade for the Hereafter and a splendid guesthouse of the All-Merciful.

Belief showed with certainty that the only fruit at the top of the tree of life was not a corpse, as it appears to heedless eyes, but that my spirit, which was created for eternal life and endowed with potential to gain eternal happiness, has left its worn-out home to travel through the stars.

Through its meaning and content, belief showed that my bones and the dust which was the source of my creation were not worthless dust trampled underfoot, but that the soil was the door to Divine Mercy and a veil before the hall of Paradise.

Belief also showed through the Qur'an that the world, which had appeared to my heedless eye as revolving behind me through the valleys of nothingness and the darkness of non-existence, consists of missives of the Eternally Besought-of-All and pages of the embroideries of the Divine glorification of God. When they (these missives and pages, that is, all the existent things and happenings in the world) have completed their tasks, displaying their content and meanings, they depart the world one after the other, leaving their results in existence in their place. With complete certainty the true nature of the world is made known.

Through the light of the Qur'an belief showed that the grave which is looking at me from a certain distance with eyes wide open is not the mouth of a well, but the door to the world of light, and that the highway stretching to eternity beyond the grave leads not to nothingness and non-existence but to existence and a realm of light, and eternal happiness. Since belief has shown this truth with convincing certainty, it is both a cure and ointment for my afflictions.

Furthermore, in place of a very minor ability to choose and implement, belief gives that limited human faculty of willpower a document through which it may rely on an infinite Power and be connected to a limitless Mercy in the face of these innumerable enemies and veils of darkness. Indeed, belief itself is that document in the hand of human willpower. Though this human instrument of willpower is in itself both short-range, feeble, and deficient, yet—just as when a soldier uses his limited capacities on behalf of the state, he performs duties far exceeding those capacities—through belief, if that limited willpower is used in the name of God Almighty and in His cause, it may also gain a paradise as broad as five hundred years of walking.

Belief takes from the body the reins of the willpower, which cannot penetrate the past or the future, and hands them over to the heart and spirit. Since the sphere of the life of the spirit and heart is not restricted to the present time as the body is, and since it encompasses a great many years from the past and a great many years from the future, the willpower no longer becomes limited and acquires universality. Just as through the power of belief it can enter the deepest valleys of the past and remove the darkness of the sorrows that arise from the past, so too through the light of belief it can rise as far as the farthest mountains of the future, and remove the apprehensions and anxieties that arise from there.

And so, my elderly brothers and sisters who, like me, are suffering the hardships of old age! Since, all praise be to God, we are believers, and belief contains so many light-diffusing, delightful, pleasant, and satisfying treasures; and since our old age drives us even further into the contents of those treasures, then, surely, rather than complaining about old age that is accompanied by belief, we should be offering endless thanks for it.

The eighth hope

At a time when grey hairs, the sign of old age, were appearing on my head, I returned to Istanbul from captivity as a prisoner of war (in Russia) after the turmoil of the First World War, and this made the deep sleep of youth even heavier. In addition to the great celebrity and honor accorded to me, the kind treatment and attention far exceeding my due that I received from everyone, from the caliph, the shaykhul-Islam, and the commander in chief of the army to the students of religious schools, the intoxication of youth, and the mood produced by my position made the sleep of youth so heavy that I saw the world as perpetual and myself cemented in it as if there were no longer death.

Then, one day in the holy month of Ramadan, I went to Bayazid Mosque in Istanbul to listen to the sincere reciters of the Qur'an. Through the tongues of the reciters, the Qur'an of miraculous expression was proclaiming with its exalted heavenly address the decree, *Every soul is bound to taste death* (3: 185), which most powerfully declares the inevitable death of the human being and of all living creatures. It entered my ear, and established itself in the very center of my heart, shattering the extremely thick layers of my sleep of heedlessness and intoxication. I went out of the mosque. Because of the stupor of the sleep, which had for so long settled in my head in which now a tempest was raging and a fire was burning producing smoke, for several days I saw myself as a boat which had lost its course. Every time I looked in the mirror, the grey hairs told me, "Be careful!" And so the reality showed itself through the warnings of my grey hairs.

I noticed that my youth, which had so captivated me with its pleasures and in which I had so trusted, was saying farewell to me, and this worldly life in which I was so lovingly involved was beginning to fade; the world which I so loved and with which I was closely connected was seeing me off, warning me that I would be leaving this guesthouse. It was itself, while bidding farewell, preparing to depart. From the encompassing content of the verse, *Every soul is bound to taste death*, the following meanings were unfolding in my heart: humankind is a soul—it will die in order to be resurrected; the earth is a soul—it will die in order to assume an eternal form; and the world too is a soul—it will die in order to assume the form of the Hereafter.

So, while in this state, I considered my situation. I saw that youth, which is the mine of pleasures, was going away, being replaced by old age—the source of sorrow. Life, which shines so brightly, was departing, and death, which is apparently dark and terrifying, was preparing to take its place. The lovable world, which is thought to be perpetual and is the beloved of the heedless, was hastening to its demise.

In order to delude myself and plunge my mind into heedlessness once more, I considered the pleasures of the social position I enjoyed in Istanbul, which was far exceeding my due, but it was of no use at all. All the regard, attention, and consolation of people could only attend me as far as the door of the grave, which was so near me; there it would be extinguished. And since I saw a repugnant hypocrisy, cold pretension, self-adulation, and temporary stupefaction under the embellished veil of glory and renown, which is the greatest aim of those who chase celebrity, I understood that these things which had deluded me until then could provide no solace for me and that there was no light to be found in them.

I again turned to the reciters in the Bayazid Mosque in order to hear the heavenly teaching of the Qur'an and to be awakened once more. Then from its exalted instruction I heard glad tidings through such sacred decrees as *And give glad tidings to those who believe...*

Through the radiation provided by the Qur'an, I sought consolation, hope, and light, not beyond but within the matters that had provoked in me horror, desolation and despair. A hundred thousand thanks be to God Almighty, I had found the cure within the affliction itself, I had found the light within the darkness itself, and I had found the solace within the horror itself.

Firstly, I looked in the face of death, which terrifies everyone and is imagined as being the most terrible thing. Through the light of the Qur'an I saw that although death's veil is black, dark, and ugly, for believers its true face is luminous and beautiful. We have convincingly expressed this truth in several parts of the *Risale-i Nur*. For instance, as we explained in the Eighth Word and the Twentieth Letter, death is not extinction and eternal separation; it is rather the introduction to eternal life, its beginning. It is a rest from the hardships of life's duties, a demobilization. It is a change of residence. It is meeting with the caravan of one's friends who have already migrated to the Intermediate World of the grave, and so on. I saw death's true, beautiful face through realities such as these. It was not with fear but with a certain yearning that I looked at the face of death. Indeed, in a sense, it was with yearning, and I understood some meaning of the Sufis' "contemplation of death."

Then I looked at my departed youth, which had been spent in heedlessness—the youth which infatuates everyone and whose departure makes them weep. I saw that within its beautiful embellished garb was the ugliest, most drunken and stupefied face. Had I not learnt its true nature, in return for intoxicating and amusing me for a few years. If I remained in the world a hundred years, it would have caused me to weep that long. One such person lamented, "If only one day my youth had returned, I would have told it of the woes old age has brought me."

Indeed, elderly people who, like that person, do not know the true nature of youth, think of their own youth, and weep with regret and longing. But youth spent in worship, good works, and trade for the Hereafter by believers with sound minds and hearts is the most powerful means of earning and the most agreeable and pleasant means of doing good works. For those who know their religious duties and do not misspend their youth, it is a precious and enjoyable Divine favor. When it is not spent in uprightness, modesty, and God-consciousness, youth poses numerous risks. When unrestrained, it ruins eternal happiness and the life in this world. Indeed, in return for the pleasures of a few years' youth, many years of grief and sorrow are caused in old age.

Since youth is harmful for most people, we elderly people should thank God that we have been saved from its dangers and harm. Like everything else, the pleasures of youth are transitory. If youth has been spent in worship and good works, its fruits remain perpetually in place and will be the means of gaining youth in eternal life.

Next, I looked at the world, which most people love with deep attachment. Through the light of the Qur'an, I saw that there are three universal worlds, one within the other:

The first relates to the Divine Names; it is a mirror to them.

The second relates to the Hereafter; it is an arable field for it.

The third relates to worldly people; it is the playground of the heedless.

Moreover, everyone has his own particular world within this world. It is as if there are worlds, one within the other, equal to the number of human beings. But the pillar of everyone's private world is their own life. When their bodies are destroyed, their world collapses on their head, and it is doomsday for them. Since the heedless do not realize that their world has such a nature, which is bound for such speedy destruction, they suppose it to be perpetual as the general world appears to be and adore it. I thought to myself, "I too have a private world that will quickly collapse like the worlds of other people. What value does this private world of mine, this short life of mine, have?"

Through the light of the Qur'an, I saw that both for myself and everyone else this world is a temporary market place set up on the road for the passers-by to shop in, a guesthouse which is every day filled and emptied, an ever-renewed notebook of the Eternal Inscriber, in which He continuously writes and erases; every spring is a gilded letter of His and every summer a well-composed ode. It is formed of mirrors that reflect the ever-renewed manifestations of the All-Majestic Maker's Names; it is a seedbed of the Hereafter, a flowerbed of Divine Mercy, and a temporary workshop producing tablets that will be displayed in the Realm of Eternity.

I offer a hundred thousand thanks to the Creator of Majesty, Who has made the world in this way. I understood that while humankind has been endowed with love for the beautiful, inner faces of the world, which look to the Hereafter and Divine Names, many have wasted that love on its transient, ugly, harmful, heedless face, and so realized the meaning of the *hadith*, "Love of this world is the source of all errors."[112]

And so, elderly brothers and sisters, I realized this truth through the light of the wise Qur'an, and the warnings of my old age and belief opened my eyes; I have demonstrated this with decisive proofs in several parts of the *Risale-i Nur*. I have found a true solace, powerful hope, and radiant light. I am happy that I am old; and I am glad that my youth is gone. You do likewise: do not weep, but offer thanks. Since there is belief and since the truth is thus, it is the heedless who should weep and the misguided who should lament.

The ninth hope

In the First World War, I was in the distant province of Kosturma in north-eastern Russia as a prisoner of war. There was a small mosque there belonging to the Tatars beside the famous Volga River. I became weary among my friends, the other officers. I wished for solitude, yet I could not stroll about outside without permission. Then they allowed me out on bail to the Tatar quarter, to that small mosque on the banks of the Volga. I would stay in the mosque alone. Spring was close. I would be awake for quite long times during the long, long nights of that northern land. The pathetic splashing of the Volga and the moving patter of the rain and the sad blowing of the wind during those dark nights in that dark exile temporarily awakened me from the deep sleep of heedlessness. I did not yet consider myself old, but those who experienced the World War were considered to be old. For those were the

112 al-Bayhaqi, *Shu'ab al-Iman*, 7:338; al-Mundhiri, *at-Targhib wat-Tarhib*, 3:178. (Tr.)

days that, as though manifesting the meaning of the verse, *A Day which will turn the children gray-headed* (73: 17), made even children old. So, although I was forty years old, I felt as if I were eighty. In those long, dark nights during that sorrowful exile and melancholy, I felt despair of life and for my homeland. In the face of my powerlessness and loneliness, my hope failed.

Then, while I was in that state, the wise Qur'an came to my aid. My tongue uttered, *God is sufficient for us; and how excellent a guardian is He* (3: 173); and weeping, my heart cried out:

I am a stranger, I am lonely and weak, and I am powerless:
I beg mercy, ask forgiveness, and I cry for help from Your Court, O my God!

And, thinking of my old friends in my homeland, and imagining myself dying in exile there, like Niyazi Misri, I said as follows:

Renouncing the world's grief,
Taking flight into nothingness,
Flying constantly with ardor,
I call in each breath, Friend! Friend!
My spirit was searching for its friends.

In any case, my neediness and weakness became such powerful intercessors and means at the Divine Court in that long, melancholy, pitiful, separation-afflicted night in exile that now I still wonder at it. For, several days later, I escaped in an extremely unexpected manner, on my own, not knowing Russian, across a distance that would have taken a year on foot. I was saved in a wonderful way through Divine favor, which came as a response to my neediness and impotence. Then, passing through Warsaw and Austria, I reached Istanbul. Being saved in this way, so easily, was quite extraordinary. I completed the long flight with an ease and facility that even a Russian-speaking, boldest and most cunning person might not have been able to accomplish.

That night in the mosque on the banks of the Volga made me decide: I will pass the rest of my life in caves. It is enough that I have long mixed in the social life of people. Since, finally, I will enter the grave alone, I will from now on choose solitude in order to become accustomed to loneliness.

But, regretfully, things of no use, like having many and important friends in Istanbul, and the glittering worldly life there, and in particular the fame and honor accorded to me which was far greater than my due, caused me to temporarily forget my decision. It was as though that night in exile was the iris and pupil of my life's eye, and the glittering white daytime of Istanbul, the lightless, white part of it, so that it could not foresee the future, and fell into sleep again. It was only two years later that *Ghawth* al-Jilani opened my eyes once more with his book *Futuhu'l-Ghayb* ("The Conquests Concerning the Unseen").

And so, elderly men and women! Know that the weakness and powerlessness of old age are means for attracting Divine grace and mercy. Just as I have observed this in myself on numerous occasions, the manifestation of mercy on the face of the earth demonstrates this truth clearly. For the most powerless and weakest of animals are the young. But it is also they who are favored with the sweetest and most beautiful manifestation of mercy. The powerlessness of a young bird in the nest at the top of a tree employs its mother like an obedient soldier as a manifestation of mercy. Its mother flies all around and brings it food. As soon as its wings grow strong and the nestling forgets its powerlessness, its mother says, "Go and search for your own food by yourself!" and no longer listens to it.

Just as this reality of mercy is in force for the very young, so too is it in force for the elderly, who are like the young in weakness and impotence. There have been many experiences that have given me the certain conviction that, in the same way that infants are sent their sustenance in a wonderful fashion by Divine Mercy because of their impotence, flowing forth from the springs of their mothers' breasts, so too the sustenance of the believing elderly, who have acquired innocence, is sent in the form of miraculous abundance. The part of a *hadith* which says, "Were it not for the elderly with their bent backs, calamities would descend on you in floods,"[113] makes clear that a family's source of abundance is the elderly among it, and it is the elderly who preserve the family from the visitation of calamities.

Since the weakness and powerlessness of old age are the means of attracting Divine mercy to this extent; since the wise Qur'an through the verses *Should one of them, or both, attain old age in your lifetime, do not say 'Ugh!' to them (as an indication of complaint or impatience), nor push them away; and always address them in gracious words. Lower to them the wing of*

---

[113] at-Tabarani, *al-Mu'jam al-Kabir*, 22:309; Abu Ya'la, *al-Musnad*, 11:287. (Tr.)

humility out of mercy, and say: "My Lord, have mercy on them even as they cared for me in childhood (17: 23–24), calls children, in the most wonderfully eloquent fashion, in five ways to be kind and respectful towards their elderly parents; since the Religion of Islam orders respect and compassion towards the elderly; and since human nature also requires respect and compassion towards the elderly; we elderly people certainly enjoy, in place of the temporary physical pleasures roused by appetites of youth, substantial, continual mercy and respect from Divine Grace and innate human feelings of tenderness, and the contentment of spirit that arises from such respect and compassion. This being the case, we should not wish to exchange this old age of ours for a hundred youths. I can tell you certainly that if they were to give me ten years of the Old or Former Said's youth, I would not give in exchange one year of the New Said's old age. I am content with my old age, and you too should be content with yours.

The tenth hope

After returning from captivity in Russia heedlessness overcame me for a year or two in Istanbul. During the days when the political atmosphere drew my attention away from myself to the outside world, I was once sitting on a high spot in the Eyüp Sultan graveyard overlooking the Golden Horn. I had a look around the horizons of Istanbul. I was suddenly overcome by such a state of mind that it was as if my private world was dying with my spirit being withdrawn in certain respects. Wondering whether the inscriptions on the gravestones were giving me such illusions, I withdrew my gaze. I looked not at the distance, but at the graveyard itself. Then the following was imparted to my heart: "This graveyard around you contains Istanbul a hundred times over, for Istanbul has been emptied here a hundred times. You cannot be an exception who can be saved from the judgment of the All-Wise and Powerful One, Who has poured all the people of Istanbul into here. You too will go."

I left the graveyard and with that awesome experience entered a small cell in Eyüp Sultan Mosque where I had stayed many times before. I thought to myself: I am a guest in three respects: I am a guest in this small room, I am also a guest in Istanbul, and in this world. A guest has to consider the journey. In the same way that I will leave this room, so one day I will leave Istanbul, and yet another day I will leave this world.

Amidst these reflections, my heart was overwhelmed by a most pitiful, grievous sorrow. For I was not losing only one or two friends; I would be parted from thousands of friends whom I loved in Istanbul, and I would also part from Istanbul, which I loved dearly. And as I would be parted from hundreds of thousands of friends in this world, I would also be parted from the beautiful world that I loved and with which I was infatuated. Pondering this, I went up once more to the high spot in the graveyard. Having been to the movie theater from time to time in order to reflect and take lessons, just as the movie shows the images of dead people as if they were alive, moving around, that moment, all the dead of Istanbul appeared to me as corpses walking around. I said to my imagination: Since some of those in the graveyard appear to be walking around like people shown to move on a movie screen, so you should see those who are bound to enter the graveyard in the future as though they have entered it—they too are corpses, walking around.

All of a sudden, through the light of the Qur'an and through the guidance of *Ghawth al-A'zam*, Shaykh al-Jilani, my sorrowful state changed into a joyful, happy one. It was like this:

In the face of that sorrowful state, the light coming from the Qur'an reminded me: You had a few officer friends while you were in exile in Kosturma in the northeast of Russia. You knew that those friends would one day go to Istanbul. If one of them had asked you, "Would you go to Istanbul, or would you stay here?" certainly, if you had any intelligence, you would have gladly chosen to go to Istanbul. For out of a thousand and one friends, nine hundred and ninety-nine were already in Istanbul. Only one or two remained there, and they too would go to Istanbul one day. Going to Istanbul would not be a sad departure or a sorrowful separation for you. Moreover, at last, you came here and were you not happy to do so? You were delivered from the long, dark nights and cold, stormy winters in that enemy country. You came to this beautiful Istanbul, which resembled Paradise on the earth.

In the same way, from your childhood to your present age, ninety-nine out of a hundred of those whom you love have migrated to the graveyard; this is terrifying for you. You have only a few friends who are still in this world, and they too will go there. Your death in this world is not separation; it is a reunion—a reunion with all those friends. They—those everlastingly alive spirits—have left behind under the soil their worn-out dwellings, some traveling about the stars and some through the levels of the Intermediate Realm.

The Qur'an and belief demonstrate this truth so certainly and convincingly that unless one is entirely lacking in heart and spirit, or unless misguidance has suffocated one's heart, it must be believed as though seeing it. For, most certainly and self-evidently, the All-Munificent and All-Compassionate Maker, Who adorns this world with His uncountable varieties of favors and gifts and so demonstrates His Lordship in an all-munificent and caring manner, preserving even the least significant things like seeds, would not annihilate or waste humanity—the most perfect, most comprehensive, and most important and beloved among His creatures—by sending it into eternal extinction or never-ending separation from those they love. Rather, as proven in the Tenth and Twenty-Ninth Words, like the seeds a farmer scatters over the earth, the All-Compassionate Creator temporarily takes that beloved creature of His under the ground, which is a door of mercy, in order to produce shoots in another life.

And so, after receiving this reminder from the Qur'an, the graveyard became more lovable to me than Istanbul. Solitude and seclusion became more pleasurable to me than conversation and company with people. And I found a place of seclusion for myself in Sarıyer on the Bosphorus. There, *Ghawth al-A'zam* al-Jilani, may God be pleased with him, became a master, doctor, and guide for me with his *Futuhu'l-Ghayb* ("Conquests Concerning the Unseen"), and Imam Rabbani, may God be pleased with him, a companion, a tender-hearted friend, and teacher with his *Mektubat* ("The Letters"). Then I was extremely pleased I had entered upon old age, renounced the pleasures of modern civilization, and withdrawn from social life. I thanked God.

And so, respected people who have entered upon old age like me and frequently remember death through its warnings! In accordance with the light of the teachings of belief in the Qur'an, we should look favorably on old age, death, and illness, and even love them in one respect. Since we have an infinitely precious gift like belief, old age is agreeable, and illness and death likewise. If there are things that are disagreeable, they are sins, dissipation, heresy, unacceptable innovations in the Religion, and misguidance.

The eleventh hope

After my return from captivity, I was living together with my nephew Abdurrahman in a villa on the hill of Çamlıca in Istanbul. In respect of worldly life, my situation could have been thought to be the happiest for people like us: I had been saved from captivity, and in the *Darul-Hikmet al-Islamiya*[114] ("The House of Islamic Wisdom"), we were enjoying success in teaching and serving knowledge to the highest degree suited to my profession of teaching. The honor and attention afforded me was far greater than my due. I was living in Çamlıca, the most beautiful place of residence in Istanbul. Everything was perfect for me. I was together with my late nephew Abdurrahman, who was extremely intelligent and self-sacrificing, and was both my student, and servant, and scribe, and who was like a son to me. While in this situation knowing myself to be more fortunate than anyone else in the world, one day I looked in the mirror and I saw grey hairs in my hair and beard.

Suddenly, the spiritual awakening I had experienced in the mosque in Kosturma while in captivity began again. As a result, I began reflecting upon the circumstances and causes to which I was inwardly attached and which I supposed to be the means of happiness in the life of the world. Whichever of them I thought about, I now saw it as rotten, unworthy of attachment, a delusion of sorts. In the meantime, I suffered an unexpected and unimaginable act of treachery and betrayal at the hands of a friend I had supposed to be most loyal. I felt frightened of the world. I said to my heart, "Have I been utterly deluded? I see that many people look with envy at our situation, which in reality should be pitied. Are all these people crazy, or am I now going crazy so that I see all these world-adoring people as such?"

Anyway, as a result of that intense awakening brought on by old age, first of all I took note of the transience of the short-lived things to which I felt attached. Then I took note of myself, and saw myself to be utterly powerless. Thereupon my spirit, which desired eternity and yet was deeply attached to transient things, supposing them to be eternal, pronounced most emphatically, "Since I am mortal regarding my body, what good can come from these mortal things? Since I am powerless, what can I expect from these powerless things? What I need is an All-Powerful, Everlasting One Who will provide a remedy for my ills." And I began to search.

---

114 *Darul-Hikmet al-Islamiya* ("The House of Islamic Wisdom"), which was established in August 1918, was an Islamic academy. It was established in order to answer the questions posed to Islam, clarify the doubts raised concerning its precepts, and publish books to teach it. Bediüzzaman Said Nursi was one of its leading members. (Tr.)

Then, before all else, I had recourse to the learning I had been studying for so long, and searched for a consolation, a hope. Unfortunately, up to that time I had filled my mind with "natural" sciences and the sciences of philosophy as well as Islamic ones, and had mistakenly imagined those philosophical and "natural" sciences to be the source of personal development and means of enlightenment. However, those philosophical issues had greatly muddied my spirit and hindered my spiritual development. Suddenly, thanks to the Mercy and Grace of God Almighty, the sacred wisdom contained in the wise Qur'an came to my aid. As explained in several parts of the *Risale-i Nur*, it washed away and cleansed the dirt of those philosophical issues.

For instance, the spiritual veils of darkness coming from "natural" sciences had caused the outer world to suffocate my spirit. In whichever direction I turned to seek enlightenment, I could find not a beam of light in those matters, nor could I breathe. And so it continued until the extraordinarily brilliant light of Divine Unity taught by the Qur'an with the declaration, "There is no deity but God," dispersed all those veils of darkness, and I breathed easily. But based on what they had learnt from the people of misguidance and philosophers, my carnal soul and Satan attacked my reason and my heart. Thanks be to God, the ensuing debate with my soul resulted in the victory of my heart. Those exchanges have been narrated in part in several parts of the *Risale-i Nur*. Without needing to go further, in order to show one thousandth part of that victory of the heart, I will explain here only one proof out of thousands. I hope that it may also purify, to a certain extent, the spirits of certain elderly people who have dirtied their spirits in their youth and caused their hearts to be diseased, spoiling their souls with matters that are in part misguidance and in part trivialities—the matters taught or studied in the name of what they call modern philosophy or certain modern sciences. And may their spirits be saved from the evil that Satan and the carnal, evil-commanding soul provoke concerning Divine Unity.

The one proof out of a thousand is as follows:

My carnal, evil-commanding soul said in the name of science and philosophy, "Due to their very nature, things have a share in the existence and operation of the universe. Everything depends on a cause. The fruit has to be demanded from the tree and seed from the soil. So what does it mean to seek the tiniest and least insignificant thing from God and to entreat Him for it?"

Through the light of the Qur'an, the meaning and mystery of Divine Unity then unfolded and my heart said to my soul as follows:

> The tiniest and least significant thing, just like the greatest and largest, issues directly from the Power of the Creator of the entire universe and emerges from His treasury. It cannot occur in any other way. Causes are merely a veil. For, in respect of art and creation, sometimes the creatures we suppose to be the tiniest and least significant are greater than the largest ones. Even if a fly is not greater than a chicken in art, it is not lesser than it. So, we should not make a difference between great and small. Either all should be attributed to material causes, or all should be ascribed at once to a single Being. And just as the former alternative is inconceivable, the latter is necessary and inevitably acceptable.
>
> For if things and beings are attributed to a single Being, that is, to One Who is Eternal and All-Powerful, since His Knowledge—the existence of which the order of the universe and uncountable instances of wisdom in it establish and demonstrate with utter certainty—encompasses everything; and since all things are determined in His Knowledge, each with a certain, particular measure; and since, manifestly, things and beings, infinitely full of art, constantly come into existence from nothing with infinite ease; and since, as has been convincingly demonstrated in many parts of the *Risale-i Nur* with numerous powerful proofs, the All-Knowing and All-Powerful One is absolutely able to create anything whatsoever with the command of *"Be!" and it is*, as simply as striking a match, He has limitless Power—this being so, the extraordinary ease and facility we observe in things coming into existence are due to the all-encompassing nature of that Knowledge and the limitless immensity of that Power.
>
> For example, if the appropriate chemical solution is applied to a book written in invisible ink, that book suddenly reveals its existence and makes itself read. Just so, the particular form and nature of everything are determined in the all-encompassing Knowledge of that Eternal, All-Powerful One with a certain, particular measure. Like the chemical solution applied to invisible writing, through His limitless Power and penetrating Will, the Absolutely All-Powerful One applies with the command of *"Be!" and it is* a manifestation of His Power to the being which exists as knowledge, giving it external existence with utter ease and facility. He makes read the embroideries of His Wisdom.
>
> If all things are not all at once attributed to that Eternal, All-Powerful One, the Knower of all things, then as well as having to assemble, for example, the body of the tiniest thing like a fly from the great

variety of beings in the world, in a precise measure, the particles operative in that tiny fly's body will also have to know the mysteries of the fly's creation and its perfect art in all its minutest details. For, manifestly and as agreed by all intelligent people, natural or physical causes cannot create something from non-existence. If they were able to create, they would be assembling the body of even the tiniest being from most of the species of beings. And if they were to be assembling it, no matter which animate being, as there are within each being samples of most elements and most species, as each living creature is like a seed of the universe or an extract from it, they would necessarily have to obtain a seed from the entire tree or animate being from the entire earth, carefully putting them through a fine sieve and measuring them with the most sensitive balance. However, natural causes are ignorant and lifeless, and they have no knowledge that will allow them to determine a plan, a content, model, or program according to which they can melt and cast the particles to shape the exact form of any being without allowing dispersal or deformation. Moreover, there are infinite alternatives for a thing or being to take on a particular form; this requires that the lifeless and ignorant natural causes know which form they should give to each thing and thus gather and hold together, according to a certain, particular measure, the particles of the elements that flow like floods. So, anyone who does not suffer from blindness in their heart will see how distant from probability and reason is the idea that natural causes can create all these beings, each with an extraordinarily well-ordered body.

As a corollary of this truth, according to the meaning of the verse, *Those whom, apart from God, you deify and invoke will never be able to create even a fly, even if all of them were to come together to do so* (22: 73), if all physical causes were to come together and if they had willpower, they could not assemble all the systems and organs of a single fly in the exact order and balance particular to it to form its body. Even if they were able to assemble them, they could not retain or preserve them in the specified measure required by the existence of that body. Even if they were able to retain or preserve them thus, they could not make the particles in that body, which are constantly renewed or replaced by new ones coming from the outside world, work in order. Therefore, self-evidently, physical causes cannot claim ownership of things, and their True Owner is someone else.

Indeed, their True Owner is One for Whom, according to the verse, *Your creation and your resurrection are but as (the creation and resurrection) of a single soul* (31: 28), He revives all the living beings on the earth as easily as He revives a single fly. He creates the spring as easily as He creates a single flower, for He has no need to assemble things to create. Since He possesses the command *"Be!" and it is* and

> since every spring, in addition to the physical elements forming the bodies of beings, He also creates the innumerable attributes, states, and forms of innumerable beings from nothing, and since the plan, model, contents, and program of everything are already determined in His Knowledge, and since all particles and atoms move within the sphere of His Knowledge and Power, He creates everything with infinite ease, as though striking a match. And nothing confuses this motion in the least. In the same way that the planets are His obedient army, particles and atoms too move like a regular, well-ordered army for Him.
>
> Since they move in dependence on that eternal Power, and operate in accordance with the principles of that eternal Knowledge, all things and beings come into existence with the invention of that Power. So, they should not be considered insignificant because they are small in body. Through the power it has because of its connection with that Power, a fly can destroy a Nimrod, an ant can ruin Pharaoh's palace, and the tiny seed of a pine caries the burden of a tree that is as tall as a mountain. We have proved this truth in numerous places in the *Risale-i Nur*. In the same way that due to his connection with the state as a member of the army, an ordinary soldier can take a king prisoner, thus far exceeding his own personal capacity, so too, due to their connection with the eternal Power, all things can be favored with and display miracles of art exceeding the capacity of their natural causes by hundreds of thousands of times.
>
> In short, the fact that all things come into existence with both infinite art and infinite ease shows that they are the works of an Eternal All-Powerful One Who has all-encompassing Knowledge. Otherwise, because of hundreds of thousands of impossibilities, far from being possible, their existence would be absolutely unimaginable.

Through this most subtle, powerful, profound, and self-evident proof, my carnal, evil-commanding soul, which had been a temporary student of Satan and the spokesman for the people of misguidance and deviant philosophy, was silenced, and, all praise be to God, came to believe completely. It said:

> I need such a Creator and Lord that He should know the least and most secret occurrences to my heart and my most secret appeals. And, just as He should answer the most hidden needs of my spirit, He should also have the power to replace this mighty world with the Hereafter in order to give me eternal happiness, and to create the heavens as easily as a fly, and to place a particle in the pupil of my eye just as He fastens the sun as an eye in the face of the sky. For one who cannot create a fly cannot do anything in relation to the

> thoughts of my heart and cannot hear the appeals of my spirit. One who cannot create the heavens cannot give me eternal happiness. In that case, my Lord is He Who both corrects and purifies the occurrences to my heart, and, as He fills and empties the skies with clouds in an hour, He will replace this world with the Hereafter, make Paradise, and open its doors to me, telling me to enter.

So, my elderly brothers and sisters, who, misled by some unfortunate considerations as my soul was, having spent part of your lives on lightless materialist philosophy and scientism! Understand from the sacred decree of *There is no deity but He*, which is perpetually pronounced by the Qur'an, just how powerful and true, how unshakeable and impregnable, how unchanging and sacred a pillar of belief this is, and how it disperses all spiritual darkness and cures all spiritual wounds!

In any case, due to the grey hairs appearing in my hair and beard and the treachery of an old friend, I felt disgust at the pleasures of Istanbul's glittering and apparently pleasant worldly life. My soul searched for spiritual pleasures in place of the pleasures with which it had been infatuated. It desired a light, a solace, in this old age, which the heedless think to be cold, burdensome, and unpleasant. And all praise be to God and countless thanks, just as I found the true, lasting, and sweet pleasures of belief in *There is no deity but He* and in the light of Divine Unity in place of all those false, unpleasant, fleeting and fruitless worldly pleasures, so too through the light of Divine Unity, I saw old age (which the heedless think cold and burdensome) to be most light, and warm, and luminous.

And so, elderly men and women! Since you have belief and since you regularly pray and offer supplications which illuminate and strengthen belief, you can view your old age as eternal youth. For you can gain eternal youth through it. The old age that is truly cold, burdensome, ugly, dark, and full of pain is the old age of the people of misguidance; indeed, their youth is thus as well. They should weep and utter sighs and regrets. But you, respected believing elderly people should thank God and rejoice, saying, "All praise and thanks be to God for every state!"

The twelfth hope

I was once being held in the district of Barla in the province of Isparta in distressing captivity under the guise of exile. I was in an extremely wretched state, suffering both illness and old age, and continuous separation from home, and in a village alone with no one, banned from all company and communication. Then, out of His perfect Mercy, God Almighty bestowed a light on me regarding the subtle points and mysteries of the wise Qur'an, which was a means of consolation for me. With it, I tried to forget my pitiful, grievous, sorrowful state.

I was able to forget my native land, my friends and relatives, but alas, there was one person I could not forget. That was Abdurrahman, who was both my nephew, although more like a son to me, and my most self-sacrificing student and most courageous friend. He had parted from me six or seven years before. He did not know where I was and thus he could not hasten to help or console me, nor did I know his situation so that I could correspond with him and confide in him. In that old age of mine, I was in need of someone faithful and self-sacrificing like him.

Then all unexpectedly, someone gave me a letter. I opened it and saw it was from Abdurrahman; it was a letter that showed his true nature. Exhibiting three manifest instances of wonder-working, part of which has been included in the Twenty-Seventh Letter.[115] It made me weep much; indeed, it still makes me weep. In the letter, the late Abdurrahman wrote earnestly and sincerely that he hated the pleasures of the world and that his greatest desire was to reach me and serve me in my old age just as I had taken care of him when he was a child. He also desired to help me with his powerful pen in publicizing the truths of the Qur'an, my true duty in this world. He even wrote, "Send me twenty or thirty treatises and I'll transcribe twenty or thirty copies of each and get others to transcribe them."

His letter afforded me great hope in respect of my affairs. Thinking that I had found a daring student with the intelligence of a genius, one who would serve me more faithfully and closely than a real (biological) son, I forgot my painful captivity, loneliness, separation from home, and old age.

Before writing that letter, he had a copy of the Tenth Word, which is about belief in the Hereafter. It was as if the treatise had been a remedy for him, curing all the spiritual wounds he had received during those six or

---

115 This contains the communications between Said Nursi and the students of the *Risale-i Nur* and which was published as separate books under the names of *Barla Lahikası* ("Supplements of Barla"), *Kastamonu Lahikası* ("Supplements of Kastamonu"), and *Emirdağ Lahikası* ("Supplements of Emirdağ"). (Tr.)

seven years. He then wrote the letter to me as if he were anticipating his death with a truly strong and radiant belief. While I was once again thinking of spending a happy life with Abdurrahman, one or two months later I suddenly received news of his death. I was so shaken that five years later I am still under its effect. It caused a great sense of separation, grief, and sorrow, ten times exceeding that of the painful captivity, loneliness, separation, old age, and illness I was then suffering. I considered that half of my private world had died with the death of my mother, and now with Abdurrahman's death, I felt that the other half died. My ties with the world were now completely severed. For if he had lived, he could have been both a powerful help in my duties that pertain to the Hereafter, and a worthy successor to fill my place after me, as well as a self-sacrificing friend and a means of consolation in this world. He would have been my most intelligent student and companion, and a most trustworthy patron and protector of the *Risale-i Nur*.

From the viewpoint of being human, such losses are extremely painful and ravaging for people like me. It is true that, outwardly, I was trying to tolerate it, but in my spirit a fierce storm was raging. If from time to time the solace that came from the Qur'an's light had not been able to provide consolation for me, I would not have been able to bear it. At that time I used to go out alone to wander in the mountains and valleys of Barla. I sat in lonely places and, while surrounded by sorrows, pictures of the happy life I had spent in the past with my faithful students like Abdurrahman passed through my imagination like film scenes, and the grief caused by old age and exile broke my resistance. Suddenly, the meaning of the sacred verse, *Everything is perishable (and so perishing) except His "Face" (His eternal Self, and what is done in seeking His good pleasure). His alone is judgment and authority, and to Him you are being brought back* (28: 88), was unfolded to me. It made me utter, "O Everlasting One, You are the Everlasting! O Everlasting One, You are the Everlasting!" and gave me true consolation.

Then, as described in the treatise, the Stairway of the Sunna (the Eleventh Gleam), while in that sorrowful state in that desolate valley, inspired by this sacred verse, I saw myself at the head of three vast corpses:

I saw myself as a gravestone at the grave of the fifty-five dead Saids who were buried during the fifty-five years of my life.

The second corpse was the vast corpse of all my fellow human beings who had died since the time of Adam, peace be upon him, and who had been buried in the grave of the past. I saw myself as a tiny living creature like an ant moving on the face of this century, which is like the headstone of that grave.

The third corpse was the whole world which, as announced in the verse above, will one day die like human beings and the worlds that travel through it every year. This was embodied in my imagination.

Then the verse, *Still, if they turn away from you, say: "God is sufficient for me; there is no deity but He. In Him have I put my trust, and He is the Lord of the Supreme Throne"* (9: 129), came to my aid and with its true solace and inextinguishable light, it utterly removed that terrifying vision which arose from my sorrow at Abdurrahman's death. It reminded me: Since God Almighty exists, He is sufficient in place of everything else. Since He is Everlasting, He is surely sufficient. A single instance of His Grace substitutes for the whole world. And one manifestation of His Light gives life to the three vast corpses mentioned above, showing that they are not corpses, but rather they have completed their duties and have left for other worlds. As this truth has been explained in the Third Gleam, here I will only say that the two repetitions of the phrase, "O Everlasting One, You are the Everlasting! O Everlasting One, You are the Everlasting!" which indicates the meaning of *Everything is perishable (and so perishing) save His "Face"* (to the end of the verse), saved me from that most painful, sorrowful state. It was as follows:

The first time I uttered "O Everlasting One, You are the Everlasting!", like a surgical operation it began to cure the endless spiritual wounds caused by the passing of the world and the numerous friends to whom I was attached in this world, and by the severance of my bonds with them.

The second utterance of the phrase "O Everlasting One, You are the Everlasting!" was both an ointment and medication for all those innumerable wounds. It gave me the thought: "You are everlasting. Let those who depart do so; You are sufficient for me. Since You are everlasting, one manifestation of Your Mercy is sufficient in the place of all things which are decaying. Since You exist, for one who is aware of one's connection with You through belief in Your Existence, and who acts in accordance with that connection in adherence to Islam, everything exists. Transience and decay, and death and departure are a veil, a renewal; they are like traveling through different realms."

Thinking this, my burning, exile-stricken, sad, painful, dark, and terrifying mood changed into a happy, joyful, pleasurable, luminous, lovable, companionable state. My tongue and heart—indeed, through the tongue of their disposition, each particle of my being—exclaimed, "All praise be to God!"

One thousandth of that manifestation of mercy is this: I returned to Barla from that valley where I suffered sorrows and where I was in a melancholy state of mind. I saw that a young man called Kuleönlü Mustafa had come to ask me a few questions concerning the five daily Prayers and ablutions. Although I was not accepting visitors at that time, as if through a presentiment my spirit perceived his sincerity of spirit and the future valuable services he would perform for the *Risale-i Nur*,[116] I did not turn him away and accepted him.[117] It later became clear that God Almighty had sent me Mustafa as an example (of future students of the *Risale-i Nur*) in place of Abdurrahman as a worthy successor who would completely fulfill the duty of a true heir in the work of the *Risale-i Nur*, as though saying, "I took one Abdurrahman from you, but in return I will give you thirty Abdurrahmans like the Mustafa you see, who will be both students, and nephews, and son-like companions, and brothers, and self-sacrificing friends in this duty for the Religion."

All praise be to God, He gave me thirty Abdurrahmans. So I told myself, "O weeping heart! Since you have seen this example and through it He has healed the most grave of your spiritual wounds, you should be convinced that He will heal all the rest of the wounds that afflict you."

And so, my elderly brothers and sisters who, like me, have lost a child or relative they love much during their old age, and who have to bear the intense sorrows of separation together with the burdens of old age! You have understood that while I was in a much more severe situation than yours, a single verse of the Qur'an healed it. So, in the sacred pharmacy of the wise Qur'an, there must certainly be remedies to heal all your afflictions. If you have recourse to it through belief and apply those remedies

116 By transcribing more than seven hundred copies of parts of the *Risale-i Nur* with his fine pen, Mustafa's younger brother, Küçük Ali, not only became an Abdurrahman but also trained many other Abdurrahmans.

117 He truly demonstrated that he was not only worthy of being accepted, but also worthy of the future.

through regular worship, the heavy burdens of your old age and your sorrows will be greatly lightened.

The reason why this peace has been written relatively longer is to seek more prayers for Abdurrahman; let it not weary you. Also, what I pursue in showing my most painful and sordid wound in an extremely grievous and unpleasant way is to demonstrate what an extraordinary remedy and brilliant light is the sacred antidote of the wise Qur'an.

The thirteenth hope

Here I will recount an important scene from the course of my life. It has to be somewhat lengthy, but I hope it will not become boring or tax your patience.

After being saved from captivity in Russia during the First World War, service to the Religion in the *Darul-Hikmet* kept me in Istanbul for two or three years. Then, through the guidance of the wise Qur'an and the spiritual assistance and influence of *Ghawth al-A'zam* al-Jilani and the awakening of old age, I felt wearied by the civilized life of Istanbul and troubled by its busy social scene. A longing for my native land drove me there. Thinking, since I am bound to die, let me die in my native land, I went to Van.[118]

I went first to visit my *medrese* in Van, the Horhor. I saw that the Armenians had burned it down during the Russian occupation, like all the other buildings of Van. It was adjacent to Van's famous fort, which is a huge, mountain-like monolith. My true friends, brothers, and close students of the *medrese*, which I had left seven or eight years before, were embodied before my eyes. Some of those self-sacrificing friends of mine had truly become martyrs, while others had died due to that calamity and become martyrs by default.

I could not help weeping. I climbed to the top of the fort, which overlooks the *medrese*, towering above it to the height of two minarets. I sat down there. I went back in memory seven or eight years. Having a powerful imagination, I wandered all around that time in my mind. Being alone, there was no one around to distract me from these imaginings or draw me back from that time. I saw enough changes over seven or eight years to fill a century.

---

118 Van is a province of Turkey in Eastern Anatolia, bordering western Iran. (Tr.)

I saw that the parts of the town at the foot of the fort and surrounding my *medrese* had been completely burnt and destroyed. Seeing this filled me with such sadness; it was as if two hundred years had passed between then and the time I had seen it before. Most of the people living in those houses had been my friends and acquaintances. The majority of them had died in the migrations, may God have mercy on them; they had become wretched in exile. Apart from the Armenian quarter, all the Muslim houses of Van had been demolished. My heart felt a very sharp pain. I was so sorrowful that if I had had thousands of eyes, they would all have wept together. I had returned to my homeland from exile and supposed that I had been saved from exile. But alas! The most woeful exile I suffered was in my homeland. I saw that hundreds of my students and friends, with whom I had been connected in spirit, like Abdurrahman, who is mentioned in the Twelfth Hope above, had entered the grave and their places were all in ruins.

There was a saying that had long been in my mind, but which I had not been able to understand completely. Now in the face of that sorrowful scene I understood it completely. The saying was this: "If there were to be no separation from friends, death could find no way to our souls enabling it to take them."[119] That is to say, what causes humans to die most is separation from friends. Nothing had caused me as much suffering or sorrow as that situation. If help had not come from the Qur'an and belief, my grief and suffering would have almost made my spirit fly away.

Since early times, in their verses poets have lamented the destruction wreaked by time on the places where they were together with their beloveds. Now I witnessed this with my own eyes in the most painful form. With the sorrow of one passing by the residences of beloved friends after two hundred years, my heart and spirit joined my eyes, and they all wept together. Then, one by one, the pleasing scenes of the life I had spent for nearly twenty years working with my dear students, when the places now lying in ruins before my eyes had been prosperous, joyful, and happy, came to life before me like pictures at the movies, then died away and vanished. These embodied scenes continued to pass before my eyes for some time.

---

119 This saying is from Abu Tayyib al-Mutanabbi (for whom see footnote 59 at the end of the Eleventh Gleam): al-Hamawi, *Hizanat al-Adab*, 1:136. (Tr.)

Then I felt greatly astonished at worldly people: how can they deceive themselves? For the scene mentioned showed clearly that the world is transitory and that human beings are guests in it. I saw with my own eyes how true the continuously repeated words of the people of truth are: "The world is cruel, treacherous, evil; do not be deceived by it!" I also saw that just as humans are connected to their own bodies and households, so too are they connected with their town, their country, indeed with the whole world. For while weeping with just two eyes out of sorrow for the old age of my own being, I wanted to weep with ten eyes not only at the old age of my *medrese*, but also at its death. And I felt the need to weep with a hundred eyes at the half-death of my beautiful homeland.

There is a *hadith* that every morning an angel calls out, "You are born to die, and construct buildings to be destroyed."[120] I was not just hearing this truth with my ears now, but also seeing it with my eyes.

Ten years later when I recall that situation of mine, I still weep in the same way that it caused me to weep at that time. The houses at the foot of the old citadel, which had been standing there for thousands of years, were all in ruins, the town had aged eight hundred years within eight years, and my *medrese*, which had been quite prosperous and had acted as the gathering-place of friends, had died with the great monolith of Van's fort becoming a gravestone to it, indicating the spiritual grandeur of its corpse; this was a sign of the death of all the *medreses* in the Ottoman State.[121] It was as if my students, who had been together with me in the *medrese* eight years before, were weeping in their graves together with me. Indeed, the ruined walls of the town and its scattered stones were weeping with me. I saw them weeping.

Then I understood that I could not bear that exile in my homeland. I thought that I would either have to join them in the grave, or retreat into a cave in the mountains and await my death there. I told myself, "Since there are unbearable, burning separations which break patience and resistance in the world, surely death is preferable to life. Such a severe aspect of life cannot be endured."

---

120 al-Bayhaqi, *Shu'ab al-Iman*, 7:396; ad-Daylami, *al-Musnad*, 4:51. (Tr.)

121 All the *medreses* were banned and abolished in the early years of the Republican Era in Turkey. (Tr.)

I then cast my eyes in the six directions and saw them all to be dark. The unawareness of truth that arose from my intense grief showed me the world as a terrifying, void, desolate place that was about to collapse over my head. My spirit sought a point of support in the face of uncountable hostile calamities, and a source of help to satisfy its endless desires extending as far as eternity, and awaited consolation in the face of the sorrow and grief that arose from endless instances of separation, devastation, and death. All at once, the reality expressed by the following verse of the Qur'an of miraculous exposition manifested itself: *Whatever is in the heavens and the earth glorifies God; and He is the All-Glorious with irresistible might, the All-Wise. To Him belongs the sovereignty of the heavens and the earth. He gives life and causes to die. He has full power over everything* (57: 1–2).

It saved me from that pitiful, separation-stricken, terrible, sad imagining and opened my eyes. I saw that the fruits at the tops of the fruit-bearing trees were looking upon me with a smile. "Note us as well; do not look only at the ruins!" they were saying. The truth expressed by the verses brought the following thought to mind:

> Why does a letter in the form of a town, which was inscribed by the hands of people who were guests on the page of Van's plain, and finally fell and was wiped out in a disastrous torrent called the Russian invasion, sadden you to this extent? Instead, consider the Eternal Inscriber, the True Owner and Master of everything, and see how His missives on this page of Van continue to be written in the same splendid fashion as you used to see. Your weeping because these places have become desolate ruins arises from the error of forgetting their True Owner, from not thinking that people are guests, and from imagining them to be in lasting possession.

A door to the truth opened up from that error and that burning scene, and my soul was prepared to accept it completely. Just as iron is put in the fire so that it becomes pliable and may be given a useful form, it was in the same way that that sorrowful state and terrible situation functioned as the fire that shaped my soul. Through the truth of the above verses, the Qur'an of miraculous exposition showed to my soul the radiation of the truths of belief, causing it to accept them.

All praise and thanks be to God, as is convincingly demonstrated in parts of the *Risale-i Nur* like the Twentieth Letter, through the radiation of belief, the truth expressed by the verses mentioned gave such a point of support to the spirit and heart—a support which can be developed in proportion to everyone's strength of belief—that it equipped me with the power to be able to resist calamities a hundred times more dreadful than the situation I then experienced. It reminded me: Everything is subjected to the command of the True Owner of this country, Who is your Creator. The reins of all things are in His hands. Your connection with Him is sufficient.

When I came to recognize my Creator and rely on Him, all the things that had appeared hostile no longer were so; and the sorrowful situations that had made me weep started to give me happiness. As we have demonstrated with sure proofs in many parts of the *Risale-i Nur*, the light issuing from belief in the Hereafter afforded such a source of help against my countless desires that it was sufficient not only for my attachment to my friends and connection with them in this insignificant, transient, and brief, worldly life, but also for my innumerable far-reaching desires in the world of permanence and eternal happiness. For through one manifestation of His Mercy, the All-Merciful and All-Compassionate One every spring lays on the table of that season innumerable delightful, artful bounties on the face of this earth, which is His temporary guesthouse and one of the mansions in the universe, in order to please His guests for one or two hours. Then, after presenting these to them as an appetizer, He fills eight eternal Paradises with innumerable varieties for the eternal life of His servants. So, those who rely on the Mercy of such an All-Merciful and Compassionate One through belief and are aware of their relation with Him certainly find such a source of help that even its least degree provides for innumerable ambitions that extend as far as eternity, enabling their realization.

Furthermore, through the truth expressed in the above-mentioned verses, the light issuing from the radiation of belief showed itself so brightly that it lit up the six dark directions like daytime. It removed my sorrow that arose from the death of my students and friends and the destruction of my *medrese*, reminding me, "The world where your friends have gone is not dark. They have merely changed locations; you will meet with them again." It brought an end to my tears and made me understand that I would find others who resembled them and who would take their place in this world.

All praise and thanks be to God, with the *medrese* of Isparta He raised to life the dead *medrese* of Van, and, in one sense, He raised my friends there to life with the more numerous and valued students and friends here. So I came to know that the world is not void or meaningless, and that my thinking of it in the form of a ruined wasteland had been wrong. Rather, as required by the Wisdom of the True Master, the world changes its scenes that are made by people and renews His missives. Like the new fruit of a tree taking the place of those that have been harvested, death and separation in humankind are in fact renewal and refreshment. From the perspective of belief, they are a renewal which should not cause painful sorrow due to the want of friends, but a sweet sorrow that arises from parting in order to meet again in another, better place.

The verses also illuminated the face of the beings in the universe which had appeared dark because of the former appalling situation. Therefore, I wanted to offer thanks for this, and the following lines occurred to me in Arabic; they described that very reality. I said:

> All praise be to God for the light of belief, which shows that those who were thought to be strangers, antagonistic, lifeless, terrifying, and weeping orphans, in fact are lovable ones, brothers and sisters, living companions, employed for meaningful results, joyful, glorifiers of God and reciters of His Names.

Since I have the right to think of all the beings in my personal world, as well as in the entire world, as engaged in the praise and glorification of God, and through the intention to make use of them in these duties, together with all those beings, who praise and glorify God individually and collectively through the tongue of their disposition, I say, "All praise and thanks be to God for the light of belief."

Moreover, the true pleasures of life, which had been reduced to nothing because of my former heedless and appalling state of mind, and my hopes which had withered up entirely, and the bounties bestowed on me, which had been constricted, as has been explained in many other parts of the *Risale-i Nur*, so expanded that narrow sphere around my heart all at once through the light of belief that it contained the whole universe. In place of the bounties which had withered up in the garden of the Horhor *Medrese* and which had lost their taste, they made this world and the Hereafter each a merciful table of bounties. The light of belief showed not the ten or so human members like the eyes, ears, or the heart, but rather each of the hundred members in the form of such an extremely long arm which believers might stretch out each according to their degree that they could gather the bounties from all sides of those two tables of the All-Merciful. Therefore, in order to express this elevated truth and to give thanks for these limitless bounties, I uttered the following words:

> All praise and thanks be to my Creator for the bounty of the light of belief, for it shows the two realms of the world and the Hereafter as being full of bounties and mercy, from which every believer can rightfully benefit with their numerous senses able to develop by the leave of their Creator.

Since belief has so great an effect in this world, in the Realm of Eternity it will certainly have such fruit and radiation that they cannot be comprehended or described by the mind in this world.

And so, you elderly people who, like me, suffer the pains of separation from numerous friends because of old age! However much older than me in years the oldest of you is, in effect, I must be older than he. For since I feel extreme pity for my fellow beings due to the excessive compassion ingrained in my nature, and, because of that very compassion, I have suffered the pains of thousands of my brothers in addition to my own, I feel as though I have lived for hundreds of years. In addition, however much you may have suffered from the disaster of separation, you cannot have been exposed to that disaster to the degree that I have. For I have no child that I should think only of him or her. My deep innate feeling of pity and compassion causes me to feel pain and sympathy in the face of the sorrows of thousands of children, and even innocent animals. Neither do I have a house of my own that I should care for it only. Rather, being a Muslim, I am deeply bound to this country, and, in fact, the whole Muslim world, as though each were my own house. I feel great pain at the suffering of my fellow Muslims in these two great houses, and I am sorrowful at being separated from them.

And so, in the face of all these sorrows of mine that result from old age and the calamity of separation, the light of belief was enough for me; it gave me an inextinguishable hope and light and unending solace. So, it must certainly be more than enough for you in the face of the darkness, heedlessness, sorrow, and pains brought on by old age. In reality, the old age that is utterly dark and bereft of light and solace, and the most painful and terrible separation, is the old age and separation of the people of misguidance and the dissipated. In order to experience the belief which gives such hope, light, and solace, and its effects, one should be in a consciously worshipful attitude that is worthy of old age and appropriate to Islam. We cannot experience this by trying to imitate the young, plunging our head into heedlessness, and forgetting old age.

Consider the *hadith*, the meaning of which is, "The best of the young among you are those who resemble the old in care and avoidance of vice, while the worst of your elderly are those who imitate the young in vice and heedlessness."[122]

My elderly brothers and sisters! There is another *hadith* which says, "Divine Mercy is ashamed to leave unanswered the prayers offered to the Divine Court by an elderly believer of sixty or seventy years."[123] Since Divine Mercy holds you in such respect, be respectful towards this respect by worshipping Him!

The fourteenth hope

The Fourth Ray, explaining the luminous Qur'anic statement, *God is sufficient for us* (3: 173), says in the beginning, in summary:

Due to the worldly people having isolated me from everything, I was suffering five sorts of separation. Without looking to the consoling and helpful lights of the *Risale-i Nur*, because of heedlessness arising from distress, I turned to my heart and spirit. I saw that together with an infinite impotence and boundless neediness, an extremely powerful love of permanence, an intense attachment to existence, and a great yearning for life were dominating me. But an awesome mortality was extinguishing that permanence. In that mood, I exclaimed like the poet who suffers separation:

While my heart desired permanence, God, the Truth,
judged the mortality of my body;
I am afflicted with an incurable ill; how pitiful it is that
Luqman is unaware of it!

I bowed my head in despair. Suddenly the verse, *God is sufficient for us; how excellent a Guardian He is!* (3: 173), came to my aid, and asked me to read it attentively. So I recited it five hundred times every day. While reciting it, out of its numerous invaluable lights, nine aspects of God's sufficien-

122 at-Tabarani, *al-Mu'jam al-Kabir*, 22:83; Abu Ya'la, *al-Musnad*, 13:467. (Tr.)

123 at-Tabarani, *al-Mu'jam al-Awsat*, 5:270. (Tr.)

cy[124] were unfolded to me, not only at the level of "certainty coming from knowledge," but at that of "certainty coming from observation."

The first luminous aspect of God's sufficiency

My innate love of permanence, which essentially arises from a manifestation in my being of a Name of the One of Perfection and Majesty, Who is naturally loved because of His absolute Perfection, and which should therefore have been directed towards the Essence, Perfection, and Permanence of that Absolutely Perfect One, had lost its way and become attached to the shadow due to heedlessness. It had sought the permanence of the worldly life, which is nothing more than a transitory mirror of what is essentially eternal. Then the Qur'anic statement, *God is sufficient for us*, came and lifted up the veil. I observed and felt and experienced with the degree of "absolute certainty" that the true pleasure and happiness of my permanence lay accurately and in more perfect form in the Permanence of the Everlasting One of Perfection and in believing and confirming that He is my Lord and Deity. The proofs for this have been explained in the Fourth Ray (included in *The Rays*), the treatise on the verse *God is sufficient for us*, in twelve consecutive paragraphs in a fine, profound way.

The second luminous aspect of God's sufficiency

At a time when old age, exile, solitude, and isolation were added to my endless impotence in nature, when "the worldly" were attacking me with their schemes and spies, I told my heart, "Armies are attacking a single man whose hands are tied, and who is ill and weak. Is there not a point of support for me?" I had recourse to the verse, *God is sufficient for us; how excellent a Guardian He is*, and it informed me of the following:

Through the document of belief you become connected to such a Ruler of Absolute Power that every spring He equips in perfect order all the armies of plants and animals on the earth, which is composed of hundreds of thousands of different nations. In addition, as the All-Merciful, He places in tiny protective cases the sustenance of all animals and humans in the form of the extracts of all kinds of foods, which we call seeds and grains and which may be likened to the meat, sugar and other food extracts discovered

124 Six aspects of God's sufficiency are mentioned here. (Tr.)

recently, but a hundred times more perfect than them. He includes in those extracts the instructions of Divine Destiny concerning their growth and development into edible foods. The creation of those tiny cases and their growth into elaborate tables of food take place with such speed, ease, and abundance in the factory of *Kâf–Nûn*, forming the command of "*Kun!* [Be!]," that the Qur'an states that the Creator merely commands and it comes into being.[125] Since you have such support through the connection to Him enabled by the document of belief, you can rely on an infinite strength and power. As I learned this lesson from the verse, I found such a moral strength that I felt I had enough power of belief to challenge not only my present enemies, but the entire world. With all my spirit I proclaimed, "*God is sufficient for us; how excellent a Guardian He is!*"

The third luminous aspect of God's sufficiency

Having found my attachment to the world to have been severed after suffering the oppression of those exiles and illnesses, belief recalled to me that I was destined for perpetual happiness in an eternal world, an everlasting realm. I then gave up sighing regretfully, which only caused further grief and yearning, and became cheerful and happy. However, this ideal or goal of the spirit and the final result of human nature could only be realized through the infinite Power of an Absolutely All-Powerful One, Who knows and records the action and rest and conduct and states, in word and deed, of all His creatures, and through His conferring limitless favor and importance on humans, whom He takes as His friends and addressees, and to whom He has given a rank superior to all beings despite their absolute impotence. Reflecting on these two points—namely, the activity of such a Power and the importance in reality of apparently impotent and insignificant human beings—I sought an explanation that would deepen belief and satisfy the heart. Again I had recourse to the verse, *God is sufficient for us; how excellent a Guardian He is*, and it told me to note the suffix "*-na*," ("for *us*") and to be attentive to the beings that are saying, "*God is sufficient for us*," with me either verbally or through the tongue of their disposition.

125 The writer refers to the verse, *When He wills a thing to be, He but says to it "Be!" and it is* (36:82). (Tr.)

I at once looked and saw that innumerable birds and flies (which are miniature birds) and innumerable animals, plants and trees were, like me, reciting, *God is sufficient for us; how excellent a Guardian He is!* through the tongue of their disposition. They recall to everyone the following fact: that they have such a Guardian Who guarantees all their essential necessities of life that before our eyes and particularly in the spring, His vast and all-majestic Power creates in utmost abundance, with the greatest ease, on a vast scale, with the greatest art, and in balanced and well-ordered fashion, and in forms all different from one another, with no defect, fault, or confusion at all, from eggs, drops of fluids, grains, and seeds that look very much like each other and whose component elements are the same, a hundred thousand species of birds, hundreds of thousands of animals, hundreds of thousands of types of plants, and hundreds of thousands of varieties of trees. The similarity and resemblance among all these beings despite the infinite difference demonstrate to us His Unity and Oneness, and inform us that there cannot be any interference or participation in those acts of His Lordship and Creativity. Those who want to understand my personal identity and human nature as a believing man, which is like that of all believers, should look at the meaning of the 'I' included in the first person plural 'us' in *God is sufficient for us*. What is my apparently insignificant, needy being, or that of any believer? What is life? What is humanity? What is Islam? What is certain, verified belief? What is knowledge of God? How should love be? They can find the answers to all these questions.

The fourth luminous aspect of God's sufficiency

Once, when in an instance of heedlessness in which I felt overpowered by circumstances like old age, exile, illness, and defeat, I was painfully anxious about my being, to which I was intensely attached and with which I was infatuated. I was anxious that my being, as well as all other creatures, were heading for death, were being stripped of existence. So, once again, I had recourse to the verse. It said to me, "Note my meaning; look at it through the telescope of belief!"

So I looked with the eye of belief and saw that like all other believers, my minuscule being was the mirror of an Unlimited Being, and through infinite expansion, the means of gaining innumerable existences, and a word of wisdom yielding the fruits of numerous permanent existences more valuable than itself. So, I knew with the certainty of knowledge that to live in connection with that Being, even for an instant, was as valuable as eternal existence. For I understood through the consciousness of belief that my being was a work of art and a manifestation of the Necessarily Existent Being. So, being saved from the essentially groundless anxieties of loneliness and from innumerable separations and their pains, I formed relations and bonds of brotherhood with beings that I love, to the number of Divine acts and Names responsible for beings and especially living ones, and I knew that there was a permanent union with all of them after a temporary separation. And so, through belief and connection with the Creator and all of His creatures through belief, like all believers, my being gained the lights of innumerable existences untainted by separation. Even when my being departs, as they remain behind, it is as happy as if it too had remained.

In short, death is not separation, it is union; it is a change of location; it is producing an eternal fruit.

The fifth luminous aspect of God's sufficiency

At another time, my life was once more shaken by very harsh conditions, and drew my attention to itself. I saw that my life was going swiftly, drawing close to the Hereafter; it had started to be extinguished under harsh conditions. I thought sorrowfully that, as explained where the Divine Name, the All-Living is discussed in the *Risale-i Nur*[126] with its important functions and great merits and benefits, life did not deserve to be so swiftly extinguished, but rather should endure a long time. I again had recourse to my teacher, the verse, *God is sufficient for us; how excellent a Guardian He is!* This time it said to me, "Consider life from the perspective of the All-Living and Self-Subsisting by Whom all subsist, Who gives you life!"

I did so and saw that if my life looks to me in one respect, it looks to the All-Living and the Self-Subsisting in a hundred. And if, out of its results, one looked to me, a thousand looked to my Creator. Therefore, one instant of its endurance within the bounds of God's good pleasure and approval is sufficient; a long time is not required. This truth has been explained in five indications and four matters in the Thirtieth Gleam in this book. Those who are not dead or who want to be alive should seek the

126 It is discussed in the Fifth Part of the Thirtieth Gleam in this book. (Tr.)

nature and reality of life and its true rights in these indications and matters; they will find them and be raised to life!

A summary is as follows: the more life is grasped, causing it to look to the All-Living and the Self-Subsisting, and the more belief becomes the life and spirit of life, the more it becomes perpetual and yields enduring fruits. It also becomes so elevated that it receives the manifestation of eternity. It is no longer a consideration whether life is short or long.

The sixth luminous aspect of God's sufficiency

At a time when old age was reminding me of my personal departure from the world amidst the events of the end of time, which suggest the overall destruction of the world—the time of general parting, my innate love of beauty and fondness for perfection were being developed in an extraordinarily sensitive manner. With extraordinary awareness and sorrow I saw that transience and decline, which are always destructive, and death, which is the continuous cause of separation, were pounding this beautiful world and these lovely creatures in a terrible manner and destroying their beauty. When my innate love of creation boiled up intensely and rebelled against this situation, once more I had recourse to the verse *God is sufficient for us; how excellent a Guardian He is!* to find consolation. It said to me, "Recite me and consider my meaning carefully!"

So I entered the observatory of verse 35 of *Surat an-Nur*, *God is the Light of the heavens and the earth* (to the end of the verse), and looked through the telescope of belief to the most distant levels of the verse, *God is sufficient for us; how excellent a Guardian He is!* and through the microscope of the insight of belief at its most subtle meanings. I saw the following:

Mirrors, pieces of glass, transparent things, and even bubbles manifest the various hidden beauties of the sun's light and the seven colors in its light; and through their disappearance, renewal, and replacements with new ones and with different capacities and refractions, they cause the renewal and re-manifestations of these beauties. In the same way, in order to act as mirrors to the sacred Beauty of the All-Gracious, Beautiful One of Majesty, the Eternal Sun, and to the permanent beauties of His All-Beautiful Names, and to cause the ever-renewal of their manifestations, these beautiful creatures, these lovely beings arrive and depart in a constant flux. As explained in detail in the *Risale-i Nur* with powerful evidence, they demonstrate that the beauties manifested by them are not their own property, but the signs, indications, gleams, and manifestations of an eternal, transcendent, sacred Beauty Which wants to become manifest. Anyone with a sound mind and heart who reads them will understand and confirm that their existence, as well as the existence of everything, is a miracle, and they will try to develop it.

The fifteenth hope

When I was once in enforced residence in Emirdağ,[127] in what was virtually solitary confinement, I became wearied of life because of the torments inflicted on me through unbearable surveillance and pressure. I regretted having been released from prison and longed for Denizli Prison with all my spirit, even wishing to enter the grave. But, even as I was thinking that prison or the grave were preferable to a life like this, Divine Grace came to my aid and bestowed on me the students of the *Medresetu'z-Zehra* , whose pens were like the duplicating machines that had just been invented. All at once, five hundred copies of each of the valuable collections of the *Risale-i Nur* appeared; one pen had become five hundred. The fact that this work gained new hearts on a wider scale made me love that distressing life, causing me to offer endless thanks.

A while later, the covert enemies of the *Risale-i Nur* could no longer bear its victories, and provoked the government against us. Again life started to become difficult for me. Then suddenly, Divine Grace showed itself: the officials connected with the case, who were in fact most in need of the *Risale-i Nur*, studied the confiscated copies of it in connection with their duties with great curiosity and care, and their hearts became friendly to it. When they began to appreciate this work instead of criticizing it, the *Risale-i Nur* circle of study greatly expanded. It produced spiritual profits a hundred times greater than our material losses, reducing our anxiety and distress to nothing.

Then, secret, hypocritical enemies drew the government's attention to my person. They recounted my political activities during my days of the Old or Former Said. They caused both the justice department, and the education authorities, and the police, and the Ministry of Internal Affairs to be suspicious of me. Due to certain political trends and the provocation of certain communists, who were in fact anarchists, the suspicions became more

[127] Emirdağ is a district of Afyon, a province in the west of Turkey. (Tr.)

widespread. They started to pressure us and arrest us, and confiscate those parts of the *Risale-i Nur* that came into their hands. The activities of the *Risale-i Nur* students came to a standstill. With the thought of disgracing me in the sight of people, a number of officials made false accusations so absurd that no one could have believed them at all. They tried to spread the most incredible slander, but they could not make anyone believe it.

Then on some most trivial pretext they arrested me during the intensely cold days of winter, and kept me in solitary confinement in prison, in a large and extremely cold cell that had no form of heating. When in my small room I had been accustomed to light my stove several times a day, and had always had live coals in the brazier because of my weakness and illness. Despite this, I was only able to endure the cold with great difficulty because of my weakness and illness. While struggling in the cell, suffering both from fever caused by the cold and from a dreadful distress and anger, a truth unfolded in my heart through Divine Grace. What follows occurred to my spirit:

You called prison the "Medrese-i Yusufiya"—the School of the Prophet Joseph. And while in the Denizli prison, circumstances a thousand times greater than your distress caused such spiritual gain that other prisoners benefited from the *Risale-i Nur*, and its conquests were on a larger scale; this caused you to offer thousands of thanks instead of complaining. They made each hour of your imprisonment and hardship equal to ten hours of worship, and those transient hours became eternal. God willing, the fact that those who suffer imprisonment in your third School of Joseph will benefit from the *Risale-i Nur* and find consolation in it will warm this cold, severe hardship of yours and transform it into joy. If those with whom you are angry have been deceived, then they are ill-treating you unknowingly. So, they do not deserve anger. But if they are tormenting you and causing you suffering knowingly, out of spite and on account of misguidance, soon they will enter the solitary confinement of the grave through the eternal execution of death, where they will suffer incessant torment. On account of their oppression, you are both earning merit and spiritual pleasures, and making your transient hours eternal, and performing scholarly and religious duties with sincerity.

With all my strength I uttered, "All praise and thanks be to God!" Being a human, I pitied those tyrants and prayed, "O my Lord, reform them!" As I wrote in my statement to the Ministry of Internal Affairs, those responsible for this new incident, which was completely unlawful in at least ten respects, were themselves the guilty ones. Those tyrants had acted unlawfully even in the eyes of human law. Through the most incredible pretexts they had contrived such slanders and fabrications that those who heard them laughed and lovers of truth wept, demonstrating to the fair-minded that they had been completely unable to find a way to attack the *Risale-i Nur* or its students according to the law or to justice, and therefore they had deviated into lunacy.

For instance, the officials who had spied on us for a month could find nothing to accuse us of, so they wrote a note that said, "Said's servant bought *raki* from a shop and took it to him." Unable to find anyone to sign the note, they finally picked up a drunken, uncivilized man and tried to bully him into signing it. Even he said, "God forgive us! Who would sign this most incredible lie?" So they were compelled to tear it up.

A *second example:* Someone I did not know personally and still do not know loaned me his horse so that I could take an excursion into the country. Because of my illness and in order to take some air, I would go out most days for a couple of hours in summer. Following my rule and in order not to feel indebted to anyone, I had promised the owner of the horse and the carriage (that came with it) books worth fifty *lira.* Is there any danger in such a thing? But as though it was an important political event or an incident that affected public security, the governor, the court officials, and the police asked us nearly fifty times who the horse belonged to. In order that this meaningless questioning might come to an end, out of human tenderness, one person said that the horse was his and another that the carriage was his. They were both arrested with me. We faced numerous childish games such as these and sometimes we laughed and sometimes we cried. We understood that those who attacked the *Risale-i Nur* and its students only made fools of themselves.

A peculiar conversation from among these incidents is as follows: On the paper authorizing my arrest it was recorded that it was for "disturbing public order." Without having seen the document, I told the public prosecutor, "I spoke behind your back last night. I said to a police officer who was questioning me on behalf the Chief of Police, 'If I have not served the public security of this country to the same degree as a thousand public prosecutors and a thousand police chiefs—I repeated this three times—may God damn me!'"

Then at that point, in those freezing conditions, I was almost overcome by anger and annoyance with those whose hatred and ill intentions had sent me into this unbearable exile, isolation, arrest, and oppression at a time when I was most in need of rest, of avoiding catching cold and being anxious about the world. Divine Grace came to my aid, and it occurred to my heart as follows:

> Divine Destiny, which is pure justice, has a large part in the oppression which these people are inflicting on you. You have food to eat in this prison; that provision of yours called you here. You should respond with contentment and resignation. The Wisdom and Mercy of the Lord have also a significant part in this situation: you should try to enlighten those in this prison and console them, so you might gain reward. Your response should be thousands of thanks and great patience. Your soul also has a part in this situation because of certain faults you may be unaware of. Your response should be repentance and seeking forgiveness, telling your soul that it deserved this blow. Also, some of your secret enemies have a part in it, through their deceitful intrigues that provoke certain ingenuous and suspicious officials to such oppression. In response to this, the powerful immaterial blows dealt by the *Risale-i Nur* to those hypocritical ones have sought your revenge completely. That is enough for them. Finally, the officials who were the actual means of bringing about this situation have a part in it. Your response should be—so that they may benefit from the *Risale-i Nur* through belief, whether they want to or not, and even if they came to it with the intention of criticizing it—to forgive them according to the rule, *The God-revering, righteous ones—those who .... ever-restrain their rage (even when provoked and able to retaliate), and pardon people (their offenses)* (3: 134); that would be an act of magnanimity.

Due to the perfect contentment and gratitude I felt as a result of this veritable warning, I decided to remain in this new "School of Joseph," and even to commit some harmless offence which would inflict upon me a prison sentence so that I might help even those who were opposed to me. Furthermore, I was seventy-five years old, without any worldly attachment, and out of seventy of those whom I loved only five remained alive. Besides, seventy thousand copies of the *Risale-i Nur* collection were in free circulation and would perform my duties, and in addition, I had brothers and sisters and heirs who would serve belief with thousands of tongues in place of my one tongue. Therefore, the grave was a hundred times better for me than this prison. And the prison was a hundred times more comfortable and more beneficial than liberty outside that had no freedom and which was subject to tyranny and oppression. For in place of having to suffer all alone outside the oppression of hundreds of officials, in prison, with hundreds of other prisoners, one only had to suffer the slight "formal" oppression of one or two people, like the prison governor and chief warder. But one receives the brotherly kindness and consolation of many companions in prison. In addition, Islamic compassion and human innate tenderness lead to the kind treatment of the elderly in such a position, thus turning the hardship of prison into mercy. In consideration of all these, I became resigned to prison.

When I went to court for this third trial, because of my difficulty in remaining standing due to weakness, old age, and illness, I sat on a chair outside the door of the trial room. The judge suddenly appeared and angrily asked in a spiteful manner, "Why isn't he waiting standing up?" I became angry at this mercilessness in the face of old age. Suddenly, I saw that a large number of Muslims had gathered around us and were watching with complete affection and brotherly compassion, and not dispersing. The following two truths occurred to me:

The first: The secret enemies of myself and the *Risale-i Nur* had deceived certain ingenuous officials in the hopes that in this way they could put a stop to the *Risale-i Nur*'s conquests by destroying the public's good opinion of me and damaging my reputation—something that in any case I did not want. They had provoked those officials to act disdainfully towards me in that way. But in place of that one man's insults, see these hundred people as a Divine favor for the *Risale-i Nur*'s service to belief! Appreciating your service, they pity you and are offering their sympathy, and they welcome you and see you off. Indeed, the next day while I was answering the public prosecutor's questions, about a thousand people gathered in the courtyard outside the court windows, showing their concern. It was as though they wished to tell the authorities not to oppress me. The police were unable to make them disperse. It occurred to me that in this perilous age these people desire true solace, an inextinguishable light, a powerful belief, and certain glad tidings about eternal happiness—by their very nature, they were searching for these. They must have heard that what they were searching for existed in the *Risale-i Nur*, and this was the reason why they showed my unimportant person such attention and regard for the little service I had performed for belief—the attention and regard that far exceeded my due.

The second truth: It occurred to me that in return for the insulting ill-treatment of a few deceived individuals which they inflicted on us due to their ungrounded suspicions that we were disturbing public order and with the intention to prevent our service for belief and to destroy public acclaim and regard for us, came the applause and appreciation of innumerable people of truth and forthcoming generations.

Through the strength of certain, verified belief, in every part of this country the *Risale-i Nur* and its students have halted the dreadful corrupting efforts of anarchy that shelter under the veil of communism and which are trying to destroy public order. The *Risale-i Nur* and its students work to maintain public order and security, and as a result in over twenty years three or four courts and the police in ten provinces have not been able to find or record any incidents of public order violation by the *Risale-i Nur* students, who are very numerous and found in every part of the country. And some fair-minded police officers in three provinces have stated, "The *Risale-i Nur* students are moral police. They help us with the preservation of public order. Through certain, verified belief, something is left in everyone's head who reads the *Risale-i Nur* that prevents them from committing any offense. They work to secure public order."

An example of this was Denizli prison. When the *Risale-i Nur*, including in particular *Meyve Risalesi* (The Treatise on the Fruits of Belief), which was written in that prison, entered there, within a period of three or four months the prisoners, numbering more than two hundred, became so extraordinarily obedient and acquired such religious, righteous conduct that a man who had killed three or four people held back from even killing bedbugs. They became completely compassionate, harmless and beneficial members of the nation. The officials observed this change in amazement and appreciation. Before receiving their sentences, some youths even said: "If the students of the *Risale-i Nur* remain in prison, we will try to have ourselves convicted so that we can be taught by them and become like them. We will reform ourselves through their teaching."

So, those who accuse the *Risale-i Nur* students, who are of that quality, of disturbing public order are surely seriously mistaken, or have been deceived, or knowingly or unknowingly are deceiving the government for the sake of anarchy, and trying to crush us through oppression. We say the following to them:

> Since death cannot be killed and the grave is not to be closed, and the travelers in this guesthouse of the world, convoy after convoy, enter the earth with great speed and ado, and disappear, certainly we

> too will part from one another very soon. You will receive the punishment for your oppression in a terrible fashion. You will mount the gallows of death, which is a door to eternal punishment for you but the discharge papers for the oppressed people of belief. The passing pleasures you have received in this world, which you imagine to be permanent, will change into everlasting, grievous pain.

Regrettably, our covert hypocritical enemies sometimes attach the name of "Sufi order" to the truth of Islam, which has been gained and preserved with the efforts of hundreds of millions of martyrs of the rank of saints and heroic veterans of this religious nation. While the way of Sufi orders is only a single ray of the Sun of Islam, they attempt to show it as the sun itself, and deceive certain careless government officials. Labeling the *Risale-i Nur* students, who in fact work effectively for the truths of the Qur'an and belief, as "followers of a Sufi order" and "members of a political society," they wish to provoke such officials against us. We say to them, and to those who lend an ear to them against us, what we told the fair court at Denizli:

> Let us too be sacrificed for a sacred truth, for which hundreds of millions of others have been sacrificed! Even if you set fire to the world to burn us, we who sacrifice ourselves for the truths of the Qur'an will not lay down our "arms" before heresy; by God's will and help, we will not abandon our sacred duty!

And so, because of the sacred solace for the pains and despairing condition of my old age that emanates from belief and the Qur'an, I would not exchange even the most distressing year of my old age for ten of the happiest years of my youth. Particularly so, as every hour in prison of those who repent and perform the obligatory Prayers is equal to ten hours of worship under normal conditions, and each transient day spent in illness and oppression gains the reward of ten days of perpetual life, I have understood how deserving of thanks are these days for someone like me who is awaiting his turn at the door of the grave. I utter, "Endless thanks be to my Lord!" and am content with my old age and pleased with my imprisonment. For life does not cease; it passes swiftly. If it passes in pleasure and happiness, since the disappearance of pleasure is pain, it causes regret and grief, and due to thanklessness and heedlessness, it departs leaving sins in its wake. Whereas, if it passes in prison or hardship, since the disappearance of pain is a pleasure in spirit, and since it is considered to be a sort of worship, it becomes perpetual in one respect, and through its good fruits, gains permanence. It becomes atonement for the sins committed in the past and the mistakes that were the cause of imprisonment, purifying them. From this perspective, those among the prisoners who perform at least the compulsory parts of the obligatory Prayers should offer thanks in patience.

The sixteenth hope

Once in my old age I was released from the Eskişehir prison after serving a year's sentence. They exiled me to Kastamonu (in northern Turkey), where they kept me for two or three months as a guest in the police station. It may be understood how much distress someone like me suffered in a place like that; how difficult this was for one who prefers solitude, one who is wearied by meeting even loyal friends, and one who cannot endure the change of his classical, native dress. While in such tormenting conditions, Divine Grace suddenly came to the aid of my old age. The inspector and police officers in the police station became like faithful friends. They did not once warn me about how I dressed, and, as if they were my servants, they used to take me for trips around the town.

Then I took up residence in Kastamonu's "*Risale-i Nur Medrese*," opposite the police station, and started to write more of the *Risale-i Nur*. Heroic *Risale-i Nur* students like Feyzi, Emin, Hilmi, Sadik, Nazif, and Salahaddin attended the *Medrese* in order to duplicate the treatises in their handwriting and distribute them. We held scholarly debates even more profound than those I had held in my youth with my former students.

Then our secret enemies aroused the suspicions of some officials and some egotistical *hojas* and *shaykhs* concerning us. They caused us and the *Risale-i Nur* students from five or six provinces to be gathered together in the "School of Joseph" of Denizli prison. The details of this Sixteenth Hope are to be found in the short letters sent from Kastamonu and those I secretly sent to my brothers while in Denizli prison, and in the collection containing the court defense speeches. So referring the details to those letters and to my defense speech, I will cut it short here:

I hid certain confidential and important treatises under the coal and firewood so that they might be published after my death or after the top-ranking authorities in the capital city listened to the truth and came to their senses. While I was feeling relaxed about this, some detectives and the assistant public prosecutor suddenly raided my house. They pulled out those confidential and important treatises from under the wood. Afterwards, they arrested me and sent me to Isparta prison, although I was in bad health. While I was greatly upset and extremely saddened at the harm that had come to the *Risale-i Nur*, Divine Grace came to our aid. The authorities began to read with great care and curiosity these important treatises which had been hidden, and of which they were much in need, and the government offices became like *Risale-i Nur* study centers. Having started to read with the intention of criticizing, they began to appreciate them. Even in Denizli, although we were unaware of it, numerous official and unofficial people read the secretly printed edition of *Ayetü'l-Kübra* (The Supreme Sign), and their belief was strengthened. This reduced to nothing the disaster of prison that we were suffering.

Later they took us to Denizli prison, and put me into solitary confinement in a stinking, cold, damp cell. While struggling with old age, illness, and the unhappiness that arose from the troubles my friends were suffering because of me, as well as the grief and distress caused by the confiscations of the parts of the *Risale-i Nur* and the cessation in its activities, Divine Grace suddenly came to my aid. It changed that huge prison into a *Risale-i Nur Medrese*, proving it to be a School of Joseph. The *Risale-i Nur* started to spread through the diamond pens of the heroes of the *Medresetu'z-Zehra*. In those severe conditions, one of those heroes, who is the most advanced in serving the *Risale-i Nur*, copied out more than twenty copies of the Fruits of Belief and the Collection of Defense Speeches in the space of three or four months. They began to conquer minds and hearts both within the prison and outside. This changed our losses in that disaster into great gains and our distress into joy. It once again demonstrated the truth in the verse, *It may well be that you dislike a thing but it is good for you* (2: 216).

Then due to the harsh criticisms of the first Experts Committee, based on incorrect and superficial official reports, and due to the dreadful attacks by the Education Minister and the statement he published against us, as well as some press releases, things went so far that they even tried to have some of us executed. While in these circumstances, Divine Grace came to our aid. First of all, against all expectations, an appreciative report came from the Experts Committee in Ankara. In addition, we proved in court that certain points that they had shown to be errors in the *Risale-i Nur* collections were completely correct, and that they themselves had been in error. Also, we showed almost ten errors they had made in their five pages of report. Then, while awaiting severe, threatening reproaches in return for the Fruits of Belief and Collections of Defense Speeches Collections, which we had sent to seven government offices, and for the entire *Risale-i Nur*, which had been sent to the Ministry of Justice, and in particular the strong criticisms that had been laid against certain important persons in confidential treatises, they responded extremely leniently. Even like the reassuring letter that had been sent to us by the Prime Minister, they were conciliatory, far from attacking us. All these proved decisively that, as a miracle of Divine Grace, the truths of the *Risale-i Nur* had caused them to study its treatises like a guide, and made those broad circles into a sort of study circle, securing the belief of numerous hesitating or bewildered people, causing us spiritual joy and profit a hundred times greater than our distress.

Then our secret enemies poisoned me and at the same time the late Hafiz Ali, the martyred hero of the *Risale-i Nur*, went to hospital and from there traveled to the Intermediate Realm of the grave in my place; we wept in despair. Before this disaster, I had repeatedly exclaimed on the mountain at Kastamonu, "My brothers, don't give meat to the horse or grass to the lion!" That is, "Don't give all the treatises to everyone, lest they misunderstand them and use them to attack us." At the time when I had so exclaimed, as if he had heard via his spiritual telephone from a distance of seven days' march, Hafiz Ali, may God have mercy on him, wrote to me, "Indeed, my teacher, it is a wonder of the *Risale-i Nur* that it does not give meat to horses or grass to lions. Rather, it gives horses grass and lions meat so that it gave that lion-like *hoja* the treatise on Sincerity." I received his letter seven days later. We made the calculations, and discovered that at the very moment I was shouting out those words on the mountain, he was writing them in his letter.

Thus, just at the time when we were feeling depressed by the death of that hero of the *Risale-i Nur* and the intrigues that our hypocritical enemies undertook against us so that we would be suspected and punished, and when we were worried that I would be taken to hospital on official orders as I was ill from the poison, Divine Grace suddenly came to our aid. Through the sincere prayers of my blessed brothers, the risk of my death from the poison disappeared. According to powerful signs, Hafiz Ali, that blessed martyr, was occupied in his grave with the *Risale-i Nur*, and answered with the *Risale-i Nur* to the questioning angels; and the Denizli hero, Hasan Feyzi, may God have mercy on him, who would serve in his place and work according to his system, and his friends, were serving the *Risale-i Nur* effectively. Since the other prisoners were being reformed by the *Risale-i Nur*, even our enemies supported our being released from prison. Resembling the Companions of the Cave,[128] the *Risale-i Nur* students turned that place of ordeal into a cave of the ascetics of former times, and endeavored to write and publish the parts of the *Risale-i Nur* with contented hearts. All of these proved that Divine Grace had come to our aid.

It also occurred to my heart that since leading scholars of the Law such as Imam A'zam Abu Hanifa[129] had suffered imprisonment; since a supreme defender of Islam like Imam Ahmad ibn Hanbal[130] had been severely tormented in prison for the sake of a single issue related to the Qur'an, and had borne it in perfect patience, not remaining silent about the matter in question; and since numerous religious leaders and scholars had offered thanks in complete patience, without being shaken, although they had been subjected to torments far greater than ours, then certainly we were obliged to offer endless thanks for the few troubles we had to suffer in return for the great reward that we gained from the many truths of the Qur'an. Let me describe briefly a manifestation of Divine Grace amidst humankind's wrongful tyranny:

When I was twenty years old I used to repeatedly say, "Like the recluses who withdrew into caves in former times, towards the end of my life I will retreat from social life into a cave or onto a mountain." Also, when I was a prisoner of war in the northeast of Russia during the World War I, I decid-

---

128 The Companions of the Cave were seven youths who proclaimed their faith in God's Unity in the presence of the polytheist king of the country, and therefore had to shelter in a cave. As a Divine miracle, they slept in the cave for three hundred years, and were awakened to find that their faith had become the official religion of their nation. Having witnessed this, they died and were buried in the cave. See, the Qur'an, 18:9–26. They are known as, the Seven Sleepers, in the West. (Tr.)

129 Imam A'zam Abu Hanifa, Nu'man ibn Thabit (d. 768): Founded the Hanafi School of Law and one of the greatest Muslim scholars of jurisprudence and deducer of new laws from the Qur'an and Sunna. He was also well-versed in theology. (Tr.)

130 Imam Ahmad ibn Hanbal (d., 855): The founder of one of the four Sunni schools of law in Islam. He valiantly suffered persecution for the sake of his religious conviction. His *Musnad* is famous, containing about 40,000 Traditions that he collected. (Tr.)

ed that I would spend the remaining part of my life in caves. I would withdraw from political and social life. I had had enough of them. Now I see that, in a way far better than my decision and wish, out of compassion for my old age, the Grace of the Lord and the justice of Divine Destiny changed those caves, which I had thought of withdrawing into, into prisons, retreats, and places of ordeal in loneliness and solitary confinement. It had given me Schools of Joseph that are far superior to the mountain caves of ascetics and recluses, and places of solitary confinement so that I might not waste my time. It had both granted me the benefits of the Hereafter that are expected of retreat in caves, and enabled me to carry out a sacred service to the truths of belief and the Qur'an, which is a kind of *jihad*. I had even thought of feigning guilt of some offense and remaining in prison following the acquittal of my friends, with bachelors like Husrev and Feyzi. On some pretext I would have remained in the cell for solitary confinement in order not to meet with people or not to waste my time on useless conversation or egotistical affectation. But Divine Destiny sent us to another place of ordeal. In accordance with the Divine rules, "That which God chooses is what is good," and *It may well be that you dislike a thing but it is good for you* (2: 216), out of compassion for my old age and so that we should work harder in the service of belief, we were charged with duties beyond our will and power in this third School of Joseph.

There are instances of wisdom and three important benefits for the service of the *Risale-i Nur* in the Divine Grace compassionately turning the caves I had thought to withdraw into during my youth, when I had no powerful, secret enemies, into the solitary confinement cells of prison for my old age:

First instance of wisdom and benefit: At this time the *Risale-i Nur* students can gather only in the School of Joseph without harm. Their coming together outside would have both been expensive and caused suspicion. In such a situation it might even have happened that some of those who came to visit me would have spent forty or fifty *liras* but would have had to return after only seeing me for twenty minutes or not seeing me at all. Therefore, I would have willingly chosen the hardship of prison in order to be closer to some of my brothers. This means that prison is a favor and mercy for us.

Second instance of wisdom and benefit: The service to belief at this time through the *Risale-i Nur* is possible through publicizing it everywhere and drawing the attention of those who are in need of it. Thus, our imprisonment draws attention to the *Risale-i Nur* and contributes to its being known. Those who are most stubborn and in most need can find it and preserve their belief; their stubbornness is defeated and they are saved from the danger of going to the other world without belief, and thus the *Risale-i Nur*'s circle of study is widened.

Third instance of wisdom and benefit: The *Risale-i Nur* students who are imprisoned learn from one another's conduct, character, sincerity, and self-sacrifice, and they no longer seek worldly benefits in their service through the *Risale-i Nur*. Indeed, since in the School of Joseph they have observed with their own eyes ten or even a hundred spiritual benefits and good results for every hardship and trouble they suffer, through the good results and extensive sincere service to belief, they are able to attain pure sincerity, no longer lowering themselves by seeking lesser, personal benefits.

There is, however, a sorrowful but agreeable point concerning these places of ordeal that concerns me alone. It is as follows:

I have observed the same situation here that I saw in the old *medreses* in my hometown during my youth. For traditionally in the Eastern Provinces, a portion of the needs of the *medrese* students were met from outside the *medrese*. In some *medreses*, their meals were prepared in the *medrese* itself. And there are several other ways in which the *medreses* resembled this place of ordeal. As I watch the prison with a feeling of pleasurable regret and longing, I travel in my imagination to those former sweet times of youth, and forget the difficulties of old age.

The Twenty-Seventh Gleam

The Twenty-Seventh Gleam consists of the speeches from the Eskişehir trials. Since they have been published in *Tarihçe-i Hayat* ("The Life History of Said Nursi"), they have not been included here.

The
Twenty-Eighth Gleam

The Twenty-Eighth Gleam

The place of flies in the ecological system and balance • Some aspects of the element of air • A Discussion on Divine Speech • Why the Qur'an says that iron and cattle have been sent down from above • There is an immediate reward in good deeds, and an immediate punishment in bad ones • The intended meaning hidden under the apparent meaning • The times of sleep • On calling God's blessings and peace upon the Prophet Muhammad • An explanation of the Transcendental Unity of Being or Existence • What should we do on religious festive days • On the carnal, evil-commanding soul and some of its temptations • How everlasting punishment for unbelief during a short life can be justice • On spying jinn and evil spirits and their repulsion from the heavens

This comprises some of the shorter consoling pieces I wrote for my brothers who were (in the cell) opposite me in the Eskişehir prison, at a time when I was forbidden to mix or speak with them.

In the Name of God, the All-Merciful, the All-Compassionate

A pleasing conversation with Süleyman Rüşdü, known for his loyalty and distinguished by his purity of heart.

It was almost the time when flies are discharged from their duties in autumn. Because of the insignificant annoyance they give, some selfish humans applied insecticides to our prison cell to kill them. This aroused acute pity in me. However, the flies, in resistance to those humans, multiplied even more. There was a clothes-line in our cell. In the evening those tiny birds would be lined up in an orderly fashion on the line. One day Süleyman Rüşdü rose to hang up the washing, and I said to him, "Don't bother those tiny birds; hang it up somewhere else." He replied in complete seriousness, "We need the line; let the flies find somewhere else for themselves."

Anyway, in the early morning a discussion started in connection with this small incident about small creatures like flies and ants, which exist in great numbers. I said the following to him:

The species which exist and multiply in great numbers have important duties and great value. Like an important book whose copies are multiplied, because of their significant duties, the All-Wise Creator greatly multiplies these tiny missives of Divine Destiny, these words of Divine Power. The Wise Qur'an announces:

> *O humankind! A parable is struck, so pay heed to it: Those whom, apart from God, you deify and invoke will never be able to create even a fly, even if all of them were to come together to do so. And if a fly snatches away anything from them, they cannot recover that from it. Powerless indeed is the seeker, and (so is) the sought!* (22: 73)

That is to say, the creation of flies is such a miracle of the Lord's creativity that if all things and beings to which creativity is attributed were to come together, they would be unable to create even a fly. They would not be able to imitate that miracle of the Lord.

When, in the face of the annoyance they cause, the Prophet Moses, upon him be peace, complained to God about these creatures, which form an important topic in the above verse, and which caused the death of Nimrod—saying, "O my Lord! Why do You so greatly multiply these irritating creatures?"—the following answer was inspired unto him:

> You have objected about the flies once, but the flies ask many times: "O our Lord! These humans with huge heads mention and praise You with only one tongue. And sometimes they neglect to do that. If you had created us out of only their head, there would have been creatures mentioning and praising You with thousands of tongues!"

So, the species of flies, having defended the wisdom of their creation against the Prophet Moses' complaint a thousand times more powerfully than the objection and demonstrating their love of cleanliness by continually cleaning their faces, eyes, and wings as though taking ablutions, must certainly have important duties. The modern scientific approach has a short-range view when perceiving the instances of wisdom in creation; it is unable to comprehend those duties completely.

Indeed, in order to preserve the sea from being polluted with the corpses of sea-creatures[131] that die every day in their millions, God Almighty has created species of carnivorous beings which function like public health officials. If these public health officials of the sea did not carry out their duties in a perfectly regular fashion, the sea would not sparkle like a mirror; it would rather display a sorrowful and distressing turbidity.

Also, in the same way that eagles and certain other carnivorous birds which, through a drive given to them by Divine Grace, are wonderfully able to perceive the location of a corpse from a distance of five or six hours, and go and remove it, God Almighty has created other wild animals which, functioning like public health officials, collect every day millions of dead animals and thus cleanse the surface of the earth, saving conscious beings from such distressing and sorrowful sights. If it were not for these health officials of the land who carry out perfectly orderly duties, the face of the earth would display a scene that would cause us all to weep.

God's laws of life have appointed the flesh of dead animals to be the licit food of carnivorous and scavenging animals. A *hadith* declares that "the rights of the hornless (weak and oppressed) animal will be restored from the horned on Resurrection Day," pointing out that the spirits of animals continue to live after their bodies perish, and there will be reward and punishment among them in a manner appropriate for them in the Eternal Realm.

Also, ants are charged as both cleansing and health operatives, collecting the corpses of miniature creatures and the small particles and fragments of their bounty, allowing these food particles and fragments to be preserved

---

131 One fish produces thousands of eggs and thousands of young; roe is comprised of about a million eggs. Therefore, in order for the balance in the sea to be maintained, there must be as many instances of death as there are births. It is another manifestation of Divine Compassion that since the mother fish cannot enter the places where its young hide and superintend them because of the great difference in size, the All-Wise and Compassionate One chooses one from among the young to be their supervisor, and employs that tiny creature in the duties of the mother.

from waste, or from being trodden underfoot, disdained, or rendered useless. In the same way flies are dutiful about cleaning away noxious substances or germs that cause disease. By sucking up and absorbing harmful germs, they destroy them, and they cause noxious or poisonous substances to change into other harmless forms, thus preventing the spread of many contagious diseases. A sign that they are both laborers for health and cleansing operatives and chemists, serving many instances of wisdom, is the fact that they exist in extremely great numbers. For the things that are valuable and beneficial are multiplied.[132]

O you egotistical human being! Apart from thousands of instances of wisdom in the life of flies, consider only the following small benefit that they provide for you and abandon your hostility towards them: In addition to keeping you company in your solitude and loneliness when in exile, they prevent you from falling into heedlessness or confusion of thought. You see how through their delicate manners and their washing of their faces and eyes, as though taking ablutions, they teach and remind you of human duties, such as cleanliness, performing the Prayers, and taking ablutions.

Moreover, in addition to giving you honey to eat, which is the sweetest and most pleasant of bounties, bees, which may be considered to be similar in many ways to flies, are mentioned in the Qur'an of miraculous exposition as being distinguished with Divine inspiration. So, as we must love them, hostility to flies or other similar animals that always come to the aid of humanity in friendliness and which suffer a multitude of hardships in their service, is wrong and unjust. We may combat harmful creatures only to prevent their causing us harm. For example, we can fight against wolves to protect our sheep from attack. Is it not possible that mosquitoes and fleas are natural healers, attacking when there is more blood than necessary for the body during hot weather, sucking out the old tired blood in the vessels which may well carry certain harmful substances? *All-Glorified is He at Whose art the mind is amazed*!

When I was once struggling with my carnal, evil-commanding soul, which was thinking the bounties which it saw in itself to be its own prop-

---

132 How beautiful and subtle are the following lines by the famous poet Yunus Emre, which indicate what wonderful works of Divine art the fly's wings and body are:

I loaded a single fly's wing onto forty ox carts;
Forty of them could not pull it; it remained spread out where it was placed.

erty, my soul became conceited, proud and boastful. I said to it, "This property is not yours; it is a trust." So then the soul abandoned its conceit and pride, but began to display laziness, saying, "Why should I care about something that is not mine? Let it perish!" Suddenly I saw that a fly had alighted on my hand and had begun to thoroughly clean its eyes, face, and wings, which were its trust from God. The fly was cleaning itself as a soldier cleans the rifle and uniform given to him by the state in trust. I said to my soul, "Look at that fly!" It looked and learned an important lesson. The fly became a teacher to my conceited and idle soul.

It is not far from Divine Wisdom that flies may be machines of transformation and purification for thousands of different harmful substances, germs, and noxious matters. Apart from bees, there are other species of flying insects[133] that eat various decaying substances and then provide syrup in place of the filth. Transforming these rotten, noxious substances into sweet and healing syrup like quails raining onto the leaves of trees (the Qur'an, 2:57; *Genesis*, 16:4–31), these insects demonstrate that they are machines that can transform one substance into another. They demonstrate what a mighty nation these tiny individuals belong to. Through the tongues of their disposition they say, "Do not consider our smallness, consider instead the vastness of our species, and pronounce, 'All-Glorified is He!'"

* * *

[133] There is one species of flying insect which is created in spring in the form of a black mass stuck on the branches of almond and wild apricot trees, and remains there. They continuously produce something like honey and other species of flies gather round them and suck it up.

Yet another species is employed in the pollination of the flowers of some plants and trees, like the fig. Just as the firefly, which flashes and sparkles, is worthy of watching, there are also other species that glisten like gold, deserving attention. We must not forget flies that are armed with lances, and wild bees, which are like brigands among them. If the All-Merciful Creator did not control them but rather allowed them to attack human beings, like fleas, just as those armed species killed Nimrod, these insects would cause serious harm to the human race. They would exhibit one of the implicit meanings of the Qur'anic declaration, *And if a fly snatches away anything from them, they cannot recover that from it* (22: 73). Thus, the fact that this kind of creation has almost a hundred known species is of great importance, and the following mighty verse, which contains the above-mentioned declaration, takes them as its subject:

> *O humankind! A parable is struck, so pay heed to it: Those whom, apart from God, you deify and invoke will never be able to create even a fly, even if all of them were to come together to do so. And if a fly snatches away anything from them, they cannot recover that from it. Powerless indeed is the seeker, and (so is) the sought!*

In the Name of God, the All-Merciful, the All-Compassionate.

When He wills a thing to be, His command is but say to it "Be!" and it is (36: 83).

This verse indicates that creation occurs with a command. The treasuries of Divine Power are in the *Kaf* and *Nūn*, (the letters which constitute the command, *Kun!* ("Be!"). A few of the numerous aspects of this subtle reality have been mentioned in various places of the *Risale-i Nur*. Here, in order to make more understandable the *hadiths* about the qualities, virtues, and material effects of the letters of the Qur'an, particularly the "disjointed" or "isolated" letters that are found at the start of some *suras* to the materialist view of this century, we will make this point with a material example.

The All-Majestic One, the Owner of the Supreme Throne, has four Thrones through which He directs the creatures on the earth, the center of the universe and its heart and *qibla*:

The first Throne is the Throne of Preservation and Life, which is earth. This is the manifestation of the Divine Names, the All-Preserving and the Giver of Life.

The second Throne is the Throne of Bounty and Mercy, which is the element of water.

The third is the Throne of Knowledge and Wisdom, which is the element of light.

The fourth is the Throne of Command and Will, which is the element of air.

We see with our own eyes that minerals and innumerable and various plants are formed from simple earth; with these the innumerable needs of animals and human beings are met. This means that a single simple element like earth is the means of the formation of almost infinitely multiple things and an infinite variety of species in perfect order; innumerable and perfectly orderly embroideries are inscribed on a single, plain page. Also, innumerable miracles of the Divine Art are manifested through water, and particularly through animal sperm, which is a simple fluid like water; this shows that like these two Thrones, despite their simple nature, light and air are also the means of the manifestation of the amazing miracles of the Pen of Divine Knowledge, the Command and Will of the Eternal Inscriber, the All-Knowing One of Majesty.

Putting to one side the element of light for now, we will try to remove, to some extent, the veil over the wonders of Command and Will in the element of the air, which is the Throne of the Divine Command and Will for the earth.

We sow letters and words with the air in our mouths, and they sprout and send forth shoots all at once. That is to say, in an instant, in no time at all, a word becomes a seed sown and sprouting in the air. It produces innumerable copies in the surrounding air. We consider the element of air and we see that it is so obedient and subjugated to the command of "*Be!" and it is* that it is as if it is a soldier in a well-organized army, with each of its particles being always prepared to carry out the orders that come from the Commander, and thus demonstrating its complete submission to the commands that issue from the command of "*Be!*"

For example, the fact that no matter where it is left in the air, human speech can be heard everywhere on the earth at the same moment by means of radio transmitters or receivers demonstrates how perfectly each particle of air obeys the command of "*Be!*" *and it is*. So, as a result of this perfect obedience, the letters of a sacred text or speech, which have an unstable existence in the air, may manifest many physical effects and material qualities. It seems that they have qualities which can be said to transform spirituality to materiality and invisibility to visibility.

Innumerable signs like these show that letters have existence in the air, especially the sacred and Qur'anic letters, and in particular the isolated letters at the beginning of some *suras*, which are certain Divine ciphers, and are infinitely sensitive. It is as if they are listening to the instantaneous commands and acting accordingly; because of their sacredness and because they are the decrees of the Divine Will, and due to the perfect obedience of the particles of air to the command of "*Be!*" *and it is*, these letters will surely manifest material qualities and transitory, wonderful effects.

It is due to this mystery that the expressions of the Qur'an of miraculous exposition which contain the decrees of the Divine Will and Power, Which create instantly and completely subjugate and command things, function like the Power and Command itself. That is to say, the letters that issue from the creative Command govern the existence of beings like a physical force; that creative Command manifests itself as the Power and Will Itself.

Indeed, these extremely subtle and physical "embodiments" of Will and Command in the element of air appear to have effects as if they were the Power Itself that exists in beings with a semi-material or a semi-immaterial existence. And in order to draw attention to those beings that have some sort of existence lying between the material and the spiritual, the Qur'an of miraculous exposition declares, *When He wills a thing to be, His command is but say to it "Be!" and it is* (36:83).

It is thus perfectly reasonable that the sacred isolated letters—those Divine ciphers—such as *Ha Mim*. *Ta Sin*, and *Alif Lam Mim*, which exist at the start of some *suras*, function as switches that cause the wires of the hidden, subtle relations to vibrate among the particles of air and therefore enable sacred "wireless" communications to exist between the earth and the Divine Throne.

In addition to the duties of each and every particle of air in connection with wireless and telecommunication duties or the reception and conduction of subtle forces such as electricity, I have observed a further particular duty they perform in the blossom of almond trees. The blossoming of almond trees has convinced me that trees, like a well-ordered army on the face of the earth, receive and obey the command of "*Be!*" through the particles of air, which function as transmitters through the breeze that wafts through the trees. This means that the air is a servant of the All-Merciful, All-Compassionate One, and this servant is always prepared to carry out His commands and serve His guests on the earth; in addition, all its particles deliver the sacred commands of that All-Merciful One to plants and animals. Not only does it cool creatures off by fanning them and by being the means of their respiration, it serves for the purification of their blood and the kindling of their bodily heat, the fire of life; moreover, the element of air is the means for the formation of words in mouths, and carries out many other important duties like those discussed in obedience to the command of *"Be!" and it is*.

It is because of this quality that when existing in air, the letters which acquire sacredness, that is, the letters of the Qur'an, particularly those isolated at the beginning of some *suras*, function as the receivers and conductors of Divine Commands, or even as the Commands themselves, and become like the sensitive switches of hidden relations between the Divine Throne and the earth. Just as their existence in the air has this quality, their existence in the mind or even in the written form may acquire a similar quality and carry out similar functions. That is to say, medication, healing cures or some other goals may be achieved through the reading or writing of those letters.

Said Nursi

* * *

In the Name of God, the All-Merciful, the All-Compassionate.

> *Say: "If all the sea were ink to write my Lord's words (the acts, decrees, and manifestations of all His Names and Attributes), the sea would indeed be exhausted before my Lord's words would be exhausted, even if We were to bring the like of it in addition to it."* (18: 109)

This mighty verse is a vast, elevated, broad ocean. One would have to write a large volume in order to describe all of its jewels. Saving these precious jewels for another time, for now I will try to encapsulate with a few words the rays of a subtle point which appeared to me from afar a few days ago while making recitations after the daily Prayer.

THE FIRST WORD: Being a Divine Attribute, like Knowledge and Power, Divine Eternal Speech is also infinite. Certainly, if the seas were ink (to write with), they could never be enough for an infinite purpose.

THE SECOND WORD: The most apparent and most powerful thing that suggests someone's existence is their speech. Considering the fact that hearing someone's speech proves their existence as clearly as a thousand proofs, indeed, as clearly as seeing them, the verse quoted above alludes:

> If the seas were ink and the trees, pens, they would not be able to suffice to write down the Divine Speech, which demonstrates the All-Majestic Lord's Existence. Just as any speech bears witness to the existence of the one who spoke it at the degree of seeing him, so too the testimony of Divine Speech to the Unique, Besought-of-All is beyond measure.

THE THIRD WORD: Since the Qur'an of miraculous expression teaches the truths of belief to all levels of understanding, it contains apparently repetitive statements that are required by the wisdom of establishing and verifying a truth and convincing others of the same. So, this verse is also an allusive answer to the entirely unjustifiable attacks by Jewish scholars, who were the learned People of the Book at the time of the revelation of the Qur'an on the most illustrious Prophet, upon him be peace and blessings, concerning this, in the face of his being unlettered. The answer is as follows:

> The verse says: Many instances of wisdom, such as verification and persuasion, require the repetition of a truth that contains numerous benefits and results so that it may be established in the hearts of all people, and particularly in the hearts of those who are ordinary among them. Therefore, the repetition of the pillars of belief does not arise from a lack of words or intellectual deficiency or a lack of the required capital; every matter of belief has the value of a thousand other matters and contains thousands of truths, in different and miraculous ways. Indeed, if the seas were ink, if conscious beings were scribes, if plants were pens, and the particles were the pens' nibs for enumerating the words of eternal Divine Speech, which is the source of the Qur'an and which addresses the visible world on account of the world of the Unseen and which speaks to humans and the jinn, spirits, and the angels, resounding in the ears of every individual, an end would never be approached. For the former are finite, while Divine Speech is infinite.

THE FOURTH WORD: Clearly, the issuing of speech from something unexpected increases the importance of the speech, making it heeded. In particular, speech-like voices that emanate from large bodies like the atmosphere or the clouds make everyone listen to them. The songs from a gramophone the size of a mountain would attract the attention of even more ears. As for the heavenly voice of the Qur'an, which takes the heavens as gramophones, it is issued from Divine Speech in order to make the whole earth hear and listen to it. So, serving as the receivers or transmitters of its letters, the particles of air become like mirrors, tongues, needle points, or ears for the sacred Qur'anic letters. So, alluding to this fact and indicating how important, valuable, significant, and alive these letters are, the verse means:

> The Qur'an, which is the Divine Word, is so alive and valuable that if all the seas were ink, and the angels scribes, and atoms and sperms and plants and hairs pens, they could still never come to the end of the ears that hear and listen to it or to the end of the sacred words that enter those ears.

Indeed, they could never come to the end of them, because, considering how God Almighty multiplies the weak and lifeless speech of human beings millions of times in the air, certainly each word of the Speech of the peerless Sovereign of the heavens and the earth, which addresses all conscious beings in the earth and heavens, will comprise words to the numbers of the particles of air.

THE FIFTH WORD: This consists of two letters.

The first letter: Just as the Divine Attribute of Speech has words, the Power also has embodied words. Likewise, Divine Knowledge has wise words of Divine Destiny, which comprise all things and beings. Living beings and small creatures in particular are each words of the Lord which indicate the Eternal Speaker in a way more powerful than speeches. So this verse alludes to the fact that if the seas were ink, they would never come to the end of them.

The second letter: All the inspirations that come to angels and humans, and even to animals, are a sort of Divine Speech. The words of this Speech are certainly infinite. The verse suggests how numerous and indeed infinite are the Divine Command's inspirations and words which the innumerable hosts of the Absolute Sovereignty constantly receive.

True, exact knowledge of everything is with God alone. None knows the Unseen save God.

* * *

In the Name of God, the All-Merciful, the All-Compassionate.

And We have sent down iron, in which is stern might and benefits for humankind. (57: 25)

This is a brief reply to an important question about the above verse, with which a person of a certain standing who had knowledge of modern science was able to silence a number of *hojas*.

QUESTION: Iron is mined from the earth; it does not come down from above. So why is it said in this verse *We have sent down* rather than "We have extracted?" Is this not contrary to an apparent reality?

THE ANSWER: By saying *We have sent down*, the Qur'an of miraculous exposition draws attention to how great and important a bounty iron is. For it does not mention iron only for itself—if it did so, it would say "We have extracted"—rather, it emphasizes the tremendous Divine bounty in iron and how much humankind is in need of it. Any bounty does not come upwards from below, but rather is sent down from the treasury of Mercy.

The treasury of Mercy is certainly high in degree, so the bounty descends from "above" and humankind, which is needy of bounties, is below. Surely, the rank of giving bounty is superior to neediness, so the correct way to express the fact that bounty comes from the treasury of Mercy to the aid of humankind's need is *We have sent down*, not "We have extracted."

Also, extraction is a gradual process and is performed by humankind. Thus, the heedless view of humanity does not have the impression that iron is a bounty. It is true that when considered for its material existence, iron is extracted from the earth, but as a Divine bounty it has been sent down from above. The verse in question draws our attention to the fact that iron is a Divine bounty and therefore focuses on its immaterial value. A bounty that issues from the treasury of Mercy, which is a manifestation of the infinitely high rank of the All-Merciful, is certainly sent down from the highest rank to the lowest level. Thus, the correct expression to be used is *We have sent down*. With this expression, the verse reminds humankind that iron is one of the greatest bounties of God Almighty.

Indeed, the source of all the industries of humanity, of its material progress and the means of its power is iron. So, in order to emphasize the importance and greatness of iron as a bounty, drawing attention to God's bounties and bountifulness and in a perfectly majestic style, the Qur'an declares,

> *And We have sent down iron, in which is stern might and benefits for humankind.* (57: 25)

In the same way that the Qur'an declares about a very important miracle granted to the Prophet David, upon him be peace:

> *And We also made iron supple for him.* (34: 10)

That is, it declares that God softened iron as a great miracle and bounty for a great Prophet.

Secondly: "Above" and "below" are relative concepts. We say that something is above or below according to its position related to the earth's center. In fact, something which is below in relation to ourselves is above from the viewpoint of other continents. This means the position of substances that come from the earth's center to its surface changes according to the position of those who are on the surface.

With the tongue of miraculousness, the Qur'an of miraculous exposition says:

> Iron contains so many benefits and such extensive uses that it is not some ordinary substance to be extracted from the store of the earth, which is the home of humankind. Nor is it some natural substance to be used to meet any random need. Rather, in order for the important needs of the inhabitants of the earth to be met, iron has been sent down from the Creator's treasury of the Mercy of the universe and prepared in the vast workshop of the universe by the Creator Himself, as the Lord of the heavens and earth. Like rain, heat, and light, which descend from the skies, iron contains such extensive benefits that it is sent from the workshop of the universe, not from the narrow stores of the earth. Having been prepared in and sent from the great treasury of Mercy in the palace of the universe, and situated in the stores of the earth, it is extracted little by little over the centuries in proportion to need.

The Qur'an of mighty stature does not will that iron should be regarded as something ordinary which exists in this small store (the earth) to be consumed there; rather, in order to state that the All-Majestic Creator sent down that mighty bounty to meet many of humankind's needs from His supreme treasury together with the earth when He separated the earth from the sun, it uses the expression, *We have sent down*. One of the things most necessary for the house of the earth is iron, and many of humanity's needs are met with iron. The wise Qur'an also means in a miraculous fashion, "Use iron in your works and try to extract it and make use of it."

By saying, ... *iron, in which is stern might and benefits for humankind*, the verse describes two important uses of iron as a bounty. That is, it is used both for repelling enemies (in war) and attracting other benefits. Iron had been put to important uses for humanity before the revelation of the Qur'an, but with the phrase, *in which is stern might*, it offers a gleam of miraculousness, predicting that in the future iron will be used in an amazing fashion and display a crushing power throughout the world. Its present use for manufacturing weapons and traveling through the sea, air, and land prove this prediction of the Qur'an.

* * *

While discussing the subtle Qur'anic point above, the subject of the Prophet Solomon's hoopoe was introduced into the discussion. One of our brothers who persistently asks questions (but shows laziness in transcribing the Treatises, parts of the *Risale-i Nur*) asked, "Why is it that on an extreme occasion the hoopoe described God Almighty as One *Who brings to light what is hidden in the heavens and the earth* (27: 25), which is a relatively insignificant attribute among more significant Divine Attributes?"

THE ANSWER: One of the virtues of eloquence is that it suggests the craft that the speaker is most occupied with. Like the Bedouin diviners who through their insight amazingly discovered the places where water was to be found in the Arabian deserts, as a diviner among birds and other animals, Solomon's hoopoe was a blessed bird who served the Prophet Solomon as a diviner. It considered God Almighty from the viewpoint of its own craft, and stated that God has the exclusive right to be worshipped and prostrated before because He makes known the things hidden in the heavens and earth.

Indeed, the hoopoe understood the truth well, for the natural tendency of uncountable seeds and minerals under the earth cannot be to emerge upwards from below. Since bodies which have certain weight but no spirit, will, or consciousness are unable to go upwards by themselves, they can only go or fall downwards. It is particularly impossible for a body under the weight of the earth to shake the heavy load off its shoulders by itself and come out into the air. This means that such a small seed or mineral can come out only through an exceptional Power.

It is because the hoopoe discovered, through its divination, one of the most hidden and important proofs of God's being One Who is to be worshipped and prostrated before that the wise Qur'an added an instance of miraculousness to its statement concerning it.

* * *

In the Name of God, the All-Merciful, the All-Compassionate

He has sent down for you eight in pairs of cattle. He creates you in the wombs of your mothers, one act and phase of creation after another, in three veils of darkness (39: 6)

This verse contains the same truth we explained in connection with the verse, *And We have sent down iron*; it both corroborates it, and is corroborated by it.

By saying in *Surat az-Zumar*, *He has* sent down *for you eight in pairs of cattle*, not *He has* created *for you eight in pairs of cattle*, the Qur'an of miraculous expression states that God has sent down to us eight pairs of blessed cattle from His treasury of Mercy; it is as if He had sent them down from Paradise as bounties. Their wool or hair is used by nomads to make tents and clothes, their flesh for food, their milk as sustenance, their hides to make shoes and similar things, and their manure to fertilize the land and give warmth; it is as though those blessed animals are pure bounty and embodied mercy. It is because of this that, just as rain is called "mercy" (*rahma*), those blessed animals are called "bounties" (*an'am*). It is as if mercy embodied becomes rain, and bounty embodied takes on the form of goats, sheep, oxen and cows, water buffalo, or camels. Even though their physical bodies are created on the earth, since their being a bounty and mercy takes priority over their being physical creatures, the phrase *He has sent down* expresses that the All-Compassionate Creator has sent down these blessed animals to the earth directly from the exalted rank of His Mercifulness and His elevated, immaterial Paradise as gifts from His treasury of Mercy.

Indeed, like a fly, miniature in body but great in respect of the art of the Lord it contains, there may be things that are worth almost nothing in material but contain arts of high worth, and therefore have great value in respect of their art without taking into consideration their material worth. By contrast, there may be other things that are materially valuable but worth almost nothing in art, and therefore their value is restricted to their material being.

In just the same way, there are some material things whose aspect of being a bounty or mercy is a hundred times more important than their physical being. They are viewed from the perspective of their being a bounty without drawing any attention to their physical being. Thus, just as the tremendous benefits of iron and the numerous products it yields conceal its material aspect, so too is the physical being of these blessed animals, bounty from head to foot, transformed into a bounty. It is because of this that the immaterial aspects of their being cause their physical being to be ignored, and therefore the Qur'an uses for them the expression of *sending down*.

Together with this subtle reality, the use of *sending down* miraculously expresses an important meaning in respect of eloquence. It is as follows:

Iron is a strong mineral and is extracted from the depths of underground. But its area of usage is extremely broad and it has been equipped with the quality of being easily softened. Therefore, in addition to other instances of wisdom contained in iron, in order to express that iron is easily obtained and used everywhere by everyone, the phrase, *We have sent down* indicates that it is as if iron tools have been sent down from a workshop like "natural," heavenly bounties to be delivered into the hands of humans. Also, although being much greater in size than many species of animals, from the mosquito to snakes, and scorpions, wolves, and lions that are harmful to humans, large beasts like water buffalo, oxen, and camels, which are among the most important animals, are extremely docile and submissive. They are so submissive that they may be led by even a child. In order to express the meaning of their submissiveness, the sentence, *He has sent down for you eight in pairs of cattle* states that it is as if these blessed beasts were not among worldly animals, as they are neither wild nor dangerous. It is as if they were animals that belonged to an immaterial Paradise; they are beneficial and gentle; they have been sent down from above, that is, from the treasury of Mercy. It may be because of this that some Qur'anic commentators say that these animals have been sent from Paradise.[134]

It should not be thought that we are writing too much by writing one page to explain even a single letter of the wise Qur'an, for it is God's Word. It is therefore not wasteful to write two or three pages about the expression, *We have*, or *He has*, *sent down*. Sometimes one letter of the Qur'an is the key to a treasury.

* * *

[134] By saying, "the origin of these beasts is the heavens," some Qur'anic commentators also imply the following: These animals, called "*an'am*," subsist through sustenance, and their sustenance is fodder, the existence of which depends on rain. Rain is the water of life and mercy; therefore, sustenance also comes from the heavens. The verse, *And in the heavens there is your sustenance* (51: 22), indicates this. Since the continuously renewed existence of these beasts is possible through rain, which comes from the skies, the phrase *He has sent down*, which expresses the meaning of having been sent down from the sky, is apt.

A very valuable, significant point

Out of His perfect munificence, compassion, and justice, God Almighty has included in good deeds an immediate reward and in bad ones an immediate punishment. He has included in good deeds spiritual pleasures that recall the rewards of the Hereafter, and in bad ones, spiritual recompenses that recall the torments of Hell.

For example, love between believers is a good deed for the people of faith. Included in this good deed is spiritual pleasure, contentment, and exhilaration which recall the physical rewards of the Hereafter. Anyone who turns to their heart will feel this pleasure. While on the other hand, enmity and hostility between believers are evil, causing noble spirits to feel torment of the conscience that is great enough to suffocate the heart and spirit. I myself have, perhaps more than a hundred times, experienced that when I feel enmity towards a believing brother, I have suffered such torment that it has left me in no doubt that this was an immediate punishment for my evil deed.

Another example: Being respectful towards those who are worthy of respect, and compassionate to those who are worthy of compassion, and serving them are good deeds. There is such great pleasure and contentment in these good deeds that the rewards of the Hereafter are felt, leading one to show respect and compassion to the extent that they make one ready to sacrifice one's very life. The pleasure and reward a mother receives from the compassion she feels for her child are such that they may cause her to sacrifice her life. The hen which attacks a lion in order to save her chick is an example of this truth in the animal kingdom. This means that there is an immediate reward in compassion and respect. Noble people of magnanimity and endeavor feel this, and thus they have a heroic character and attitude.

And for example, in greed and wastefulness there is a punishment—continuous complaints, dissatisfaction, worry, and heartache cause greedy, wasteful people to lose their senses. And in envy there is an immediate punishment that scorches the one who feels it. While in contentment and trust in God we find an immediate, pleasurable reward which removes all the tribulations and pains of poverty and neediness.

As another example, pride and conceit are such heavy burdens that a proud person demands respect from everyone. Since they are despised because of this desire, they suffer constant torment. Respect is given; it is not to be sought.

Another example: The pleasurable reward in humility and the abandonment of egotism save one from the heavy, despicable burden of trying to make oneself liked.

And for example, there is an immediate punishment in thinking ill of or misinterpreting people's words and actions. According to the rule, "Whoever strikes is struck," those who think ill of others are also thought ill of. The actions of those who misinterpret the actions of their believing brothers and sisters are also misinterpreted, and thus they suffer the punishment for this misinterpretation.

And the list goes on; all good and bad deeds and good and bad morals should be considered according to this standard. I hope and expect from Divine Mercy that those who experience or taste the Qur'anic miraculousness in spirituality and morality that is manifested at this time through the *Risale-i Nur* also experience these spiritual pleasures, and I hope that they will not suffer from bad morals, God willing.

Another important point

In the Name of God, the All-Merciful, the All-Compassionate.

> *I have not created the jinn and humankind but to (know and) worship Me (exclusively). I demand of them no provision, nor do I demand that they should feed Me. Surely God—it is He Who is the All-Providing, Lord of all might, and the All-Forceful.* (51: 56–58)

I will briefly explain three aspects of the extremely beautiful and sublime meanings of the above verses.

The first aspect

In order to honor and ennoble His Messenger, God Almighty sometimes attributes to Himself certain states that could pertain to the Messenger. While saying in the verses above, "I have created you to worship Me; not to demand provision from you," God actually means, "My Messenger does not demand a wage or reward from you, or to be fed by you, in return for his duty of Messengership and his service of conveying to you the duties of worship."

The second aspect

In order that humanity, so excessively preoccupied with its provision, should not think that working to obtain provision prevents one from the duties of worship, nor use obtaining provision as a pretext for neglecting worship, the verse declares, "You have been created for worship. The main aim of your creation is not to work to obtain provision for yourself, or your family, or animals. That is to say, you have not been created to procure the provision which I have undertaken to provide for you. I am the All-Providing, and provide for you and your dependents, My servants, with whatever is essential to life. Therefore, although working to obtain your provision, which I have created and have undertaken to convey to you, is a form of worship, do not make it an excuse to neglect the essential duties of worship!"

It is an established rule of eloquence that if the apparent meaning of a word is clear and self-evident, what is intended by that word is not that meaning but the meaning necessitated by it or dependent on it. For example, if you say to someone who is known by everybody to have memorized the Qur'an, "You are a *hafiz*," you are stating what is already known. So, the intended meaning is this: "I know that you are a *hafiz*." You are informing them of something they do not know.

Thus, based on this rule, the meaning of the verse which states that God is not One to be fed is this: "You have not been created to provide for yourselves or My other creatures, whose provision I have undertaken. Your essential duty is worship. Striving to procure your provision in accordance with My commands is also a form of worship, but there is the condition that it should not prevent you from the essential duties of worship."

The third aspect

As the apparent meaning of, *He begets not, nor is He begotten* (112: 3) in *Surat al-Ikhlas* is obvious and self-evident, the intended meaning is this: "Those having parents and children cannot be gods." So, in order to declare that neither the Prophet Jesus or the Prophet Uzayr (Ezra), upon them be peace, nor the angels, nor the celestial bodies, nor any other objects deified by any people can be gods, the verse emphasizes God Almighty's being absolutely free from any limits of time and space or other attributes particular to the creation. Likewise, by saying that the All-Providing of Majesty,

Who is your sole object of worship, does not want provision from you, nor have you been created to feed Him, the verse under discussion means, "Those in need of provision or provided with food cannot be deities and are not worthy of worship."

Said Nursi

* * *

In the Name of God, the All-Merciful, the All-Compassionate

... *or when they were taking their ease in the noontime* (7: 4).

This was written in answer to the question of Rafet Bey concerning ... *or when they were taking their ease in the noontime*, and to prevent his diamond-like pen from idleness due to lethargy that arises from his sleeping after the early morning Prayer in the prison, like other prisoners who are not *Risale-i Nur* students.

Sleep, in the sense of napping, is of three sorts:

THE FIRST is *Ghaylula*, which is the sleep from dawn, the early time of the early morning Prayer to the end of the time during which Prayer is prohibited (approximately forty-five minutes after sunrise). According to a *hadith* this form of sleep causes a decrease and unproductiveness in provision, and is contrary to the practices of the Prophet, upon him be peace and blessings. The time most appropriate for preparing to work for one's sustenance is when it is cool, the early hours of the day.[135] When this time has passed, lethargy descends. It has been established through numerous experiences that not only is lethargy unfavorable for daily work and gaining one's livelihood but it also causes unproductiveness.

THE SECOND sort of sleep is *Faylula*. This is from the afternoon Prayer to sunset. It causes a reduction in life. That is, it shortens the day and causes it to pass in a state of semi-sleep. Also, since most of the material and immaterial results of the day are obtained after the afternoon Prayer, spending that time in sleep prevents one from obtaining these results, and makes it as if the day has not been lived.

---

135 *at-Tirmidhi*, "Buyu'" 6; *Abu Dawud*, "Jihad" 78. (Tr.)

THE THIRD is *Qaylula*. This is around noon and commendable according to the practice of the Prophet,[136] upon him be peace and blessings, since it is helpful in rising at night to pray. It is further strengthened as a commendable practice by the fact that in the Arabian Peninsula this "siesta" allows a temporary rest from work at noon, when it is hottest. This sleep is a cause of increase in both life and provision, for half an hour's *qaylula* equals two hours' sleep at night. This means that it adds one and a half hours to a person's life every day. It rescues one and a half hours from the grip of sleep, the brother of death, and adds it to the time of working for one's livelihood.

Said Nursi

* * *

"This is good as well"

While reciting, "Thousands upon thousands of blessings, and peace thousands upon thousands of times be upon you, O Messenger of God!" among the recitations after the early morning Prayer, a subtle meaning occurred to me from afar. Unable to grasp all of it, I will only relate one or two sentences by way of alluding to it.

I saw that nighttime is like a newly opened mansion of the world. I entered that mansion during the late evening or early night (*'isha*) Prayer. Due to the extraordinary expansion of the imagination and the innate connection of the human to the whole of creation, I saw the huge world as nothing more than a mansion. Human beings and other living creatures became so tiny that they were invisible. With the imagination I only observed the collective personality of Muhammad, upon him be peace and blessings, which cheered, made lovable, and illuminated that mansion. In the same way that a person greets those present when he enters a house,[137] I

---

136 *al-Bukhari*, "Isti'dhan" 16, 39; *Muslim*, "Fada'il" 84. (Tr.)

137 The mercy reaching the person of Ahmad (Muhammad), upon him be peace and blessings, essentially relates to the needs of his whole Community through all eternity. For this reason, endless greetings are in place. Consider this: if someone enters a vast house that is like the world, desolate, empty, and dark through heedlessness, how frightened, dismayed, and agitated he will be. Then suddenly the house is lit up and a familiar, friendly, lovable, beloved, and noble Lieutenant appears. If he describes and makes known the house's Compassionate and Generous Owner through all its fittings and furnishings, you can un-

was overwhelmed with the desire to say, "Peace, thousands upon thousands of times be upon you, O Messenger of God!" It was as though I was greeting him as many times as there were humans and jinn in the world. That is to say, I offered greetings. I uttered: I have renewed my allegiance to you, I have accepted your mission, I submit to the laws and commands you brought, and I state through these greetings that they will be safe from our assaults. By making all the members, that is, all the conscious beings of my world—all the jinn and humans—speak, I offered peace in the name of each, intending all the meanings mentioned above.

Since just as the Prophet Muhammad, upon him be peace and blessings, illuminates my world through the light and gifts he brought, he also illuminates and fills the worlds of everyone with bounties, I exclaimed in grateful response, "Thousands upon thousands of blessings be upon you, O Messenger of God!" I meant, "We are unable to respond to this goodness of yours, so we display our gratitude to you by entreating that mercy reach you from our Creator's treasury of Mercy, to the number of the inhabitants of the heavens."

In respect of his worship and servanthood and on account of his turning from the creation to the Creator, the person of Ahmad (Muhammad), upon him be peace and blessings, requires blessings, which have the meaning of mercy, while in respect of his Messengership—being a messenger from the Creator to creation—he requires peace. Just as he deserves as much peace as there are jinn and human beings, and we offer a general renewal of our allegiance to that same degree, he also deserves as many blessings from the treasury of Mercy as there are inhabitants in the heavens and in the name of each. For with the light he has brought, the perfection of all things has become apparent, the value of all existent things and beings has been made manifest, the duty of every creature assigned to it by the Lord can be observed, and the Divine purpose for the existence of every creature has come to be known. Therefore, since everything is certain to utter, "Peace and blessings be upon you, O Messenger of God!" pronouncing this in the tongue of its disposition, we say in the name of all, "Thousands upon thousands of blessings, and peace, thousands upon thousands of times

---

derstand what joy, familiarity, happiness, light, and exhilaration it would give. You can appreciate the value and pleasure of the greetings for the Messenger, upon him be peace and blessings, from this.

be upon you, O Messenger of God, and to the number of jinn and humans, and of angels and stars!"

> It is enough for you that God Himself grants His Messenger blessings, and His angels also send him blessings and peace.

Said Nursi

* * *

About the doctrine of the Transcendental Unity of Being (Wahdat al-Wujud)

My Dear Brother!

You want an explanation of the Transcendental Unity of Being. You can find sufficient and convincing explanations about this doctrine of Muhyid-Din ibn al-'Arabi[138] in some parts of the *Risale-i Nur*. For now we just say the following:

Teaching the doctrine of the Unity of Being to people at the present time could cause serious harm. Like metaphors and similes being considered to be literally true when they pass from the hands of the learned to those of the uneducated ignorant people,[139] when profound matters like the Unity of Being are included among the discussions of the heedless common people, who view everything from the perspective of causality, they confuse this with naturalism, and the following three significant instances of harm appear:

The first instance: While the doctrine of the Unity of Being is based on simply denying the universe on account of God Almighty, when it is adopted by the heedless common people and, in particular, when it enters minds tainted by materialistic thoughts, it becomes a form of denying God on account of the universe and materiality.

The second instance: The way of the Unity of Being rejects the Lordship of anything other than God so intensely and powerfully that it denies every-

138 Muhyid-Din ibn al-'Arabi (1165–1240): One of the greatest and most famous Sufi masters. His doctrine of the Transcendental Unity of Being, which most have mistaken for monism and pantheism, made him the target of unending polemics. He wrote many books, the most famous of which are *Fusus al-Hikam* and *al-Futuhat al-Makkiyyah*. (Tr.)

139 Consider how the two angels, called the Ox and the Fish, on which a *hadith* tells us the earth stands, came to be supposed by the common people to be a huge ox and an enormous fish. For an explanation of this *hadith*, see the First Station of the Fifteenth Gleam.

thing but God, removing duality. It essentially denies recognizing the independent existence of anything, let alone that of the carnal, evil-commanding soul. However, the predominance of the idea of attributing creativity to nature at present, and the inflation of the carnal, evil-commanding souls with pride and egotism, and oblivion, to a degree, of the Hereafter and the Creator have led some to fall under the control of their evil-commanding souls and to assume Pharaoh-like positions, taking their own selves as the object of worship. So, suggesting the doctrine of the Unity of Being to such people can inflate the evil-commanding soul to such an extent that—may God preserve us from such a thing—it can no longer be contained.

The third instance: The All-Majestic One is absolutely free and exempt from and exalted above all change, alteration, division, and being comprehended in time or place. The doctrine of the Unity of Being gives rise to concepts which are not appropriate for His necessary Existence, Divinity, and the fact that He is free from all defect, and thus leads to false suggestions and associations.

One who speaks of the Unity of Being must have such great profundity in mind and spirit that they can mentally rise from the ground to go beyond the heavens, leaving the universe behind and fix their gaze on the sublime Supreme Throne of God, and being so absorbed in the Existence of God Almighty that they are unable to see the physical universe, and with strength of belief they perceive everything as being annihilated in the Single One of Uniqueness. Otherwise, if they stand on the earth, looking at the universe from the ground, viewing everything and every event from the perspective of cause and effect, it is possible that they will fall into the swamp of naturalism and become immersed in causality. One who rises in their mind as high as the Supreme Throne can say, like Jalalud-Din ar-Rumi,[140] "Listen! You can hear the words you hear being uttered by everyone as if they are coming from God Almighty (through "natural" gramophones)." But if you say to one who cannot rise as high as Jalalud-Din, or who cannot see that all the beings from the ground to the Supreme Throne are in the form of a mirror, "Lend an ear! You will hear the Divine speech

140 Jalalud-Din ar-Rumi, Mawlana (Mevlana) (1207–1273): One of the most renowned figures of Islamic Sufism. He was the founder of the Mawlawi (Mevlevi) Order of the whirling dervishes, and famous for his *Mathnawi*, an epic of religious life in six volumes. For Western readers, ar-Rumi is a powerful voice among the poets of Sufism. (Tr.)

from everything," they will become so entangled in false conceptions that it will be as if they are falling from the Supreme Throne to the ground.

> *Say: "God," and then leave them to their game of plunging into vanities* (6: 91).

> How can it be possible for one stuck in earth to ascend and know the Lord of the Worlds?

> All-Glorified is the One Who, in respect of His Essence, is absolutely pure of and free from having anything similar to Him, and in respect of His Attributes is exalted above any resemblance, and to Whose Lordship all His signs bear witness, all-exalted is His Majesty, and there is no deity but He.

The answer to a question

I have no time to evaluate or compare the ideas of Mustafa Sabri[141] and those of Musa Bekuf.[142] I will only say that both went to extremes in opposite directions. Although in the matter he defended Mustafa Sabri was more correct than Musa Bekuf, it is not right to disparage someone like Muhyid-Din ibn al-'Arabi, who was a miracle of the Islamic sciences.

Indeed, Muhyid-Din was rightly-guided and acceptable, but it is not possible that he can be a true guide or a good teacher in all his works. Since he frequently did not observe the balance in teaching the truths, at times he opposed the rules of the Ahl al-Sunna, and some of his words appear to be misguided, although he himself is free of misguidance. Sometimes, a word may appear to be unbelief, but the one who spoke it is not an unbeliever. Mustafa Sabri did not take these points into consideration; he went to extremes concerning certain points due to his excessive devotion to the rules of Ahl al-Sunna.

As for Musa Bekuf, because of his ideas excessively in favor of innovations (*bid'ah*), and the concessions he made to modernity, he was very much in error. He corrupts some of the truths of Islam with his false interpreta-

141 Mustafa Sabri Effendi (1869–1954). He was a religious scholar and Shaykhul-Islam in the last years of the Ottoman State. Having left Turkey in 1922, he remained in exile in Egypt until his death. (Tr.)

142 Musa Jarullah Bigiyef (Bekuf). He was a native of Turkistan and a "reformist" Muslim scholar. He was sent into exile by the Russians in 1904. He wrote many works.

tions. Since he held Abu'l-'Ala al-Ma'arri,[143] who had been rejected (by verifying Muslim scholars) above authoritative scholars of verification, and favored disproportionately the ideas of Muhyid-Din that opposed the Ahl al-Sunna because they suited his own, he went to great extremes.

Muhyid-Din said, "Those who are not one of us (those do not know our station) should not read our books." What he meant is that these books may be harmful for such people. Indeed, at this time it is harmful to read Muhyid-Din's books, especially his concepts concerning the Unity of Being.

Said Nursi

* * *

In the Name of God, the All-Merciful, the All-Compassionate.

While watching from my prison window through the lens of the consideration of the future and our end in the world, the cheers of human beings, which in fact should be wept for, during a glittering night of celebration, a scene was unfolded before my imagination. In the same way that those who are lying dead in the cemetery are shown to be alive on the movie screen, it was as if I had seen the moving corpses of those who would be the residents of the cemetery in the near future. I wept for those merry-makers. All of a sudden a feeling of isolation and pity came over me. I turned to my intellect and asked of the truth, "What about this imagining?" The truth replied, saying:

> In fifty years time, out of a hundred of those who are merry-making now in great joy fifty-five will be old, about seventy years of age, with backs bent, while the remaining forty-five will have rotted in the cemetery. Those beautiful countenances and that joyful laughter will have changed into their opposites. Since according to the rule that "everything that is coming is close," it is a reality of a certain degree that we can see the things that are bound to happen in the near future as having already happened; thus surely what you see is not imagination.

---

143 Abu'l-'Ala al-Ma'arri (973–1057): A Syrian Arab writer of poems, commentaries, elegies, and religious tracts. He was born and lived most of his life in Ma'arra, in Syria. He was blind from childhood. Following his mother's death, he lived in a cave and adopted ascetic habits. (Tr.)

Since the heedless laughter of this world is therefore a veil over bitter facts, which in fact should be wept for, and is temporary and subject to decline, then most certainly it is only the kind of the enjoyment which is religiously permissible, thankful, and innocent and which leads to awareness of God's omnipresence and dispels heedlessness, and the pleasures which are eternalized via the reward they bring—it is only this kind of enjoyment and pleasures that will make happy humans' eternity-adoring hearts and their spirits infatuated with permanence. For this reason, there are Prophetic reports that strongly encourage giving thanks to God and remembrance of Him on religious festive days so that heedlessness should not prevail or lead to religiously forbidden acts. It is hoped that through thanksgiving and God's remembrance, the bounty of joy and happiness on these days may be transformed into thankfulness, which in turn may cause that bounty to continue and increase. Giving thanks increases bounty and dispels heedlessness.

Said Nursi

* * *

In the Name of God, the All-Merciful, the All-Compassionate.

This is about one of the meanings of the verse, *Assuredly the human carnal soul always commands evil* (12: 53), and the *hadith*, "The most harmful of your enemies is your carnal, evil-commanding soul in your breast."[144]

One who has an uneducated and unpurified carnal soul and who loves and appreciates themselves cannot love others. Even if they apparently love someone, they cannot do so sincerely. They love only the benefits and advantages that come to them from or through the other. Such people always try to make themselves liked, and do not ascribe faults to themselves; rather, they defend themselves like a lawyer and claim to be free of error. By praising and exalting themselves through exaggeration and even lying to justify themselves, they make themselves subject to the punishment of the verse, *Who has taken his lusts and fancies for his deity* (25: 43).

Such self-praise and trying to make oneself loved have the reverse effect, and cause a person to be despised and treated coldly. They also lose sincerity and purity of intention in their actions that pertain to the

144 ad-Daylami, *al-Musnad*, 3:408. (Tr.)

Hereafter and are tainted with hypocrisy. Led by emotions which are blind to the consequences and which do not consider the results, infatuated with the pleasures at hand and having lost their way in defeat to the carnal desires, such a person serves a year's prison sentence because of one hour's pleasure. They pay a punishment of ten years in return for one minute's gratification of pride or revenge. Like a foolish child who sells the last part of the Qur'an he is studying to buy a single sweet, in order to have his emotions flattered and to gratify their desires and appetites, such a person makes their diamond-like good deeds the means of their egotistical pleasures, like insignificant fragments of glass, and thus suffers a loss in profitable works.

> O God! Preserve us from the evil of the carnal, evil-commanding soul and of Satan, and from the evil of jinn and humans.

* * *

A Question

How can everlasting, tormenting confinement in Hell in return for unbelief for a short duration be justice?

THE ANSWER: In the world they punish a murder that takes only a minute with seven million, eight hundred and eighty-four thousand minutes of imprisonment. One minute's unbelief is the same as at least a thousand murders. So, according to the law of human justice, someone who lives a life of twenty years and then dies in unbelief deserves imprisonment for fifty-seven trillion, five hundred and three billion, two hundred million years. It can be understood from this how conformable with Divine justice is the verse, *(They will) abide therein forever* (4:169; 33:65).

The reason for the great gap between these two numbers—the duration of unbelief and that of its punishment—is this: offenses such as murder and unbelief are destruction and aggression against the rights of others. One minute's murder causes, on average, the loss of at least fifteen years of the victim's life, so the murderer suffers imprisonment in return for those years. As for unbelief, it means the denial of a thousand and one Divine Names with all their inscriptions, the violation of the rights of the universe and the rejection of its perfections, as well as the contradiction of innumerable evidences of Divine Oneness and the rejection of their testimony. So one minute of unbelief throws the unbeliever among the lowest of the low for more than a thousand years, and a whole life of it imprisons them everlastingly.

Said Nursi

* * *

In the Name of God, the All-Merciful, the All-Compassionate

They cannot hear anything from the High Assembly (of the angels), and (whenever they attempt to hear) become targets of missiles from all directions, repelled; and for them is a perpetual punishment—excepting one who snatches something by stealth, and is pursued (and destroyed) by a piercing shooting star. (37: 8–10)

And, indeed, We have adorned the lowest heaven (the heaven of the world) with lamps (stars), and made (out of) them missiles to drive away devils; and for them, We have prepared (in the Hereafter) the punishment of the Blaze. (67: 5)

In connection with criticisms made by some people of misguidance, an important point concerning verses like those above will be explained. It is as follows:

Before the advent of our Prophet, upon him be peace and blessings, spies from among the jinn and devils eavesdropped on the conversations of the inhabitants of the heavens and whispered them to soothsayers, mediums, and some spiritualists as news from the Unseen. In order to prevent such reports casting doubts about the truth of Divine Revelation, they were prevented from their attempts at spying by shooting stars fired on them when the Qur'an began to be revealed. What follows is a brief reply to a triple question concerning the above-mentioned verses, which are about this matter:

Question

As can be understood from the verses in question (before the advent of our Prophet, upon him be peace and blessings), spying devils used to gain access to the extremely distant lands of the heavens in order to hear about some minor and even personal events pertaining to the Unseen. However, it does not seem to be logical or reasonable that a minor event would have been talked about in all the corners of this extremely vast realm, and that any particular devil could have penetrated wherever it wished and heard about any event, even vaguely, thus to bring it to the earth.

Second, as indicated in the Qur'an (3: 37) and reported from the Prophet, upon him be peace and blessings, some from among the Messengers and saintly people would sometimes obtain the fruits of Paradise—Paradise being located above the heavens—as if plucking them from close by, and gazing on Paradise from near at hand. This suggests an infinite distance is contained in infinite nearness, which is unacceptable to the modern mind.

Thirdly, it does not seem to be in conformity with the wisdom in the perfectly wise administration of the universe that some minor state of an individual should be talked about by the High Assembly in the universal, vast land of the heavens. Nevertheless, all these three matters are considered to be among the truths of Islam.

The Answer: *Firstly:* The fact that the spying devils are repulsed from the heavens with shooting stars, which is expressed in the verse, *And, indeed, We have adorned the lowest heaven (the heaven of the world) with lamps (stars), and made (out of) them missiles to drive away devils* (67: 5), is convincingly explained in the Fifteenth Word (included in *The Words*) in seven steps.

Secondly: We will try to present the three truths questioned above and which are supposed to be far from reason through a comparison that will help those with narrow minds to understand.

Suppose that a country has its military office in the east, its ministry of justice in the west, its education ministry in the north, its religious affairs department in the south, and its civil service in the center. When these offices or departments are connected and communicating with one another by means of radio, telephone, and telegraph, and when they are carrying out their functions in the most regular and orderly fashion, the entire country will quite simply be the army office at the same time that it is the ministry of justice, and the department of religious affairs and civil service.

Just to cite another example, a country that is made up of federal states or colonies has authority over all its dependent parts through trade, colonial or federal relations. Each state is connected with the people of the country through these types of relationships. The affairs of these states, no matter how distant they are from one another, touch one another, and they intersect with each other in every house, even in every person in the country. The minor matters of the citizens can be concluded in a minor department due to this contact; they are not referred to the central government. However, since the laws and regulations are dependent upon the general constitution, it is as if those matters that are concluded in minor departments were actually settled by the central government.

So, as in these two comparisons, although the land of the heavens is extremely far from the earth, particularly in respect of its "center" and "capital," it has a network of communication able to reach the hearts of the people on the earth. Moreover, there are not only connections with the world of corporeal beings, but since the land of the heavens comprises the World of Spirits and the World of the Inner Dimension of Things, in one respect it encompasses the whole manifest world.

Furthermore, despite the almost infinite distance, Paradise, which is included in the Realm of Eternity, has immaterial connections with all realms of existence that lie beneath the veil of the manifest sphere. In the same way that the human senses are able to affect and control the entire body, despite their centers being in different locations in the head, through the Wisdom and Power of the All-Wise and All-Majestic Maker, the universe, this macro-human, comprises thousands of worlds, one within the other like concentric circles. The events that occur in them are considered and treated according to the universality or particularity and insignificance or importance of each. That is, minor or particular issues are concluded in minor departments, while the important, universal ones are settled in universal, vast centers or offices.

However, it sometimes occurs that a minor, particular incident resounds in all corners of the universe. And sometimes some comprehensive mobilization is carried out, not against the enemy's forces, but to make a show of pomp and majesty. For example, it was both due to the fact that the advent of the Prophet Muhammad, upon him be peace and blessings, and the revelation of the Qur'an were the most important, sacred events in the whole land of the heavens, and as a Divine indication to the matchless degree of the Qur'anic Revelation's majesty, magnificent sovereignty, and undoubted truth, that sentries were posted on the distant, towering bastions of the vast heavens, and shooting stars were fired in greater numbers than ever. This also signaled the repulsion of spying devils. The Qur'an of miraculous exposition interprets these cosmic proclamations and heavenly signs, making them heard and known.

Indeed, spying devils can surely be blown away by the breath of an angel. Therefore, mobilizing angels against them, an event that was staged and announced as a tremendous, heavenly sign, was surely to show the majesty of the sovereignty of the Qur'anic Revelation. Also, the magnificent announcement of the Qur'an and the vast heavenly mobilization was not to express that the jinn and devils have enough power to force the inhabitants of the heavens to fight and defend themselves, but rather to indicate that the jinn and devils cannot interfere anywhere on the long way from the Supreme Divine Throne and the world of the heavens to the heart of Muhammad, upon him be peace and blessings. Since the Qur'anic Revelation was a majestic truth that was talked about by all the angels in the heavens, in order to draw close to it a little the devils felt compelled to rise to the heavens; they hoped to be able to interfere with it to some degree, but they were instantly repulsed and killed with the "missiles" that were fired. This shows that the Revelation which came to the heart of Muhammad, upon him be peace and blessings, and Gabriel, who came to his presence, and the truths of the Unseen which were clearly manifested to his view were absolutely sound and free from all doubts. The Qur'an of miraculous exposition informs us of this reality in a miraculous fashion.

As for the fact that despite its great distance and despite its being one of the realms of eternity, some people of Prophethood or sainthood can see Paradise and sometimes pick some of its fruits, as may be understood from the two comparisons above, this transient, visible world is a veil to the World of the Unseen and the Eternal Realm. Although the supreme center of Paradise as the realm of eternity is extremely distant from us, it can be seen everywhere by means of the mirror of the World of Immaterial Representations or Ideal Forms. Also, by means of belief at the degree of absolute certainty and based on experience, Paradise may have, so to speak, some types of colonies or ministries in this transient world, and there may occur some sort of communication between it and some elevated spirits through the cable of the heart, and its gifts may reach them.

As for a universal sphere concerning itself with a particular personal matter, that is to say, the reality that is described in Qur'anic commentaries as devils rising to the heavens and eavesdropping in order to bring information of the Unseen to soothsayers, but then bringing only false, confused news, this must be as follows: what is meant is not that the devils go as far as the capital of the land of the heavens and receive particular news. Rather, the country of the heavens, which also encompasses the atmosphere, has certain places like posts—the metaphor should not be mistaken for the reality itself—which have connections with the earth. The devils eavesdrop on particular events at these particular stations. The human heart is even one of these stations where the angel of inspiration and Satan do battle.

As for the truths of belief and the Qur'an and the events connected with the Prophet Muhammad, upon him be peace and blessings, even those that are the most particular among them are discussed in every corner of the spheres of the Supreme Throne and the heavens as being among the greatest and most universal significant events. It is as if they were published in—the comparison should not be taken literally—the immaterial official newspapers that publicize the decisions made and the events concerning the universe. Also, since the devils are in no way able to interfere with the Revelation of the Qur'an from the heart of the Prophet Muhammad, upon him be peace and blessings, to the sphere of the Divine Supreme Throne, they can do nothing apart from listening to the heavens. So, it should be displayed and proclaimed most eloquently, indeed, miraculously, how elevated and great a truth is the Qur'anic Revelation and the Prophethood of Muhammad, upon him be peace and blessings, and it should be reiterated that it is impossible to find anything wrong in them or to draw close to them with ploys.

Said Nursi

All-Glorified are You. We have no knowledge save what You have taught us. Surely You are the All-Knowing, the All-Wise.

The Twenty-Ninth Gleam

The Twenty-Ninth Gleam

Reflections on God's infinite Greatness

In the Name of God, the All-Merciful, the All-Compassionate

To introduce

With many statements like *...that you may reflect* (2: 219, 266); *...that they may reflect* (7: 176; 16: 44; 59: 21); *Do they not reflect upon themselves (even once)? God has not created the heavens and the earth and all that is between them save with truth and for an appointed term?* (30: 8); and *...there are signs for a people who reflect* (10: 24; 13: 3; 45: 13), the Qur'an of miraculous exposition orders and encourages reflection. Also, the *hadith*, "An hour's reflection (on God's signs and Divine truths) is better than a year's (supererogatory) worship,"[145] makes it clear that on occasion an hour's reflection may be equal to a year's worship, and powerfully urges us to reflect. Therefore, for the last thirteen years, following these Qur'anic and Prophetic injunctions with both my mind and heart, in order to preserve for myself the extensive lights and comprehensive truths that emerge in my mind and heart as a result of reflection, I have recorded a number of words and phrases, not to demonstrate these lights and truths, but to indicate their existence and to facilitate reflection, and thus make it possible to follow an ordered way in reflection. Formerly, I would mention these words and phrases with a variety of Arabic terms when I embarked on

145 al-Ghazzali, *Ihya'u 'Ulum ad-Din*, 4:423; al-Qurtubi, *al-Jami' li Ahkam al-Qur'an* 4:314. (Tr.)

reflection. It does not weary me that I have repeated them thousands of times over this long period, nor has the pleasure they give decreased, nor has the spirit's need of them disappeared. As these reflective words and phrases are gleams of Qur'anic verses, the quality of never wearying and preserving their freshness and sweetness, which are among the qualities of the verses, are represented to a degree in the mirror of that reflection.

I have recently realized that the parts of the *Risale-i Nur* have their source of life and their lights in these sequences of reflection. Thinking that they may have the same effect on others as they have had on me, even though greatly important parts of them have already been included in the *Risale-i Nur*, I intended to write them all down towards the end of my life, as a further power and value are to be found when they are gathered together.

Since when life will end is not certain, and since the conditions of my present imprisonment have taken on a form worse than death, instead of waiting for my life to come to an end, and at the importunate insistence of my brothers, these sequences of reflections have been written down as seven chapters. Only the Third Chapter, which is on *God is the All-Great*, is included here.

The third chapter

This is about the ranks of *Allahu akbar* (God is the All-Great).

We will mention here seven of the thirty-three ranks. Some important ranks have been explained in the Second Station of the Twentieth Letter, and at the end of the Second Station of the Thirty-Second Word and at the beginning of its Third Station. Those who wish to understand the truth of these ranks can refer to those two Words.

The first rank

> *And say: "All praise and gratitude are for God, Who has neither taken to Him a child, nor has a partner in the sovereignty (the dominion and ownership of the whole creation), nor (being exalted above all want or insufficiency) has He a guardian against neediness and weakness. And exalt Him in His immeasurable greatness* (17: 11).

We are at Your command, O Lord!

Exalted is His Majesty! God is the All-Great, greater than all things in power and knowledge,

for He is the Creator and Fashioner Who through His Power has made humanity like the universe and inscribed the universe with the "pen" of His Destiny as He has inscribed humanity with the same pen. For that macrocosm (the universe), like that microcosm (humanity), is the artifact of His Power and the inscription of His Destiny. He has invented the universe as a "mosque," and has made human beings worshippers in it. He has brought the former into existence as an abode, and given existence to the latter as a servant inhabiting it.

His Art in the universe has been manifested as a book, while His coloring of humanity has flourished as speech. His Power in the universe displays His Majesty, while His Mercy towards humanity arranges His provision. His Majesty in the universe bears witness that He is One, while His provision for humanity announces that He is the Unique. His stamp on the universe, both on it as a whole and on its parts, shows itself in apparent calmness in never-ending motion, while His seal is on the human body as well as on each of its parts, down to each cell and particle.

Look at His works, which are stable and well-ordered: you will see as clearly as daylight absolute order despite absolute abundance, absolute measure and balance despite absolute speed, absolute stability despite absolute facility, absolute beauty of art despite absolute heterogeneity, absolute harmony and correlation despite absolute distance, absolute distinction despite absolute compositeness, and absolute worth and value despite infinite economy. This obvious quality of existence is enough of a witness for a sensible person, and compels even a foolish hypocrite to admit that this art and unity is truly the work of the Absolute Power, and that the One possessing that Power is absolutely the All-Knowing.

Existence can be explained with absolute ease if it is attributed to One Divine Being. If you try to explain it by attributing it to various origins, insurmountable barriers are encountered. If you attribute it to the One Divine Being, the whole universe will be as easy to create as a palm tree, and a palm tree will be as easy to create as a piece of fruit. If, by contrast, you ascribe it to multiple origins, creating a palm tree will be as difficult as creating the universe, and creating a piece of fruit will be as difficult as creating all the trees in the universe.

This is because a single being, with a single movement, can produce an effect and deal with the whole with no difficulty. If that effect or treatment is expected of multiple beings, it will be obtained, if at all, only with extreme difficulty and after much controversy. It would be like referring the duty of an officer to the soldiers, or that of a master builder to the stones of the building, or that of the earth to all other planets, or that of a water jet to drops of water, or that of the center of a circle to the points on its circumference.

When existence is attributed to One Divine Being, the connection between existence and that Being becomes like a boundless power. Because of this connection, a single cause or means does not have to possess all the power required for the existence or occurrence of something, and the work produced becomes valuable in proportion to the Being to Whom it is attributed, and the cause can have a great effect. Otherwise, a cause or means would have to possess all the power by itself, and the resulting effect would be restricted to the size and/or quality of the cause alone. It is because of this that an ant and a fly can defeat tyrants, and a tiny seed becomes a huge tree.

When all things are attributed to One Divine Being, they do not have to be created from absolute non-existence, for creation means giving external, material existence to things that already exist in Divine Knowledge. It is like developing the image that is reflected on the mirror at the back of a camera onto photographic paper or revealing words written in invisible ink by rubbing a special substance on the piece of paper. However, if things are ascribed to causes or existential multiplicity, they have to come into existence from absolute non-existence, and this is the most difficult of things, if not inconceivable.

The ease with which One Divine Being does this makes the existence of things not only easy but absolutely necessary; the difficulty in ascribing existence to multiple things or causes is beyond measure. The wisdom in the Oneness of the Agent makes it possible to create a thing from non-existence instantaneously and without matter, or to pour particles to form an object into the mold that exists in Knowledge. All intelligent beings agree that it is impossible for a multiplicity of material agents or causes to create something from non-existence, because a living being's existence requires that the particles that form it, which are spread out in the soil, water, and air, should come together. In addition, since there would have to be molds that exist in or are formed by an eternal, all-encompassing knowledge, each particle or atom would have to have universal knowledge and absolute will in order for the particles to be able to form a well-ordered body or for its maintenance to be enabled. In addition, anything or anyone with such knowledge and will would be independent of having or needing its likes. Furthermore, there are no signs in the universe that such things exist. Therefore, there must be a perfect, infinite power (possessing that knowledge and will) so that the existence of the heavens and the earth could be possible. This power is absolutely independent of having any partners. Or else, it would have to be limited by another power. An infinite power does not need partners and is not obliged to accept them, even if they were to exist (and they do not).

Not only does this Power have no partners, It also has no assistants or ministers. Material causes are only a thin veil before the operation of this Eternal Power, and they have no creative effect on the existence of things. Human beings, the noblest cause, and being equipped with willpower, have only a very small part even in those of their acts that are carried out through free will, such as eating, speaking, or thinking. Seeing that we do not have complete control over ourselves despite our free will, how can animals, plants, and inanimate objects (and the laws that are lifeless, blind, and deaf, and which have only nominal existence) be partners with the Creator of the heavens and the earth in creating and controlling things?

Obviously, the "envelope" in which a king puts his gifts, or the "handkerchief" in which he wraps his offerings, or the "soldier" with whom he sends his presents cannot be partners with him in His kingdom. In the same way, nature and causes, which are the "soldiers" by means of which the Absolute Sovereign sends His bounties to us, are only the envelopes or chests in which He stores His offerings for us; they are the handkerchiefs in which He wraps His gifts for us. These cannot be His partners or a means of a creative effect in the execution of His commands.

The second rank

> *Exalted is His Majesty! God is the All-Great, greater than all things in power and knowledge,*

for He is the Creator, the All-Knowing, the Maker, the All-Wise, the All-Merciful, and the All-Compassionate. All earthly creatures and heavenly objects are obviously the miracles of the Power of this All-Knowing Creator. The multicolored and decorated plants and innumerable species of adorned animals that are distributed throughout the garden of the earth are the wonders of the All-Wise Maker's Art. The smiling flowers and bedecked fruits of the earth are gifts from the Mercy of the All-Merciful, the All-Compassionate.

These miracles of Power bear witness, these wonders of Art proclaim, these gifts of Mercy announce that their Creator, Fashioner, and Bestower is powerful over all things, that He knows everything, and encompasses all things in His Mercy and Knowledge. In relation to His Power, minute particles and stars, and the few and the abundant, and the little and the great, and the limited and the unlimited are all equal. And all the events of the past and its marvels are the miracles of that All-Wise Maker's Art, which bear witness that the Maker is powerful over all future contingencies and marvels and that He can do whatever He wills in the future, for He is the All-Knowing Creator, the All-Wise, and the All-Mighty.

All-Glorious is He Who has made the garden of the earth an exhibition of His Art, the assembling ground of His Creativity's products, a place where His Power and Wisdom are manifested, a garden where His Mercy blossoms, a field to be sown for Paradise, and a place where creatures come and depart in a continuous flux according to fixed measures.

Ornamented animals, bedecked birds, fruit-bearing trees, flowering plants—all are miracles of His Knowledge, marvels of His Art, gifts of His Generosity, and proofs of His Favor. Blossoms smiling with the adornment of fruits, birds singing at dawn, raindrops splashing on the cheeks of flowers, mothers' compassion for their infants—all are instances of an All-Loving One making Himself known, an All-Merciful One making Himself loved; all are imprints of the Compassion of an All-Pitying One and the Pitying of a Most Kind One for the jinn, humanity, spiritual beings, angels, and animals.

Seeds, fruits, grains, and flowers are miracles of Wisdom, marvels of Art, gifts of Mercy, proofs of (Divine) Oneness, and witnesses of His Graciousness in the Hereafter. They are truthful witnesses testifying that their Creator is powerful over and knows all things, and that He encompasses all things in Mercy, Knowledge, Creativity, Sustaining, Making, and Fashioning.

In respect of creation, arrangement, maintenance, making, and fashioning, the sun is no different from a seed, a star from a flower, or the earth from a grain—none of them can bear the responsibility of creating, maintaining, making, or fashioning. Seeds and fruit mirror (Divine) Unity in the realm of multiplicity and they are signs of Destiny and indications of Power. They show that the source of multiplicity (the universe and its contents) is the realm of Unity. Multiplicity testifies to the Creator's Oneness in originating and fashioning, and ends in a Unity that indicates the Maker's Wisdom in creating, sustaining, and maintaining. Seeds and fruit are also signs of Wisdom indicating that the Creator of everything looks, with His all-encompassing view, both at the particular and the parts. (As He considers all the trees) He also considers the fruit, because the fruit is the most obvious aim of the tree's creation. And humanity is the fruit of the universe, so humanity is the Creator's most manifest purpose in creating the universe. The heart is like a seed or the nucleus (of a person), and it is the brightest mirror of the Maker of creation. This instance of Wisdom shows that humanity—this microcosmic being—is the pivot of the universe upon which the wheel of creation turns and for the sake of which the universe is continually destroyed or changed, transformed or renewed.

God is the All-Great: O Great One! O God, You are One Whose Grandeur intellects cannot grasp.

All things announce in unison: There is no deity but He;
Continually beseech for the requirements of their lives,
Saying, O Truth, the Ever-Constant; and altogether say: O Living One!

The third rank

God is the All-Great, greater than all things in power and knowledge,

for He is the All-Powerful, the All-Determining, the All-Knowing, the All-Wise, the All-Fashioning, the All-Munificent, the All-Subtle, the All-Decorating, the All-Favoring, the All-Loving, the One Who makes Himself Known, the All-Merciful, the All-Compassionate, the All-Pitying, the All-Gracious and the All-Beautiful, the One with Absolute Beauty and Perfection, and the Eternal Designer. The truths of the worlds—everything that exists and happens—in whole or in parts, of creation as a whole or in parts, or in coming into existence, or in its permanence are nothing but the lines drawn by the "pen" of His Decree and Destiny according to a definite ordering, determination, knowledge, and wisdom, and the designs made by the "compasses" of His Knowledge and Wisdom according to a definite art and fashion. They are all but decorations made by the "bright hand" of His Art, Fashioning, Decorating, and Illustrating with favor and munificence; and the flowers of His Favoring, His Munificence, Making Himself Known and Loved with mercy and bountifulness; and the fruits of the overflowing spring of His Mercy, Bountifulness, Pitying, and Affection with grace and perfection. They are all but the radiations of an everlasting Beauty and perpetual Perfection, as attested to by the fact that the mirrors (reflecting these truths—that is, all creatures) are mortal and the reflections disappear, while manifestations of Beauty and bestowal of Bounty continue to confer bounties through days, seasons, centuries, and ages despite the mortality of their recipients.

The mortality of mirrors and the decay of creatures, despite the perpetual manifestation (of Divine Names, Attributes, and acts) in utmost abundance, is a clear sign and convincing argument that the manifest beauty and flowering perfection do not belong to those on whom they are manifested. This is a most eloquent explanation and evidence of the abstract Beauty and ever-renewed Benevolence of the Necessarily Existent and the All-Loving, Permanent One.

Indeed, a perfect work self-evidently indicates a perfect act. A perfect act necessarily indicates a perfect name and a perfect agent. A perfect name undoubtedly betokens a perfect attribute. A perfect attribute definitely shows an essential capacity. An essential capacity certainly demonstrates the perfection of the Being through what is befitting for that Being, Who is the Most Evident Truth.

The fourth rank

Exalted is His Majesty. God is the All-Great,

for He is the All-Just and the source of justice, the All-Judging, the All-Ruling, and the All-Wise. He founded the tree of this universe in "six days" according to the principles of His Will and Wisdom, divided it into branches according to the prescripts of His Decree and Destiny, arranged it according to the rules of His usual way of acting, decorated it according to the precepts of His Favor and Mercy, and illuminated it through the manifestations of His Names and Attributes. The orderliness and balance of His creation;

the decorations of His creatures; the similarity, correct proportions, mutual assistance and responding among them; and the firm, conscious artistry in all things that Destiny has determined for each, according to its capacity, all attest to this.

- The comprehensive, all-inclusive wisdom in the ordering of creation;
- the perfect favoring in the equipment of each thing with the necessary parts and organs, as well as in its being made handsome and well-proportioned;
- the all-encompassing mercy in the gratification of the needs of every creature;
- the all-inclusive provision in each creature's raising and breeding;
- the amazing life conferred on each living thing or being to make it an exhibition of the All-Originating's essential Qualities;
- the beauties granted to it for certain purposes;
- the permanence of the manifestations of His Grace despite the decay of the creatures that receive them;
- the creation's innate love for its Object of Worship;
- the attraction the creation feels towards Him evident in its ecstasies;
- the unanimous agreement of its perfected, conscious members about the unity of its Originator;
- the benefits that are achieved in all its parts;
- the wise planning displayed by all plants;
- the munificent nurturing of all animate beings;
- the perfect order in the changes in the creation's basic parts;
- the extensive goals followed in its order as a whole;
- its instantaneous creation with perfect art and beauty, without need for either time or matter;
- the infinitely wise and purposeful individualization despite the unlimited possibilities;
- the gratification of each creature's needs just on time on which it does not reckon, despite the infinite multiplicity and diversity of creation and the creatures' inability to meet ever the least of their demands;

- the absolute strength manifested in its weakness;
- the absolute power manifested in its helplessness;
- the life apparent in its lifelessness;
- the comprehensive consciousness manifested in its ignorance;
- the perfect order and arrangement in the changes it undergoes requiring the existence of One Who causes to change but Himself does not change;
- the concord—like that of concentric circles—in its glorifications;
- the acceptance of its prayers it does in the tongues of capacity, essential neediness, and utter constraint and privation;
- the supplications it makes and some hidden truths being unveiled to it and the radiations it is favored with in its worship;
- the measure and balance in its acts of worship;
- the peace and contentment it attains through remembrance of its Originator;
- its worship being the line uniting its beginning and end; and
- the cause of its perfections being brought forth and the purposes of its Maker for its existence being realized.

All these qualities and states of creation and many others unmentioned are witnesses that this universe is managed by a single All-Wise One, sustained and raised by a single, All-Munificent Lord, One Who is Besought-of-All. All things serve a single Master and are at the disposal of a single Ruler. Also, the origin of creation is a single Power, the multiple stamps of Whose Unity appear on each of Its "missives" inscribed on each of the "pages" of Its creatures.

Every flower and fruit, plant and tree, animal or rock, every sand particle or stone, in all the valleys and mountains and deserts is a manifest seal that demonstrates to any careful examination that the One Who has made it is the "Inscriber" of this space which is full of lessons, and the "Inscriber" of the surface of the land and the bottom of the sea. He is also the Designer of the sun and moon on the page of the heavens that is full of lessons. Exalted is the Majesty of that Designer. He is God, the All-Great.

Whence the world sings in unison: There is no deity but He.

The fifth rank

God is the All-Great,

for He is the Creator, the All-Powerful, the Fashioner, and the All-Seeing. All heavenly bodies and pearl-like stars are proofs of His Divinity and Grandeur; they are witnesses of His Lordship and Grandeur. They attest to and proclaim the splendor of His Lordship's Kingdom, the vastness of His Rule and Wisdom, and His Power's magnificence and greatness.

Now consider the verse, *But do they, then, never observe the sky above them, how We have constructed it and adorned it* (50:6). Look at the sky and see the serene silence, the wise and purposeful motion, and the magnificent glittering smile with its orderly creation and well-proportioned art. Its "lamp" shines for the changing of seasons; its "lantern" radiates for the illumination of the world; its stars glitter for the decoration of the worlds. Everything proclaims the boundless Sovereignty in the universe's organization and maintenance to those of common sense and discernment.

This All-Powerful Creator knows all things and has a Will so comprehensive that whatever He wills to be is, and whatever He wills not to be is not. He is powerful over all things by an absolute, all-encompassing Power that is essential to His Divine Being. Just as it is inconceivable for the sun to exist without light or heat, so too is it inconceivable that there be God, the Creator of the heavens Who does not possess an all-encompassing Knowledge or absolute Power. He knows all things by an all-encompassing Knowledge that is essential to His Divine Being. Nothing can escape this Knowledge, by virtue of Its relation with all things and Its omnipresence, penetrative capability and comprehensiveness.

Whatever is observed in the whole of creation, such as orderliness, balance, and harmony, all-inclusive wisdom, perfect favoring, well-established measures, well-arranged dispensation, fruitful decrees, appointed final ends, regular provision, wise precision and faultlessness, pleasing care (given to all things), as well as the perfect differentiation, measurement, order and stability, and absolute ease—all testify to the all-encompassing Knowledge of the Knower of the Unseen and of all things. The verse, *Is it conceivable that One Who creates should not know? He is the All-Subtle, the All-Aware* (67:14), indicates that the existence of something requires full knowledge of it; the light of existence in things requires the light of full knowledge of them. If the beauty of art in one's work indicates one's consciousness to the extent of the infinitesimal light of a firefly on a pitch-dark night, humanity's creation indicates its Creator's Knowledge to the extent of the sun's splendor at noon.

As He knows all things, His Will encompasses all things. Nothing takes place without His Will. Power produces the effect, Knowledge distinguishes, and the Will apportions and individualizes. This is how things come into existence. There are as many witnesses of the Almighty's Will as there are characteristics, attributes, and states of things.

The creating and fashioning of each thing with its distinguishing character and attributes purposefully chosen for it out of innumerable alternatives and potentialities in an infinitely diverse flux, forming each most delicately and with most sensitive measures; and the creating of diverse, well-formed living beings from simple, inanimate elements (e.g., creating humanity with its senses and all other systems and physical organs from a sperm and an egg, a bird and its physical being from an egg, a tree with all its parts from a seed) witness that everything is given its individual character and attributes by the Almighty's Will and Choice. All-Glorious is He.

The correspondence in physical structures and basic systems among the members of a species shows that their Maker is One and Unique. However, the fact that each member is different and distinguishable among others demonstrates that the One and Unique Maker does whatever He wills and judges however He wills. Exalted is His Majesty.

In the same way that the All-Knowing and All-Willing Creator has an all-encompassing Knowledge and all-inclusive Will, He has a perfect Power that issues from and is essential to His Divine Being. That Power has no opposite, for that would require the agreement or combination of two opposites, which, by universal assent, is inconceivable. There can be no grades in that Power, so in relation to It, the particles and the stars, the few and the many, the particular and the universal, humanity and the universe, seeds and trees are all equal.

The transparency of the immaterial dimension of existence with which that Power deals, the interrelation among things, the exact balance in creation, the perfect order of existence, and the utmost obedience of existence to that Power testify to this. The absolute order, harmony, balance, and differentiation or individualization in creation, despite absolute speed, ease, multiplicity and diversity also testify to this fact.

The One Who has that Power can create anything, without exception, with great ease because He is the One and Unique Who has absolute control over everything as a whole and over individuals; He exists by Himself and is totally different from the created; He is unrestricted, indivisible, and uncontained by space. Nothing impedes Him; rather, like the veins in our bodies or metal wires that conduct electricity or other subtle forces, whatever seems to be an impediment serves as a means of ease although He has no need for any help in conducting or executing His commands. Whatever He creates has the same quality of art—particles, parts, particulars, the few, the small, the human, and the seed are in no way less beautiful or lesser in art than the stars, universals, the many, the great, the universe, and the trees. Whoever creates the latter creates the former. The One Who creates a seed, which is a small-scale copy of a tree into which the Creator has included the tree by the principles of His Knowledge, must undoubtedly be the Creator of the tree. It is not difficult for the Power Who brings the particulars into existence to create the universals.

Just as the copy of the "Qur'an of wisdom" that is inscribed in an atom with ether particles has the same quality of beauty and art found in the copy of the "Qur'an of grandeur" written on the pages of the heavens in the ink of stars and suns, so creating a honeybee or an ant requires no less skill or artistry than creating a date palm or an elephant. The art contained in a rose is not less than the art contained in a pearl-like star. While the utmost and perfect ease of creating things causes the misguided to confuse creation with self-formation, which requires accepting impossibilities and superstitions that contradict sound reasoning and judgment, it leads people of truth to the certainty that planets and minute particles are the same in relation to the Power of the Creator of the universe.

Exalted is His Majesty, and sublime is His Name. There is no deity but He.

The sixth rank

> *Exalted is His Majesty, and sublime is His Name. God is the All-Great, greater than all things in power and knowledge,*

for He is the All-Just, the All-Wise, the All-Powerful, the All-Knowing, the One, the Unique, and the Eternal Sovereign. All worlds are at the disposal of His "Hands" of order and balance, arranging and measuring, Justice and Wisdom, and Knowledge and Power. They observably show His Unity—all-encompassing manifestations of His Names as a whole—and Oneness—the concentration of the manifestations of some of His Names on individual things. Nothing in the universe is excluded from His order or balance, or from His arranging or measuring; these are two "chapters" of the Manifest Record and the Manifest Book, which in turn are the titles of the Knowledge and Command of the All-Knowing and All-Wise, and the Power and Will of the All-Mighty and All-Compassionate. The order and balance in this Book, together with that Record, are two proofs for anyone with reason in their head or eyes to be able to observe with, to understand that nothing in existence or time is outside the disposal of the All-Merciful, the ordering of the All-Pitying, the decorating of the All-Gracious, and the measuring of the All-Ruling.

In summary: The manifestations of the Divine Names "the First" and "the Last" in creation refer to the beginning and end, the origin and issue, the past and future, the command and knowledge, and indicate the Manifest Record. The manifestations of the Names "the Outward" and "the Inward" on things that are connected with God's Attribute of Creation indicate the Manifest Book.

The universe is like a huge tree, and each world or realm in it is also like a tree. A tree has an origin (its seed) and an issue that carries on its task after its death (the seeds in the fruit). Its beginning and end manifest the Divine Names "the First" and "the Last." Through its composition and the purposes it serves, the original seed is an index or code for the tree's formation. Thus it manifests "the First." The seeds in the tree's fruits manifest "the Last."

Seeds are like miniature treasure chests of Wisdom that contain the Pen of Destiny's inscribed index and code for forming new trees that will exactly resemble the original one. A tree's exterior manifests the Name "the Outward." Through its perfect, well-ordered structure, decoration, and the purposes it serves, the tree is like a perfectly beautiful dress made with perfect wisdom and favor to fit the tree. The tree's interior manifests the Name "the Inward." Through its perfect, amazing organization and the conduct of the food required for the life of the tree into all of its parts with perfect order, its interior is like an extraordinary machine or factory working in perfect order and balance.

The tree's beginning resembles an amazing list of instructions, its end an extraordinary index, and both indicate the Manifest Record. With its exterior resembling an artistically woven dress and its interior resembling an extremely well-ordered machine, the body of the tree points to the Manifest Book. Like human memory, which indicates the Supreme Preserved Tablet, all the original seeds and fruits of the tree indicate the Manifest Record, and their exteriors and interiors symbolize the Manifest Book. Compare with that particular tree the "tree" of the earth, with its past and future; compare the "tree" of the universe with its beginning and future, and the "tree" of a person with his or her ancestors and descendants.

Exalted is the Majesty of their Creator, and there is no deity but He. O All-Great One! You are the One Whose Grandeur cannot be described by minds and Whose Dominion cannot be comprehended.

The seventh rank

> *Exalted is His Majesty. God is the All-Great, greater than all things in power and knowledge,*

for He is the Creator, Opener, All-Acting, All-Knowing, Bestower of gifts, Distributor of Blessings, and Eternal "Sun." All worlds and their contents are shadows of His lights, works of His acts, colors of the embroidery of the manifestations of His Names, lines of the "pen" of His Destiny and Decree, and mirrors that manifest His Attributes of Beauty, Majesty, and Perfection. All of this is attested to by the Eternal Witness—the Almighty Himself—with all His Books, Pages or Scrolls; by the consensus of the signs of creation and the verses of the Qur'an. It is also attested to by the consensus of the earth and all that is on it, with their manifestations of absolute riches and wealth, despite the essential destitution and need of each, and by the consensus of the Prophets, saints and the purified, exacting scholars who have enlightened intellects and illuminated hearts with their verifications, spiritual discoveries, and supplications, and the blessings with which they are favored.

All of the above, with their endless certain testimony and the acceptance of the testimony of signs of creation, the verses of the Qur'an, and the testament of the heavenly Books and Pages that contain the testimony of the Necessarily Existent One—all of these witnesses, including the earth and all other heavenly and earthly bodies, unanimously agree that all creatures are works of His Power, inscriptions of His Destiny, mirrors of His Names, and images of His lights.

Exalted is His Majesty, and there is no deity but He.

The
Thirtieth Gleam

The Thirtieth Gleam

About the six Names of God having all-comprehensive manifestations

Being a fruit of Eskişehir Prison, this Gleam consists of six parts about the six Names of God that have all-comprehensive manifestations.

Meyve Risalesi ("The Fruits of Belief," included in *Şualar* ["The Rays"]) was the great lesson of the Denizli School of Joseph, and *el-Hüccetü'z-Zehra* ("The Radiant Proof," included in *The Rays*) was a most valuable lesson of the Afyon School of Joseph. This Gleam is a powerful lesson of the Eskişehir School of Joseph. It is about God Almighty's six Names which have all-encompassing manifestations.

The first part
An aspect of the Divine Name the All-Holy

In the Name of God, the All-Merciful, the All-Compassionate.

And the earth, We have spread it out like a couch; and how excellent We are in spreading it. (51: 48)

One aspect of the meaning of the above-mentioned verse and one manifestation of the Divine Name, the All-Holy, which is one of the Divine Names that have all-encompassing manifestations, or one of the six lights of the All-Encompassing Name of God became clear to me towards the end of the month of Sha'ban in

Eskişehir Prison. It showed both the existence of God most manifestly and His Unity most clearly. I saw it as follows:

The universe is a vast, constantly working factory and the earth is a hostel or guesthouse which is continuously filled and emptied. Generally, such continually working factories, hostels and guesthouses become much dirtied with filth, debris and rubbish, and putrid matter accumulates throughout them. If they are not kept with the utmost care or not cleaned or swept, it is impossible to dwell in them; humans would suffocate there. But the factory of the universe and the guesthouse of the earth are so pure and clean and so untainted and fresh that there is no useless, unnecessary thing, not even random dirt, in either. Even if some becomes visible, it is quickly thrown into a transformation machine and cleaned.

This means that the One Who looks after this factory does so very well. That Owner of the factory is such that He sweeps and cleans and orders this vast factory, this extensive palace, as though it were only a small room. Although there must be dirt and rubbish in proportion to the size of this huge factory, care is also given to its cleanness and tidiness in proportion to its size.

If someone does not wash themselves or clean their small room for a month, both will become extremely dirty and soiled. So, we can conclude that the cleanliness, purity, and luminosity in this palace of the world arise from a continuous, wise, and sensitive cleaning and purification. But for this cleaning, sweeping and careful tending, hundreds of thousands of animal species would have been choked on the earth within one year. Also, the debris of the globes, satellites, and stars in space and the heavens, which are bound to die, would have crashed down not only on our heads and those of the other animals, but also on the head of our world. They would have rained down on our heads rocks the size of mountains and driven us away from our earthly homeland. Although a long time ago a few meteorites fell as a result of destruction and reconstruction, as if a warning, in those elevated realms, they did not hurt any human.

Furthermore, because of the exchange and struggle between life and death, the corpses of hundreds of thousands of animals and the debris of hundreds of thousands of plants would have so utterly dirtied the faces of land and sea that conscious beings, rather than loving those faces, would have felt disgust at such ugliness and preferred death.

Just as a bird cleans its wings and a scribe his pages easily, so too, the wings of the plane of the earth and the "birds" of the sky and the pages of the book of the universe are so cleansed and made so beautiful that those who do not see the infinite beauty of the Hereafter or consider it with belief become lovers of this cleanliness and this beauty of the world, adoring it.

Considering this fact, this palace of the world and that factory of the universe are the objects of the universal manifestation of the Divine Name the All-Holy. It is by reason of this fact that not only the carnivorous cleaners of the seas and the eagles of the land, but also the cleansing officials of the earth, such as worms and ants, which gather up corpses, obey the commands of cleaning that issue from that sacred Name. Furthermore, both the red and white blood corpuscles that flow in the body and the respiratory system obey these sacred commands of cleaning as well and carry out the cleansing in the body's cells and purify the blood.

And just as the eyelids obey the command to clean the eye and a fly the command to brush its wings, the vast atmosphere and the clouds obey as well. The air blows away the pieces of dust and soil that settle on the face of the earth, and cleans it. The sponges of the clouds sprinkle water on the garden of the earth, settling the dust and dirt. Then, in order not to pollute the sky, the air quickly collects the rubbish and withdraws and hides it with perfect orderliness. It exhibits the beautiful face and eye of the skies that have been swept and polished, all shining brightly.

Also, as the stars, elements, minerals, and plants obey that command to cleanse, all particles and atoms obey it as well; they are careful of cleanliness amidst the astonishing tumults of change and transformation. They never assemble anywhere unnecessarily or get in the way. And if they become soiled, they are quickly cleansed. They are moved by a hand of Wisdom so that they acquire the cleanest, neatest, and brightest states and the most beautiful, pure and pleasing forms.

Thus, this single act and truth, that is, cleansing, is a comprehensive manifestation of the Divine Name, the All-Holy, which shows itself throughout the universe. Like a telescope, it shows the existence of God with His All-Beautiful Names and His Unity to our eyes as brightly as the sun.

It has been established with decisive proofs in many parts of the *Risale-i Nur* that since the act of ordering and order, which are a manifestation of the Divine Attribute of Wisdom and the Divine Name of the All-Wise, and the act of making balanced and balance, which are a manifestation of the Attribute of Justice and Name of the All-Just, and the act of equipping and benevolence, which are a manifestation of the Names the All-Gracious and All-Munificent, and the act of rearing, nurturing and bestowal, which are a manifestation of the Names the Lord and the All-Compassionate, are each a single truth and a single act observed throughout the universe, they demonstrate the necessary existence and Unity of a Single Being. In exactly the same way, the act of purifying and making clean, which is a manifestation of the Name the All-Holy, demonstrates like the sun the existence of the Necessarily Existent One, and His Unity like daylight.

And as the wise acts of ordering, balancing, equipping, adorning and making clean mentioned above indicate a Single Maker by reason of their being complementary to one another and together causing the same all-encompassing result in the maximum sphere of existence, each of the All-Beautiful Names has such a comprehensive manifestation in the maximum sphere as well. And the act that proceeds from that manifestation points to the Single Unique One with clarity and decisiveness in relation to its extensiveness.

The obvious realities and the acts indicate a single source which illuminates the universe and makes it smile, such as the universal wisdom that causes all things to obey its law and order, the comprehensive munificence which adorns and satisfies all things, the all-embracing mercy that makes all things pleased and happy, the universal providing of sustenance which nurtures and gives pleasure to all things, and the life and giving of life which connects all things to and makes them benefit from one another—all such obvious realities and acts point to a single source that indicates an All-Wise, All-Munificent, All-Compassionate and All-Providing One, and an All-Living Giver of Life as plainly as the light indicates the sun.

If even one of these hundreds of extensive acts, each one of which is a clear, profound proof of God's Unity, is not attributed to the Single Unique One, each necessarily becomes impossible in hundreds of respects. For example, let alone the obvious realities and proofs of unity of the source, such as wisdom, munificence, mercy, provision and the giving of life, if only the act of cleansing is not attributed to the Creator of the universe, then the way of unbelief followed by the people of misguidance would require the following:

Either all the creatures would have a share in the universal act of cleansing, from particles and flies to the universal elements and the stars; each would have to have the capacity to know and consider the adorning, balancing, ordering, and cleaning of the vast universe and would act accordingly; each would have to possess the sacred Attributes of the Creator of the universe, or there would have to be a consultative committee the size of the universe in order to decide and regulate all those acts together, balancing the incomings and outgoings of the universe, and the innumerable particles, flies, and stars would have to be members of that committee. Hundreds of such superstitious and nonsensical impossibilities would have to occur for the universal, comprehensive, and exalted acts of equipping, adorning, and cleaning that are observed everywhere to exist. This is impossible not just once, but hundreds and thousands of times over.

If daylight and the reflected miniature suns in all the shining objects on the earth are not attributed to the sun and they are not accepted as the manifestations of the sun's reflection, then it is necessary to accept that there is a sun in all the fragments of glass, in all the drops of water and snowflakes that glisten on the face of the earth, and even in all the particles of air, so that all-encompassing light can exist.

Thus, wisdom also is a light; all-embracing mercy is a light; adorning, balancing, ordering, and cleansing are each an encompassing light—these are all the rays of the Eternal Sun. So, see how misguidance and unbelief have entered a swamp from which there is no way out! See just how ridiculous the ignorance of misguidance is! Say, "Praise be to God for the Religion of Islam and perfect belief!"

Surely, this exalted, universal act of cleansing, which keeps the palace of the universe clean, is the manifestation and requirement of the Divine Name the All-Holy. And just as the glorification of all creatures is also directed to the Name the All-Holy, the Name the All-Holy also requires the cleanliness of all of them.[146]

It is because of this sacred connection of cleanliness to the Divine Name the All-Holy that some *hadiths* connect cleanliness with belief.[147]

---

146 We must not forget that bad qualities, false beliefs, sins and heresies are all instances of moral and spiritual filth.

147 *Muslim*, "Tahara" 1; *at-Tirmidhi*, "Da'awat" 86. (Tr.)

And the verse, *Surely God loves those who turn to Him in sincere repentance and He loves those who cleanse themselves* (2: 222), shows that cleanliness is a means of attracting God's love.

The second part
The Divine Name the All-Just

> *There is not a thing but the stores (for its life and sustenance) are with Us, and We do not send it down except in due, determined measure.* (15: 21)

One aspect of the meaning of the above-mentioned verse and one manifestation of the Divine Name the All-Just, which is one of the Divine Names that have all-encompassing manifestations or one of the six lights of the All-Encompassing Name of God, appeared to me from afar while in Eskişehir Prison. In order to make it understandable, again by means of a comparison, we say the following:

The universe is such a palace that in it is a "city" which is being continuously shaken by destruction and repair. And in the city there is a "country" which is incessantly surging up in war and emigration. And within the country is a "world" which is constantly revolving amidst death and life. But such an astonishing balance, equilibrium, and act of ordering prevail in the palace, city, country, and world that it obviously proves that all the changes, incomings, and outgoings which occur in these innumerable beings are measured and weighed on the scales of a Single Being Who every moment sees and supervises the whole universe. For considering that, for example, a single fish lays a thousand eggs at one time and a single flower like a poppy produces twenty thousand seeds, if causes—all creatures—were free and unrestrained, being ever able to destroy the balance and overrun everything through the onslaught of incessant changes and the elements flowing in floods; or if they were under the control of aimless, purposeless "chance," anarchic blind forces, or unconscious dark nature; then the balance in beings or the balance of the whole universe would have been so utterly destroyed that within a year, indeed within a day, there would have been chaos. The seas would have been filled with things in total disorder and confusion and would have become putrid; the atmosphere would have been poisoned with noxious gases and the earth would have turned into a refuse heap, slaughterhouse, or swamp. The world would have suffocated.

Thus, everything in the universe from the cells of an animate body, the red and white corpuscles in the blood, the transformations of minute particles, and the proportion and relationship among the body's organs, to the water coming in and out of the seas, and the income and expenditure of springs under the earth, the birth and death of animals and plants, the destruction of autumn and the reconstruction of spring, the duties and motion of the universal elements and the stars, and the alternations, struggles and clashes of death and life, light and darkness, and heat and cold, is ordered and weighed with such a sensitive balance, so fine a measure that the human mind can nowhere see any waste or futility, just as human science sees and indicates the most perfect order and beautiful balance everywhere. Indeed, human science is a manifestation and interpreter of that order and balance.

So, come and consider the balanced relationship between the sun and its twelve planets. Does it not indicate as clearly as the sun the All-Majestic One Who is the All-Just and All-Powerful? And in particular our ship, that is, the earth, which is one of the planets, travels an orbit of about eighty thousand years in human distances in one year. Despite that extraordinary speed, it does not scatter or shake the things heaped or arranged on its face, nor does it throw them off into space. If its speed had been less or more to a certain degree, it would have thrown its inhabitants off into space and scattered them. And if the balance in its movement and placement were to be destroyed for a minute, or even a second, this would destroy the world. Indeed, it would crash with another body and cause overall destruction.

In particular, the compassionate balance on the earth in the births, deaths, livelihoods, and lives of hundreds of thousands of plant and animal species shows a single All-Just and All-Compassionate One as clearly as light shows the sun.

And in particular the organs, faculties, and senses of just one of the innumerable members of those species are related to one another in such a sensitive balance that it self-evidently indicates an All-Wise and All-Just Maker.

And in particular, the cells and blood vessels in the bodies of animals, and the corpuscles in the blood, and the particles in the corpuscles are so sensitively balanced and have such a fine relationship with one another that it clearly proves that they are being maintained and administered through the balance, law, and order of a single All-Just and All-Wise Creator, Who has in His hands the reins of all things, and the key to all things, and directs all things as easily as a single thing without the direction of one thing impeding the direction of others.

If someone who, deeming it unlikely, does not believe that the deeds of jinn and humans will be weighed upon His supreme scales of Justice at the Last Judgment notes carefully this vast balance which they can see in this world with their own eyes, they will surely no longer consider it unlikely.

O wasteful, unjust, dirty one, disrespectful of economy, justice, and cleanliness! Since you oppose the whole universe by not observing economy, cleanliness, or justice, which the whole universe and all other beings observe as basic principles in their acts, you have become the object of their anger and disgust. On what are you based and on what do you rely that you make all beings angry through your wrongdoing, disequilibrium, wastefulness and uncleanliness?

Indeed, the universal wisdom in the universe, which proceeds from the most comprehensive manifestation of the Divine Name the All-Wise, observes economy and lack of waste, and orders economy. And the all-embracing justice in the universe that issues from the most comprehensive manifestation of the Name the All-Just administers the balance of all things and orders humanity to justice. The word "balance" is mentioned four times in the following verses of *Surat al-Rahman*:

> *And the heaven—He has made it high (above the earth), and He has set up the balance, so you must not go beyond (the limits with respect to) the balance; and observe the balance with full equity, and do not fall short in the balance*. (55: 7–9)

This indicates four degrees and four types of balance, showing its supreme importance in the universe. Just as there is no wastefulness in anything, there is no disorder or imbalance in it either. Likewise, the act of cleansing and cleanliness that issue from the Name the All-Holy cleans and makes beautiful all the beings in the universe. Unless the polluting hand of humanity interferes, there is no uncleanness or ugliness in anything in the true sense of the word.

You may therefore understand from this how fundamental the principles of justice, economy, and cleanliness are to human life; these are truths of the Qur'an and of Islamic principles. And know how closely interconnected with the universe the commandments of the Qur'an are; they have spread their firm roots everywhere and enveloped and permeated all its corners. Know that it is impossible to destroy these truths in the same way that it is impossible to destroy the universe or change its form.

Moreover, like these three most comprehensive lights, hundreds of other comprehensive realities, such as mercy, munificence, and recording and preserving, require the Resurrection and the Hereafter. Is it therefore possible that the Resurrection will not happen and the Hereafter will not be established, and so all these powerful and comprehensive realities, namely mercy, munificence, justice, wisdom, economy, and cleanliness, which prevail not only in the universe but also with all beings, change into mercilessness, injustice, a lack of wisdom, wastefulness, uncleanness, and futility?

God forbid, a hundred thousand times, God forbid! Would a mercy and wisdom which compassionately preserve the rights to life of a fly violate the endless rights to life of all conscious beings or the boundless rights of numberless other beings by not bringing about the Resurrection? And if it is permissible to say so, would the Majesty and Magnificence of a Lordship Which shows infinite sensitivity and care concerning mercy, compassion, justice, and wisdom, and the Sovereignty of a Divinity Which adorns the universe with its countless wonderful arts and bounties in order to display Its perfections and make Itself known and loved, allow the non-occurrence of the Resurrection, which would reduce to nothing all the creatures and perfections of this universe, causing the denial of these perfections? God forbid! An absolute Beauty and Grace such as that clearly would not allow such absolute ugliness.

Indeed, one who attempts to deny the Hereafter must first deny the entire world with all its realities. Otherwise, with all its realities, the world would contradict them with a hundred thousand voices, proving that they are liars a hundred thousand times over. The Tenth Word (included in *The Words*) proves with certain proofs that the existence of the Hereafter is as certain and indubitable as the existence of this world.

The third part
The Divine Name the All-Wise

Call to the way of your Lord with wisdom (16: 125).

One aspect of the meaning of the above-mentioned verse and one manifestation of the Divine Name the All-Wise, which is one of the Divine Names that have all-encompassing manifestations or one of the six lights of the All-Encompassing Name of God appeared to me in the holy month of Ramadan. In order to indicate it, the following five points have been written in haste.

First point

As pointed out in the Tenth Word, the all-embracing manifestation of the Divine Name the All-Wise has made the universe into such a book that hundreds of books have been written on every page of it, and hundreds of pages have been included in every line of it, and there are hundreds of lines in every word of it, and every letter of it contains hundreds of words, and a short index of the book is to be found in every point. The book's pages and lines, down to the very points, demonstrate its Inscriber and Author in hundreds of respects with such clarity that an observation of that book of the universe establishes the Existence and Unity of its Scribe to a degree that is hundreds of times greater than the proof of the book's own existence. For if a single letter exhibits its own existence to the extent of a letter, the same letter exhibits its Scribe to the extent of a line.

One page of this macro-book is the face of the earth. As many books as there are plant and animal species can be seen to be written on this page in the spring one within the other, together, at the same time, without error, and in the most perfect form.

One line of the page is a garden. We see with our eyes that on this page well-composed odes to the number of flowers, trees, and animals in the garden are written all together, one within the other, and without error.

One word of the line is a tree which has blossomed and put forth its leaves in order to yield its fruit. This word comprises meaningful passages that laud and praise the All-Wise One of Majesty to the number of its orderly, well-proportioned, adorned leaves, flowers, and fruit. It is as if, like all other trees, this tree too is a well-composed ode, singing the praises of its Inscriber.

It is also as though the All-Wise One of Majesty wants to look with thousands of eyes on His wonderful, venerable works, thus displaying them in the exhibition of the earth.

And it is as though the bejeweled gifts, decorations, and uniforms accorded to the tree by that Eternal Monarch have been made with such incredibly adorned, well-proportioned, orderly, and meaningful forms in order that they might be presented to His view in the spring, the tree's particular festival and parade, that each of these gifts, decorations, and uniforms—the flowers, leaves, and fruits—bears witness to the Existence and Names of the Inscriber in numerous ways and with many proofs, one within the other.

For example, each blossom or fruit displays a perfect organization and balance. The balance is maintained through an unceasing and ever-renewed act of ordering; the act of ordering follows perfect art and decoration, and this art and decoration is combined with exceptional scents and purposeful tastes. Thus, each blossom indicates the All-Wise One of Majesty to the number of the blossoms on the tree.

The tree, which itself is a word, grows from a seed, which is a letter. This letter is a small coffer containing the future content and program of the entire tree. And so on. To continue the same analogy, the manifestation of the Name the All-Wise not only makes every page of the book of the universe, but it also creates its lines, words, letters, and points, as miracles; thus even if all the causes—living or non-living—should gather together, they would not make the like of a single point, nor could they dare to compete with it.

Since each of the creational signs of this mighty Qur'an of the universe displays miracles to the number of its points and letters, then surely, purposeless chance, blind force, aimless, anarchic, unconscious nature can in no way interfere with that wise, insightful, and particular balance or most sensitive order. If they were able to interfere, some traces of confusion would certainly have been apparent. However, no trace of disorder is to be observed anywhere.

Second point

This consists of two matters.

First matter: As expounded in the Tenth Word, it is "natural" and "inevitable" that an infinitely perfect beauty and infinitely beautiful perfection tend to observe and manifest themselves. It is because of this basic universal rule or tendency that the Eternal Inscriber of the mighty book of the universe makes Himself known with His Grace and Perfections, and makes Himself loved through the universe, through all its pages, lines and even letters and full stops.

So, O heedless human! While the All-Wise One of Majesty and Grace wants to make Himself known to you and loved by you through each of His creatures in such brilliant and endless ways, if, in return, you do not recognize Him with belief or you do not make yourself loved by Him with your worship, you should know just what a bottomless, compounded ignorance this is and what a loss it will be; so, come to your senses!

Second matter: There is no room for partnership in the dominion of the All-Powerful and All-Wise Maker of the universe. For, as an infinitely perfect order prevails in everything, it cannot admit partners. For, if many hands intervene in one matter, they will confuse it. If there are two kings in a country, two governors in a town, or two headmen in a village, disorder will reign in all matters in the country, town, or village. Moreover, the fact that even the most minor official does not accept the interference of others in his duties shows us that the most essential characteristic of dominion and sovereignty is independence. This means that order necessitates unity, and sovereignty requires independence.

If such a temporary shadow of sovereignty, manifested on powerless humans who are in need of assistance, rejects interference, then certainly absolute sovereignty, enjoyed by an absolutely Powerful One at the degree of Lordship over the entire universe, will certainly reject interference with all its might. If there were even the most minuscule interference, the order would be spoilt.

However, the universe has been so created that the creation of a seed requires as much power as is needed to create the entire tree. And in order to create a tree, there must be as much power as there is to create the entire universe. And if there were a partner who interfered in the universe, they would have to have a part in the existence of the tiniest seed. For the seed is a sample of the universe. So, two different Lordships, for which there is not the least room in this vast universe, would have to find room for themselves in a seed, or even in a minute particle. This is the most inconceivable and meaningless of impossibilities and false conceptions. Unbelief and associating partners with God mean attributing impotence to the absolutely

Powerful One, Who holds and maintains the entire universe in all its states and circumstances, in the balance of His Justice and the order of His Wisdom, even down to the creation of a single seed. Know from this what an infinitely compounded opposition to the truth, (what an unforgivable) error, and (what monstrous) falsehood are unbelief and associating partners with God, and what an infinitely compounded truth and reality is Divine Oneness and belief in it. Know this and say, "All praise and thanks be to God for belief!"

Third point

Through His Name the All-Wise, the All-Powerful Maker has included thousands of well-ordered worlds in this world. Among those worlds, He has created humanity as a center and pivot in which His instances of Wisdom and the purposes behind the existence of the universe are concentrated. The most important of these instances of wisdom and purpose relate to humanity; He has made provision the focal point of the human sphere. Most of the purposes that are followed and the instances of wisdom in the human world relate to provision and are manifested through it. Consciousness in humanity and the pleasure provision gives display a manifestation of the Name the All-Wise in a brilliant fashion. And each of the hundreds of sciences invented by means of human consciousness describes one manifestation of the Name the All-Wise in one aspect of existence.

For example, if the science of medicine were to be asked, "What is the universe?", it would certainly reply, "It is an extraordinarily orderly and perfect vast pharmacy. All remedies are prepared and stored in it in the best and most proper way."

And if the science of chemistry were asked, "What is the earth?" it would answer, "It is a perfect, exceptionally ordered chemist's shop."

And the science of engineering would reply, "It is a perfect factory with no faults."

And the science of agriculture would reply, "It is an infinitely productive, well-ordered field and garden which produces all kinds of crops just in time."

The science of trade would reply, "It is an extremely well-arranged exhibition, orderly market, and shop full of the most artistic wares."

The science of economics would reply, "It is an outstandingly well-ordered warehouse containing every kind of goods."

The science of dietetics would reply, "It is a kitchen built and prepared by the Lord and a cauldron made and filled by the All-Merciful in which hundreds of thousands of the most delicious types of food are cooked all together in the most orderly fashion."

The science of military affairs would reply, "The earth is a military camp. Although every spring in that army there are hundreds of thousands of different nations newly armed with their tents pitched on the earth, they are given their rations, uniforms, weapons, training, and discharges, all different and particular for each nation, in perfect order, with no confusion and none being forgotten, through the command, power, and compassion of a single Commander in Chief, from His treasury; they are all administered in the most regular fashion."

And if the science of electricity were to be asked, "What is this world?" it would certainly reply, "The roof of this magnificent palace of the universe has been adorned with innumerable, exceptionally well-made and arranged electric lamps. There is such an extraordinary order and balance in their composition and arrangement that although all these heavenly lamps, primarily the sun, which is a thousand times larger than the earth, unceasingly burn, they do not spoil their balance, nor do they explode or cause fires. Their expenditure is boundless, so where does their income or fuel come from? Why do they not consume their source? Why is the balance in their burning not destroyed? A small lamp goes out if it is not tended regularly. Consider the Wisdom and Power of the All-Wise One of Majesty, Who makes the sun, which astronomy tells us hundreds of thousands of times is larger than the earth and hundreds of millions of years older, continuously burn without being extinguished,[148] and say, 'All-Glorious God is!' Say to the number of the seconds of the sun's age, 'What wonders God wills!

[148] Let it be reckoned just how much fuel would be necessary for the stove or lamp of the sun, which heats and illuminates the palace of the world. According to astronomy, piles of wood equal to a million earths and thousands of oceans of oil would be required for it to burn every day. Now think and say, "All-Glorious is God! What wonders God wills! Whatever and however He wills is! How well God does it, and how blessed and supreme He is! to the number of the sun's particles in the face of the Majesty, Wisdom, and Power of the All-Powerful One of Majesty, Who makes it give light continuously.

Whatever and however He wills is! How well God does it, and how blessed and supreme He is! There is no deity but He!' and reflect: These heavenly lamps are in a wonderful order, and they are tended with the greatest care. It is as though the boiler of these huge, numerous masses of fire, these light-diffusing lamps, is a Hell whose heat is never exhausted; it supplies them with lightless heat. While the machinery and central factory of those electric lamps is an everlasting Paradise; it supplies them with light; and through the broadest manifestation of the Name the All-Wise they continue to burn in orderliness."

And so on. As hundreds of sciences like these certainly testify, the universe has been adorned with innumerable instances of wisdom and usefulness, and purposes within a faultless, perfect order. And through His all-encompassing Wisdom, He pursues the same instances of order and wisdom as He has pursued for the whole of the universe in seeds and the tiniest living creatures in small measures. It is obvious that there is a purposeful choice or will and intention in pursuing certain aims, purposes, instances of wisdom, or benefits. Therefore, these intended purposes, instances of wisdom, and blessings can never be the work of unconscious causes or nature, which lack will, choice, and purpose; neither can they interfere in them.

Consequently, it cannot be described how most ridiculously ignorant it is not to recognize or how foolish it is to deny that the All-Wise Maker, the One Who does whatever He wills, and Whom the universe requires and demonstrates with all the endless instances of order and wisdom observed in all the creatures it contains. Indeed, if there is anything that we can say is the most shocking thing in the world, it is such denial. For while the most perfect order and endless instances of wisdom in all the creatures of the universe testify to His existence and Unity, even the most infinite in ignorance and blindness understand what blindness and ignorance it is not to see or recognize Him. I might even say that among the people of unbelief, the Sophists, who are regarded as foolish because they denied the universe's existence, are the most intelligent. For since they saw that it was not possible to explain the existence of the universe without believing in the Existence of God, the Creator of the universe, they denied the universe's existence. They denied themselves as well. Claiming, "There is nothing that exists," they abdicated their intelligence, and saved themselves from the boundless irrationality—under the guise of rationalism—of the other deniers; in one sense they drew close to rationality.

Fourth point

As pointed out in the Tenth Word, no one with consciousness can accept that a wise master builder carefully pursues hundreds of instances of wisdom in each stone of the palace he builds, but then he fails to construct the palace's roof, allowing it to fall into ruin and thus losing all the innumerable purposes and instances of wisdom. Similarly, it is not possible for an exceptionally wise one to pursue hundreds of benefits and purposes in a tiny seed and then to allow all the expenditure they have made on the tree to go waste by obtaining a single fruit from it, thus following a completely wasteful way that is contrary to wisdom.

In just the same way, the All-Wise Maker attaches hundreds of instances of wisdom to each of the beings in the palace of the universe, and equips them with hundreds of duties, assigning every tree instances of wisdom and duties to the number of its fruits and blossoms. So, His not bringing about the Resurrection would mean rendering countless instances of wisdom and duties as meaningless, useless or fruitless and allowing them all to go to waste, thus imputing absolute impotence to His absolute, perfect Power, infinite futility and purposelessness to His perfect Wisdom, total ugliness to His absolute and perfect Beauty and Grace, and boundless injustice to His Justice. This would be paramount to simply denying the wisdom, mercy, and justice which everyone observes in the universe. This is the most bizarre inconceivability, containing endless fallacies. So, let the people of misguidance come and see just what a terrifying darkness there is in their misguidance and what kind of nest of vipers and scorpions it is, exactly as their graves will be. So, let them know that belief in the Hereafter is a way that is as beautiful and luminous as Paradise, and thus embrace belief.

Fifth point

This consists of two matters.

First matter: As a manifestation of His Name the All-Wise, the All-Majestic Maker follows the lightest way, the shortest path, the easiest fashion, the most beneficial form in everything. This shows that there is no wastefulness, futility, or absence of benefits in the nature of things. As wastefulness is contrary to the Divine Name the All-Wise, the manifestation of this Name requires economy, which is one of its fundamental principles.

O wasteful human! Know how contrarily to the truth you act by not following economy, which is one of the most basic principles in the universe! And understand what an essential, comprehensive principle is taught by the verse, *Eat and drink, but do not be wasteful* (7: 31).

Second matter: The Name the All-Wise obviously points to and necessitates the Messengership of the noblest Messenger, upon him be peace and blessings.

Indeed, since a most meaningful book requires a teacher to teach it, and an exquisite beauty requires a mirror to see and reflect itself, and a most perfect art requires a herald to announce it, certainly there will be a perfect guide, a supreme teacher among humankind, which is addressed by the mighty book of the universe, in every letter of which there are hundreds of meanings and instances of wisdom. This teacher will show and teach the sacred and true wisdom the book contains, and he will be the means of the appearance, or even the realization, of the Lord's purposes for the creation of the universe. He will also mirror and make known the perfect art of the Creator and the beauty of His Names, which He particularly wills to be displayed throughout the universe.

And since the Creator wants to make Himself loved through all His creatures and wills His conscious creatures to respond with love and worship, one from among them will certainly respond with comprehensive worship in the name of all of them in the face of the manifestations of the all-encompassing Lordship. Through a resounding manner of making known and glorification, which will bring the land and sea to ecstasy and cause the heavens and earth to reverberate, he will also turn the gazes of these conscious creatures to the Maker of all these creatures that are full of art. Again, He will turn the attention of all beings with reason to Him through a sacred instruction and teaching. The noblest Messenger, upon him be peace and blessings, did all this through the Qur'an of mighty stature, as well as demonstrating in the best way the purposes of that All-Wise Maker (for the existence of the universe and humanity). He responded in the most perfect way to the manifestations of all His instances of wisdom and of His Grace and Majesty. In short, the existence of such a one is as necessary, as essential for the universe as the existence of the sun. This being the reality, all the wisdom in the universe necessitates the Messengership of Muhammad, upon him be peace and blessings, as much as the sun necessitates light, and the light, the day.

Just as through their most comprehensive manifestations, the Name the All-Wise necessitates the Messengership of Muhammad, upon him be peace and blessings, to the maximum degree, so too, through their broadest manifestations observed in the universe, do many of the All-Beautiful Names like God, the All-Merciful, the All-Compassionate, the All-Loving, the Bestower of bounties, the All-Munificent, the All-Gracious, and the Lord necessitate the Messengership of Muhammad, upon him be peace and blessings, to the maximum degree and with absolute certainty.

For example, the all-embracing mercy which is the manifestation of the Name the All-Merciful manifests itself, first of all, through the one who was sent as "a mercy to all the worlds," upon him be peace and blessings. And God Almighty's will to make Himself known and loved as a manifestation of the Name the All-Loving gives fruit through that Beloved of the Lord of all the worlds, and finds response in him. And all instances of beauty, which are the manifestation of the Name the All-Beautiful and Gracious, that is, the beauty of the Divine Essence, the beauty of the Divine Names, the beauty of His Art, and the beauty of creatures, are seen and displayed in the mirror of Muhammad, upon him be peace and blessings. And the manifestations of the magnificence of the Lordship and sovereignty of Divinity are known, become visible and understood, and are confirmed through the Messengership of Muhammad, the herald of the dominion of Lordship, upon him be peace and blessings. And so on. Like these examples, each of the majority of the All-Beautiful Names is a shining proof for the Messengership of Muhammad, upon him be peace and blessings.

To sum up: Since the universe exists and cannot be denied, then surely, observable realities such as wisdom, munificence, mercy, beauty, order, balance, and adornment, which are in effect the colors, embellishments, lights, arts, lives, and bonds of the universe, can in no way be denied. Since denying these attributes and acts is not possible, certainly the Necessarily Existent One, the All-Wise, the All-Munificent, the All-Compassionate, the All-Beautiful and Gracious, and the All-Just, the One Who is signified by these attributes, and Who is the Performer of these deeds, and the Sun and Source of these lights, can in no way be denied. And certainly the Messengership of Muhammad, upon him be peace and blessings, who is the supreme guide, the most perfect teacher, the most eminent herald, the solver of the enigma of existence, the mirror of the Eternally Besought-of-All, the beloved of the All-Merciful, and the means of these attributes and acts being manifested, indeed of their perfection, and even of their being realized, can in no way be denied. Like the lights of the world of reality and of the reality of the universe, his Messengership is the most brilliant light of the universe.

Blessings and peace be upon him and his Family and Companions to the number of seconds of the days and the particles of the creatures.

All-Glorified are You. We have no knowledge save what You have taught us. Surely You are the All-Knowing, the All-Wise.

The fourth part
The Divine Name the All-Independent, Single One

In the Name of God, the All-Merciful, the All-Compassionate.

Say: "He—(He is) God, (Who is) the Unique One of Absolute Oneness." (112: 1)

One aspect of the meaning of the above-mentioned verse and one manifestation of the Divine Name the All-Independent, Single One, which also comprises the Names the One of Unity and the Absolutely Unique One, and is one of the Divine Names that have all-encompassing manifestations or one of the six lights of the All-Encompassing Name of God appeared to me in Eskişehir Prison in the month of Shawwal. Referring the details of Its manifestations in the broadest sense to certain other parts of the *Risale-i Nur*, we will here expound briefly in seven short Indications the Divine Unity that was manifested clearly and indubitably, which the Name the All-Independent, Single One demonstrates with Its comprehensive manifestation.

First indication

The Twenty-Second Word and the Thirty-Third Letter have demonstrated in detail that through the broadest manifestation, the Name the All-

Independent, Single One has placed a stamp of Divine Unity on the universe as a whole and on each species of creature in it, and on each individual being. Here, we will indicate only three stamps.

The first stamp: The manifestation of Divine Independence and Oneness has placed such a seal of Unity on the face of the universe that it has made it an indivisible whole. One who does not have power of control or disposal over the entire universe cannot be the true owner of any part of it. The stamp is the following:

Like the perfectly well-ordered parts of a factory, the parts and species of beings that comprise the universe help one another, and work to complete one another's functions. Through their solidarity and cooperation, and through their hastening to the aid of one another, embracing one another and being one within the other, they form such a united existence that, like the organs of the human body, they cannot be separated from one another. One who takes the reins of one part or element in their hand cannot maintain their control over it unless they take the reins of the whole of the universe.

Thus, this universal cooperation, solidarity, mutual response, and embracing one another form a most brilliant supreme stamp of Divine Unity.

The second stamp: Through the manifestation of the Name the All-Independent, Single One, such a brilliant seal of Divine Oneness and a stamp of Unity are shown on the face of the earth and the countenance of spring that it proves that one who cannot administer all the living creatures on the earth, together with all their individuals and conditions and states, and who does not know or see all of them all together, and cannot create them, cannot possibly have any part in creation. The stamp is the following:

Disregarding the most orderly, yet hidden, stamps of the mineral substances, the elements, and the inanimate creatures of the earth, consider the following stamp that is woven with the threads of hundreds of thousands of animal species and hundreds of thousands of plant species: we see with our own eyes that on earth in spring, despite having different duties and different forms, and being one within the other and all mixed up together, all things are given their sustenance and equipment without confusion or error, with complete distinction and differentiation, with extremely sensitive balance, without difficulty, at exactly the right time, from unexpected places. This situation, this planning, this administration forms such a seal of Divine Unity and stamp of Oneness that one who cannot create all these creatures at once from nothing and administer them all together can have no part at all in Lordship or creation. If they were to have a part, the all-embracing balance of administration would have been spoilt. However, humans apparently serve the fine application of these laws of Lordship by God's leave and command.

The third stamp: This stamp of Divine Oneness is on the human face. Rather, the human face itself is such a stamp of Divine Oneness that one who does not hold in their view all the human beings who have come and who will come from the time of Adam until the end of the world, and who cannot place on each face hundreds of distinguishing marks, indeed, who cannot make each face a distinguishing mark for each individual human being, can have no part at all in the creation of even a single face with its particular, distinguishing features. The One Who places the stamp in question on each individual human being's face must surely hold within His view and encompass with His Knowledge all the members of the human species. For although all faces resemble one another in respect of their basic features like eyes and ears (and all are made of the same material), they are all different and distinguishable from one another. While the fact that the faces of human beings are all alike in respect of their basic features and their structure or composition is a stamp of Unity that shows that the Maker of the human species is One, many wise differences—unlike in other species—that distinguish one individual human from another so that they should not be confused and the rights of each human being should be preserved demonstrate the Maker's absolutely free choice or will. In addition, these differences make each face a subtle stamp of Divine Unity, which shows that one who cannot create all humans and animals, indeed, the whole universe, cannot impress this stamp.

Second indication

The worlds, species, and elements of the universe are so intertwined and interrelated with one another that an agent which does not hold in possession and control the entire universe cannot have control over any of its elements. It is as though the manifestation of unity that issues from the Divine Name the

All-Independent, Single One has made the entire universe a single, unitary entity so that whatever there is in it displays the Unity of its Maker.

For example, just as the world is illuminated with a single lamp, the sun, so too the element of air that readily hastens to the aid of living beings is a single, unitary entity. Also, fire, which cooks the food of living beings, is a single, unitary entity, like the sponges of clouds that water the garden of the earth, and the rain that comes to help all living beings. In addition, most of the animal and plant species spread freely over the entire earth, and each species forms a unity, and each has the same habitat. All these and many other instances of unity decisively bear witness that, together with their habitats, all creatures are the property of a single Being.

Following this analogy, all the parts or elements of the universe that are so intertwined and interwoven have made the universe such a single, unitary entity that it cannot admit more than one Creator. An agent that cannot dominate the entire universe can in no way have a part in the creation or administration of even a single thing nor make even a single particle obey it.

Third indication

Through Its all-inclusive manifestation, the Name the All-Independent, Single One has made the universe into innumerable missives of the Eternally Besought-of-All, each of which bears as many seals of Divine Unity and stamps of Oneness as the number of its words and indicates its Scribe to the number of these stamps.

Indeed, every flower, every fruit, every grass, and even every animal and tree is a seal of Divine Oneness and stamp of His being the Eternally Besought-of-All; together with the places where they are found, which take the form of missives, they are all signatures showing the One who has inscribed that place. For example, a flower in a garden is in effect a seal of the garden's Inscriber. To Whomever the seal of the flower belongs, all flowers of that sort on the earth clearly indicate that they too are His words and that any garden where they are found is a piece of His writing. This means that each individual thing ascribes everything to the One Who has created it, thus indicating the Divine Unity in a most comprehensive way.

Fourth indication

Besides being as clear as the sun, Divine Unity that is demonstrated by the most comprehensive manifestation of the Name the All-Independent, Single One is so reasonable that it can inevitably be affirmed and accepted with infinite ease. On the other hand, association of partners with God, which is infinitely contradicted by this manifestation, is endlessly difficult to accept, unreasonable, or even inconceivable. Numerous proofs that demonstrate this reality have been explained in various parts of the *Risale-i Nur*. For the present, referring the details of these proofs to those parts, we will here expound only three Points.

The first point: We have convincingly explained with the most certain proofs briefly at the end of the Tenth and Twenty-Ninth Words and in detail at the end of the Twentieth Letter, that the creation of the greatest thing is as easy for the Power of the All-Independent, Single and Unique One as the smallest. He creates the entire spring as easily as one flower. Every spring, He invents thousands of samples of the Resurrection before our eyes. He administers a large tree as comfortably as a small piece of fruit. Whereas if referred to numerous causes or agents, each fruit becomes as intricate and difficult as a tree, and a flower as hard and troublesome as spring.

If the equipment of an army is made on the orders of a single commander in a single factory, it becomes as easy to make as the equipment of a single soldier, whereas if each set of equipment of the soldiers is made in a different factory and the army is to be administered by many commanders at the same time, then to equip each soldier will require factories to the number of the army's soldiers. In just the same way, when everything is attributed to the All-Independent, Single and Unique One, the creation and administration of innumerable members of an entire species becomes as easy as a single member. However, if attributed to causes or different ages, each becomes as difficult as the entire species.

Indeed, both unity and union are possible when everything is created and administered by the One of Unity, and when they are dependent on Him. This connection and dependence gain beings boundless power and strength, through which a small thing may perform works thousands of times greater than its individual strength. However, something very powerful in itself that does not rely on the All-Independent, Single and Unique

One may only perform small works in relation to its individual strength, and the results diminish accordingly.

For example, no matter how bold and strong he is, a soldier who does not heed the army's regulations has to carry his own ammunition and provisions by himself; he can temporarily resist against, at the most, ten enemy soldiers. For his individual power can be sufficient for that alone. But a soldier, who through regular membership in the army is connected to and enjoys the support of the commander in chief, does not have to carry his own sources of strength and provisions. His connection and the support he enjoys become an inexhaustible strength for him, like a treasury, through which he may capture a field marshal of the defeated enemy army, together with thousands of others.

That is to say, as a manifestation of Divine Unity and Divine Singleness and through the strength of the connection to the All-Independent, Single One, an ant can defeat a Pharaoh and a fly a Nimrod and a microbe a tyrant, and a seed as tiny as a chickpea can bear on its shoulders a pine tree as huge and impressive as a mountain. Indeed, by virtue of the strength and moral power he finds in the army of which he is a member, a private may achieve remarkable things in the name of the army's commander. Similarly, even though the Eternal Monarch, Who is the All-Independent and Single, suffices for everything by Himself without needing any intermediary force to be sent to the aid of His servants; if He wills to do so, He may mobilize the entire army of the universe to help one single thing. Therefore, anything in the universe can rely on a power as great as the universe, and, if need were to arise, everything could become like the All-Independent, Single Commander's power in the face of any single thing. But for the Oneness of the Divine Being, everything would lose all this strength and become as nothing, with their results being reduced to nothing also.

Thus, the emergence of all the wonderful results from the most insignificant things, which all the time we observe with our eyes, obviously demonstrates Divine Singleness and Divine Oneness. Had it not been for them, the results or fruits of everything would have only been limited to their own size and individual physical strength, and nothing would have remained of all those things around us that exist in excessive abundance and which are extremely inexpensive despite their great value. We would not have been able to obtain a melon or a pomegranate, which we now buy for a very small sum, for a fortune. Indeed, all the ease, abundance, and cheapness in the world arise from Divine Unity and testify to Divine Singleness.

The second point: Beings are given existence in two ways; one is through creation from nothing, called "origination" or "invention," and other is the giving of existence by bringing together existent elements and things, called "composition" or "formation." The Unity and Singleness of the One Who creates makes the act of giving existence infinitely easy—so easy as to make it necessary and inevitable. If it had been otherwise, if there had been more than one Creator, the existence of things would have been inconceivable, impossible, and unreasonable. The fact that things and beings in the universe come into existence with infinite ease and in perfect form, self-evidently demonstrates the manifestation of Divine Singleness and proves that everything is directly the art of the All-Independent, Single One of Majesty.

Indeed, the All-Independent, Single One of Unity appoints for each thing a certain measure like an immaterial mold through His all-encompassing Knowledge, and creates through His boundless Power, the immensity of Which is perceived through Its works, as if striking a match. The particles of all things are situated easily in the mold that is existent in the mirror of His Knowledge, according to the form determined by Destiny, and they preserve their positions in good order. Even if it is required to gather together particles from round about, the particles move in strict accordance with the comprehensive principles of the Power Which set them to move and control them and the laws of Knowledge. Therefore, like the soldiers of an obedient army, they come in a regular fashion and enter the mould which Divine Destiny has determined for the thing for which they have already been appointed, forming its body. Like the reflection in the mirror of a camera being developed on paper, and thus clothed in external existence, or a letter written in invisible letters appearing when a special substance is applied, with the greatest ease, Power clothes with external existence the natures or forms of things that exist in the mirror of the All-Independent, Single One of Unity's eternal Knowledge. By clothing them with external existence, Power transfers them from the World of Meaning to the World of Emergence, and shows them to us.

If beings are not attributed to the All-Independent, Single One of Unity, it would be necessary to collect all the particles to form a fly's body from all around the earth and the universal elements—quite simply, it would be necessary to sift the face of the earth and the elements to collect all the particles to form its body so full of art, and situate them in proper order in the mold of its body. This would require the existence of physical molds to the number of the members of the fly's body and drawing its fine, subtle, immaterial faculties like the spirit from the immaterial worlds in a particular measure.

Thus, the creation of a fly in this way would be as difficult as that of the universe; rather, completely impossible and inconceivable. For all the people of religion and science are agreed that nothing apart from the All-Independent, Single One can create from nothing. When referred to causes and nature, the existence of each individual thing would require controlling or mastery over the entire universe, with all its material and immaterial realms.

The third point: We will explain briefly two or three comparisons which were mentioned in other parts of the *Risale-i Nur* to demonstrate how, if attributed to an All-Independent, Single One of Unity, all things become as easy as a single thing, while if ascribed to causes and nature, the existence of a single thing becomes as difficult as that of all things.

For example, if the administration of a private is referred to ten officers, it will be ten times more difficult than commanding a battalion. For those who command him will form obstacles to one another, and the ensuing disorder will cause the soldier to have no peace. However, if the result and situation expected of a battalion is referred to a single officer, he can achieve the result and the situation easily. If that result and situation are expected of soldiers who form a battalion without a commander, the desired result and situation can only be achieved with much dispute and difficulty, and in great disorder.

A *second comparison:* For example, if a master builder is appointed to build the dome of a mosque like Ayasofya (Haghia Sophia) by arranging its stones, he can do it easily. But if it is referred to the stones themselves, they will all have to be both absolutely dominant over each other as well as dominated by one another so that they can support each other and stand in a suspended position. This would become a task a hundred times greater than that which a hundred master builders could perform.

A *third comparison:* For example, since the earth is an official, a soldier, of the All-Independent, Single One of Unity, which obeys that single One's command in great rejoicing with two movements of revolution like an ecstatic Mawlawi (Mevlevi) dervish, magnificent results like the change of the seasons, the alternation of day and night, and the lofty, majestic motions and movie-scene-like changes in the heavens are obtained most easily, regularly, and in a most orderly way. It is as though that single soldier is commanding magnificent maneuvers in the universe.

If not attributed to an All-Independent, Single One Whose rule of Divinity and sovereignty of Lordship encompass the entire universe, and whose command and rule dominate all beings, these results—these heavenly maneuvers, earthly seasons, and daily changes—could only be obtained by millions of stars and spheres a thousand times larger than the earth traveling the long distance of millions of years every twenty-four hours and every year.

Thus, the achievement of these majestic results through the two Mawlawi-like motions of a single official—the earth—on its axis and in its orbit, is an example that shows the infinite ease in Divine Unity. It also demonstrates what falsities and impossibilities are entailed by unbelief and association of partners with God, which would require endlessly long and millions of times more difficult ways to obtain the same results.

Consider this comparison as well in order to see the ignorance of those who adore causes and nature: an exceptionally skilled person makes and prepares perfectly the parts or machinery of an extraordinary factory, or a wonderful clock, or a magnificent palace, or a perfectly fine book. Then, without assembling the parts easily and setting them to work by himself, he incurs great expense and makes each part, each mechanism, and each sheet of paper and pen into extraordinary machines merely to construct the factory, palace, and the clock, and to write the book. Thus, he refers to them his exceptional art, skills, and mastery, which he has a great desire to display. You will understand how unreasonable and what ignorance such a supposition is.

In just the same way, those who ascribe creation to causes and nature fall into ignorance much greater than that displayed in this supposition. For nature and causes or apparent agents themselves are, like other creatures, extraordinarily well-ordered works of art. The one who makes them thus produces their results too, and displays them together. The one who makes the seed, also makes the tree over it; and the one who makes the tree, is the one who makes the fruit on it. Otherwise, for other, different natures and causes or apparent agents to come into existence, further well-ordered natures and causes would be necessary. And so on, *ad infinitum*. One would have to accept the actual existence of an infinite, meaningless, impossible chain of illusory fancies. This would be the most eccentric type of ignorance.

Fifth indication

With decisive proofs we have demonstrated in many places of the *Risale-i Nur* that the most essential characteristic of sovereignty is independence and the rejection of partnership. Even the weak shadow of sovereignty enjoyed by impotent humans vehemently rejects the interference of others so that it can preserve its independence. This rejection of interference has led many kings mercilessly to put to death their innocent children and beloved brothers. This means that the most basic, indispensable characteristic of sovereignty is independence and the rejection of interference by others.

It is because of this most basic characteristic that Divine sovereignty, which is at the degree of absolute Lordship over the whole creation, absolutely rejects partnership and interference by others, and that the Qur'an of miraculous exposition insistently and sternly points out and stresses the affirmation of Divine Unity, rejecting with severe threats the association of partners with God.

Thus, the Divine sovereignty of Lordship both absolutely requires Divine Unity and most clearly and decisively explains a most powerful and necessitating cause for it. Also, the infinitely perfect order and harmony in the universe, most clearly apparent and observable, from its totality down to the stars, animals, and minerals, from these down to the particulars, individuals, and minute particles, are an indubitably truthful witness to and a clear, profound proof of that Oneness and Unity. For, were there interference by others, this most sensitive balance, order, and regularity of the universe would have been spoilt and signs of disorder would have been apparent. As stated in the verse,

> *But the fact is that had there been in the heavens and the earth any deities other than God, both (of those realms) would certainly have fallen into ruin* (21: 22),

if this were the case, the wonderful, perfect order of the universe would have been destroyed. Whereas as declared in the verse,

> *Look yet again: can you see any rifts?* (67: 3),

from minute particles to the planets, from the ground to the Divine Supreme Throne, there is no sign of fault, defect, or confusion. Thus, the order, balance, proportion, and regularity throughout the universe, with whatever is in it, demonstrate most brilliantly the all-encompassing manifestation of the Name the All-Independent, Single One and testify to Divine Unity.

Moreover, due to the concentrated manifestations on each creature of certain Names of the All-Independent, Single One, the tiniest living creature is a miniature sample of the universe and a small index of it. Therefore, the One Who owns it can be only He in Whose Power the whole universe is grasped. And since, in respect to creation, a seed is not inferior to a tree, and a tree is a small universe, and all living beings too are like small universes or small worlds, the above-mentioned Divine manifestation has made partnership with God impossible. Since through this manifestation the universe is not only an indivisible whole, but also, in respect of its nature, is a whole that rejects the interference of more than one hand, each part of it represents the whole, and the whole of it is a single entity which makes the participation of multiple hands impossible. Together with this concentrated manifestation of certain Divine Names on each creature, the all-encompassing manifestation of the Name the All-Independent, Single One self-evidently proves Divine Oneness.

Indeed, the fact that the realms and species of beings in the universe are interwoven and intertwined, and the duties of each are related to the entire duty of the universe makes the universe an indivisible whole in respect of Divine Lordship and creation. Similarly, the all-encompassing Divine acts in the universe operate one within the other. That is, for example, within the act of giving life, the acts of providing and maintaining manifest themselves at the same instant. And the acts of ordering and decorating the bodies of living creatures are observed at the same instant as the acts of giving life and providing manifest themselves. And together with these acts of giving life, providing, ordering, and decorating, the acts of giving form, raising, and caring strike the eye. And so on. Since such all-encompassing Divine acts are interwoven and intertwined, displaying an overall, united manifestation that resembles the seven colors of the prism being manifested as white, and as each of these acts encompasses most things and beings in a way that exhibits the same nature, and as each of them belongs to the same Being, and pervades the whole universe and unites them with the other acts in cooperation—it is because of these characteristics of Divine acts that the universe is an indivisible whole, with each living creature in it being like a seed, index, or sample, and the universe rejects the existence of more than one Lord over it. That is to say, the universe is such a totality that to be the Lord of a part of it is only possible by being the Lord of the whole. It is such a whole entity that making any one single member of it submit to any lordship over it is only possible by subjugating it as a whole.

Sixth indication

As the Oneness of Lordship and the Unity of Divinity are the means and basis of all perfections,[149] and the source and origin of the purposes for and wisdom in the universe's creation, so too are they the source and sole means for conscious beings and particularly for human beings to attain their desires and expectations. But for the Oneness of Divine Lordship, all human desires and expectations would be extinguished. Also, the results of the universe's creation would not have been realized and the majority of perfections which either exist or are certain to exist would have been annihilated.

For example, humanity has an intense, passionate desire for eternity. Only One Who on account of His Oneness holds the whole universe in His grasp and Who can close down this world and open up the Hereafter as easily as closing down one house and opening up another can fulfill that desire. And like this desire, humanity's thousands of other desires which extend to eternity and are spread throughout the universe depend on the realization of Divine Singleness and Unity. If it were not for the All-Independent, Single One Who has absolute control over the entire universe, these desires would not be fulfilled. And even supposing they were to be fulfilled, they would not be fulfilled in a sufficient manner.

---

149 Indeed, the unity of creation as the result of Divine Unity is the clearest, most powerful evidence for endless Divine Perfections and Beauty to be manifested and known. For the recognition of the universe's Maker as the Unique One of Unity is the means of all the perfections and beauties in the universe being known as the shadows, manifestations, and signs of His sacred Perfections and Beauty. Otherwise, the perfections and beauties of the universe would be attributed to the creatures and causes themselves, and the eternal treasury of Divine Perfections would be without a key to be discovered and therefore would remain unknown to the human mind.

It is because of this mighty reality that, just as the Qur'an of miraculous exposition teaches Divine Unity and Oneness repeatedly and fervently and with lofty eloquence, so too do all the Prophets, purified, saintly scholars, and saints find all their greatest pleasure and happiness in the Oneness of God.

Seventh indication

Since the Messengership of Muhammad, upon him be peace and blessings, taught, proved, and proclaimed perfectly the true affirmation of Divine Unity in all its degrees, his Messengership must be as certain as Divine Unity. For all the arguments that prove Divine Unity decisively prove his Messengership, the authenticity of his mission, and the rightness of his cause. Indeed, a Messengership which encompasses thousands of elevated truths, and truly discovers and teaches Divine Oneness and Unity is most definitely required by such a Singleness and Unity.

Thus, out of numerous proofs that establish the unparalleled importance and sublimity of the collective personality of Muhammad, upon him be peace and blessings, proving that he is the Sun of the Universe, we will point out the following three:

The first: In accordance with the rule, "The cause is like the doer," all the good deeds which have so far been performed and will be performed in the future by his Community are also recorded in the book of the good deeds of Muhammad, upon him be peace and blessings. In addition, the fact that since the calling of God's blessings and peace upon the Prophet Muhammad by his Community, which is something performed every day, is certainly accepted, the station and degree that these endless prayers necessitate show what kind of a Sun in the universe is the collective personality of Muhammad, upon him be peace and blessings.

The second: Consider the extraordinary capacity and potential of the essence of Muhammad, upon him be peace and blessings, which is the origin, seed, life, and means of the mighty tree of the world of Islam, and his spiritual progress that has been contributed to by his sacred worship, recitations, and glorifications which he does the best of all and which form the spiritual aspect of the world of Islam. Understand from this how much more elevated than other sainthoods was the sainthood of Muhammad's servanthood to God, by which he rose to the degree of being the beloved of God.

At one time, a single glorification unfolded to me in one of my Prayers that was close to how the Companions of the Prophet perceived it; this appeared to me as important as a month's worship. I understood from this the Companions' great worth. This means that at the start of Islam, the spiritual gifts and light originating from the sacred words of worship had a different quality. On account of their freshness, they had a different flavor, subtlety, and pleasure, which with the passage of time became hidden, diminished, and obscured under the veil of heedlessness. For the Prophet Muhammad, upon him be peace and blessings, received them with his extraordinary capacity, new and fresh from their original source, the Most Pure and Holy One, and absorbed and assimilated them. As a consequence, he could receive as much radiation from a single glorification as others could receive from an entire year of worship, with all its acts and dimensions.

Thus, from this perspective one can understand to what degree the Prophet Muhammad, upon him be peace and blessings, has progressed through the limitless ranks of perfections.

The third: Humankind is the pivot of all the purposes of the Creator for the existence of the universe, and the most intelligent of the audiences to whom the speeches of the All-Glorious One are addressed. Since through his accomplishments and works the Prophet Muhammad, upon him be peace and blessings, is the most renowned, most perfect, and most magnificent member of humanity, the All-Independent, Single One of Majesty took him as His addressee in the name of all humankind, indeed, of the entire universe, enabling him to receive His endless gifts and spiritual radiations through the ranks of limitless perfection.

Thus, there are numerous other points like these three that prove decisively that, just as the collective personality of Muhammad, upon him be peace and blessings, is the spiritual Sun of the universe, so too is he the supreme sign of the mighty Qur'an that is called the universe, and of the Greatest Name of that Supreme Distinguisher between truth and falsehood—the Qur'an—and the mirror of the most comprehensive manifestation of the Divine Name the All-Independent, Single One. And we beseech the All-Independent, Single, Unique, Eternally Besought One that blessings and peace to the total number of all the particles of the universe, multiplied by all the seconds of all the minutes of all time, descend upon Prophet Muhammad, upon him be peace and blessings, from His infinite treasury of Mercy.

> All-Glorified are You. We have no knowledge save what You have taught us. Surely You are the All-Knowing, the All-Wise.

The fifth part
The Divine Name the All-Living

In the Name of God, the All-Merciful, the All-Compassionate.

> *Look, then, at the imprints of God's Mercy—how He revives the dead earth after its death: certainly then it is He Who will revive the dead (in a similar way). He has full power over everything.* (30: 50)

One aspect of the meaning of the above-mentioned glorious verse, together with one from the following glorious verse,

> *God, there is no deity but He; the All-Living, the Self-Subsisting (by Whom all subsist). Slumber does not seize Him, nor sleep* (2: 255),

and one manifestation of the Divine Name the All-Living, which is one of the Divine Names that have all-encompassing manifestations or one of the six lights of the All-Encompassing Name of God, appeared to my mind from afar in the month of Shawwal while in Eskişehir Prison. It was not recorded at that time; we could not capture that sacred bird. Now, after it has faded into the distance, by way of a number of signs we will at least briefly indicate a few rays of that supreme truth and light.

The first sign

Life is a comprehensive manifestation of the Divine Names the All-Living and Giver of Life. What follows is an index-like answer to the questions "What is life?" and "What is life's true nature and purpose?"

Life is:

- the most important aim of the universe, and
- its greatest result, and
- its most brilliant light, and

- its subtlest and most pleasant leaven, and
- a pure extract distilled from it, and
- its most perfect fruit, and
- its most elevated perfection, and
- its most beautiful countenance, and
- its most beautiful adornment, and
- the secret of its unitary nature, and
- the bond of its unity, and
- the source of its perfections, and
- something that has spirit and which is most extraordinary in respect of art and nature, and
- a miraculous reality that makes the tiniest creature like a universe, and
- a miracle of Divine Power which, as though serving as the means of the universe being situated in a tiny living creature, shows in that creature some sort of index of the huge universe, and connects the creature to other things and beings; and
- it is a wonderful Divine art which makes a tiny part as great as the whole and some part of a whole represent the whole itself, showing that in respect of the Lordship over it the universe is an indivisible whole or a universal entity interconnected with all its parts and which allows no participation; and
- life is the most brilliant, the most decisive, the most perfect of proofs testifying to the necessary Existence and Oneness of the All-Living and Self-Subsistent One; and
- among Divine works of art life is both the most hidden and the most apparent, and the most valuable and the most inexpensive, and it is the purest, most shining, and most meaningful embroidery of the Lord's Art; and
- life is a graceful, refined, delicate manifestation of the Mercy of the All-Merciful which makes other beings serve itself; and
- it is a most comprehensive mirror of the essential Qualities that are indispensable to His Essence; and
- it is a wonder of the Lord's creation that comprises the manifestations of numerous All-Beautiful Names, such as the All-Merciful,

the All-Providing, the All-Compassionate, the All-Munificent, and the All-Wise, subjecting to itself many realities like provision, wisdom, grace, and mercy, and it is the source and origin of all the senses like sight, hearing, and touch; and

- life is such a transformation machine in the vast workshop of the universe that it continuously cleans and purifies everywhere, allowing progress and illuminating. And it makes living bodies, which are its dwellings, guesthouses, schools, or barracks for the caravans of atoms so that they may be refined and brought up to perform their duties. Quite simply, through the machine of life, the All-Living One, the Giver of Life, beautifies, makes pleasant, and illumines this dark, transient, lowly world, and gives it a sort of permanence, preparing it to go to another, everlasting world; and
- both of the two faces of life, that is, both its outer and inner faces, are bright, sublime, and unsoiled and without defect. It is an exceptional creature in the creation of which the direct operation of the Divine Power has not been veiled by physical causes, so that it can clearly be shown that it has emerged directly without veil or means from the hand of the Lord's Power; and
- the reality of life relates to the six pillars of belief, supporting them in meaning and indirectly. That is to say, it is a luminous reality which relates to and proves the absolutely necessary, eternal existence of the Necessarily Existent One, the Hereafter and eternal life, and the existence of angels, and other pillars of belief;
- also, just as life is the purest essence of the universe, distilled from all of it, so too is it a mighty mystery generating thanksgiving, worship, praise, and love, which are the most important Divine purposes for the existence of the universe and the most important results of the world's creation.

So consider all these significant, valuable merits and properties and these elevated, comprehensive duties of life, and then look and see the magnificence of the Name the All-Living behind the Name the Giver of Life. And understand from these immense properties and fruits of life how comprehensive a Divine Name is the Name the All-Living.

Also understand that since life is the greatest result of the universe, as well as its most comprehensive aim and most valuable fruit, it must have a great aim and result as vast as the universe. For as the tree's result is its fruit, the fruit's result, too, by means of the seed, is a future tree. Indeed, just as the aim and result of this life is eternal life, so too, one of its fruits is thanksgiving to the One All-Living and Giver of Life and worship and praise of Him and love for Him. And just as this thanksgiving, love, praise, and worship are the fruit of life, so too are they the aim of the universe. Understand from this what ugly ignorance and what a blasphemous manner, paramount to unbelief, lies in the claim of those who say that the aim of life is to live comfortably, enjoy oneself heedlessly, and indulge oneself in pleasure, degrading and insulting the most valuable bounty of life, the gift of consciousness, and the bounty of reason; what appalling ingratitude they display.

The second sign

To explain all the degrees, attributes, and duties of life, a most comprehensive manifestation of the Names the All-Living and Giver of Life, and which is mentioned in the First Sign, would require as many treatises as those attributes. However, since some of them have been explained in various parts of the *Risale-i Nur*, we will indicate only a few here.

Both of the two faces of life—physical or corporeal and metaphysical or spiritual—are transparent and free of dirt, for the Lord's Power has not employed physical causes in its creation. The meaning of this property of life is as follows:

Indeed, there is good and beauty in everything in the universe, while evil and ugliness are very minor and function as units of measurement that show the degrees of good and beauty and how multiple are the truths they contain. In this way, evil becomes goodness and ugliness, beauty. But, so that the complaints and resentment that may arise from whatever seems to the superficial view of conscious beings to be ugly, evil, or disastrous should not be directed against the All-Living and Self-Subsistent One, and so that the direct contact of sacred, pure Divine Power with apparently vile and filthy things should not offend the dignity of Power, apparent causes have been made a veil to these operations of Power. The causes are absolutely unable to create, but they exist to serve as the target for unjust complaints and objections that may emanate from conscious beings, and preserve the dignity, sacredness, and unblemished nature of Divine Power.

As explained in the Introduction to the Second Station of the Twenty-Second Word, the Archangel Azra'il, upon him be peace, prayed to God Almighty about his duty of taking out the spirits of the dying. He said, "Your servants will be resentful of me." It was said to him in reply, "I will place the veil of illness and disaster between your duty and the dying, and they will fling their arrows of complaint and objection at those veils, not at you."

Just as the duty of Azra'il, upon him be peace, is to function as a veil between God Almighty and death so that the resentment and complaints of those who do not see the beauty in death for the people of belief and do not realize the manifestation of mercy in it are not directed against the All-Living and Self-Subsistent One, so also do other causes act as veils. *Indeed, God's Dignity and Grandeur require apparent causes to be veils to the Hand of Power in the view of the mind, while Divine Unity and Majesty demand that causes draw back their hands from the effect.*

However, since both the outer and inner faces of life are free from dirt, defect, or fault, and since life contains neither anything to invite complaints or objections, nor any filth or ugliness that is contrary to the dignity and sacredness of Divine Power, it has directly been submitted to the hand of the Names the Giver of Life and the Reviver of the All-Living and Self-Subsistent One. Light is the same as life, and so are existence and the giving of existence. For this reason, creation and the giving of existence depend directly on the Power of the All-Majestic One. Moreover, as rain is a sort of life and mercy, the time of its descent has not been made subject to a regular law, so that whenever need arises, hands will be raised to the Divine Court to beseech mercy. If, like the rising of the sun, rain is subject to a law, that vital bounty would not have been sought through praying at times of need.

The third sign

It was said in the last property of life that in the same way that the result of the universe is life, thanksgiving and worship are the results of life, the cause and ultimate reason for the creation of the universe, and its desired result.

Indeed, the All-Living and Self-Subsistent Maker of the universe certainly wants thanks and love from living creatures in return for His making Himself known and loved through such boundless varieties of bounties of His; He demands their praise and laudation in return for His precious arts and their worship and obedience in response to His commands as their Lord.

And so, since the thanksgiving and worship required by Divine Lordship are the most important purpose of all sorts of life and therefore of the whole universe, the Qur'an of miraculous exposition urges thanks and worship with fervor, intensity, and sweetness. And it repeatedly states that worship is for God exclusively, and thanks and praise are due only to Him. It is in order to state that this thanks and praise must go directly to their True Owner that verses like,

> *He it is Who gives life and causes to die, and the alternation of night and day* (23: 80); *He it is Who gives life and causes to die; and When He decrees a thing to be, He does but say to it "Be!" and it is* (40: 68); .... *and revives with it (rain) the earth after its death* (30: 24),

explicitly reject intermediaries and attribute life directly and exclusively to the All-Living and Self-Subsistent One's hand of Power. Also, the verses,

> *Surely God—it is He Who is the All-Providing, Lord of all might, and the All-Forceful* (51: 58); *And Who, when I fall ill, heals me* (26: 80); *He it is Who sends down the rain, useful in all ways, after they have lost all hope* (42: 28),

show that things like provisions, healing, and rain, which after life are the means of thanksgiving and gratitude and which provoke a feeling of love and praise, are exclusively particular to the All-Providing, the All-Healing, and to the Power of the All-Living, Self-Subsistent One. With restrictive expressions such as *It is He Who*, and *He it is Who*, they state that provision, healing, and rain come directly from Him without a veil. It is the True Healer alone Who gives medicines their properties and creates their effects.

The fourth sign

It was also stated among the properties of life that life relates to the six pillars of belief and that it offers proof for them.

Indeed, since the most important result and fruit of the universe and the purpose of its creation is life, certainly that elevated reality cannot be restricted to this fleeting, brief, deficient, painful worldly life. The aim of the tree of life, the immensity of which is understood through the properties mentioned—its fruit that is worthy of its tremendousness—is rather eternal life or the life of the Hereafter; it is the life in the realm of eternal, perfect happiness, the very stones, trees, and earth of which are alive. Or else, the tree of life, equipped with numerous significant members, would be without fruit, benefit, purpose, or any reality for conscious beings, including, in particular, humanity. Humanity, which in respect of its capital and faculties is, say, twenty times greater than a sparrow, and which is the most exalted and important creature in the universe, would fall twenty times lower than a sparrow with regard to the happiness of life, and become the most unhappy, the most debased of wretches. Furthermore, through preoccupation with the pains of the past and fears of the future, reason, the most precious of bounties, would continuously wound the human heart; because it muddies a single pleasure with nine pains, it would become the most calamitous affliction. So, the claim that there is no eternal life is a manifold falsehood. As a result, the life of this world, which every spring displays before our eyes hundreds of thousands of examples of the Resurrection, proves decisively the pillar of belief in the Hereafter.

Is it at all possible that the All-Powerful Disposer of Affairs, Who prepares with wisdom, grace, and mercy in your body, garden and country all the things and members that are necessary for your life, and makes them reach you just in time, Who knows and hears even the particular prayer for food offered by your stomach through its desire for maintenance, and Who shows that He accepts its prayer by gratifying it with innumerable delicious foods—is it at all possible that He does not see you or know you, or that He does not prepare all that is necessary for eternal life, humankind's greatest goal, or that He does not accept humankind's most urgent, important, general, and most necessary and proper prayers for eternity by not constructing the Hereafter and creating Paradise, or that He does not hold humankind, the ruler and result of the earth, as important as the stomach, that He ignores its most powerful, general prayer, which reverberates from the ground to the Divine Throne, thus causing His perfect Wisdom and endless Mercy to be denied? God forbid, a hundred thousand times, God forbid!

And is it at all possible that He should hear the most secret voice of the tiniest living creature, heed its plea, answer its need, nourish it with perfect care and concern, and cause even His large creatures to serve it, but should not hear the thunderous voice of the greatest, most valuable, immortal, and most delicate "life"? Is it possible that He does not take into consideration its extremely important plea and prayer for eternity? Is it possible that He should equip and maintain a mere soldier with the greatest care while ignoring a magnificent, obedient army? Is it possible that He should see an atom and not see the sun? Is it possible that He should hear the buzzing of a mosquito and not hear the roar of thunder? God forbid! A hundred thousand times, God forbid!

And could reason in any way accept that an All-Powerful and All-Wise One Who is infinitely merciful, loving, and affectionate, and Who greatly loves His own Art and makes Himself much loved and loves greatly those who love Him, would condemn to eternal non-existence both the life, which loves Him more than anything else and is lovable and loved and by nature adores its Maker, and the spirit, the essence and substance of life; thus making that beloved friend of His resentful of Himself for all eternity, and wounding them in such terrible fashion that He both denies and causes to be denied the mystery of His Mercy and the light of His Love? A hundred thousand times, God forbid! The absolute Grace and Beauty Which adorns the universe with its manifestation and the absolute Mercy Which makes happy all creatures are most certainly free of such infinite ugliness; they are absolutely exalted above such complete wrong and mercilessness.

Conclusion: Since there is life in this world, certainly those who understand the mystery of life and do not misuse their lives will be favored with eternal life in the abode of eternal permanence and everlasting Paradise. In this we believe!

Transparent objects on the earth shine with the sun's reflections, and bubbles on the surface of the sea and rivers glisten and die away with gleams of light, while the bubbles that follow on after them act again as mirrors that reflect miniature suns. This obviously shows that those gleams, those reflected suns in transparent objects and bubbles are the reflected images of a single sun high above. They sing the sun's existence with a myriad of voices, and point to it with their fingers of light.

In just the same way, through the all-comprehensive manifestation of the All-Living and Self-Subsistent One's Name of the Giver of Life, the living creatures shine on the earth and in the sea through Divine Power, and then in order to make way for those to follow, utter, "O Living One!", disappearing under the veil of the Unseen, thus indicating and testifying to the eternal Life and necessary Existence of the eternally All-Living and Self-Subsistent One. Likewise, all the evidence that bears witness to the Divine Knowledge Which the order of the universe manifests, and all the proofs that demonstrate the Divine Power Which controls the entire universe, all the realities that establish the Divine Will Which directs the universe, all the signs and miracles which prove the Prophetic missions as the channels of the Divine Speech and Revelations, and all the evidence that testifies to the seven Attributes of God Almighty—all these unanimously indicate and bear witness to the Life of the All-Living, Self-Subsistent One. For something having sight is certain to have life, hearing is a sign of life, speaking indicates the existence of life, and will or free choice demonstrates life. Thus, all-encompassing Attributes such as absolute Power, all-inclusive Will, and all-embracing Knowledge, the existence of Which is evidently demonstrated by their work in the universe, together with all the evidence that establishes their existence, bear witness to the necessary existence of the All-Living, Self-Subsistent One and testify to His perpetual Life Which illuminates the whole universe with just one of Its shadows, giving life to the entire realm of the Hereafter with all its particles with just one manifestation.

Life also relates to belief in the angels, and proves this belief indirectly. As the most important result in the universe is life, as living creatures are the most widelyspread and most abundantly created beings because of their value, as they cheer the guesthouse of the earth with their caravans that arrive and depart one after the other, as the earth has been filled with so many varieties of living creatures and is continually being emptied and refilled owing to the Divine purposes for their constant renewal and multiplication, as even rotting and corrupt substances become the media of the creation of numerous kinds of creatures, allowing the earth to become a place through which innumerable microorganisms swarm, and as consciousness and intelligence, which are the purest extracts of life distilled from life, and spirit, its most subtle and stable essence, are created in great abundance on the earth, with the result that the earth is revived with life, intelligence, consciousness, and spirits—because of all these it is not possible that the heavens, which are more refined and more spacious than the earth, should be left without life and consciousness. It is due to the meaning and purpose of life that there must be living, conscious beings who inhabit the heavens, suns, and stars particular to each. This displays the result of the creation of the heavens, showing them to be alive and receiving Divine addresses. These beings are the angels.

The essential nature of life also relates to the pillar of belief in the Prophets, and proves it indirectly. Indeed, since the universe has been created to yield life, and since life is the greatest manifestation of the Eternal All-Living and Self-Subsistent One, as well as the most perfect embroidery of His and His most beautiful work of Art, and since the everlasting life demonstrates itself and is known through the sending of the Messengers and the revelation of the Divine Scriptures, and since speech shows that the one who speaks is alive—all these illustrate that it is the Prophets and the Divine Scriptures that were sent through them that have made known the speeches of the One Who speaks, orders, and prohibits from beyond the realm of the Unseen veiled by the corporeal universe. Just as the life in the universe most certainly testifies to the necessary Existence of the Eternally Living One, so too does it also relate to pillars of the sending of the Prophets and the revelation of the Scriptures, which are rays, manifestations, and communications of that eternal life, and so too does it prove them allusively. In particular, the Messengership of Muhammad, upon him be peace and blessings, and the revelation of the Qur'an—since they are like the "spirit" and intelligence of life—can be said to be as certainly true as the existence of life.

Indeed, just as life is a pure extract distilled from the universe, just as consciousness and sense perception are extracts distilled from life, and intelligence is an extract distilled from consciousness and sense perception, and spirit is the pure essence of life—indeed, it is life itself, stable and autonomous—so too is the physical and spiritual life of Muhammad, upon him be peace and blessings, the most refined extract distilled from the life and spirit of the universe. The Messengership of Muhammad, upon him be peace and blessings, is the purest extract distilled from the sense perception, consciousness, and intelligence of the universe. Indeed, as testified to by his works, accomplishments, and legacy, the physical and spiritual life of Muhammad, upon him be peace and blessings, the very life of the universe's life, and his Messengership are the light and very consciousness of the universe's consciousness. And the revelation of the Qur'an, as borne witness to by its truths, all of which are ever-alive, is the spirit of the universe's life and the intelligence of its consciousness.

If the light of Muhammad's Messengership, upon him be peace and blessings, one day leaves the universe, the universe will die; and if the Qur'an leaves it, the universe will go mad and the earth will lose its reason and strike its then unconscious head on a planet, causing the destruction of the world.

Life also relates to the pillar of belief in Divine Destiny and proves it allusively. This is because, as life is the light of the physical, visible world throughout which it permeates, and as it is the result of the aim of existence, and since it is the most comprehensive mirror to the Creator of the universe and the most perfect epitome and index of the acts of Divine Lordship, and—if we may say so—is like some sort of program for these acts, then certainly, life necessitates that the creatures in the worlds of the seen and Unseen, that is, in the past and in the future, should be identified in an order known and predisposed to obey the rules of God Almighty's creation and operation in the universe.

The original seed of a tree and its roots, as well as the seeds of its fruit, are all alive, just like the tree is itself as a whole entity; indeed, they follow the laws of life more subtly than does the tree. Similarly, the seeds and roots left by the last autumn, as well as the seeds and roots that will be left to future springs after this spring has ended—they all have life, just like spring, and are subject to the laws of life. In just the same way, the branches and twigs of the tree of the universe each has a past and a future. They have a chain of existence that consists of their past and future states and stages. The various, multiple existences and states of each species and each member of each species, which are contained in Divine Knowledge, form a chain of existences pertaining to or recorded in that Knowledge. Just like their external existence, their existence which exists in Divine Knowledge bears a ray of immaterial life from the universal, all-encompassing Life. All the states and stages of their material life occur according to these tablets of Divine Destiny, which are all alive.

The fact that the world of spirits, one form of the World of the Unseen, is full of spirits, which are life itself or the essences or substances of life, certainly requires that the past and future—which are another form of the World of the Unseen and its second section—should also be favored with some sort of life. Furthermore, the perfect order, the meaningful arrangement, and the living fruits and stages that are inherent in the existence of a thing in God's Knowledge also demonstrate that that thing has a sort of life in Knowledge. As the life in Knowledge is a light from the Sun of the Eternal Life, life cannot be restricted to the visible or physical world, this present time, or the observed, external existence. Rather, each world receives a manifestation from that light in accordance with its capacity, and the universe is alive and illuminated through it with all its worlds. Otherwise, as the misguided imagine, with the exception of this apparent, temporary (physical) life, each world would have been a vast and terrible corpse, a dark ruin.

Thus, the pillar of "belief in Divine Destiny and Decree" is understood in a broad sense through the mystery of life and is established by it. That is, the orderliness of the visible world with whatever is in it and the results it produces manifest its life and vitality. Similarly, belonging to the World of the Unseen, the creatures of both the past and the future (which clearly indicate orderliness in their arriving in and departing from the world and through their worldly lives) have an immaterial living existence and an immaterial presence in God Almighty's Knowledge. The trace of this life and presence is manifested and observed by means of the Tablet of Destiny and Decree and through all the stages of their worldly lives.

The fifth sign

Also, it was said concerning the sixteenth property of life mentioned in the First Sign above that when life enters a thing, it makes it like a world; if it is a part, it makes it like a whole, if it is something of a particular nature that belongs to an indivisible whole, it gives it the comprehensiveness of that whole.

Indeed, life is of such a nature that it is a comprehensive mirror that reflects God's Oneness on particular things in the concentrated manifestations of many of His Names. When life enters a body, it makes it a small world; it becomes some sort of seed of the tree of the universe, containing its compacted content, (like the contents page of a book). Therefore, just as a seed can only be the work of a Power able to make the tree that bears it, so too, the One Who creates the tiniest living being is certainly the Creator of the whole universe.

Thus, through such comprehensiveness, life demonstrates in itself a most subtle mystery of Divine Oneness. That is, like the huge sun that is present through its light, reflection, and seven colors in every drop of water and fragment of glass that faces it, so too are the Divine Names and Attributes, Which encompass the universe, manifested together in each living being. From this point of view, in regard to the creation and Lordship over it, life makes the universe into an indivisible whole, indeed, a single, whole entity, all parts of which are indivisibly interconnected with both one another and the universe itself.

Indeed, the stamp He has placed on your face obviously shows that the One Who created you is the One Who creates all humankind. For all of humanity is of the same essential nature. Also, by means of life, the parts of the universe are like the individual members of humankind, and the universe, like humankind itself. As the universe displays the stamp of Divine Oneness in it as a whole, it also shows the stamp of God's Oneness and His being the Eternally Besought-of-All on each of its individual parts, thus negating and falsifying the association of partners with God in all aspects and kinds.

Also, the Art of Divine Lordship has such extraordinarily wonderful miracles in life that a power which cannot create the whole universe cannot create even the tiniest living creature. Indeed, like writing the entire Qur'an on a chickpea, only a pen that inscribes in a tiny seed the summarized and compact content of the huge pine tree and its future life in all its stages can surely be the Pen Which has inscribed the heavens and the stars. And only the one who places in the tiny head of a honeybee the ability and faculties to recognize the flowers in the garden of the universe, to build relations with most of its elements, to convey a gift of Divine mercy like honey, and know on the day it comes into the world the conditions of life can surely be He Who is the Creator of the entire universe.

In short, life is a shining stamp of Divine Unity on the face of the universe and in respect of life, every living being is a stamp of Divine Oneness; the embroideries and the art in every living being form a seal of God Almighty's being the Eternally Besought-of-All. All living creatures sign their signatures with their lives on the missive of the universe in the name of the All-Living and Self-Subsistent One. These are the seals of Divine

Unity and the stamps of Divine Oneness and of God Almighty being the Eternally Besought-of-All. Similarly, just as all living beings are, like life, seals of Divine Unity in this book of the universe, so too has a seal of Divine Oneness been placed on the faces and features of each.

Furthermore, just as life forms signatures and seals that bear witness to the Unity of the All-Living and Self-Subsistent One to the number of all living creatures and the individual members of each, so too does the act of raising and restoring to life set the signatures to Divine Unity to the number of beings. For example, the raising to life of the earth, which is a single individual, bears witness to Divine Unity as brilliantly as the sun. For while the earth is being raised to life in spring, hundreds of thousands of species and the innumerable individual members of each species are restored to life, one within the other, without fault or defect, in perfect, regular order. The one who performs with a single act innumerable other orderly acts must surely be the Creator of all beings and the All-Living, Self-Subsistent One, and the Single One of Unity, to Whom any partnership in His Lordship is impossible.

For now, this small number of the properties of life has been briefly described, and we refer the explanation and detailed discussion of other properties to other parts of the *Risale-i Nur* and to another time.

Conclusion

The Greatest Name of God or the Divine Name that has the most comprehensive manifestation is not the same for everyone; it may differ according to individuals. For example, for Imam 'Ali, may God be pleased with him, it was these six Names: the All-Independent, Single One, the All-Living, the Self-Subsistent (by Whom all subsist), the All-Wise, the All-Just, and the All-Holy. For Imam al-A'zam Abu Hanifa, it was two Names: the All-Wise and the All-Just. While for *Ghawth al-A'zam* 'Abdul-Qadir al-Jilani, it was O All-Living One. For Imam Rabbani, the Greatest Name was the Self-Subsistent, and so on; many other people considered the Greatest Name to be yet others.

In relation to this Fifth Part being about the Name the All-Living as both a blessing, a witness, evidence, sacred proof, and a prayer for ourselves, as a proper conclusion to this part, we quote the following, uttered by the most noble Messenger, upon him be peace and blessings, in his supreme supplication called *al-Jawshan al-Kabir*, which shows the extremely elevated and comprehensive degree of his knowledge of God. We will travel in the imagination to his time, and saying "Amen" to what the most noble Messenger, upon him be peace and blessings, said, will recite the following part of that supplication with the voice of Muhammad, upon him be peace and blessings, as though reciting it ourselves:

O All-Living, Who was living before all living beings;
O All-Living, Who will continue to live after all living beings;
O All-Living, like Whom there is nothing whatever;
O All-Living, resembling Whom there is nothing whatever;
O All-Living, Who needs no other living being;
O All-Living, with Whom no living being can be a partner;
O All-Living, Who causes all living beings to die;
O All-Living, Who provides the sustenance of all living beings;
O All-Living, Who restores to life the dead;
O All-Living, Who never dies;
All-Glorified are You; there is no deity but You!
Mercy! Mercy! Save us from the Fire! Amen!

All-Glorified are You. We have no knowledge save what You have taught us. Surely You are the All-Knowing, the All-Wise.

The sixth part
The Divine Name the Self-Subsistent (by Whom all subsist)

An apology

Since the following very important matters concerning the profound and comprehensive manifestation of the Name the Self-Subsistent occurred to me as separate gleams and were written with great haste, and since they have remained in the form of an extremely ill-arranged, rough copy, many deficiencies and much disorderliness are to be found in the phrasing and manner of expression. Forgive my defects for the sake of the beauties of the matters discussed.

A reminder

Since the matters concerning the Divine Names which have the most comprehensive manifestations are wide-ranging to the utmost degree and are also extremely profound, and particularly as the matters concerned with the Name the Self-Subsistent, including those that are discussed under the heading of the First Ray, have been discussed very deeply as they primarily concern materialists, not everyone will be able to understand every matter in all its aspects. However, everyone will have a share in each matter to some extent. According to the rule that "even if a thing is not wholly obtained, it still should not be abandoned completely," it is not reasonable to give up reading them with the excuse, "I cannot pick all the fruits in this immaterial garden." However much fruit a person is able to pick, that amount will be of benefit to them.

In the same way that some matters concerning the Greatest Name are so comprehensive that they cannot be comprehended, there are also others that are so subtle that the mind cannot distinguish them. Not all minds may be able to comprehend the matters concerning the Names the All-Living and the Self-Subsistent, or, in particular, the allusions that life makes to the pillars of belief, particularly to the pillar of Divine Destiny and Decree, which are discussed above, or the matters that will be discussed below concerning the Name the Self-Subsistent under the heading of the First Ray. However, they will not remain without some share of them and, in any event, these matters will strengthen their belief. The strengthening of belief, which is the key to eternal happiness, is of tremendous importance. Even an iota's increase in belief is a treasure. Imam Rabbani Ahmad al-Faruqi, said, "A small matter of belief being unfolded and known in plainer terms is preferable to me than experiencing hundreds of spiritual pleasures or working wonders."

In the Name of God, the All-Merciful, the All-Compassionate.

> *So, All-Glorified is He in Whose Hand is the absolute dominion of all things* (36: 83); *His are the keys of (the treasures of) the heavens and the earth* (39: 63); *There is not a thing but the stores (for its life and sustenance) are with Us* (39: 21); *No living creature is there but He holds it by its forelock and keeps it under His complete control.* (11: 56)

One aspect of the meaning of the above-mentioned verses, which proclaim God's absolute Self-subsistence by which everything subsists, and the second of the two of the lights of the Divine Greatest Name, or a most comprehensive manifestation of the Divine Name the Self-Subsistent, which is the sixth of the lights of the Divine Name having all-encompassing manifestations, appeared to me in the month of Dhi'l-Qa'da.

Due to the conditions of Eskişehir Prison, I will not be able to explain fully that Greatest Light. However, since Imam 'Ali, may God be pleased with him, attached the greatest importance to these six Divine Names in his supplication of the Ode of *Arjuza* under the name of *Sakina*, as well as in his Ode of *Jaljalutiya*, as the most comprehensive Names, and since I find great consolation in his recitation of them, in addition to our discussion of the five preceding Names, we will briefly explain the Name the Self-Subsistent with five rays.

The first ray

The Majestic Creator of the universe is Self-Subsistent, that is, He subsists and eternally exists by Himself. All things subsist, continue, and have permanence by Him. If the universe's connection with His being the Self-Subsistent by Which all subsist was severed for even a fraction of a second, the universe would be utterly destroyed.

Furthermore, besides being the Self-Subsistent by Whom all subsist, as the Qur'an of mighty stature decrees, that All-Majestic Being is also *the One like Whom there is nothing whatever* (42: 11). That is, neither in His essence, nor in His Attributes, nor in His acts has He either like, equal, peer, or partner. Indeed, it is inconceivable that there be any like, equal, partner, or peer for the All-Holy One, Who holds in the grasp of His Lordship the entire universe with whatever is or happens in it, and Who administers, sustains, and nurtures it with perfect order as though it were a house or a palace.

He is such an All-Living, Self-Subsistent One of Majesty that the creation of the stars is as easy for Him as that of particles, and the greatest thing is subservient to His Power in the same way as the most minute thing is, and His doing one thing can in no way prevent Him from doing another thing, and innumerable things are present before His View all at the same time as if a single thing, and He hears all voices simultaneously and is ever able to answer the limitless needs of all simultaneously, and, as testified to by the order and balance in all corners of the universe, there is nothing, no action or state that is outside the sphere of His Will, and although absolutely not limited by space, He is omnipresent everywhere with His Power and Knowledge, and although everything is infinitely distant from Him, He is infinitely close to all things. Certainly, such an All-Living, Self-Subsistent One of Majesty can in no way have any like, equal, partner, deputy, opposite or peer; it would be impossible. We can only consider His sacred essential Qualities and Attributes through parables and metaphors. All the comparisons and allegories in the *Risale-i Nur* are of this sort of parable and metaphor.

However, despite His being the Necessarily Existent One Who has no like, and Who is absolutely free of matter and space; despite His being One for Whom division is inconceivable in every respect, as is any sort of change or alteration; and despite His being infinitely exalted above neediness and impotence; a group of the people of misguidance suppose certain manifestations of that All-Sacred One on the pages of the universe and in His realms of beings to be the All-Sacred One Himself and ascribe the attributes and acts of the Divinity to certain creatures, thus attributing some of the All-Majestic One's works to nature.

However, it has been convincingly demonstrated in numerous places in the *Risale-i Nur* that nature is a Divine art and that it cannot be the artist. It is something inscribed by the Lord and it cannot be the scribe. It is a design and it cannot be the designer. It is a register and it cannot be the registrar. It is a law and it cannot be the power. It is a pattern and it cannot be the source. It is a passive recipient and it cannot be the author. It is an order and it cannot be the orderer. It is a system of creation and it cannot be the establisher of the system.

If, to suppose the impossible, the tiniest animate creature was referred to nature and nature was told, "Make this," as has been convincingly demonstrated in many places in the *Risale-i Nur*, ignoring its being unconscious, ignorant and devoid of will, it would then be necessary for nature to provide molds, or rather machines, to the number of the tiny creature's members and bodily systems so that it could fulfill that task.

Also, a group of the people of misguidance called materialists has perceived a comprehensive manifestation of the creativity of Divinity and the power of Lordship in the orderly motions of minute particles or atoms. However, since they are unable to know from where the manifestation comes and cannot understand from where the universal force is being directed, which originates from the manifestation of the Eternally Besought-of-All's Power, they suppose matter and force to be pre-eternal and attribute the Divine works to atoms and their motion. All Glorified is God! How can human beings be so ignorant that they attribute the acts and works of One Who is beyond space, but also ever-present everywhere in such a way that He is able to see, know, and direct all things in the creation of all things, to particles or atoms or their motion, which are lifeless, blind, and unconscious, and which whirl about continuously and in utter confusion? Anyone with the least bit of intelligence must see just what an ignorant and superstitious idea this is.

Indeed, since these people withdraw from seeing and accepting absolute unity, they have fallen into a limitless, absolute multiplicity. That is, since they do not accept the One and Single God, they are compelled to accept numberless gods. In other words, since their corrupted minds are unable to grasp how a Single, All-Holy One can be pre-eternal and the Creator of all things—though pre-eternity and creativity are indispensable to the Divine Being—their approach compels them to accept the pre-eternity, indeed the divinity, of those numberless, lifeless particles. So, come and consider this boundless degree of ignorance!

Certainly, the comprehensive manifestation of the creativity of Divinity and the power of Lordship over particles or atoms has made that mass of particles into an orderly and magnificent army. If the Commander-in-Chief's Command and Power were withdrawn, even for a second, that disparate, lifeless, unconscious mass would become like irregular soldiers; it would altogether cease to exist.

Furthermore, another group of people are even more ignorantly misguided. As if able to see even further, they imagine the matter of ether to be the origin and author of creation. Whereas, being an extremely subtle, fine, obedient and subjugated page for the All-Majestic Maker's acts, being a means for the transmission of His commands, being an extremely delicate veil for the execution of His decrees, being refined ink for His writing, being a finest raiment to clothe His acts of creation, being a fundamental component in His artifacts and a field in which to sow His seeds, ether acts as a mirror for the manifestations of the Lordship of God.

Ether is a kind of matter that is lifeless, unconscious, and devoid of will; it is more subtle and finer than the minute particles in which materialists are drowned, but denser than the primordial matter to which the ancient philosophers were stuck fast. It would be infinitely wrong to attribute this matter, which has limitless divisibility and is equipped with conductivity and the qualities or duties of being the medium in which God's commands are executed—it would be infinitely wrong to attribute to it, indeed, to its minute particles, which are far more minute than particles of other matter, the acts and works that exist only through a Will and Power that can see, know, and direct all things in all things.

The act of creation observed in beings is such that it clearly demonstrates that it proceeds from a Power and Will that see and know all things simultaneously and know and secure each and every living creature's relationship with the entire universe. It thus demonstrates that it can in no way be the act of causes, which are material, and which are not all-encompassing. It is due to the mystery of God Almighty's Self-Subsistence that even a most particular creative act bears the supreme quality that indicates that it is directly the act of the Creator of the entire universe. For example, an act pertaining to the creation of a bee demonstrates that it is peculiar to the Creator of the universe in two respects.

The first respect: The fact that all the other bees throughout the world display the same act at the same time demonstrates that the particular act displayed by an individual bee and all bees is the tip of a comprehensive act which embraces the entirety of the earth. Therefore, whoever is the author of that comprehensive act must also be the author of the particular act.

The second respect: In order to be the author of an action connected with the creation of the bee in question, there must be a power and will that are encompassing enough to know and secure conditions for the life of the bee, and all its members, and its relationship with the universe. Therefore, only the one who authors the particular act will be able to perform it so perfectly by having authority over the entire universe.

Thus, even the most particular and insignificant act demonstrates in two respects that it is peculiar to the Creator of all things.

What is most remarkable and surprising is this: it is the Necessarily Existent One Whose Existence is absolutely necessary and indispensable and forms the firmest level of existence. Being free of matter is the reason for the most stable degree of existence; absolute freedom from space is the state of existence furthest from termination; unity is the soundest quality of existence and the one absolutely exalted above change or non-existence. The Necessarily Existent One possesses all these attributes of existence and eternality is His most particular Attribute. Yet materialists attribute pre-eternity and permanence to matter and things like ether and particles which form the weakest and least stable level of existence and which have the least tangible, the most changeable and the most varying state of existence, and which are the most dispersed through space. Fancying matter and things like particles or atoms to be pre-eternal, and supposing them to be the origin of some of the Divine works is infinitely unreasonable and contrary to truth and reality. This has been demonstrated through convincing arguments in numerous places in the *Risale-i Nur*.

The second ray

This consists of two matters.

The first matter

> *Slumber does not seize Him, nor sleep* (2: 255); *There is not a thing but the stores (for its life and sustenance) are with Us* (39: 21); *His are the keys of (the treasures of) the heavens and the earth.* (39: 63)

One aspect of the mighty truth that is indicated by these verses, which point to a most comprehensive manifestation of the Divine Name the Self-Subsistent, is as follows:

All the heavenly bodies in the universe continue to exist or subsist by God's Self-Subsistence or by His making them subsist. If the manifestation of that Self-Subsistence was to turn away its face for a moment, millions of spheres, some of which are a thousand times larger than the earth, would be scattered into the endless void of space, and, colliding with one another, they would crash into nothingness.

For example, imagine a power which keeps thousands of stately palaces in place in perfect order and makes them travel like planes through space. Its capacity to make them subsist is measured through the order, regular movements, and continuance of those palaces in space. Similarly, the Self-Subsistent One of Majesty keeps and causes to travel innumerable heavenly bodies within ethereal matter in perfect order and stability, making them subsist or hold up, without support, in space all those bodies, some of which are a thousand and some even a million times larger than the earth. He also entrusts them all with duties and causes them to submit in perfect obedience, like a majestic army to the decrees issuing from the command of *"Be!" and it is*. All this is a measure to understand the all-encompassing manifestation of the Name the Self-Subsistent (by Whom all subsist), and demonstrates that the particles or atoms of all beings also subsist, like the stars, through God Almighty's Self-Subsistence.

The particles in the body of a living creature do not disperse, but are assembled and remain in groups and systems peculiar to each limb, and without scattering, preserve their position amidst the storms of the elements, which flow like floods, remaining in order. Since such a phenomenon self-evidently does not occur by itself, but by God's Self-Subsistence and by His making all subsist, the result is that each body remains like a well-ordered regiment and each species like a regular army, with all living creatures remaining and moving on the earth and among the stars in space; thus, these particles or atoms proclaim the mystery of Self-Subsistence in innumerable voices.

THE SECOND MATTER

This subject requires that some of the benefits and instances of wisdom in things that are connected with Divine Self-Subsistence are mentioned.

The wisdom and Divine purposes for the creation and existence of all things have three comprehensive results.

The first result relates to the thing itself and humanity, together with humanity's benefits.

The second result, which is more important, is that as a sign, a missive, a book, and an ode to be studied by all conscious beings and which makes known the Names of the All-Majestic Originator, everything states multiple meanings for innumerable readers.

The third result relates to the All-Majestic Maker Himself. If the benefits and results of everything that relate to the thing itself are one, those relating to the All-Majestic Maker are hundreds. The All-Majestic Maker beholds the wonders of His Art Himself, and observes the manifestations of His Names in beings He Himself has made. Considering this third, mighty result, anything living, even for a second, is sufficient.

Divine Self-Subsistence has another mystery that requires the existence of all things which will be explained in the Third Ray below.

At one time I was investigating the talisman of the universe and the riddle of creation; I concentrated upon the instances of wisdom and benefits in creation. I wondered why these things appear for some time and then swiftly decline and vanish. I noticed their features: they have been dressed up and adorned in an orderly, purposeful fashion and sent to this exhibition. But then they disappear within one or two days, and some of them within a few minutes even; in appearance, they go without purpose. What is the reason for them to appear to us for such short a time? I was most curious. At that time, through Divine favor, I found out one important instance of wisdom in beings, particularly living beings, coming to this worldly school. It was as follows:

Each being, and particularly each living being, is an extremely meaningful word, missive, an ode of Divine Lordship, and Divine proclamation. After it has been studied by all conscious beings and has stated its meaning to innumerable readers, its corporeal form, which is like the letters that form it, vanishes.

For about a year this instance of wisdom was sufficient for me. Then many wonderful and subtle miracles of art that are found in creatures, and particularly in animate ones, were unfolded to me. I understood that these wonderful subtleties of art are not only for the study of conscious beings. Even though innumerable conscious beings may study each creature, their studying is limited and none of them may be able to penetrate all the subtleties of art in those living creatures. That is to say, the most important result of the creation of living beings and the most significant purpose of their creation is that the Eternal Self-Subsistent One presents to His Own View the marvels of His Art and the compassionate gifts and bounties that He bestows.

I was content with this purpose for a long time. I had understood that the great "expenses" spent on living creatures or the countless subtleties of art present in beings, particularly in animate beings, serve the purpose of exhibiting the Art of the Eternally Self-Subsistent One.

Some time later I realized that the subtleties of art in the beings and their forms are not constant; they are changing and are renewed at a great speed; they are transformed in endless activities by Divine creativity. I started to ponder the wisdom in this creativity and activity, and realized that it must necessarily be as extensive as the activity itself. Then, the two instances of wisdom mentioned above began to appear insufficient. With great curiosity I began to search for a further purpose and instance of wisdom.

All praise be to God, through the radiation of the Qur'an of miraculous exposition, after some time a vast and limitless wisdom and purpose appeared related to Divine Self-Subsistence through Which all subsist. And through it, a Divine mystery called "the talisman of the universe" and "the riddle of creation" was understood. (Referring its detailed explanation to the Twenty-Fourth Letter, here we will mention briefly two or three points, in the following Third Ray.)

Look from this point at the manifestation of the mystery of Divine Self-Subsistence: it takes all beings out of non-existence, and as stated in the verse,

God it is Who has raised the heavens without pillars you can see (13: 2), causes each to remain in infinite space, bestowing on them stability and permanence. If there was not this support, nothing at all could continue to exist by itself. Everything would topple over into an infinite void and tumble into decay.

Furthermore, just as all beings depend on the All-Majestic, Self-Subsistent One for their existence and subsistence, so too are there thousands of chains or lines—like telephone and telegraph lines, if the comparison is permissible—meeting which are responsible for the connectivity among everything in the lives and subsistence of all beings; they end in the ultimate reality stated in the verse, *and to Him alone is the whole matter referred* (11: 123). If they were not dependent on that luminous point of support, there would have to be thousands of sequences of causes, or rather, as many sequences of causes as there are beings. According to thinkers and scholars, this is an impossible and false notion. For example, one thing (preservation or light or existence or provision, for instance) in one respect relies on the next thing, and that on the next, and that on the next, until finally, since this cannot continue endlessly, it must end in an original source.

Thus, the end of all such lines and sequences lies in the Divine Self-Subsistence by Which all subsist. When Divine Self-Subsistence is understood properly, it is not necessary to imagine chains or sequences of causes to explain the absolutely regular and ordered subsistence of beings. For everything directly depends on Divine Self-Subsistence by Which all subsist.

The third ray

> *Every (moment of every) day, He is in a new manifestation (with all His Attributes and Names as the Divine Being)* (55: 29). *One Who freely does whatever He wills* (85: 16). *He creates however He wills* (30: 54). *All-Glorified is He in Whose Hand is the absolute dominion of all things* (36: 83). *Look, then, at the imprints of God's Mercy—how He revives the dead earth after its death.* (30: 50)

By means of a few introductory points, we will try to explain to a small degree the manifestation of Divine Self-Subsistence that accompanies Divine creativity and the activities of Divine Lordship.

THE FIRST: When we look at the universe, we see that some creatures, which are ceaselessly active in the flood of time and which follow one after the other, convoy after convoy, come for a second and then immediately disappear. Another group comes for a minute and then vanishes. One species stops by in the corporeal world for an hour, and then enters the world of the Unseen. Some of them come and settle in the corporeal world for a day, some of them for a year, some for a century, and some for hundreds of years; they perform their duties and then depart.

This astonishing traveling and flow or flux of creatures is directed with such order, balance and wisdom, and the One Who commands these convoys does so with such insight, wisdom and deliberation that even if all minds were to unite and become one mind, it would be unable to comprehend the essence of this wise direction; it would be unable to find any fault in it and so would not be able to criticize it.

Thus, through this activity of His Lordship, He Who commands the flux of creatures keeps under His absolute control all of these pleasing creatures that He loves, in particular living creatures, and dispatches them to the world of the Unseen, continuously filling the guesthouse of the world and emptying it without needing to ask the guests' opinions. Making the earth like a board for writing and erasing, the Pen of Destiny and Decree ceaselessly renews Its writings on the earth through the manifestations of *He gives life and causes to die* (2: 258). This activity of Lordship and Divine creativity has three most important and comprehensive purposes and instances of wisdom.

The first of these purposes is this: Every sort of activity, whether particular or universal, gives pleasure. Rather, there is pleasure in every activity. Indeed, activity is pure pleasure; or the manifestation of existence, which is pure pleasure, and a movement to escape non-existence, which is pure suffering, rising to the realm of existence.

Indeed, everyone with ability pursues with pleasure the development of their abilities through activity. The manifestation of innate talents through activity arises from a pleasure and results in pleasure. Everyone with certain perfections pursues with pleasure their manifestation and development through activities.

Since in every activity there is perfection and pleasure, which is thus loved and sought after, and as activity itself is perfection; and since the manifestations of a boundless love and infinite compassion that originate from a perpetual and eternal Life are apparent in the world of living creatures, these manifestations show that as an indispensable attribute of the eternal Life, the All-Sacred One, Who thus loves and is compassionate and makes Himself loved, has sacred, essential Qualities like Divine intense, sacred love, and sacred pure pleasure fitting His Holiness and the absolute necessity of His existence. And it is these essential Qualities that continuously renew, cause to ceaseless move, and change the universe through that endless activity and infinite creativity.

The second instance of wisdom in the limitless Divine activity connected with Divine Self-Subsistence relates to the Divine Names. It is a fact that everyone who possesses perfect beauty desires to both see and display their beauty; that everyone who has some skills desires and loves to attract attention to their skills by exhibiting them; and that a beautiful truth and meaning that has remained unrevealed or undiscovered wishes and loves to be manifested and find its "customers."

These fundamental rules are in force in all things according to the intensity in each of them. Certainly, as testified to by the universe and demonstrated by their manifestations and embroideries, each of one thousand and one All-Beautiful Names of the All-Majestic, Self-Subsistent Being has absolute, true beauty, perfection, grace, and truth in Its every degree of manifestation. Indeed, in every degree of the manifestation of every Name there are endless varieties of beauty and innumerable beautiful truths.

It is the universe with whatever is in it that serves as a mirror reflecting the sacred beauties of these Names, and that forms the scenes that display their beautiful embroidery and the pages that demonstrate their beautiful truths. So, in order to present their boundless manifestations and infinite, meaningful embroideries and books both to the witnessing View of the All-Majestic, Self-Subsistent One, Whom they signify, and to the examination of uncountable, conscious, living creatures, and in order to display countless scenes out of a finite and limited thing, numerous individuals out of a single individual, and multiple truths out of a single truth, these permanent and eternal Names entirely and unceasingly renew and change the universe through their manifestations as a consequence of that sacred Divine love and because of the mystery of Divine Self-Subsistence.

The fourth ray

The third instance of wisdom in the constant and astonishing activity in the universe is the following:

Everyone who is compassionate feels happy to please others; everyone who is kind feels pleased when they make others happy; everyone who loves rejoices at making those who are worthy of being happy joyful; everyone who is noble-hearted takes pleasure at making others happy; everyone who is just is happy to uphold justice and gain the gratitude of those whose rights have been vindicated by punishing those who deserve it; and every skilful artist takes pride in exhibiting their work, and in its functioning as they have imagined and planned it would function, and in its yielding the desired results.

Thus, each of these principles is a fundamental rule that operates throughout the universe and the world of humankind. Three examples that demonstrate these rules also have functions in the Divine Names that have been explained in The Third Station of The Thirty-Second Word. Since it is appropriate to summarize them here, we will say as follows:

For example, prompted by his or her innate exalted qualities, an extremely merciful, generous, munificent, noble-hearted person boards the poor and needy onto a large ship, satisfies them with large banquets and gifts, and sails with them over the seas around the world. This benefactor watches his guests happily from a position above, taking pleasure at the satisfaction and gratitude of these needy people, and feels proud.

If a human being, who is merely like a distribution official, takes such pleasure and delight at holding a particular banquet, then consider the following: the All-Living and Self-Subsistent One has boarded all animals and humans and countless jinn, angels and other kinds of spiritual beings onto the ship of the earth, which is a vessel of His all-encompassing Mercy; He spreads the earth before them as a table of His Lordship, laden with a variety of food, and the things which will satisfy all their senses; He takes these needy, thankful, grateful and happy creatures through the regions of the universe. Not being content with making them happy in this world just with these bounties, He also makes each of the eternal Gardens of His Paradise a table of unending banquets in the Eternal Realm. Thus, it is the manifestations of His Lordship or His essential Divine Qualities that are alluded to through designations such as "the sacred happiness," "the sacred pride," and "the holy pleasure"—the manifestations that arise from the thanks, gratitude, joy and delight of those creatures, and we are in fact unable to describe—which necessitate the constant activity and ceaseless creativity in the universe.

Another example: if a skilful craftsman were to make a gramophone which required no records and it played just as he wishes, how proud and delighted he will be, and he will say to himself, "What wonders God wills; whatever and however He wills comes into being!" If an insignificant work of art, made without creation from nothing, engenders a feeling of such pride and pleasure in the craftsman's spirit, then consider the following:

The All-Wise Maker of all beings has made the entire universe like a Divine orchestra and an amazing, wonderful workshop which gives forth countless songs and hymns, praising and glorifying; He puts on a show of all the species, all the worlds; this occurs in the universe through different miracles of art and different styles of craftsmanship. Not only does He fashion a set of machines in the heads of animate creatures, including even the smallest, that operate like a gramophone, camera or telegraph, but He also fashions in the heads of all human beings not just a gramophone that plays without records, a camera without a lens, a telegraph without wires, but a machine that is many times more wonderful. It is therefore the same manifestations of His Lordship or His essential Qualities which are called by the designations "the sacred pride" and "the holy pleasure" that issue from His creating such machines and their operating in the way He wills, producing the results He wants, that necessitate this unceasing activity.

Yet *another example*: the fact that a just ruler takes pleasure and is satisfied and feels proud at restoring the rights of the oppressed from the oppressors in order to uphold justice, at protecting the poor against the wrongdoing of the powerful, and at giving to everyone their due is a fundamental rule of rulership and justice. So, consider the following:

The All-Living and Self-Subsistent One, Who is the All-Wise Ruler and is Absolutely Just, bestows on all His creatures, particularly on living ones, the necessary conditions for life, which are known as "the rights of life"; He grants them the abilities and members necessary for the preservation of their lives; He compassionately protects the weak from the evil of the powerful; as a requirement of His Justice, He gives each among His creatures its due and punishes the wrongdoers. In addition, His absolute embracing Justice will be fully realized at the Supreme Tribunal in the Hereafter. So, it is all such executions of His Lordship and manifestations of His essential Qualities as those mentioned that necessitate the unceasing activity in the universe.

Thus, as these three examples show, each of the All-Beautiful Names of God Almighty is the means for the manifestation of certain sacred Divine essential Qualities in this unceasing activity and they demand unceasing creativity. And every ability and capacity gives joy, pleasure, and exhilaration through development, flourishing, and the yielding of results; everyone charged with a duty feels a great feeling of relief and happiness when the duty is completed and they have been released from it. To obtain numerous fruits from a single seed and to gain a hundredfold profit from a single thing is the most pleasurable trade. Similarly, the All-Living, Self-Subsistent One causes the innumerable capacities of all creatures to develop, and discharges all creatures after employing them in valuable duties. Rather, He raises them to higher positions, raising elements to the level of minerals, minerals to plant life, plants to the level of animal life by making them their provision, and animals to the high level of human conscious life.

When a living thing departs from the world with its external or corporeal existence (as explained in The Twenty-Fourth Letter), it leaves behind its other types of existence, such as its spirit, nature, form, all the instances of its life that are embodied in the World of the Ideal Forms, its existence in the minds and Divine Knowledge, its astral body, and the sheath of its spirit. Thus, it may be understood from all these acts of creativity and divinity by the Divine Lordship how important are the sacred meanings of the Divine Lordship that originate from Its acts.

AN IMPORTANT QUESTION

One group of people of misguidance say that the One Who changes and transforms the universe with unceasing activity must Himself be changeable.

THE ANSWER: God forbid! A hundred thousand times, God forbid! The fact that the mirrors reflecting the sun on the earth change demonstrates not that the sun in the sky also changes, but, on the contrary, that its manifestations are being renewed. Furthermore, change and alteration are inconceivable for the All-Sacred Divine Being, Who is eternal, permanent, absolutely perfect, self-sufficient and absolutely independent in every respect, Who is absolutely free of matter, restriction, and contingency, like being contained in time or space. Change in the universe indicates not His changing but His being absolutely free of change or undergoing transformation. Because, one who unceasingly causes innumerable things to move or change in perfect order must themselves be unchanging and not move. For example, if you spin a large number of balls which are tied to one another with pieces of string and cause them all to move unceasingly within an order, then it is necessary that you must remain in one place and not move, or else you destroy the order. It is clear that one who makes objects move in orderliness must themselves not move, and one who makes objects change without ceasing must themselves be unchanging so that these actions can continue in orderliness.

Secondly: Change and alteration arise from being created, and from needing renewal in order to be perfected, from need, and from being material and contingent. Since the All-Sacred Being is both eternal, and in every respect absolutely perfect and absolutely self-sufficient and independent, as well as being absolutely free of matter, and necessarily existent, most certainly change and alteration are inconceivable for Him.

The fifth ray

This consists of two matters.

The first matter

If we wish to see the all-encompassing manifestation of the Name the Self-Subsistent (by Whom all subsist), we may make our imagination into two telescopes that can observe the entire universe. One of these two telescopes will show the most distant objects, the other the most minute particles. We look through the first telescope and see that by the manifestation of the Name the Self-Subsistent (by Whom all subsist), of the millions of spheres or stars thousands of times larger than the earth, some have been made apparently stationary in the matter known as ether, which is subtler than air, while others have apparently been made to travel as their duty.

Next we look through the second telescope, which is the microscope of the imagination, so that we may see minute particles. It is again by the Divine Name the Self-Subsistent (by Whom all subsist) that the particles or atoms forming the bodies of earthly creatures take up an orderly position like the stars, moving and performing significant duties. We see that in particular the cells known as red corpuscles and white corpuscles in the blood, which are formed of minuscule particles, move, like the planets, with two well-ordered motions like Mawlawi (Mevlevi) dervishes.

A *summary*: In order to see the sacred light formed of the six Divine Names Which have all-encompassing manifestations, which make a harmonious combination like the seven colors in light, it is appropriate to make a summary of all the explanations above. It is as follows:

Look beyond the all-encompassing manifestation of the Divine Name the Self-Subsistent, Which upholds and gives permanence and continuity to all the beings in the universe: the all-encompassing manifestation of the Name the All-Living has set aflame all living beings and illuminated the universe. This Name makes all living beings shine with Its manifestation.

Now look again: beyond the Name the All-Living, the all-encompassing manifestation of the Name the All-Independent, Single One includes the entire universe with all its elements and parts in unity. It puts a stamp of Unity on the forehead of each being. It puts a seal of Oneness on each being's face. This Name has Its manifestation proclaimed with countless tongues.

And now consider the all-encompassing manifestation of the Name the All-Wise beyond the Name the All-Independent, Single One: It includes each of the beings we observe through the two telescopes of the imagination, from the stars to the particles, whether of a universal or a particular nature, from the greatest sphere to the most minute, in a fruitful order, wise regularity, and purposeful harmony appropriate to each. It adorns and makes shine all beings.

Then look beyond the all-encompassing manifestation of the Name the All-Wise: through Its all-encompassing manifestation, which was explained in the Second Part, the Name the All-Just governs the entire universe with all its beings in ceaseless activity with such balance, equilibrium, and measure that should just one of the heavenly bodies lose its balance even for a second, that is, should it break free of the manifestation of the Name the All-Just, it would cause chaos among the stars and this would be like Doomsday. Thus, encompassed and governed by this manifestation, all beings and all the different realms of beings, from the army of the stars to the army of minute particles, from the largest galaxy known as the Milky Way to the sphere of the motion of red and white corpuscles in blood, which stand and move in a way appointed and established with the finest balance and measure, demonstrate that all of them obey the commands issuing from *"Be!" and it is*, with utter subjugation.

Now, look beyond the all-encompassing manifestation of the Name the All-Just to the all-encompassing manifestation of the Name the All-Holy, which was explained in the First Part: this Name renders all the beings in the universe so clean, pure, clear, beautiful, adorned and shining that It has given the universe as a whole and all the beings in it the form of beautiful mirrors that are worthy of and fitting for the infinite essential Beauty of the Absolutely Beautiful One and His All-Beautiful Names.

In short, these six Greatest Names or six lights of the Divine Greatest Name or the Name having an all-encompassing manifestation have wrapped the universe and all beings in shining veils with ever differing and various colors, embroideries and adornment.

THE SECOND MATTER

As the Divine Name the Self-Subsistent (by Whom all subsist) has an all-majestic manifestation throughout the universe as a whole, so too does It also have a gracious, particular manifestation on the human being, the center, pivot, and conscious fruit of the universe. In this way the human becomes a mirror in which the overall manifestation of the Divine Name the Self-Subsistent is reflected throughout the universe. That is to say, just as the universe subsists by the manifestation of God's being the Self-Subsistent by Whom all subsist, so too does it subsist in one respect on account of the human's being the perfect medium for the manifestation of the Name the Self-Subsistent. As most of the wisdom, aims, purposes, and benefits in the existence of the universe relates to humanity, it is as if the manifestation of Divine Self-Subsistence throughout it is a support for the universe.

Indeed, it may be said that the All-Living and Self-Subsistent One willed the existence of the universe for the sake of humanity and therefore created it for humanity. For, due to the comprehensiveness of its nature, humanity can understand the Divine Names and experience their manifestations. In particular, it can understand numerous Divine Names through the pleasure that is found in provision. But the angels cannot know them through that pleasure.

As a result of this important comprehensiveness of human nature, in order to make humanity experience the manifestations of all of His Names and taste all varieties of His bounties, the All-Living and Self-Subsistent One has given humans a stomach with an appetite for which He has generously laden the table of the earth with His endless varieties of food. He has also made life a stomach too, like the biological one, and spread for it a vast table of bounties. Through its senses, life enjoys numerous varieties of benefits from that table and offers all kinds of thanks.

In addition to the stomach of life, He has endowed human beings with the stomach of humanity, which demands provision and bounties in a wider sphere than life. As if the hands of this stomach, intelligence, mind, and imagination benefit from the table of mercy, which is as broad as the heavens and the earth, and offer thanks.

And in addition to the stomach of life, in order to spread another, infinitely vast table of bounties, He has made the tenets of Islamic belief and principles of Islamic life like an immaterial stomach that requires a great deal of provision. He has made its table extend beyond the sphere of contingency and included in it the Divine Names. Thus, through this stomach, humanity perceives the Names the All-Merciful and the All-Wise as the greatest pleasure of provision and exclaims, "All praise be to God for His being the All-Merciful and the All-Wise!" And so on. Humans can benefit from limitless Divine bounties through this vast immaterial stomach. And the pleasure of Divine love provided by this stomach has another sphere.

Thus, the All-Living and Self-Subsistent One has made humanity a center and pivot for the whole universe; He has spread before it a table of bounties that are as extensive as the universe, and He has subjugated the universe to it. The reason for this and the reason the subsistence of the universe has been made dependent, in one respect, on humanity's being the mirror for the manifestation of Divine Self-Subsistence are the following three important duties of humanity:

The first is the arrangement of all the bounties that are spread throughout the universe through humanity. The All-Living, Self-Subsistent One arranges them on the string of the benefit of humanity like prayer beads on a string; the ends of the strings of bounties are tied to our heads, thus making humanity like a list of all the varieties of His treasures of Mercy.

The second important duty of humanity is that, by reason of its comprehensive nature, humanity should be the most perfect addressee of the All-Living and Self-Subsistent One; with appreciation of His astonishing arts, humanity should be the loudest herald of His arts; through all varieties of conscious thanksgiving, humanity should give praise to Him and offer thanks for all the varieties of His bounties and the limitless types of His gifts.

Humanity's third duty is that through its life it should act as a mirror to the All-Living and Self-Subsistent One with His essential Qualities and all-encompassing Attributes in three respects.

The first respect: Through its own essential impotence, humanity perceives the absolute Power of its Creator, and through the degrees of its impotence, humanity perceives the degrees of His Power's manifestation. Humanity understands, through its own absolute poverty, His Mercy with Its degrees of manifestation, and through humanity's own weakness, His Strength, and so on. In short, through its own defective attributes, humanity is a mirror that is like a unit of measurement for the Creator's Attributes of perfection. In the same way that light appears brighter at night and the darkness of night is a perfect mirror to display electric light, humanity also acts as a mirror to the Divine Perfections through its own defective attributes.

The second respect: Humanity builds and owns its own house through its partial will, tiny knowledge, minute power, and apparent ownership. It deduces from this and mirrors in proportion to the vastness of the universe the fact that the Master Builder of the universe has Art, Will, Power, and Knowledge.

The third respect: There are two aspects of humanity's acting as a mirror in this respect:

The first: It is to display in itself the ever differing embroideries of the Divine Names. To put this more simply, by reason of its comprehensive nature, humanity is like a tiny index and miniature specimen of the universe and thus displays the embroideries of all Divine Names.

The second aspect: Humanity acts as a mirror to the Divine Attributes. That is to say, just as humanity indicates the Life of the All-Living and Self-Subsistent One through its own life, so too, by means of its own senses, such as hearing and sight which develop during its life, humanity acts as a mirror to make known the Attributes, like Hearing and Sight, of the All-Living and Self-Subsistent One.

Furthermore, through the numerous senses, feelings, and emotions which display themselves during life but which do not develop, but rather boil up in the form of sensitivity, humanity also acts as a mirror to the sacred essential Qualities of the All-Living and Self-Subsistent One. For example, through feelings such as loving or feeling proud, pleased, happy and exhilarated, humanity acts as a mirror to the All-Sacred One's Qualities of this sort, which are suitable and worthy for His Sacredness and His absolutely independent Self-Sufficiency.

Also, in addition to being a unit of measurement to recognize the All-Majestic One's Attributes and essential Qualities through its comprehensive life, as well as being an index of and a conscious mirror to the manifestation of His Names, and so on, the human being is also a unit of measurement, an index, a scale, and a balance to the truths of the universe. For example, a person's memory is extremely decisive evidence of the existence of the Supreme Preserved Tablet in the universe and a sample of it; the human faculty of imagination is decisive evidence of the existence of the World of Immaterial Representations or Ideal Forms.[150] And the subtle

[150] Indeed, the elements in humans indicate the elements in the universe, and their bones its stones and rocks, their hair its plants and trees, and the blood which flows in their bodies and the fluids which issue from their eyes, ears, noses and mouths the springs and mineral waters of the earth, and so on. Similarly, the human's spirit points to the World of Spirits, their faculties of memory to the Supreme Preserved Tablet, and their faculties of imagina-

powers and faculties of humanity are evidence of the existence of spiritual beings in the universe and an example of them. And so on. In a small measure and to the degree of certainty that is based on observation, humanity can indicate the truths of belief that are displayed in the universe.

Thus, humanity serves very important purposes, like the duties mentioned above. Humanity is a mirror to the Permanent Divine Beauty and it is the medium for the manifestation of the Perpetual Divine Perfection and a herald of It. Humanity is needy and thankful for the Eternal Divine Mercy. Since Beauty, Perfection, and Mercy are everlasting and eternal, certainly then humanity, which is the loving and eager mirror to that permanent Beauty, the loving herald of that perpetual Perfection, and the one that is thankful and needy for that eternal Mercy, will eventually go into an everlasting realm in order to remain there permanently and accompany that eternal Beauty, perpetual Perfection, and everlasting Mercy for all eternity. For an eternal beauty cannot be content with an impermanent lover or a mortal friend. Since beauty loves itself, it desires love in return for this love. Transience and going into non-existence transform such love into enmity. If human beings were not going to go to eternity to remain there permanently, their innate love of the Eternal Beauty would be replaced by enmity.

As described in a footnote in The Tenth Word, a beautiful woman, admired throughout the world, expelled a lover from her presence. This caused his love to turn into enmity and in order to console himself, he said, "Ugh! How ugly she is!", thus insulting and denying her beauty.

Indeed, just as humans are hostile to what they do not know, they also try in enmity to find faults in the things they cannot obtain or own. Since, as the whole universe testifies, the True Beloved and Absolutely Beautiful One causes humanity to love Himself through His All-Beautiful Names and wills humans to love Him, then most certainly He would not ingrain enmity towards Himself in humanity, whom He both loves and is loved by, thus causing them to be bitterly resentful about Him. He would also not ingrain a hidden enmity in the spirit of humanity, as this would be altogether contrary to the nature of humanity, which He has created as His exceptional, most lovable creature and which He has created to love Him. For human-

---

tion to the World of Ideal Forms, and so on. Each human member and faculty indicates a different world and bears decisive witness to the existence of the same.

ity would only be able to cure the deep wounds that might arise from eternal separation from an Absolute Beauty that they love and appreciate through enmity towards It, by being resentful about, and by denying It. It is because of this that the unbelievers are enemies of God. Therefore, in order to keep company with humanity, who is Its loving mirror, on the way to all eternity, that Eternal Beauty will surely favor humanity with a permanent life in a permanent abode.

Since the human being has been created with a nature to love and deeply desire a Permanent Beauty; and since the Permanent Beauty cannot be content with an impermanent lover; and since, in order to find consolation from the pain and sorrow that arise from some aim that they do not know or cannot attain or own, humanity reassures themselves by finding faults in that aim or by nurturing a hidden enmity towards it; and since the universe has been created for humanity and humanity has been created to know and love God; and since the Creator of the universe, together with His Names, is eternal; and since the manifestations of His Names will last eternally, then most certainly humanity is to go to a realm of permanence where they will be favored with a permanent life.

The Prophet Muhammad, upon him be peace and blessings, who is the supreme guide and perfect, universal human, made known and demonstrated in the most perfect form in himself and in his Religion the value and all the perfections and duties of humanity that we have explained above. This demonstrates that just as the universe has been created for humanity, so too the greatest aim and object that was willed for the existence of humanity and humanity's choicest and most valuable member, and its most brilliant mirror to the Single and Eternally Besought-of-All is Ahmad Muhammad, upon him be peace and blessings.

Upon him and his Family be blessings and peace to the number of good deeds of his Community.

> O God! O All-Merciful One! O All-Compassionate One! O All-Independent, Unique One! O All-Living One! O Self-Subsistent One by Whom all subsist! O All-Wise One! O All-Just One! O All-Holy One! We beseech You for the sake of Your wise Criterion of truth and falsehood, the Qur'an, and for the sake of the respect for Your noblest Beloved, and for the sake of Your All-Beautiful Names, and for the sake of the respect for Your Name that has all-encompass-

ing manifestations, to preserve us from the evil of the carnal, evil-commanding soul and from Satan and from the evil of devilish jinn and men. Amen.

All-Glorified are You! We have no knowledge save what You have taught us. Surely You are the All-Knowing, the All-Wise.

A Supplication

O God, O my Lord!

I see with the eyes of belief, and through the instruction and light of the Qur'an, and the teaching of God's noblest Messenger, upon him be peace and blessings, and the guidance of the Divine Name the All-Wise that:

There is not a single movement in the heavens that does not indicate Your Existence through its orderliness;

There is not a single heavenly body that does not indicate or testify to Your Lordship and Unity by performing its duties without noise and standing without support;

There is not a single star that it does not indicate or testify to Your Unity and the magnificence of Your Divinity through its most proportionate structure, exactly ordered position, bright countenance, or its resemblance to all other stars;

There is not a single one of the twelve planets that does not testify to Your absolutely necessary Existence nor indicate the dominion of Your Divinity through its wise movement, obedient subjugation to Your law, orderly duties, and important satellites.

Indeed, just as with all inhabitants each of the heavens testifies to Your absolutely necessary Existence, so also O Creator of the heavens and earth, with their totality, they bear witness to the absolutely necessity of Your Existence so obviously, and O One Who governs all particles or atoms together with the compounds they form, and has subjugated all the planets to His command, making them revolve with their satellites, they testify to Your Unity and Oneness so powerfully that as many luminous proofs as the stars in the heavens confirm their testimony.

With their extraordinarily large bodies, which move with an extraordinary speed, these pure heavens display the scene of an orderly army and a fireworks celebration illuminated by electric lamps. They clearly indicate the magnificence of Your Lordship and the grandeur of the Power of You Who invents everything; they indicate the limitless expanse of Your Dominion, Which dominates all the heavens, and of Your Mercy, Which embraces all living creatures; they certainly testify to the all-encompassing nature of Your Knowledge, Which penetrates and orders all the acts and states of the heavenly creatures, and to the comprehensiveness of Your Wisdom. This testimony and indication are so clear that it is as if the stars are the words of testimony of the heavens and their embodied luminous proofs.

As for the stars, which give the impression of being obedient soldiers, orderly ships, extraordinary planes, and astonishing lamps, they exhibit the splendor of the dominion of Your Divinity. As displayed by the duties that the sun, which is a member of the army of stars, performs in our globe and other satellites of its, some of the stars which are friends of the sun have a relationship with the worlds of the Hereafter, and they may be the suns of the worlds which are permanent.

O Necessarily Existent One, O the Single, Unique One!

Those wonderful stars, those breathtaking suns and moons have been subjugated, ordered and entrusted with various duties in Your domain, in Your heavens through Your Command, Power, Rule, and Management. All those celestial bodies glorify the sole Creator Who has created them, Who administers them, and makes them revolve; they magnify Him, and say with the tongue of their disposition, "All-Glorified are You," "God is the All-Great." I too declare You to be the All-Holy through their glorifications.

O the All-Powerful One of Majesty, Who is hidden due to the intensity of His manifestation and concealed because of His Grandeur!

I have understood through the teaching of the Qur'an and the instruction of God's noblest Messenger, upon him be peace and blessings, that:

In the same way that together with all their stars the heavens bear witness to Your Existence and Unity, the atmosphere also testifies to your absolutely necessary Existence and Unity through its clouds, lightning, thunder, wind, and rain. It is as follows:

Indeed, it is only by Your Mercy and Wisdom that the lifeless and unconscious cloud sends rain, which is the water of life, to the aid of living creatures that are in need of it; chance has not the least part in it.

Also, being the brightest and most powerful of electricity, urging us to benefit from it on account of its quality of illuminating, lightning sheds light on Your power in the heavens.

In addition, the thunder, which gives good tidings of the coming of rain, makes the vast heaven speak, and the roaring voice of its glorification resounds in the sky, declaring You to be the All-Sacred with the tongue of its disposition, testifying to Your being the Lord of the whole creation.

Again, entrusted with many duties, such as bringing living beings their most necessary sustenance and causing them to respire and refresh themselves, winds transform the atmosphere into some sort of tablet of effacement and confirmation due to certain Divine purposes. As they indicate the activities of Your Power and testify to Your Existence, so too does rain, which is the embodiment of mercy and is sent to the living beings through Your Mercy, bear witness to the comprehensiveness of Your Mercy and Affection through its orderly drops.

O the Ever-Active One Who controls everything, and the All-Transcending Bestower of abundant bounties!

As the clouds, thunder, wind, and rain each testifies to the absolute necessity of Your Existence independently, so too, through their helping one another and existing together despite their differences of nature, do they powerfully indicate Your Unity and Oneness. They also testify to the magnificence of Your Lordship, Which makes the vast sky a display of extraordinariness and fills and empties it a few times on some days, and to the greatness and comprehensiveness of Your Power, Which uses the atmosphere as if a tablet of effacement of confirmation and a sponge by means of which You water the garden of the earth, and to the boundless vastness and all-encompassing nature of Your Mercy and Dominion, Which embrace and maintain all creatures.

The employment of air in such wise duties and the employment of the clouds and rain for such knowledge-based benefits as require an all-embracing wisdom and an all-encompassing knowledge demonstrates that this employment is in no way possible without Your Wisdom or Knowledge.

O the One Who always does whatever He wills!

Your Power, Which performs actions such as continuously displaying samples of the Resurrection in the atmosphere, changing summer into winter and vice versa, and bringing forth a new world and sending another to the Realm of the Unseen all within an hour, gives signs of changing the world into the Hereafter and showing therein Your unending activity.

O the All-Powerful One of Majesty!

Air, clouds, rain, and thunder in the atmosphere are subservient and dutiful in Your domain, through Your Command, and by Your Power. Those atmospheric creatures, which differ in nature, declare You to be the All-Sacred, the Commander and Sovereign, Who makes them obey immediate and quick commands, and they praise Your Mercy.

O the All-Majestic Creator of the heavens and the earth!

Through the instruction of Your wise Qur'an and the teaching of the noblest Messenger, upon him be peace and blessings, I have believed in and know what follows:

In the same way that the heavens, through their stars, and the atmosphere, through its elements, testify to the absolute necessity of Your Existence and Your Oneness, the earth too bears witness to Your Existence and Oneness through all its creatures and circumstances to their number.

There are no transformations on the earth nor any changes—whether of universal or particular nature—in its plants, trees, and animals such as changing their garments every year, that do not bear witness to Your Existence and Oneness.

There is not a single animal that does not bear witness to Your Existence and Oneness through its sustenance given to it compassionately and in proportion to its need and weakness, and through being wisely equipped with the members necessary for its life.

Also, there is not a single plant or animal that is resurrected or originated before our eyes every spring which does not make You known through its remarkable art, fine organs, distinguishing features, and the perfect order and proportion in its composition and life.

All these plants and animals that fill the face of the earth as miracles of Your Power are created with perfect differentiation and rich adornment, and with no faults or flaws at all from the eggs or seeds that resemble one another and which are made up of almost the same substances. Their testimony to the Existence, Oneness, Wisdom and boundless Power of their All-Wise Maker is such that it is more powerful and brilliant than the testimony of light to the sun.

Also, there is no element, such as air, water, light, fire, or soil, that does not bear witness to Your Existence and Oneness by performing duties that require a perfect consciousness despite their unconsciousness, or by bringing perfectly formed fruits and crops of all kinds from the treasury of the Unseen, despite their distribution throughout a vast area or their invasion of the same.

O All-Powerful Originator, O All-Knowing and All-Opening, and O All-Acting and All-Creating!

In the same way that the earth testifies, with all its inhabitants, that its Creator is the Necessarily Existent One, so too O Single and Unique One, O All-Kind and All-Benevolent, and O All-Bestowing and All-Providing One, through the stamp on its face and the stamps on the faces of its inhabitants, and through the concentric manifestations of Your Names as their Lord, which cause their harmonious co-existence and mutual assistance despite vast distribution, the earth self-evidently testifies to Your Unity and Oneness to the number of the creatures on it.

Also, the fact that the hundreds of thousands of plant and animal divisions which form the global army that is encamped and performing drills on the earth are provided in perfect order with the exact members or equipment necessary for each demonstrates the magnificence of Your Lordship and demonstrates that Your Power commands everything at the same time. Similarly, it shows the all-encompassing nature of Your Mercy and Dominion that innumerable living creatures are compassionately and munificently provided with their sustenance just on time from simple soil, and that all of them obey the orders of Your Lordship with the utmost subservience.

Also, it is only possible through an all-encompassing knowledge and all-administering wisdom that all the convoys of creatures and all instances of death and life are made to follow one another on the earth in such perfect orderliness, and that all the plants, trees, and animals are administered so perfectly and regularly. This obviously indicates the all-encompassing nature of Your Knowledge and Wisdom.

Also, although humans are entrusted with limitless duties and are provided with such capacity and equipment as if they were to live eternally on the earth, and although they are allowed to command and control earthly creatures, they remain on the earth only very briefly. Therefore, such great importance given to them, and such limitless expenditure made for them, and such boundless manifestations of the Divine Lordship observed on them, and such endless addresses of the All-Glorified One, and such infinite Divine bounties conferred on them certainly cannot be for this brief, fleeting, painful, and calamity-stricken life on this transient barracks of the world or for this temporary encampment of the global army. Rather, as they can essentially be for another eternal life and for permanent happiness in another, everlasting realm, they indicate, indeed, testify to the otherworldly bounties in the realm of eternity.

O Creator of all things!

All the creatures of the earth are subservient to and administered by Your Strength, Power, Knowledge, Will, and Wisdom on Your earth, which is Your property. And Your Lordship—creation, maintenance, provision, rearing, and administration—the activities of Which are observed on the earth, display such vastness and comprehensiveness, and the administration, provision, and raising of this Lordship are so perfect and sensitive, and Its actions and operations exhibit such unity, resemblance, and coordination, that It is clearly an indivisible and universal Lordship. Furthermore, with all its inhabitants and through countless tongues more articulate than human verbal speeches, the earth glorifies its Creator and declares Him to be the All-Sacred, and through the tongue of His limitless bounties, it praises its All-Providing Majesty.

O the All-Sacred One Who is hidden due to the intensity of His manifestations and concealed because of His Grandeur!

With all the earth's glorifications of You and its declarations of You as the All-Sacred, I declare You to be absolutely exalted above any faults, impotence, or having partners, and I praise You and offer thanks to You with all their praises.

O the Lord of the land and the sea!

I have understood through the instruction of the Qur'an and the teaching of the noblest Messenger, upon him be peace and blessings, that just as the heavens, atmosphere, and the earth bear witness to Your Existence and Oneness, the rivers, springs, and streams also clearly testify to the absolute necessity of Your Existence and Your Oneness.

Indeed, there is not a single creature, indeed, not a single drop of water in the seas, which are the source of marvels and like steam boilers, that does not make its Creator known through its existence, orderliness, position, and the benefits it causes.

There is not a single member of the amazing creatures, the sustenance of which is provided through simple sand or simple water, or of sea animals created in an extremely orderly fashion, or in particular, of fish, which inhabit the seas, each laying one million eggs, that does not indicate its Creator or testify to its Provider through its creation, duties, administration, maintenance, and provision.

Also, there is not one single precious or ornamented substance in the sea with distinguishing features that does not make You known through its fine and fascinating creation or its beneficial character.

All those creatures mentioned testify to You individually. Also, although they exist in extremely wide varieties and great numbers and all are mixed with one another, their easy creation and the stamp of unity displayed by their creation bear witness to Your Unity. Furthermore, the earth remains suspended in space and revolves around the sun at great speed without its lands or seas mixing with each other or its seas invading the lands. Also, all of its minerals, substances, and marine and terrestrial life are well formed and extremely varied; these are created from simple water or soil and all those creatures are administered and nurtured perfectly and in perfect orderliness. Moreover, despite their extremely abundant existence and the fact that everyday countless numbers die, none of their corpses remains on the earth or in sea for long, with the result that both the face of the earth and the seas are always clean and pure. So, through all these clear facts, the earth testifies to the number of its creatures to Your Existence and that You are the Necessarily Existent Being. In the same way that all these creatures obviously indicate the splendor of Your Lordship's dominion and the immensity of Your Power, Which encompasses all things, they also point to the boundless comprehensiveness of Your Mercy and Dominion, Which embrace everything from the extremely large stars in the heavens above to the tiny fish at the bottom of the sea. Also, through their perfect organization and ordered existence and life, and through the benefits they give and the instances of wisdom they display, and through their well-proportioned structure and composition, they indicate Your all-encompassing Knowledge, and all-embracing Wisdom.

You have such pools of mercy in this guesthouse of the world for the travelers and You have subjugated these pools for their benefit and so that they can travel on ships. This indicates that these pools, the seas, are only very small and transitory samples of the gifts of He Who offers such innumerable marine gifts to His guests who stay only one night in that guesthouse standing on the way to eternity—He is One Who certainly has such eternal treasures of seas in His eternal domain of sovereignty. Thus, the keeping of the seas around the lands in such an extraordinary fashion and the wonderful maintenance of the creatures self-evidently demonstrate that they are subservient to Your command and that they are exclusively in Your domain and only are controlled through Your Will, Power, and Government. Through the tongue of all these facts, they declare You to be the All-Sacred as their Creator and say, "God is the All-Great."

O the All-Powerful One of Majesty, Who has made mountains as treasure-laden masts for the ship of the earth!

I have understood from the instruction of God's noblest Messenger, upon him be peace and blessings, and from the teachings of the Qur'an that just as the seas recognize You and make You known through their marvels, so too do the mountains recognize You and make You known through the instances of wisdom in their existence and the services they offer. For example, they serve the earth, keeping it solid and preserving its stability despite the stormy movements within it, and they are unperturbed by the invasion of the seas. They also purify the air of harmful gases, serve to store and preserve water, and function as storehouses for minerals and metals that are necessary for living beings.

Indeed, there is not a single one of the rocks or precious stones in mountains, or any of the innumerable varieties of substances that are used as medication or ingredients for medication, or any of the extremely diverse kinds of minerals or metals that are vital for living beings, including in particular humanity, or the varieties of plants and trees that adorn the mountains, plains, and fields with their flowers, making them prosperous with their fruits—there is not a single one of these that does not clearly testify to the absolute necessity of the Existence of an infinitely Powerful, Compassionate, and Munificent Maker through their instances of wisdom, fine arrangement and composition, fine creation, benefits, and the extreme diversity of the taste of the fruits or such minerals as salt, citric acid, quinine sulphate, or alum, despite their apparent similarity. Also, in addition to bearing witness to the Maker through their extreme variety and multifarious blossoms and fruits, despite growing in simple, uniform soil and being nurtured with the same, simple water, trees and flowers also testify to His Unity and Oneness through the unity of their administration, maintenance, origin, habitat, creation, and art, and through their abundance and cheapness despite their great worth, and the ease and speed of their creation despite each being a marvel of art.

Also, the fact that the mountains all over the world have almost the same composition, and that all kinds and species of beings are made perfectly, with no faults, in the same way, in a short time, without any confusion with other kinds or beings or without one deed impeding another indicate the magnificence of Your Lordship and the immensity of Your Power, for Which nothing is difficult. In addition, the mountains being full of large varieties of plants, trees, and minerals which gratify the endless needs of innumerable kinds of living creatures, and their different tastes and appetites, and the provision of the necessary medications for their countless kinds of illnesses indicate the boundless extensiveness of Your Mercy and the infinite vastness of Your Dominion. Although the seeds of all of these plants and trees and all the minerals exist hidden under the ground in darkness and all mixed with one another, they are grown and prepared in perfect orderliness and based on a vast knowledge and all-encompassing sight. All these facts indicate the comprehensiveness of Your Knowledge, Which encompasses everything, and the all-embracing nature of Your Wisdom, Which arranges everything perfectly. In addition, through the preparation of medications and the depositing of minerals and metals in them, mountains obviously indicate the beauties of Your Lordship's compassionate and munificent actions and the precautionary subtleties of Your benevolence.

Again, Your making these huge mountains the well-made warehouses of supplies for the future needs of Your visiting guests in this guesthouse of the world and the perfectly arranged store of many treasures of vital importance for the lives of the guests indicate, indeed, testify to the fact that a Maker so munificent and hospitable, so wise and caring, and so powerful and nurturing certainly has eternal treasures of everlasting bounties for these guests, whom He loves very much in an eternal world. The stars there will perform the duties of the mountains here in the world.

O the One powerful over everything!

The mountains are subservient in the service of humanity in Your domain by Your Power, Knowledge, and Wisdom, and so are the creatures that are in them. They glorify and declare to be All-Sacred their Creator, Who has made them subservient and dutiful in this manner.

O the All-Merciful Creator and All-Compassionate Lord!

I have understood from the instruction of God's noblest Messenger, upon him be peace and blessings, and the teaching of the wise Qur'an that in the same way that through their creatures and contents the heavens, the earth, the seas, and mountains recognize You and make You known, so too do all the plants and trees on the earth obviously know You and Make You known through their leaves, flowers, and fruits.

The leaves of all plants and trees, which make enraptured movements of remembrance of their Creator, and their flowers, which describe and define the Names of their Maker through their adornments, and their fruits, which attractively smile due to the manifestation of His Mercy—each of these leaves, flowers, and fruits self-evidently testifies to the absolute necessity of the Existence of an infinitely Compassionate and Munificent Maker through its perfect, extraordinarily artistic formation, and through the perfect balance and proportion in its formation, and the adornment that accompanies the balance and proportion, and the embroideries that contribute to the adornment, and the fine and different scents that are added to the embellishments, and the diverse tastes of the fruits together with their scents. In addition, in their totality, through their resemblance in their creation, and the relationship between their growth and provision, and the concentricity among the Divine acts and Names relating to their existence and maintenance, and through the administration of the uncountable individual members of their hundreds of thousand of varieties without any confusion, they obviously bear witness to the Unity and Oneness of that necessarily existent Maker.

In the same way that these testify to the absolute necessity of Your Existence and Your Unity, the perfect and distinctive maintenance of countless members of the host of the living beings that are formed of hundreds of thousands of "nations" on the earth indicates the splendor and uniqueness of Your Lordship, and the immensity of Your Power, Which encompasses everything and creates a spring as easily as a flower. Moreover, the preparation of countless substances of the numerous varieties of their food for innumerable animals and humans distributed throughout the earth indicates the boundless comprehensiveness of Your Mercy; the perfect order in the performance of all those acts of providing, administering, and maintaining, and the subservience and obedience of everything, indeed, of all particles or atoms to these acts and the commands concerning their accomplishment certainly testify to the all-encompassing nature of Your Dominion. Similarly, the fact that whatever relates to the existence, growth, and maintenance of each of the leaves, flowers, fruits, roots, branches, and twigs is done based on certain knowledge and insight and for many wise purposes and benefits obviously indicates the all-encompassing nature of Your Knowledge and Wisdom. And all of these, together with the acts relating to them, praise the beauty of Your infinitely perfect Art and the perfection of Your infinitely beautiful bountifulness.

In addition, such invaluable bounties and gifts offered, and such extraordinary expenditure made, and such wonderful munificence displayed, through the hands of trees and plants in this transitory guesthouse within a very short time indicates, indeed, bears witness to the fact that the All-Compassionate, Powerful, Munificent One has certainly prepared fruit-bearing trees and blossoming plants that are suited for the perpetual Gardens of eternal Paradise out of His eternal treasures of Mercy for His servants whom He will favor with eternity in an everlasting realm. This is because He never wants, in a manner which will be contrary to His will to make Himself known and loved through all His bestowals, to cause His loving friends to complain, saying, "He has made us taste of them but then sent us to eternal non-existence without allowing us to eat of them to full satisfaction." Nor does He want to reduce the infinite value of the dominion of His Divinity or cause His loving friends to deny His endless Mercy, thus changing their love to enmity. All the fruit-bearing trees and blossoming plants in the world are only examples of their eternal counterparts to be displayed to their customers.

Just as the trees and plants glorify and praise You and declare You to be the All-Sacred through all their leaves, flowers, and fruits, so too do each of these "words" proclaim Your absolute sacredness. The glorifications the fruits make through the tongue of their disposition—that is, through their attractive shapes, through their many different and fascinating colors, through their edible parts of numerous variety, through their marvelous seeds and through being offered to the guests of this guesthouse of the world from the hands of the trees or plants—manifest themselves as if verbally. All of them are subjugated in Your domain through Your Power, Will, Benevolence, Mercy, and Wisdom, and obedient to all of Your commands.

O the All-Wise Maker, the All-Compassionate Creator, Who is hidden due to the intensity of His manifestation and concealed because of His Grandeur!

I declare You to be absolutely exalted above any defect, impotence, and having partners, and praise You with the voices of all trees and plants and with all their leaves, flowers, and fruits; I praise you to the number of all of them.

O the All-Powerful Originator, the All-Wise Administrator, the All-Compassionate Governor!

I have understood from the instruction of God's noblest Messenger, upon him be peace and blessings, and from the teaching of the wise Qur'an, and believe that in the same way that plants and trees recognize You and make known Your all-sacred Attributes and All-Beautiful Names, there is not a single animal or human that does not testify to the absolute necessity of Your Existence and to Your Attributes through their perfectly and artistically made bodies or their equipment with extremely delicate and well-functioning "instruments" that have the finest order and equilibrium, and through all of their internal and external organs, which are made to operate in perfect sensitivity and orderliness, and their members and senses that are established in their bodies with perfect balance and arrangement and for extremely important benefits. For it is absolutely impossible that any blind force or unconscious "nature" or random chance should take part in the art that is delicate and wise to such degree, or in the wisdom that requires such a degree of care and consciousness, or in the perfect balance that is sensitive and purposeful to such an extent. As for their self-formation, it is a hundred times more impossible and inconceivable. For their self-formation would require that each of their particles or atoms should be as knowledgeable and powerful as if a deity so that each is able to perfectly know and create itself and all other atoms with their relations to one another, and all the universal elements having share in their existence and operation.

And the observable unity in their administration and maintenance as a whole, and the exact similarities among members of each species, as well as between species themselves, and the stamp of unity observed in their creation and nourishment, and in the fact that each of them has eyes, ears, mouths, and so on, and that each is directed towards similar goals—every one of these and similar other instances of unity decisively bear witness to Your absolute Unity. In the same way that all of Your Names are manifested in the universe, thus indicating Your Unity, they are also manifested in each of them, displaying Your Oneness.

Also, like humanity, hundreds of thousands of animal species distributed throughout the world are equipped, trained, obedient, and subjugated like a well-organized army, and the commands of Your Lordship operate in perfect orderliness in their kingdom. While this indicates how magnificent Your Lordship is, their extreme value despite their abundance, their perfect composition and organization despite their quick origination, and the perfect, peerless art they contain despite their easy creation indicate the grandeur of Your Power. As from microbes, which exist everywhere—from the east to the west and from the south to the north—to rhinoceroses, and from the tiniest flies to the largest birds, their exact provision or nourishment decisively indicates the endless comprehensiveness of Your Mercy, so too does each of them perform its vital duties without any faults; the earth, functioning like a ground for their mobilization in spring and for their demobilization in fall and winter, indicates the boundless vastness of Your Dominion.

Also, every animal is made like a miniature sample of the universe through an extremely profound knowledge and fine wisdom and without allowing any confusion in the appointment or placement of any of its atoms, compounds, members, or organs, one within the other and in complex relationships with one another. Again, each animal is given a different body and distinguishing features that have no defects, confusions, or faults at all. As these facts indicate Your all-encompassing Knowledge and Your all-embracing Wisdom to the numbers of animals, so too does the creation of each, so artistic and wise that it could but have emerged as a miracle of art and a marvel of wisdom, indicate the perfect beauty of Your Lordship's Art, Which You love very much and will to be exhibited. Also, through their delicate nourishment and the gratification of their needs and desires, all of them, in particular the young among them, endlessly indicate the extreme beauty of Your Benevolence.

O the All-Merciful, the All-Compassionate, O the All-Truthful absolutely true in His promise, and O the Master of Judgment Day!

I understood from the instruction of Your noblest Messenger, upon him be peace and blessings, and the teaching of Your Wise Qur'an the following:

Since the ultimate result of the universe is life, and the ultimate result of life is the spirit, and the ultimate choice among beings with spirit are the conscious, and the most comprehensive among the conscious is humanity; and since the whole universe serves life, and living beings are sent to the world to serve those with spirit among them and the beings with spirit are put in the service of humanity among them and help humans; and since humans love their Creator very seriously by nature and their Creator both loves them and makes Himself loved by them by every means; and since the capacities and immaterial faculties given to humanity are primarily directed towards the eternal life, and their hearts and consciousness desire eternity with all their strength, and their tongues entreat their Creator with endless prayers for eternity; then certainly the One Who loves and is much loved will never distress humans, whom He loves and by whom He is loved and whom He has created for eternal love, by making them die eternally without revival, thus transforming their love into eternal enmity. Rather, humans are sent to this world to strive for and earn an eternal life of happiness in another realm. They will be favored with the eternal manifestations of the Divine Names, Which they mirror in this fleeting, short life.

Indeed, the faithful friend of the Eternal One will be eternal, and the conscious mirror of the Everlasting One must be everlasting.

As can be understood both from authentic Prophetic Traditions and as required by reality and Divine Wisdom, Mercy, and Lordship, the spirits of animals will also remain permanently and such special members of them as the hoopoe and the ant of the Prophet Solomon, upon him be peace, and the she-camel of the Prophet Salih, upon him be peace, and the dog of the People of the Cave will go to the eternal world with their bodies and spirits, and each animal species will continue to exist as a single, representative body for occasional employment.[151]

O the All-Powerful and Self-Subsistent One!

All living creatures, spirit-possessing beings, and conscious beings have been made subservient to the commands of Your Lordship and entrusted with duties according to the nature of each in Your domain through Your Power, Will, Administration, Mercy, and Wisdom. Some among them have been put in the service of humanity not because of the power and domination of humanity, but due to their weakness and impotence. By glorifying their Maker and declaring Him to be absolutely exalted above any defects, faults, or having partners, and praising Him and thanking Him for His bounties both verbally and through the tongue of their disposition, each performs its particular form of worship.

O the All-Sacred One, hidden because of the intensity of His manifestation and veiled due to His Grandeur!

With the intention of declaring You to be the All-Sacred through the glorifications of all spirit-possessing beings, I say: All-Glorified are You, O the One Who has made every living thing from fluid!

O the Lord of all the worlds! O the Deity of all those who have come and to come! O the Lord of the heavens and the globes!

I have understood and believe from the instruction of God's noblest Messenger, upon him be peace and blessings, and the teaching of the wise Qur'an as follows:

Just as with all their members, parts, and atoms, the heavens, atmosphere, earth, land and sea, trees, plants, and animals recognize You and indicate and testify to Your Existence and Oneness, so too do the living beings, which are the essence of the universe, and humankind, which is the essence of living beings, and the saints, pure and saintly scholars, and the Prophets tell of and bear witness to the absolute necessity of Your Existence and Your Unity and Oneness through the observations and unveilings of their intellects and hearts, and through their inspirations and spiritual discoveries. Their testimony has the certainty of the consensus of hundreds of different specialist groups with absolutely true, expert knowledge, and hundreds of chains of transmitters of knowledge who have never lied during

---

151 al-Baghawi, *Ma'alim at-Tanzil*, 3:154; al-Alusi, *Ruh al-Ma'ani*, 15:226. (Tr.)

their lives. They also prove the information they provide with their miracles, wonders, and decisive proofs.

Not once is there an occurrence to sound hearts which has its source from or relates to the One Who imparts reminders to them through the veil of the Unseen that does not indicate or testify to the absolute necessity of Your Existence, all-sacred Attributes, Unity and Oneness; not once is there a single true inspiration that focuses attention on the One Who inspires, not once is there a certified creed that discovers the all-sacred Divine Attributes and the all-beautiful Divine Names with a certainty based on experience, not once is there a pure, illuminated heart, peculiar to the Prophets and saints, which observes the lights of the Necessarily Existent Being with the clarity of eyesight, not once is there an enlightened intellect, particular to the truthful, pure and saintly scholars, which confirms, based on a certainty of knowledge, the signs of the necessary Existence of the Creator of everything and the proofs of His Oneness—not once is there a single occurrence, a true inspiration, a certified creed, a pure and illuminated heart, or an enlightened intellect that does not indicate or testify to the absolute necessity of Your Existence, all-sacred Attributes, Unity, and Oneness.

And in particular, there is not a single clear miracle that confirms the tidings of the most noble Messenger, upon him be peace and blessings, who is the leader, head, and essence of all the Prophets, saints, saintly and pure scholars and those who are most advanced in truthfulness; there is not a single exalted truth that shows his absolute truthfulness; there is not a single Divine-Unity-demonstrating verse of the Qur'an of miraculous exposition, which is the essence of all sacred Scriptures and books of truth; and there is not a single sacred matter and truth of belief it contains—there is not a single one of these miracles, truths, verses, or matters that does not indicate or testify to the absolute necessity of Your Existence, Your all-sacred Attributes, Names, Unity, and Oneness.

Also, in the same way that there are hundreds of thousands of truthful ones who bear witness to Your Existence and Oneness based on their miracles, wonders, and proofs, so too do they unanimously proclaim and prove the magnificence of Your Lordship, Which has perfect knowledge of and control over everything, large or small, from the universal affairs that relate to Your Supreme Throne to the most secret occurrences of the heart and its most hidden desires and prayers; they proclaim the grandeur of Your Power,

Which invents countless things simultaneously and instantly before our eyes, and accomplishes the greatest thing as easily as the smallest one, without one impeding the other.

With their miracles and other proofs, all these truthful ones also show and demonstrate the limitless comprehensiveness of Your Mercy, Which has made this universe a perfect palace for spirit-possessing beings, and in particular humanity, and prepares Paradise and eternal happiness for the jinn and humans, and does not forget even the least being, and gratifies the most powerless heart. They also demonstrate the boundless vastness of Your Dominion, Which has subjugated all kinds of creatures from particles to galaxies, and entrusted them with certain duties, causing them to obey Your commands. Moreover, these same unanimously indicate and testify to the all-encompassing nature of Your Knowledge, Which has made the universe a cosmic book which contains as many books as there are particles and compounds in the universe, and recorded all instances of the lives of all creatures in the Manifest Record and the Manifest Book, which are the registers of the Supreme Preserved Tablet; and Which inscribes the contents and programs of all trees in each of their seeds, and the entire life histories of conscious beings in their memories. They also decisively point to and bear witness to Your all-embracing nature of Your Wisdom, Which attaches to each creature numerous instances of wisdom, such as causing each tree to yield results to the number of its fruits, and following in each living being as many benefits as its members, indeed, as its compounds and cells, and equipping the human tongue with the instruments to the number of tastes in addition to entrusting it with many duties. Furthermore, they unanimously indicate and bear witness to the fact that Your Names of Majesty and Grace, Whose exemplary manifestations are observed in this world, will continue to manifest themselves in the abode of eternity in a much brighter fashion; they testify that Your bestowals, the samples of which are experienced in this fleeting world, will last in the eternal realm of happiness in a more glittering fashion, and that the lovers of these bestowals who experience them in this world will accompany them to all eternity.

Also, based on Your promises and threats that You frequently repeat in all the Scriptures You revealed, including primarily the wise Qur'an, and relying on the dignity of Your Majesty and the dominion of Your Lordship, and on Your all-sacred Attributes and essential Qualities such as Power,

Mercy, Favoring, Wisdom, Majesty, and Grace, and through spiritual unveilings and observations, and with convictions that arise from certain knowledge, all of the Prophets with luminous spirits, including first and foremost God's noblest Messenger, upon him be peace and blessings, and the saints with illuminated hearts, and the pure, saintly scholars with enlightened intellects, all give the jinn and humankind the glad tidings of eternal happiness, and warn that there is Hell for the misguided, themselves believing in them first and foremost of all.

O the All-Powerful, All-Wise One, O the All-Merciful, All-Compassionate One, O the All-Munificent One absolutely truthful in His promises! O the All-Overwhelming One of Majesty with dignity, grandeur, and majesty!

You are infinitely free of and exalted above not bringing about the Resurrection, which would mean contradicting so many truthful friends of Yours, breaking Your vehemently repeated threats and promises, negating Your sacred Attributes and essential Qualities, annulling the decisive requirements of the dominion of Your Lordship, and rejecting the prayers of innumerable servants of Yours whom You love and who make themselves loved by You by confirming and obeying You. You are also infinitely free of and exalted above confirming the people of unbelief and misguidance in their rejection of the Resurrection, who through unbelief and disobedience and by contradicting You in Your promises insult Your Grandeur, attack the dignity of Your Majesty, offend the honor of Your Divinity, and disparage the compassion of Your Lordship. I declare Your infinite Justice, Grace, and Mercy to be absolutely free of such limitless ugliness and wrong. I wish to recite the verse, *All-Glorified is He, and absolutely exalted, immeasurably high above all that they say* (17: 43), as many times as there are particles in my body. These truthful Messengers of Yours and heralds of Your dominion point to and bear witness to Your treasures of mercy and benevolence and the extraordinarily beautiful manifestations of Your All-Beautiful Names in the world of permanence with both a certainty of experience and a certainty of observation and a certainty of knowledge. They also believe and teach others that the greatest ray of Your Name, the Ultimate Truth and Ever-Constant, Which is the origin, sun, and preserver of all truths, is this greatest truth of Resurrection.

O the Lord of the Prophets and those most advanced in truthfulness after the Prophets!

All these beloved friends of Yours are subjugated and dutiful in Your domain through Your Command, Power, Will, Administration, Knowledge, and Wisdom. Through their glorification, praise, and declarations of Your Oneness and that You are absolutely exalted above any defects, faults, or having partners, they have displayed this world as the vastest house of remembrance, and the universe as the vastest place of worship.

O my Lord, and O the Lord of the heavens and the globes! O my Creator and the Creator of everything!

For the sake of Your Power, Will, Wisdom, Sovereignty, and Mercy, Which subjugate the heavens with their stars and the earth with all its contents, and all creatures with all their states, make my carnal soul subservient to me, and subjugate my desires to me. Subjugate people's hearts to the *Risale-i Nur* purely for the service of the Qur'an and belief. And bestow on me and my brothers and sisters the perfect belief and a good end (going to the other world with perfect belief). Subjugate the hearts and intellects to the *Risale-i Nur*, just as You subjugated the sea to the Prophet Moses, upon him be peace, as you subjugated the fire to the Prophet Abraham, upon him be peace, the mountains and iron to the Prophet David, upon him be peace, the jinn and humans to the Prophet Solomon, upon him be peace, and the sun and the moon to the Prophet Muhammad, upon him be peace and blessings. And preserve me and the students of the *Risale-i Nur* from the evil of the carnal soul and Satan, and from the torments of the grave and Hellfire, and make us happy in *Jannat al-Firdaws* (the highest level of Paradise)! Amen! Amen!

All-Glorified are You! We have no knowledge save what You have taught us. Surely You are the All-Knowing, the All-Wise.

And their invocation will close with, "All praise and gratitude are for God, the Lord of the worlds!"

If I have erred by offering this lesson, which I have taken from the *Jawshan al-Kabir* ("The Great Shield"), a supplication of God's Messenger, upon him be peace and blessings, to the Court of my All-Compassionate Lord as a reflective act of worship, O my Lord, I entreat Your Mercy to forgive me for the sake of the Qur'an and the *Jawshan al-Kabir*.

Index

A

B

D

E

F

I

M

N

O

P

Q

R

S

T

U

V

W

Y

Z

Index of God's Names and Attributes

H

I

J

K

L

M

N

O

P

R

S

T

U

V

W